Legacy: Archives
Volume I

Researched and Compiled by Horace Cheeves & Denise Nicole Cheeves

Order this book online at www.trafford.com
or email orders@trafford.com

Most Trafford titles are also available at major online book retailers.

Photographs courtesy of The d'zert Club, The Library of Congress Prints and
Photographs Division, Lynn Johnson, and The Atlanta Journal-Constitution.

Edited by Bianca Morris Rhym and Krishnan Anand
Typeset by Jeffrey Henon for Henon Design
Layout by Denise Nicole Cheeves for kohl, inc.
Graphic Design by Jeffrey Henon for Henon Design
Cover Design by Denise Nicole Cheeves for kohl, inc.

Print information available on the last page.

ISBN: 978-1-4120-4360-1 (sc)

Trafford rev. 04/19/2023

www.trafford.com
North America & international
toll-free: 844-688-6899 (USA & Canada)
fax: 812 355 4082

Preface

In 1986, when the Tarbutton (a/k/a Carter) case was dismissed, I began my own investigation of what had actually occurred. Once I reviewed the records, I realized how pivotal a role the heirs played. Genealogy, I learned, creates a window to understanding our ancestry and history. Legally, you must be able to document your ancestry to receive your inheritance in questionable situations, or when there is no will or trust.

Genealogy offers tremendous insight for medical and health purposes, and provides an in-depth analysis of physical and personal character traits. Genetics and environment mold all of us and understanding those influences can be invaluable. It is the most hands-on approach to knowing oneself and our familial origins. Children deserve a more accurate documentation of their ancestry/history for future reference and research, as opposed to stringing together oral translations of the past that are unsubstantiated.

My daughter, Denise Nicole and I spent countless hours speaking with my Aunt Mattie (my father's sister), who had a keen memory of names and dates. The foundation of our genealogy was built from her recollection of people, places, and events. To validate and build on the information she provided, I gathered various documents such as birth, marriage, and death certificates; census records; plats; obituaries; family reunion booklets; tax receipts and deeds on file at county courthouses (Washington, Baldwin, Hancock, Eatonton, and Putnam). I also consulted genealogists in Washington County Georgia.

In addition, I gathered names from an array of other sources and mailed questionnaires to them. From this we found Cheeves, Trawicks, Boyers and others throughout the country, though we are not yet sure how some of them connect to us.

Ultimately, I hired other researchers and genealogists to further investigate, validate, and compile information on our families. One recorded case illustrates how important it is to investigate your own genealogy. In 1923, a Black town in Rosewood, Florida, was destroyed by a white lynch mob. Nearly 73 years after the destruction, a settlement was reached for the descendants of those Black families. In order to receive their reparations, they first had to prove their ancestry.

For this reason, committees need to be established within families to continuously research our ancestry. In Utah, the Mormon Church has compiled the genealogy of virtually everyone in the United States. Other groups such as Quakers, Jews, and the Amish, amongst others, have done so as well. It is unconscionable to depend on memory or word of mouth when we should record our ancestry as well. We owe it to our children and theirs to have a reliable record of our family's history so maybe they can trace our lineage back to a village in the Songhai region of Africa if we don't.

Thanks to the following for their contribution:

Carter | Eva Trawick Thomas, O' Neal Turner, Mary Carter Vincent, Ann Carter Green, Teresa Carter Snyder, Eloise 'Honey' Dawson Gordy, Grace Bryant

Hooks | Delores Hooks

Smith | Lucious Renfrow, Sigrid Trawick McCall

Barlow | Thelma Barlow

Mitchell | Bernice Woods

Peeler | Grady Jones

Butts | Richard Butts

Cheeves | Mary 'Town' Trawick, Marilyn 'Pos' Swint, Ernestine 'Molly' Cheeves, Annette G. Cheeves, Miriam Cheeves, Michael Cheeves, Reggie Cheeves

Mattie Cheeves Shenoster Johnson

Boyer | Ed Boyer, Phyllis Napier Green, Eliza 'Trixie' Boyer Smith, LaJude Nunlee Josey, Minnie Williams Napier, Mae Will Williams Renfroe, Norma Boyer Richardson

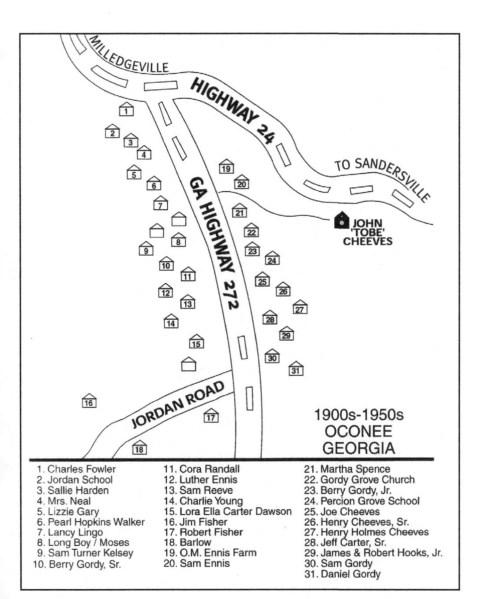

1900s-1950s
OCONEE
GEORGIA

1. Charles Fowler
2. Jordan School
3. Sallie Harden
4. Mrs. Neal
5. Lizzie Gary
6. Pearl Hopkins Walker
7. Lancy Lingo
8. Long Boy / Moses
9. Sam Turner Kelsey
10. Berry Gordy, Sr.

11. Cora Randall
12. Luther Ennis
13. Sam Reeve
14. Charlie Young
15. Lora Ella Carter Dawson
16. Jim Fisher
17. Robert Fisher
18. Barlow
19. O.M. Ennis Farm
20. Sam Ennis

21. Martha Spence
22. Gordy Grove Church
23. Berry Gordy, Jr.
24. Percion Grove School
25. Joe Cheeves
26. Henry Cheeves, Sr.
27. Henry Holmes Cheeves
28. Jeff Carter, Sr.
29. James & Robert Hooks, Jr.
30. Sam Gordy
31. Daniel Gordy

Table of Contents

Descendants of Burrell Carter

2

1870 CENSUS – UNITED STATES

State Georgia   County Washington   Town/Township Beacke Dist. 9814   P.O. Hebron   Call No. M593 roll 182
enumerated 1 July, 1870 by Jesse A. Coker

Page	Dwelling No.	Family No.	Names	Age	Sex	Color	Occupation, etc.	Value Real Estate	Value Personal property	Birthplace	Father Foreign born	Mother Foreign born	Month born in year	Month married in year	School in Year	Can't Read or Write	Eligible to vote	Date of Enumeration
340	210	207	Carter, Burrell	41	M	B	Farm Bank South			Georgia						//		
			— Mary	32	F	B	Keeping House			"						//		
			— Milly	10	F	B	Work at Home			"						/		
			— Jeff D.	8	M	B				"								
			— Gracie	6	F	B				"								
			— Burrell	2	M	B				"								

Burrell Carter, 1870 Census

1880 CENSUS – UNITED STATES

STATE Georgia   COUNTY Washington   TOWN/TOWNSHIP The 98th L Dist   CALL NUMBER T9, Roll 171

Page	Dwelling Number	Family Number	NAMES	Color	Sex	Age Prior to June 1st	Month of Birth if Born in Census Year	Relationship to Head of House	Single	Married	Widowed	Divorced	Married in Census Year	Occupation	Miscellaneous Information	Cannot Read or Write	Place of Birth	Place of Birth of Father	Place of Birth of Mother	Enumeration
7	60	60	Carter, Burrell	Mu	M	50		Head	✓					Farmer		✓	Ga	Ga	Ga	
			Mary	B	F	40		wife		✓				Keeping House		✓				
			Milly	B	F	19		dau	✓					Laborer		✓				
			Jeff	B	M	18		son	✓					Laborer		✓				
			Gracy	B	F	16		dau	✓					Laborer		✓				
			John	B	M	14		son	✓					Laborer						
			Dallie	B	F	9		dau	✓					at home						
			Virge	B	M	7		son	✓					at home						
			Susie	B	F	4		d	✓					at home						
			unamed	B	F	2/12		d	✓					at home						
			James	Mu	M	4		G. Son	✓											
			Joseph	Mu	M	2		G. Son	✓											

Burrell Carter, 1880 Census

U.S. Bureau of the Census 1880, Tenth Agriculture Census

Question No.	Column Heading	Entry
	ROW 1	
001	NAME: *Carter, Burrell* Microfilm roll #: *T1137, race 20 Washington Co. 64* ED # *138* , Page *2* , Line *4*	
002	Owner	
003	Rent for fixed money rental	✓
004	Rent for shares of production	
	Acres of Land	
	Improved	
005	Tilled, including fallow and grass in rotation (whether pasture or meadow)	*35 acres*
006	Permenant meadows, permanent pastures, orchards, and vineyards	
	Unimproved	
007	Woodland and forest	
008	Other unimproved, including "old fields" not growing wood	
	Farm Values	
009	Of farm, including land, fences & buildings	*$350*
010	of farming implements and machinery	*$25*
011	of live stock on farm June 1, 1880	*$100*
	Fences	
012	Cost of building and repair	
013	Cost of Fertilizers pruchased, 1879	*$25*
014	**Labor** Amount paid for wages for farm labor 1879 including value of board	
	Weeks hired labor in 1879 upon farm (and dairy) excluding house work	
015	White	
016	Colored	
	Estiamted value of all farm productions (sold, consumed, or on hand) for 1897	
017	(Dollars)	*$300*

Burrell Carter, 1880 Agriculture Census, pg. 1

4

Question No.	Column Heading	Entry
	Grass Lands	
	Acreage 1879	
018	Mown	
019	Not Mown	
	Products Harvested in 1879	
020	Hay	
021	Clover Seed	
022	Grass Seed	
023	Horses of all ages on hand June 1, 1880	/
024	Mules and Asses all ages on hand June 1, 1880	
	ROW 2	
	Meat Cattle and their Products	
	On hand June 1, 1880	
025	Working oxen	/
026	Milch cows	/
027	Other	4
	Movement, 1879	
028	Calves Dropped	/
	Cattle of all ages	
029	Purchased	
030	Sold living	
031	Slaughtered	
032	Died	
	Dairy Products	
033	Milk sold or sent to butter and cheese factories in 1879	
034	Butter made on the farm in 1879	15 lbs
035	Cheese made on the farm in 1879	

Burrell Carter, 1880 Agriculture Census, pg. 2

Question No.	Column Heading	Entry
	Sheep	
036	On hand June 1, 1880	
	Movement 1879	
037	Lambs Dropped	
038	Purchased	
039	Sold living	
040	Slaughtered	
041	Killed by dogs	
042	Died of disease	
043	Died of stress of weather	
	WOOL, spring clip of 1880	
044	Fleeces	
045	Weight	
046	Swine on hand June 1, 1880	*16*
	Poultry on hand June 1, 1880 exlusive of Spring Hatching	
047	Barn-Yard	*12*
048	Other	*7*
049	Eggs produced in 1879	Doz. *13*
	Rice	
050	Acres	
051	Crop	lbs.
	Row 3	
	Cereal, 1879	
052	Barley - Acres	
053	Barley - Crop	Bu.
054	Buckwheat - Acres	
055	Buckwheat - Crop	Bu.
056	Indian Corn - Acres	*15*
057	Indian Corn - Crop	Bu. *75*
058	Oats - Acres	
059	Oats - Crop	Bu.

Burrell Carter, 1880 Agriculture Census, pg. 3

6

Question No.	Column Heading	Entry
060	Rye - Acres	
061	Rye - Crop	Bu.
062	Wheat - Acres	
063	Wheat - Crop	Bu.
	Fiber, 1879	
064	Cotton - Acres	*20*
065	Cotton - Bales	*4*
066	Flax - Acres	
067	Flax - Seed	Bu.
068	Flax - straw	tons
069	Flax - Fiber	lbs.
070	Hemp - Acres	
071	Hemp - Crop	Tons
	Sugar and Molasses, 1879	
072	Cane - Acres in Crop	*1*
073	Cane - Sugar	Hhds.
074	Cane - Molasses	gals. *16*
075	Sorghum - Acres in Crop	
076	Sorghum - Sugar	lbs.
077	Sorghum - Molasses	gals.
078	Maple - Sugar	lbs.
079	Maple - Molasses	gals.

	Row 4	
	Pulse, 1879	
080	Pease *(Corn fied)*	Bu. *30*
081	Beans (Dry)	Bu.
082	Irish Potatoes - Acres	
083	Irish Potatoes - Crop	Bu.
084	Sweet Potatoes - Acres	*1*
085	Sweet Potatoes - Crop	Bu. *40*
086	Tobacco - Acres	
087	Tobacco - Crop	lbs.

Burrell Carter, 1880 Agriculture Census, pg. 4

1880 Agriculture Census

Question No.	Column Heading	Entry
	Orchards, 1879	
088	Apples - Acres	
089	Apples - Bearing trees	
090	Apples - Bushels	
091	Peaches - Acres	
092	Peaches - Bearing trees	
093	Peaches - Bushels	
094	Total Value - Dollars	
	Nurseries, 1879	
095	Acres	
096	Value of products sold in 1879	
	Vineyards, 1879	
097	Acres	
098	Grapes sold in 1879	
099	Wine made in 1879	
100	Market garden - Value of Products sold - Dollars	
	Bees	
101	Honey	lbs.
102	Wax	lbs.
	Forest Products	
103	Amount of Wood cut in 1879	cords 30
104	Value of all products sold or consumed in 1879	Dollars $10

Burrell Carter, 1880 Agriculture Census, pg. 5

8

Page 18]

No._____   MARRIAGE LICENSE.

State of Georgia, Washington County,
By the ORDINARY of said County.

To any JUDGE, JUSTICE OF THE PEACE or MINISTER OF THE GOSPEL,
You are Hereby Authorized to Join

_____

In the Holy Estate of Matrimony, according to the Constitution and Laws of this State; and for so doing, this shall be your sufficient License.

And you are hereby required to return this License to me, with your Certificate hereon of the fact and date of the Marriage.

Given under my hand and seal of office, this.....day of....................188_

_____ L.S.
                        Ordinary.

                    GEORGIA, Washington County.

I CERTIFY, that.......................................and

_____were joined in Matrimony by me,

this.......day of.................Eighteen Hundred and Eighty..........

Recorded:
_____Ordinary.

Jeff Carter and Ella Hooks, Marriage License, January 19, 1887

Jeff Carter, 1900 Census

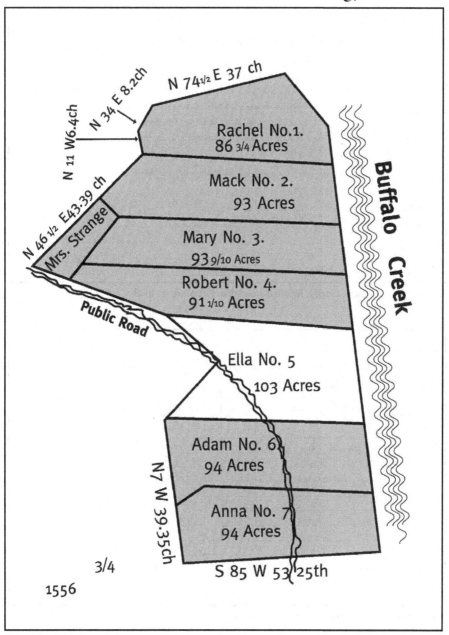

Plat of the Division of James Hooks' Estate, Washington County, Georgia; Filed and Recorded July 10, 1900

10

MARRIAGE LICENSE.   NO.

STATE OF GEORGIA, WASHINGTON COUNTY.

TO ANY JUDGE, JUSTICE OF THE PEACE, OR MINISTER OF THE GOSPEL:

You are hereby authorized to join _Jeff Carter, cd_ and _Easter Gordon cd_ in the Holy State of Matrimony, according to the Constitution and laws of this State, and for so doing this shall be your license; and you are hereby required to return this license to me, with your certificate hereon of the fact and date of the marriage.

Given under my hand and seal, this _8"_ day of _February_, 190_8_

C. D. Thigpen (L. S.)
ORDINARY.

GEORGIA, WASHINGTON COUNTY.

CERTIFICATE.

I certify that _Jeff Carter cd_ and _Easter Gordon, cd_ were joined in matrimony by me, this _8th_ day of _February_, Nineteen Hundred and _eight_

Recorded _Mar 19"_, 190_8_

G. H. Holmes M. G
C. D. Thigpen, Ordinary.

Jeff Carter and Easter Gordy, Marriage License, February 8, 1908

Jeff Carter, 1910 Census

MARRIAGE LICENSE.   No.———

STATE OF GEORGIA. WASHINGTON COUNTY.

TO ANY JUDGE JUSTICE OF THE PEACE OR MINISTER OF THE GOSPEL:

You are hereby authorized to join *Carter Jeff (col)* and *Delia Howard* in the Holy State of Matrimony, according to the Constitution and laws of this State, and for so doing this shall be your license; and you are hereby required to return this license to me, with your certificate hereon of the fact and date of the marriage.

Given under my hand and seal, this 18 day of *Feb*, 191 6.

———————————— , (L. S.)

ORDINARY.

GEORGIA, WASHINGTON COUNTY.   CERTIFICATE.

I certify that *Jeff Carter* and *Delia Howard* were joined in matrimony by me, this 12 day of *Dec*, Nineteen Hundred and *Fifteen*

Recorded *Jan. 12*, 191 7.   Ordinary.

Jeff Carter and Delia Howard, Marriage License, December 12, 1916

STATE Georgia				1920 CENSUS — UNITED STATES								SUPERVISOR'S DISTRICT # 14		SHEET NO. 5-6-
COUNTY Washington												ENUMERATION DISTRICT # 143		
TOWNSHIP OR OTHER COUNTY DIVISION				NAME OF INCORPORATED PLACE 98th Militia								WARD OF CITY —		
NAME OF INSTITUTION				ENUMERATED BY ME ON THE 12 DAY OF January , 1920								ENUMERATOR -20th A. Barksdale		

PLACE OF ABODE				NAME	RELATION	TENURE		PERSONAL DESCRIPTION				CITIZENSHIP			EDUCATIO
STREET, AVENUE, ETC.	HOUSE NUMBER OR FARM	NUMBER OF DWELLING HOUSE (VISITATION ORDER)	NUMBER OF FAMILY (VISITATION ORDER)	OF EACH PERSON WHOSE PLACE OF ABODE ON JANUARY 1, 1920, WAS IN THIS FAMILY	RELATIONSHIP TO HEAD OF HOUSEHOLD	HOME OWNED OR RENTED	IF OWNED, FREE OR MORTGAGED	SEX	COLOR OR RACE	AGE AT LAST BIRTHDAY	SINGLE, MARRIED WIDOWED, OR DIVORCED	YEAR OF IMMIGRATION TO U.S.	NATURALIZED OR ALIEN	IF NATURALIZED, YEAR OF NATURALIZATION	ATTENDED SCHOOL ANYTIME SINCE SEPT. 1, 1919
1	2	3	4	5	6	7	8	9	10	11	12	13	14	15	16
9m	88	90	Carter, Jeff	Head	O	F	M	Mu	54	M					No
		—	Delia	wife			F	Mu	36	M					Yes
		—	Crawford	son			M	Mu	16	S					Yes
		—	Minnie	dau			F	Mu	13	S				Yes	Yes
		—	Roy Dld	son			M	Mu	9	S				Yes	Yes
		—	Howard, Lizzie	Adau			F	B	17	S				Yes	Yes
9m	89	91	Carter, Jeff Jr.	Head			M	Mu	22	M					Yes
		—	Georgia	wife			F	Mu	19	M					Yes
		—	May Julia	dau			F	Mu	3	S					
		—	Lily Arthur	dau			F	Mu	1	S					

Jeff Carter, 1920 Census

12

| Date: *24 Nov 1972* | GRANTEE - GRANTOR INDEX | | File No. _____ |

Researcher _____   Ancestor *CARTEL*

| Circle one
ORIGINAL
MICROFILM
BOOK
EXTRACT | Call number | Library/courthouse *Superior Court, Washington C.*
Legible _____ Publisher _____ |

Date Recorded	GRANTOR OR GRANTEE Circle one	GRANTOR OR GRANTEE Circle one	INSTRA-MENT	TOWN	BOOK No.	PAG Nc
21 Jul 1866	Thos. J Winthur, Estate Exec	Carter, Ann	Deed		A	43
5 Aug 1866	J.N. Gilmore et al	Carter, W.W	Deed		A	48
9 Jul 1869	Thomas E. Brown	Carter, W. W.	Deed		A	56
18 June 1873	Cezek & H.O. Carter by	Carter, W.W	Deed		C	206
	Trustee					
26 Feb 1874	Benjamin D. Smith	Carter W.C. & Son	Mtg		C	34
23 Mar 1874	John C. & George Ginder	"	"	Mtg		C	37
1 Apr 1874	Matthew Johnson	"	"	Mtg		C	38
11 Mar 1893	James Lewis	Carter J James	Lien		K	74
25 Nov 1896	G L Tompkins	Carter J.J	Deed		N	44
8 Feb 1899	W J Archie (By Receiv)	Carter W.A. (Exor)	Deed		O	38
13 Apr 1901	Isabella Cotton Mill	Carter & Gillespie Elec.Co	Lien		U	266
23 Oct 1902	G.E & R.H. Gilmore	Carter, Jeff	Deed		P	421
7 Jan 1903	Jos. B. Smith	Carter, John	Deed		P	474
9 Jul 1905	W.B. Carter	Carter, Ella & Heirs	Deed		S	227
12 Dec 1905	John F. & Dot A. Page, &c	Carter, W.B	Deed		S	279
12 Oct 1906	J.J. Long	Carter, L.T.	Deed		R	57
5 Dec 1906	Butler, Stephens & Co.	Carter William B	Deed		R	60
19 Feb 1908	B.J. Whitfield	Carter, John T	Mtg		AG	23
27 Oct 1913	T.D. Davis	Carter, Jeff	Deed		W	242
3 Mar 1914	J.E. Moye	Carter, Mrs Fannie	Deed		W	32
28 Mar 1914	Mary Eva Rodgers	Carter, John	Deed		W	33
6 May 1914	Mary Eva Rodgers	Carter, J.T.	Mtg		AR	67
25 Oct 1915	Mrs. Mary Eva Rodgers	Carter, J.T.	Deed		W	505
15 Nov 1916	T.D. Davis	Carter, Jeff	Deed		Y	2
15 Nov 1916	B.J. Tarbutton Jr.	Carter, Jeff	Deed		Y	2
30 Apr 1919	F.T Horton	Carter, W.B.	Deed		AA	34
25 Nov 1919	A.D. Burau et al (By Guard.)	Carter, Mr. J.T.	Deed		AA	4
13 Nov 1920	J.L. Hattaway	Carter, W.B.	Deed & Plat		BB	488
19 June 1921	Middle Ga. Oil & Gas C.	Carter, M.W.	Deed		DD	27
20 May 1922	F.E Walker	Carter W.A & J.T.	Deed		EE	24

ix

Topic No.

Jeff Carter, Recorded Deed

"World War I Draft Card of Virgil Carter, "12 September 1918; Georgia, Washington County; World War I Draft Registration Card, Selective Service System 1917-1918 (Record Group No.163). National Archives, Southeast Region, East Point, Georgia.

14

CERTIFICATE OF DEATH
GEORGIA DEPARTMENT OF PUBLIC HEALTH
Bureau of Vital Statistics

Registered No. _____

1. PLACE OF DEATH
County _Washington_ Militia District (Number and Name) _98 - Hebron_ State of Georgia
City or Town _Sandersville_ Length of residence in this city or town: Yrs. ___ Mos. ___ Ds. ___ NON-RESIDENT (Yes or No) ___
Street and Number (No.) _____ (Street) _____ Ward _____
(If death occurred in a hospital, give its name instead of street and number)

2. FULL NAME _Virgil Carter_
Residence (City or Town) _Sandersville_ (Street and Number) _____ (State) _____

PERSONAL AND STATISTICAL PARTICULARS | MEDICAL CERTIFICATE OF DEATH

3. SEX _Male_ 4. COLOR or RACE _Negro_ 5. Single, Married, Widowed, Divorced (write the word) _married_

15. DATE OF DEATH _6-1-_ 1936 at _8:45_ G. M

17. I HEREBY CERTIFY, That I attended the deceased from _6-1-_ 1936 to _6-1-_ 1936

6. DATE OF BIRTH (month, day, year) _____
7. AGE _36_ Years _2_ Months _2_ Days If less than one day ___ Hours ___ Minutes ___

I last saw him alive on _6-1-_ 1936 death is said to have occurred on the date and hour stated above.
The principal cause of death and related causes of importance in the order of onset and duration of each:

8. OCCUPATION
(a) Trade, profession or particular kind of work done _farmer_
(b) Industry or business in which work was done _Farm_
(c) Date deceased last worked at this occupation (month and year) _May 30, 1936_ (d) Total years spent in this occupation ___

uremia one day
acute nephritis one day

9. BIRTHPLACE (P.O. Address) _Sandersville_

What test confirmed diagnosis? _clinical_

FATHER
10. NAME _Jeff Carter_
11. BIRTHPLACE (P.O. Address) _Sandersville_

If death was due to external causes (violence) fill in also the following:
Was injury an accident, suicide, or homicide? ___

MOTHER
12. MAIDEN NAME _Ella Hooks_
13. BIRTHPLACE (P.O. Address) _Sandersville_

Where did injury occur ___
Did injury occur in a home, public place or industry? ___
Manner of injury ___
Nature of injury ___

14. INFORMANT (Signed) _Mamie Carter_
(Address) _Sandersville Ga_

(Signed) _W. M. Cason_ M.D.
(Address) _Sandersville_

19. BURIAL PLACE (Cemetery) _Pleasant Springs_
(Postoffice) _Sandersville_ Date _6-5-1936_

18. FILED _6-8-_ 1936
(Signed) _W. H. Barksdale_
(Local Registrar)

20. UNDERTAKER (Signed) _M C Smith_
(Address) _Sandersville_

ite of Georgia
inty of Washington

This is to certify that this is a true and correct copy of the tificate filed with the Vital Records Service, Georgia Department Human Resources. This certified copy is issued under the authority Chapter 88-17, Vital Records, Code of Georgia, annotated, as amended.

Michael R. Lawrie
ite Vital Records Registrar
l Custodian, Director,
:al Records Service

County Custodian _Jane M. Brooker_
Issued By _Ella Tuck_ Date _6-1-93_
(Void without original signature and impressed seal)

Virgil 'Virge' Carter, Death Certificate

"World War I Draft Card of Jeff Carter Jr., "5 June 1917; Georgia, Washington County;
World War I Draft Registration Card, Selective Service System 1917-1918 (Record Group
No.163). National Archives, Southeast Region, East Point, Georgia.

16

MARRIAGE LICENSE.   No._____

STATE OF GEORGIA, WASHINGTON COUNTY.

TO ANY JUDGE, JUSTICE OF THE PEACE, OR MINISTER OF THE GOSPEL:

You are hereby authorized to join *Jeff Carter Col* and *Gervenia Fisher*

Holy State of Matrimony, according to the Constitution and laws of this State, and for so doing this shall be your license; and you are
required to return this license to me, with your certificate hereon of the fact and date of the marriage.

Given under my hand and seal, this _14_ day of _Oct._ , 191 *5*

Geo. Thigpen
, (

ORDINARY.

GEORGIA, WASHINGTON COUNTY.   CERTIFICATE.

I certify that *Jeff Carter Col* and *Gervenia Fisher* were join

matrimony by me, this _17_ day of _Oct._ , Nineteen Hundred and *fifteen*

E. H. S. Strange

Recorded _Oct 23_ , 191 *5*   *Geo. Thigpen*   On

MARRIAGE LICENSE.   No._____   *Marriage Record L page 210*

Jeff Carter Jr. and Gervenia Fisher, Marriage License, October 17, 1915

Lora Ella Carter Dawson   Virgil 'Virge' Carter Sr.   Lillie Ruth Carter Turner

16

Descendants of Burrell Carter

Generation One

1. BURRELL*¹* CARTER was born in May 1833 in Georgia. He married **Mary Ann Lane** in Georgia.

Children of **Burrell*¹* Carter** and **Mary Ann Lane** were as follows:

+   2.   i. MILLY*²*, born circa 1861 in Georgia.
+   3.   ii. JEFF SR., born circa 1862 in Georgia; married **Ella Hooks**; married **Easter Gordy**; married **Delia Howard**.
+   4.   iii. GRACE 'GRACIE', born circa 1864 in Georgia.
+   5.   iv. JOHN, born circa 1866 in Georgia.
+   6.   v. BURRELL 'BURL' JR., born circa 1868 in Georgia.
    7.   vi. SALLIE was born circa 1871 in Georgia.
+   8.   vii. VIRGIL, born circa 1873 in Georgia.
+   9.   viii. SUSIE, born February 1874 in Georgia; married **John Cheeves**; married **Jordan Lord**.
   10.   ix. (INFANT DAUGHER) was born in 1880 in Georgia.
   11.   x. MARY was born in March 1883 in Georgia.

Generation Two

2. MILLY*²* CARTER (*Burrell¹*) was born circa 1861 in Georgia.

Children of **Milly*²* Carter** and **James Smith Sr.** were as follows:

   12.   i. JAMES*³* JR. was born circa 1876 in Georgia.
+   13.   ii. JOSEPH 'JOE' SR., born December 1880 in Washington County, Georgia; married **Texann Trawick**.

3. JEFF*²* CARTER SR. (*Burrell¹*) was born circa 1862 in Georgia. He married **Ella Hooks**, daughter of **James Hooks** and **Mary (——)**, on 19 January 1887 in Washington County, Georgia He married **Easter Gordy**, daughter of **Berry Gordy Sr.** and **Lucy Hellum**, on 8 February 1908 in Washington County, Georgia He married **Delia Howard** on 12 December 1916 in Washington County, Georgia He died on 24 January 1930 in Washington County, Georgia

Children of **Jeff*²* Carter Sr.** and **Ella Hooks** were as follows:

+   14.   i. BERTHA*³*, married **Thomas Renfrow**; married **Johnnie Trawick**.
+   15.   ii. MARY ETHEL, born December 1887 in Georgia; married **Bert Lundy**; married **Charlie Young**.
   16.   iii. LUCY was born circa 1889 in Sandersville, Washington County, Georgia.
   17.   iv. ANNIE B. was born in March 1890 in Georgia.

+ 18. v. JEFF JR., born 10 September 1894 in Oconee, Washington County, Georgia; married **Gervenia Fisher.**
+ 19. vi. LORA ELLA 'LAURA', born 2 June 1895 in Sandersville, Washington County, Georgia; married **Homer Dawson.**
+ 20. vii. LILLIE RUTH, born February 1897 in Georgia; married **Samuel Turner.**
  21. viii. BOYSIE was born in August 1899 in Georgia.
+ 22. ix. VIRGIL 'VIRGE', born 15 August 1900 in Sandersville, Washington County, Georgia; married **Mamie Ethridge.**
  23. x. CRAWFORD was born in 1905 in Sandersville, Washington County, Georgia. He married **Susie** (—?—). He married **Mary** (—?—).
  24. xi. MINNIE was born circa 1907 in Sandersville, Washington County, Georgia. She married **Jesse Butts.**

Children of **Jeff² Carter Sr.** and **Easter Gordy** were as follows:
+ 25. i. RODELL³, born circa 1911 in Georgia; married **Lillian Lucille 'Seal' Cheeves.**
  26. ii. ESTHER was born on 7 May 1914 in Sandersville, Washington County, Georgia She married **Mr. Hinton** in California. She married **I.V. Scott** in 1932 in Detroit, Michigan. She died on 19 October 1985 in Los Angelos, California, at age 71.

There were no children of **Jeff² Carter Sr.** and **Delia Howard.**

4. GRACE 'GRACIE'² CARTER (*Burrell¹*) was born circa 1864 in Georgia.

Children of **Grace 'Gracie'² Carter** and **George Howard** were as follows:
  27. i. PEARL³.
  28. ii. GEORGE (JR.).

5. JOHN² CARTER (*Burrell¹*) was born circa 1866 in Georgia.

Children of **John² Carter** and **Doshia Walker** were as follows:
  29. i. ALEXANDER³.
  30. ii. GRACE was born circa 1900 in Georgia.
  31. iii. JOHN (JR.) was born circa 1904 in Georgia.
+ 32. iv. BEATRICE, born circa 1905 in Georgia.
  33. v. PENNLIE.
+ 34. vi. DEANNA, born 3 May 1906 in Washington County, Georgia; married **Herbert Irwin;** married **Lenard Usry.**
  35. vii. BURRELL 'BURL' was born circa 1908 in Georgia.
  36. viii. JOSEPH was born circa 1911 in Georgia.
  37. ix. DONNIE was born circa 1914 in Georgia.

6. BURRELL 'BURL'² CARTER JR. (*Burrell¹*) was born circa 1868 in Georgia.

Children of **Burrell 'Burl'^{2} Carter Jr.** and **Girlie 'Ann' Smith** were as follows:
38.   i. MICHAEL^3.
39.   ii. GAIL.

8. **VIRGIL^2 CARTER** (*Burrell^1*) was born circa 1873 in Georgia.

Children of **Virgil^2 Carter** and **Mary** (———) were:
+   40.   i. MAMIE^3, born in Georgia.

9. **SUSIE^2 CARTER** (*Burrell^1*) was born in February 1874 in Georgia. She married **John Cheeves**, son of **Henry Cheeves Sr.** and **Mary Ann Wise**, on 8 February 1894 in Washington County, Georgia She married **Jordan Lord** in 1910.

Children of **Susie^2 Carter** and **John Cheeves** were as follows:
+   41.   i. MARY A.^{3}, born February 1895 in Georgia; married **Major Dixon**.
+   42.   ii. SALLIE L., born November 1897 in Georgia; married **Charlie Dixon**.
+   43.   iii. JOHN JR., born March 1899 in Georgia; married **Pearl Jones**.
+   44.   iv. JULIAN, born circa 1901 in Georgia; married **Marietta Harris**.
+   45.   v. GRACE, born circa 1903 in Georgia; married **Willie Mosley**.
+   46.   vi. LUELLA 'DERRA', born circa 1904 in Georgia; married **Jim Bivins**.
    47.   vii. ETHEL was born circa 1906 in Georgia. She married **Freddie Bullock**.
    48.   viii. BESSIE was born circa 1908 in Georgia. She married **James Wright**. She died on 30 October 1966.
+   49.   ix. CLYDE, born circa 1909 in Georgia; married **Henry Mitchell**.

Children of **Susie^2 Carter** and **Jordan Lord** were as follows:
+   50.   i. BURLEY^3 (SR.), born 24 July 1911.
+   51.   ii. CENIE, born circa 1914 in Georgia.
    52.   iii. SAMUEL was born circa 1917 in Georgia. He died on 10 July 1932 in Washington County, Georgia

Generation Three

13. **JOSEPH 'JOE'^{3} SMITH SR.** (*Milly^{2}Carter, Burrell^1*) was born in December 1880 in Washington County, Georgia. He married **Texann Trawick**, daughter of **Dock Trawick** and **Violet Young.**

Children of **Joseph 'Joe'^{3} Smith Sr.** and **Texann Trawick** were as follows:
+   53.   i. JAMES BERYL 'BUDDY'^{4}, born 9 February 1909 in Sandersville, Washington County, Georgia; married **Mildred West**; married **Mary Scott.**
    54.   ii. JOSEPH D. 'JOE' (JR.) was born circa 1912 in Washington County, Georgia. He died in 1990.

55.   iii. VIRGIL was born in 1914 in Washington County, Georgia. He died in 1953.

56.   iv. MILLICENSE 'MYLIE' was born circa 1915 in Washington County, Georgia. She married **Mr. Howard**. She died in 1996.

57.   v. MARY ANN was born on 11 September 1916 in Washington County, Georgia. She married **Mr. Rayford**.

58.   vi. JULIA was born in 1920 in Washington County, Georgia. She married **Mr. Fussel**. She died in 1985.

+   59.   vii. KENNETH PAUL, born 16 August 1922 in Washington County, Georgia; married **Evelyn** (——).

14. BERTHA^3 CARTER (*Jeff^2, Burrell^1*) married **Thomas Renfrow**. She married **Johnnie Trawick**, son of **Dock Trawick** and **Violet Young**.

Children of **Bertha^3 Carter** and **Thomas Renfrow** were as follows:

60.   i. EDWARD 'BUDDY'^{4} married **Ella** (—?—).

61.   ii. THOMAS (JR.).

+   62.   iii. LUCIOUS, married **Gladys Spann**.

Children of **Bertha^3 Carter** and **Johnnie Trawick** were:

+   63.   i. EVA (JOHNNY)^4, born 31 January 1920 in Sandersville, Washington County, Georgia; married **Matthew Thomas**.

15. MARY ETHEL^3 CARTER (*Jeff^2, Burrell^1*) was born in December 1887 in Georgia. She married **Bert Lundy** in Georgia. She married **Charlie Young**.

Children of **Mary Ethel^3 Carter** and **Bert Lundy** were as follows:

+   64.   i. WILLIE BELL^4, born circa 1909 in Georgia; married **K. Jenkins**.

+   65.   ii. ELLA MAE, born circa 1911 in Milledgeville, Baldwin County, Georgia

Children of **Mary Ethel^3 Carter** and **Charlie Young** were as follows:

66.   i. CHARLIE^4 (JR.).

67.   ii. CORENE was born circa 1916 in Georgia. She married **H. Harris**.

+   68.   iii. BERTHA, born 1919 in Georgia; married **Elmer Cheeves**.

69.   iv. LILLIE married **W. Glenn**.

70.   v. LOU DESSA.

18. JEFF^3 CARTER JR. (*Jeff^2, Burrell^1*) was born on 10 September 1894 in Oconee, Washington County, Georgia He married **Gervenia Fisher**, adopted daughter of **Robert Fisher** and **Rachel** (——), on 17 October 1915 in Washington County, Georgia He died in 1930 in Washington County, Georgia

Children of **Jeff³ Carter Jr.** and **Gervenia Fisher** were as follows:
+ 71.   i. MARY JULIA⁴, born 6 October 1916 in Sandersville, Washington County, Georgia; married **Milas Butts (Jr.)**.
+ 72.   ii. LILLIAN ARTHUR, born 19 September 1918 in Sandersville, Washington County, Georgia; married **Henry Holmes Cheeves**.
+ 73. iii. RUBY CLYDE, born 20 February 1921 in Sandersville, Washington County, Georgia; married **James Nelson**.
+ 74.   iv. ENNIS, born 7 April 1925 in Sandersville, Washington County, Georgia; married **Alvonia (———)**.
+ 75.   v. JEFF RAYMOND, born 19 November 1932 in Sandersville, Washington County, Georgia; married **Leonia 'Lumpy' Adams**.

19. LORA ELLA 'LAURA'³ CARTER (*Jeff²*, *Burrell¹*) was born on 2 June 1895 in Sandersville, Washington County, Georgia. She married **Homer Dawson**, son of **Sampson Dawson** and **Mamie Robinson**. She died in October 1966 in West Palm Beach, Florida, at age 71.

Children of **Lora Ella 'Laura'³ Carter** and **Homer Dawson** were as follows:
  76.   i. SAM⁴ was born in Sandersville, Washington County, Georgia
+ 77.   ii. ROBERTA, born circa 5 November 1916 in Sandersville, Washington County, Georgia; married **Wesley Pettis**.
+ 78. iii. ELIZABETH, born 20 August 1921 in Sandersville, Washington County, Georgia; married **Lucious 'Lewis' Fisher**; married **Booker T. Whitehead**.
+ 79.   iv. TIMOTHY, born 31 August 1924 in Sandersville, Washington County, Georgia; married **Lillie Ruth Wiley**.
+ 80.   v. DEBORAH, born 29 June 1927 in Sandersville, Washington County, Georgia; married **Edward Sparks**.
+ 81.   vi. ELOISE 'HONEY', born 27 September 1929 in Sandersville, Washington County, Georgia; married **Robert Daniel Gordy**.
+ 82. vii. HOMER (JR.), born 4 January 1932 in Sandersville, Washington County, Georgia; married **Bettye Tanner**.
+ 83. viii. CORNELIUS, born 5 November 1933 in Sandersville, Washington County, Georgia; married **Delores Pinkston**.
+ 84.   ix. WILHELMINA 'CANDY', born 29 September 1936 in Sandersville, Washington County, Georgia; married **Amos Ross**; married **Frank Davis**.

20. LILLIE RUTH³ CARTER (*Jeff²*, *Burrell¹*) was born in February 1897 in Georgia. She married **Samuel Turner**.

Children of **Lillie Ruth³ Carter** and **Samuel Turner** were as follows:
+ 85.   i. SAMUEL⁴ (JR.), married **Odessa Boiling**.
  86.   ii. O'NEAL.

+ 87.   iii. BLANCHE, married **Dabney Holley.**
+ 88.   iv. MILDRED, married **James Moore.**

22. VIRGIL 'VIRGE'³ CARTER (*Jeff²*, *Burrell¹*) was born on 15 August 1900 in Sandersville, Washington County, Georgia. He married **Mamie Ethridge** on 24 December 1918 in Baldwin County, Georgia He died on 1 June 1936 in Sandersville, Washington County, Georgia, at age 35.

Children of **Virgil 'Virge'³ Carter** and **Mamie Ethridge** were as follows:
+ 89.   i. RUTH MILDRED⁴, born 30 July 1920 in Sandersville, Georgia; married **Kenneth Rawlins.**
+ 90.   ii. ANNE, born 21 March 1923 in Sandersville, Georgia; married **David Green.**
  91.   iii. DOROTHY LUCILLE was born on 29 June 1925 in Sandersville, Georgia. She married **Alfred Peachy.** She died on 26 June 1981 in Brooklyn, New York, at age 55.
  92.   iv. VIRGIL (JR.) was born on 6 October 1928 in Sandersville, Georgia.
  93.   v. MARY LILLIAN was born on 30 November 1931 in Sandersville, Georgia. She married **Timothy Vincent.** She died on 27 February 2000 in Brooklyn, New York, at age 68.
+ 94.   vi. TERESA, born 4 September 1933 in Sandersville, Georgia; married **Stanley Snyder.**

25. RODELL³ CARTER (*Jeff²*, *Burrell¹*) was born circa 1911 in Georgia. He married **Lillian Lucille 'Seal' Cheeves**, daughter of **David 'Coot' Cheeves** and **Hattie Johnson.**

Children of **Rodell³ Carter** and **Nora Davis** were:
  95.   i. BARBARA 'BOBBY'⁴.

There were no children of **Rodell³ Carter** and **Lillian Lucille 'Seal' Cheeves.**

32. BEATRICE³ CARTER (*John²*, *Burrell¹*) was born circa 1905 in Georgia.

Children of **Beatrice³ Carter** and **Will Davis** were as follows:
  96.   i. WILLIAM⁴.
  97.   ii. CALVIN.

34. DEANNA³ CARTER (*John²*, *Burrell¹*) was born on 3 May 1906 in Washington County, Georgia. She married **Herbert Irwin.** She married **Lenard Usry** in 1931 in Sandersville, Georgia.

Children of **Deanna³ Carter** and **Herbert Irwin** were:
  98.   i. MARY THERESA⁴ was born on 18 May 1922 in Sandersville, Georgia. She married **Randolph Allan Durrant** on 28 December 1985 in Philadelphia, Pennsylvania.

Children of **Deanna**^{3} **Carter** and **Lenard Usry** were as follows:
99.   i. LOIS^4 was born in Sandersville, Georgia.
100.   ii. CURTIS was born on 11 February 1934 in Sandersville, Georgia.
101.   iii. LENARD (JR.).
102.   iv. JOHN was born in Sandersville, Georgia.
103.   v. THOMAS.
+ 104.   vi. DOSHIA, born in Sandersville, Georgia.
105.   vii. WILLIAM BOB was born on 31 August 1931 in Sandersville, Georgia.

40. MAMIE^3 **CARTER** (*Virgil*^{2}, *Burrell*^{1}) was born in Georgia.

Children of **Mamie**^{3} **Carter** include:
+ 106.   i. GEORGE B.^{4}, born in Georgia.

Children of **Mamie**^{3} **Carter** and **Jeff Barlow** were as follows:
+ 107.   i. MELVIN^4, born in Georgia.
+ 108.   ii. JEFF (II), born in Georgia.
+ 109.   iii. ALFRED, born in Georgia.
+ 110.   iv. VIRGIL, born in Georgia.
+ 111.   v. KENNETH, born in Georgia.
+ 112.   vi. THOMAS, born in Georgia.
+ 113.   vii. PHELMON, born in Georgia.
+ 114.   viii. ELSIE, born in Georgia.
+ 115.   ix. DELORES, born in Georgia.
+ 116.   x. ERNESTINE, born in Georgia.
+ 117.   xi. CATHERINE, born in Georgia.
+ 118.   xii. THELMA, born in Georgia.
+ 119.   xiii. JUANITA, born in Georgia.
+ 120.   xiv. CONSTANCE, born in Georgia.
+ 121.   xv. DIANE

41. MARY A.^{3} **CHEEVES** (*Susie*^{2} *Carter*, *Burrell*^{1}) was born in February 1895 in Georgia. She married **Major Dixon**, son of **Ransome Dixon** and **Betty** (———). She died on 12 February 1942.

Children of **Mary A.**^{3} **Cheeves** and **Major Dixon** were as follows:
122.   i. JOHNNIE^4 was born circa 1913 in Georgia.
123.   ii. LILLIAN was born circa 1914 in Georgia.
+ 124.   iii. CHARLIE, born circa 1916 in Georgia; married **Elaine** (———).
125.   iv. LOZELL.
126.   v. BENJAMIN.
+ 127.   vi. WILLIAM, married **Renee** (———).

+ 128. vii. ROSALIE 'ROSE', born circa 1918 in Georgia.
129. viii. ELAINE was born circa 1920.
130. ix. ANN PEARL.
+ 131. x. ANNA JULIA

42. SALLIE L.^{3} **CHEEVES** (*Susie*^{2}*Carter, Burrell*^{1}) was born in November 1897 in Georgia. She married **Charlie Dixon**, son of **Ransome Dixon** and **Betty** (————). She died in August 1959 at age 61.

Children of **Sallie L.**^{3} **Cheeves** and **Charlie Dixon** were as follows:
+ 132.   i. HORACE^4, born 13 March 1917 in Sandersville, Georgia; married **Bertha McLemore.**
+ 133.   ii. CHARLIE (JR.)
+ 134.   iii. ED
+ 135.   iv. MINNIE, married **Mr. Woodard.**
+ 136.   v. DORIS, married **Mr. Gates.**
+ 137.   vi. JANETTE, married **Mr. Beatha.**

43. JOHN^3 **CHEEVES JR.** (*Susie*^{2}*Carter, Burrell*^{1}) was born in March 1899 in Georgia. He married **Pearl Jones.** He died on 21 March 1928.

Children of **John**^{3} **Cheeves Jr.** and **Pearl Jones** were as follows:
+ 138.   i. REATHER^4, born 16 February 1923 in Georgia; married **Ella Dixon;** married **Martha** (————).
139.   ii. JOHN III.
140.   iii. TOM.
141.   iv. BILL.
142.   v. MERIDETH.
143.   vi. ELIZABETH married **Mr. Tolston.**
144.   vii. BARBARA.

44. JULIAN^3 **CHEEVES** (*Susie*^{2}*Carter, Burrell*^{1}) was born circa 1901 in Georgia. He married **Marietta Harris.** He died in October 1943.

Children of **Julian**^{3} **Cheeves** and **Marietta Harris** were as follows:
145.   i. BERNICE^4.
146.   ii. MARIE.

45. GRACE^3 **CHEEVES** (*Susie*^{2}*Carter, Burrell*^{1}) was born circa 1903 in Georgia. She married **Willie Mosley.** She died on 13 August 1945.

Children of **Grace**[3] **Cheeves** and **Willie Mosley** were:
147.   i. CARLTON[4] was born circa 1918 in Georgia.

46. LUELLA 'DERRA'[3] **CHEEVES** (*Susie*[2]*Carter, Burrell*[1]) was born circa 1904 in Georgia. She married **Jim Bivins.**

Children of **Luella 'Derra'**[3] **Cheeves** and **Jim Bivins** were as follows:
148.   i. RUTH[4].
149.   ii. RUBY.
150.   iii. BUNCHIE.

49. CLYDE[3] **CHEEVES** (*Susie*[2]*Carter, Burrell*[1]) was born circa 1909 in Georgia. She married **Henry Mitchell.**

Children of **Clyde**[3] **Cheeves** and **Henry Mitchell** were as follows:
+ 151.   i. RUTH[4], born circa 1940; married **Lee Arthur Wright.**
152.   ii. HENRY (JR.).
153.   iii. BILL.
+ 154.   iv. WILLIE, married **Irene Flemmens.**
+ 155.   v. MILEY, married **Timothy Kelsey.**
+ 156.   vi. DORIS DOROTHY
+ 157.   vii. HAZEL, born March 1937 in Washington County, Georgia
158.   viii. MARY CLYDE.
159.   ix. ALMA JEAN.

50. BURLEY[3] **LORD (SR.)** (*Susie*[2]*Carter, Burrell*[1]) was born on 24 July 1911. He died on 6 April 1991 at age 79.

Children of **Burley**[3] **Lord (Sr.)** and **Rosa Mae Butts** were as follows:
160.   i. BERINE[4].
+ 161.   ii. MARY L., born 5 November 1935; married **Ronald Robinson;** married **John Goodson.**
+ 162.   iii. BURLEY 'SYTES' (JR.), born 6 July 1938; married **Mary Edith Hall;** married **Gloria 'Glo' Louise Trawick.**
+ 163.   iv. JEROME, born 1 April 1940; married **Priscilla Miles;** married **Patricia Pitts.**
+ 164.   v. MELVIN, born 1 October 1941; married **Anita 'Cookie' Smith;** married **Conchetta Brewer;** married **Denise Johnson.**
+ 165.   vi. RONALD C. (SR.), born 4 February 1944; married **Grace Corn.**
166.   vii. ETHEL JEAN was born on 9 January 1946.
+ 167.   viii. JACQUELINE 'JACKI', born 15 May 1948; married **Edward English.**
+ 168.   ix. JOAN, born 21 May 1949; married **Charles Moore.**

51. CENIE^3 **LORD** (*Susie*^{2}*Carter, Burrell*^{1}) was born circa 1914 in Georgia.

Children of **Cenie**^{3} **Lord** and **Al Hutchinson** were as follows:
169.   i. HENRY^4.
170.   ii. DORIS.
171.   iii. YVETTE.

Generation Four

53. JAMES BERYL 'BUDDY'^{4} **SMITH** (*Joseph 'Joe'*^{3}*, Milly*^{2}*Carter, Burrell*^{1}) was born on 9 February 1909 in Sandersville, Washington County, Georgia. He married **Mildred West**. He married **Mary Scott**. He died on 17 October 1981 in Camden, New Jersey, at age 72.

Children of **James Beryl 'Buddy'**^{4} **Smith** and **Mildred West** were:
+ 172.   i. JEAN^5, born 7 August 1934 in Philadelphia, Pennsylvania; married **Arnold Dixon Jackson Sr.**

Children of **James Beryl 'Buddy'**^{4} **Smith** and **Mary Scott** were:
173.   i. DRESSLER^5 was born on 14 September 1958 in Philadelphia, Pennsylvania. She married **Crandall Richard.**

59. KENNETH PAUL^4 **SMITH** (*Joseph 'Joe'*^{3}*, Milly*^{2}*Carter, Burrell*^{1}) was born on 16 August 1922 in Washington County, Georgia. He married **Evelyn** (———). He died on 22 October 1996 at age 74.

Children of **Kenneth Paul**^{4} **Smith** and **Evelyn** (———) were:
+ 174.   i. EVETTE^5

62. LUCIOUS^4 **RENFROW** (*Bertha*^{3}*Carter, Jeff*^{2}*, Burrell*^{1}) married **Gladys Spann.**

Children of **Lucious**^{4} **Renfrow** and **Gladys Spann** were as follows:
175.   i. CRAIG^5.
176.   ii. BEVERLY married **Robert Anderson.**

63. EVA (JOHNNY)^4 **TRAWICK** (*Bertha*^{3}*Carter, Jeff*^{2}*, Burrell*^{1}) was born on 31 January 1920 in Sandersville, Washington County, Georgia. She married **Matthew Thomas.**

Children of **Eva (Johnny)**^{4} **Trawick** and **Matthew Thomas** were as follows:
+ 177.   i. SANDRA CAROL^5, born 31 May 1946 in Philadelphia, Pennsylvania; married **Herb Connelly.**

+ 178.   ii. SIGRID ANN, born 10 March 1948 in Philadelphia, Pennsylvania; married **Howard Edward McCall Jr.**
+ 179.   iii. WANDA EILEEN, born 12 April 1950 in Philadelphia, Pennsylvania; married **John 'Donald' Bird.**

64. **WILLIE BELL**^{4} **LUNDY** (*Mary Ethel*^{3}*Carter, Jeff*^{2}, *Burrell*^{1}) was born circa 1909 in Georgia. He married **K. Jenkins.**

Children of **Willie Bell**^{4} **Lundy** and **K. Jenkins** were as follows:
180.   i. CHARLES^5.
181.   ii. JEROME.
182.   iii. JUDY.

65. **ELLA MAE**^{4} **LUNDY** (*Mary Ethel*^{3}*Carter, Jeff*^{2}, *Burrell*^{1}) was born circa 1911 in Milledgeville, Baldwin County, Georgia

Children of **Ella Mae**^{4} **Lundy** include:
183.   i. WILLIE^5.

68. **BERTHA**^{4} **YOUNG** (*Mary Ethel*^{3}*Carter, Jeff*^{2}, *Burrell*^{1}) was born in 1919 in Georgia. She married **Elmer Cheeves.**

Children of **Bertha**^{4} **Young** and **Elmer Cheeves** were as follows:
184.   i. MARY^5.
185.   ii. VIVIAN.

71. **MARY JULIA**^{4} **CARTER** (*Jeff*^{3}, *Jeff*^{2}, *Burrell*^{1}) was born on 6 October 1916 in Sandersville, Washington County, Georgia She married **Milas Butts (Jr.)**, son of **Milas Butts (Sr.)** and **Roeanor Dawson.** She died on 16 October 1943 in Philadelphia, Penn, at age 27.

Children of **Mary Julia**^{4} **Carter** and **Milas Butts (Jr.)** were as follows:
+ 186.   i. ALTON^5, born 28 October 1934 in Sandersville, Georgia; married **Marlyn Farley.**
187.   ii. VIVIAN.

72. **LILLIAN ARTHUR**^{4} **CARTER** (*Jeff*^{3}, *Jeff*^{2}, *Burrell*^{1}) was born on 19 September 1918 in Sandersville, Washington County, Georgia. She married **Henry Holmes Cheeves**, son of **Henry Cheeves Jr.** and **Clara Bell Trawick.** She died on 2 February 1966 at age 47.

Children of **Lillian Arthur**^{4} **Carter** and **Henry Holmes Cheeves** were as follows:
+ 188.   i. MIRIAM^5, born in Sandersville, Washington County, Georgia
+ 189.   ii. GLORIA, born 4 July 1941 in Sandersville, Washington County, Georgia; married **Charles Graham.**
+ 190.   iii. HORACE, born 4 September 1943 in Sandersville, Washington County, Georgia; married **Fannie Pearl Williams.**
+ 191.   iv. FOREST, born 4 September 1943 in Sandersville, Washington County, Georgia; married **Karen Kennedy.**
   192.   v. HENRY was born on 8 September 1948 in Sandersville, Washington County, Georgia
   193.   vi. DAVID was born on 10 November 1954 in Philadelphia, Penn. He died on 17 August 1995 in Detroit, Mich, at age 40.
   194.   vii. ANNETTE GAIL was born on 7 August 1958 in Philadelphia, Pennsylvania.

73. RUBY CLYDE^4 **CARTER** (*Jeff*^{3}, *Jeff*^{2}, *Burrell*^{1}) was born on 20 February 1921 in Sandersville, Washington County, Georgia. She married **James Nelson.** She died on 13 April 2002 in Philadelphia, Pennsylvania, at age 81.

Children of **Ruby Clyde**^{4} **Carter** and **Jack Cotton** were:
+ 195.   i. MICHELLE^5, born 23 February 1958 in Detroit, Michigan.

Children of **Ruby Clyde**^{4} **Carter** and **James Nelson** were:
+ 196.   i. HERMAN^5, born 4 November 1943 in Philadelphia, Pennsylvania; married **Dallay Yvonne Graham.**

74. ENNIS^4 **CARTER** (*Jeff*^{3}, *Jeff*^{2}, *Burrell*^{1}) was born on 7 April 1925 in Sandersville, Washington County, Georgia. He married **Alvonia** (————) on 12 December 1970 in Detroit, Michigan

Children of **Ennis**^{4} **Carter** include:
   197.   i. BERNICE^5 was born in 1942 in Sandersville, Washington County, Georgia
   198.   ii. HARVEY was born in November 1942 in Newnan, Georgia He died in November 1984 in Sandersville, Washington County, Georgia
   199.   iii. LEWIS was born on 7 July 1943 in Sandersville, Washington County, Georgia
   200.   iv. LOIS was born on 7 July 1943 in Sandersville, Washington County, Georgia
   201.   v. DELRA was born on 17 August 1949 in Detroit, Michigan
   202.   vi. DENISE was born on 26 July 1952 in Detroit, Michigan
   203.   vii. DONNA was born on 2 February 1956 in Detroit, Michigan

Children of **Ennis**^{4} **Carter** and **Zelma Shenoster** were:
   204.   i. DONALD 'DUCK'^{5} was born on 29 September 1948 in Philadelphia, Pennsylvania. He died on 29 June 2001 in Philadelphia, Pennsylvania, at age 52.

There were no children of **Ennis**[4] **Carter** and **Alvonia** (———).

75. **JEFF RAYMOND**[4] **CARTER** (*Jeff*[3], *Jeff*[2], *Burrell*[1]) was born on 19 November 1932 in Sandersville, Washington County, Georgia He married **Leonia 'Lumpy' Adams**. He died on 1 December 1990 in Philadelphia, Pennsylvania, at age 58.

Children of **Jeff Raymond**[4] **Carter** and **Leonia 'Lumpy' Adams** were as follows:
+ 205.   i. SHARON 'SHERRY'[5], born 18 April 1949 in Philadelphia, Pennsylvania.
+ 206.   ii. JEFF RAYMOND 'BROTHER' JR., born 1 July 1950 in Philadelphia, Pennsylvania; married **Sujuan Williams**.
  207.   iii. DENISE.
+ 208.   iv. DENNIS, born 25 December 1952 in Philadelphia, Pennsylvania; married **Marcia Earlene Jackson**.
  209.   v. RAYMOND was born in September 1959.

77. **ROBERTA**[4] **DAWSON** (*Lora Ella 'Laura'*[3] *Carter, Jeff*[2], *Burrell*[1]) was born circa 5 November 1916 in Sandersville, Washington County, Georgia. She married **Wesley Pettis**. She died in December 1954 in West Palm Beach, Florida.

Children of **Roberta**[4] **Dawson** and **Wesley Pettis** were as follows:
  210.   i. CALVIN[5].
  211.   ii. JOYCE.

78. **ELIZABETH**[4] **DAWSON** (*Lora Ella 'Laura'*[3] *Carter, Jeff*[2], *Burrell*[1]) was born on 20 August 1921 in Sandersville, Washington County, Georgia She married **Lucious 'Lewis' Fisher**. She married **Booker T. Whitehead**.

Children of **Elizabeth**[4] **Dawson** include:
+ 212.   i. SHIRLEY[5], born 29 March; married **Edward Brent**.

There were no children of **Elizabeth**[4] **Dawson** and **Lucious 'Lewis' Fisher**.

There were no children of **Elizabeth**[4] **Dawson** and **Booker T. Whitehead**.

79. **TIMOTHY**[4] **DAWSON** (*Lora Ella 'Laura'*[3] *Carter, Jeff*[2], *Burrell*[1]) was born on 31 August 1924 in Sandersville, Washington County, Georgia He married **Lillie Ruth Wiley** in 1949. He died on 26 April 1995 in Philadelphia, Pennsylvania, at age 70.

Children of **Timothy**[4] **Dawson** and **Lillie Ruth Wiley** were as follows:
  213.   i. JEFFREY[5] was born on 6 August in Sandersville, Georgia.
+ 214.   ii. BRENDA, born 18 September in Sandersville, Georgia; married **Mark Scott**.

+ 215.   iii. BENNIE LAWSON, born 6 July 1947 in Sandersville, Georgia; married **Barbara Jones.**

216.   iv. TIMOTHY (JR.) was born on 11 November 1950 in Sandersville, Georgia. He married **Volanda** (—?—).

217.   v. EMORY was born on 21 June 1951 in Sandersville, Georgia. He married **Patricia Pates.**

+ 218.   vi. LORETTA, born 30 August 1952 in Sandersville, Georgia; married **Aubrey Jones.**

+ 219.   vii. PAULINE, born 12 November 1954 in Sandersville, Georgia; married **Alfred Ford.**

220.   viii. ROBERTA was born on 19 April 1956 in Sandersville, Georgia.

221.   ix. LILLIAN was born on 6 August 1957 in Sandersville, Georgia. She married **Eddie Pulliam.**

80. **DEBORAH**^{4} **DAWSON** (*Lora Ella 'Laura*^{3}*Carter, Jeff*^{2}*, Burrell*^{1}) was born on 29 June 1927 in Sandersville, Washington County, Georgia She married **Edward Sparks.**

Children of **Deborah**^{4} **Dawson** and **Edward Sparks** were as follows:

+ 222.   i. GRACE HARRIS^5, born 22 March 1944 in Sandersville, Georgia; married **Hugh Bryant.**

223.   ii. EDWARD TRACY was born on 28 September 1958 in Syracuse, New York.

224.   iii. MICHAEL was born on 31 October 1959 in Syracuse, New York.

225.   iv. GARY was born on 13 October 1960 in Syracuse, New York.

226.   v. WILLIAM 'BILLY' KENNETH was born on 29 January 1962 in Syracuse, New York.

227.   vi. RICHARD was born on 17 July 1965 in Syracuse, New York.

81. **ELOISE 'HONEY'**^{4} **DAWSON** (*Lora Ella 'Laura*^{3}*Carter, Jeff*^{2}*, Burrell*^{1}) was born on 27 September 1929 in Sandersville, Washington County, Georgia She married **Robert Daniel Gordy**, son of **Samuel 'Sam' Gordy** and **Carrie Cheeves**, on 6 March 1950 in Sandersville, Washington County, Georgia.

Children of **Eloise 'Honey'**^{4} **Dawson** and **Robert Daniel Gordy** were as follows:

+ 228.   i. GWENDOLYN^5, born 12 March 1947 in Utica, New York; married **Julius Murphy.**

229.   ii. ROBERT DANIEL JR. was born on 27 July 1950 in Sandersville, Georgia.

+ 230.   iii. DAVID, born 13 April 1952 in Sandersville, Georgia; married **DeLois Turner;** married **Darlene Robinson.**

+ 231.   iv. DEBORAH ANNE, born 6 January 1954 in Sandersville, Georgia; married **Samuel Duggan.**

+ 232.   v. MARY LUCY, born 17 July 1956 in Sandersville, Georgia; married **Tony Owen Hurt Sr.**

233.   vi. REGINALD CORNELIUS was born on 5 September 1957 in Sandersville, Georgia. He married **Yvette** (—?—).

+ 234.   vii. BERRY RENARD, born 10 September 1958 in Sandersville, Georgia; married **Brenda Lee Lord Barlow Cardy.**

82. HOMER^4 DAWSON (JR.) (*Lora Ella 'Laura^3 Carter, Jeff^2, Burrell^1*) was born on 4 January 1932 in Sandersville, Washington County, Georgia He married **Bettye Tanner.**

Children of **Homer^4 Dawson (Jr.)** and **Bettye Tanner** were as follows:

+ 235. i. CATHERINE LORETTA^5, born 4 February 1951 in West Palm Beach, Florida; married **Douglas Fulton.**
+ 236. ii. HOMER 'BILLY' III, born 9 April 1953 in West Palm Beach, Florida; married **Brenda McCullom.**
237. iii. JEFFREY was born on 4 June 1954 in West Palm Beach, Florida. He married **Bernice (—?—).**
+ 238. iv. WENDELL, born 31 January 1957 in West Palm Beach, Florida; married **Deborah Davis.**
+ 239. v. NATALIE JEAN, born 6 April 1958 in West Palm Beach, Florida; married **Robert Smith.**

83. CORNELIUS^4 DAWSON (*Lora Ella 'Laura^3 Carter, Jeff^2, Burrell^1*) was born on 5 November 1933 in Sandersville, Washington County, Georgia He married **Delores Pinkston.**

Children of **Cornelius^4 Dawson** and **Delores Pinkston** were as follows:

+ 240. i. BEVERLY^5, born 5 February 1955 in East Palatka, Florida.
+ 241. ii. WANDA, born 1 November 1959 in West Palm Beach, Florida; married **Tim Hunt.**
242. iii. ROBBYN was born on 2 November 1961 in West Palm Beach, Florida.
243. iv. ERIC was born on 25 November 1967 in West Palm Beach, Florida.

84. WILHELMINA 'CANDY'^{4} DAWSON (*Lora Ella 'Laura^3 Carter, Jeff^2, Burrell^1*) was born on 29 September 1936 in Sandersville, Washington County, Georgia She married **Amos Ross.** She married **Frank Davis.**

There were no children of **Wilhelmina 'Candy'^{4} Dawson** and **Amos Ross.**

Children of **Wilhelmina 'Candy'^{4} Dawson** and **Frank Davis** were as follows:

+ 244. i. KAREN ' KAY' ELIZABETH^5, born 14 May 1956 in West Palm Beach, Florida; married **Willie Neal.**
245. ii. GWENETH 'RUTHIE' was born on 29 September 1957.

85. SAMUEL^4 TURNER (JR.) (*Lillie Ruth^3 Carter, Jeff^2, Burrell^1*) married **Odessa Boiling.**

Children of **Samuel^4 Turner (Jr.)** and **Odessa (———)** were:
246. i. DORICE^5.

Children of **Samuel**[4] **Turner (Jr.)** and **Odessa Boiling** were as follows:
247.   i. MICHAEL[5].
248.   ii. CAROLYN.

87. **BLANCHE**[4] **TURNER** (*Lillie Ruth*[3] *Carter, Jeff*[2], *Burrell*[1]) married **Dabney Holley.**

Children of **Blanche**[4] **Turner** and **Dabney Holley** were:
249.   i. NADINE[5].

88. **MILDRED**[4] **TURNER** (*Lillie Ruth*[3] *Carter, Jeff*[2], *Burrell*[1]) married **James Moore.**

Children of **Mildred**[4] **Turner** and **James Moore** were as follows:
250.   i. DONALD[5].
251.   ii. JAMES.
252.   iii. LILLIAN.
253.   iv. SANDRA.

89. **RUTH MILDRED**[4] **CARTER** (*Virgil 'Virge*[3], *Jeff*[2], *Burrell*[1]) was born on 30 July 1920 in Sandersville, Georgia. She married **Kenneth Rawlins**. She died on 13 August 1993 in Brooklyn, New York, at age 73.

Children of **Ruth Mildred**[4] **Carter** include:
254.   i. JOSEPH EDWARD ALEXANDER[5] was born on 5 October 1950 in Brooklyn, New York. He died on 3 June 1992 at age 41.
+ 255.   ii. AVA DIANE, born 28 June 1957 in Brooklyn, New York; married **Ricky Holden.**

There were no children of **Ruth Mildred**[4] **Carter** and **Kenneth Rawlins**.

90. **ANNE**[4] **CARTER** (*Virgil 'Virge*[3], *Jeff*[2], *Burrell*[1]) was born on 21 March 1923 in Sandersville, Georgia. She married **David Green** on 21 July 1945 in Brooklyn, New York.

Children of **Anne**[4] **Carter** and **David Green** were as follows:
+ 256.   i. RICHARD CARTER[5], born 28 October 1947 in Brooklyn, New York; married **Elaine Parson.**
257.   ii. MICHAEL DAVID was born on 23 November 1950 in Brooklyn, New York. He died on 18 December 1981 in Hawaii at age 31.

94. **TERESA**[4] **CARTER** (*Virgil 'Virge*[3], *Jeff*[2], *Burrell*[1]) was born on 4 September 1933 in Sandersville, Georgia. She married **Stanley Snyder.**

Children of **Teresa**[4] **Carter** and **Stanley Snyder** were as follows:
+ 258.   i. BARI LYN[5], born 6 February 1961 in Brooklyn, New York.
+ 259.   ii. DERON KEITH, born 16 September 1962 in Brooklyn, New York.

104. DOSHIA[4] **USRY** (*Deanna*[3] *Carter, John*[2], *Burrell*[1]) was born in Sandersville, Georgia.

Children of **Doshia**[4] **Usry** and **Frank Askew** were as follows:
   260.   i. TERRY[5].
   261.   ii. LAMONT.

106. GEORGE B.[4] **WILLIAMS** (*Mamie*[3]*Carter, Virgil*[2], *Burrell*[1]) was born in Georgia.

Children of **George B.**[4] **Williams** and **Elouise** (———) were as follows:
   262.   i. GERALD[5].
   263.   ii. VALERIE.

107. MELVIN[4] **BARLOW** (*Mamie*[3]*Carter, Virgil*[2], *Burrell*[1]) was born in Georgia.

Children of **Melvin**[4] **Barlow** and **Sarah** (———) were as follows:
   264.   i. MARGARET[5].
   265.   ii. DEBRA.
   266. iii. MARCIA.

108. JEFF[4] **BARLOW (II)** (*Mamie*[3]*Carter, Virgil*[2], *Burrell*[1]) was born in Georgia.

Children of **Jeff**[4] **Barlow (II)** and **Loretta** (———) were as follows:
   267.   i. JEFF[5] (III).
   268.   ii. BRENDA.

109. ALFRED[4] **BARLOW** (*Mamie*[3]*Carter, Virgil*[2], *Burrell*[1]) was born in Georgia.

Children of **Alfred**[4] **Barlow** and **Dana** (———) were as follows:
   269.   i. DANA[5].
   270.   ii. KHERRA.

110. VIRGIL[4] **BARLOW** (*Mamie*[3]*Carter, Virgil*[2], *Burrell*[1]) was born in Georgia.

Children of **Virgil**[4] **Barlow** and **Malinda** (———) were:
   271.   i. CLIFFORD[5].

111. KENNETH[4] **BARLOW** (*Mamie*[3]*Carter, Virgil*[2], *Burrell*[1]) was born in Georgia.

Children of **Kenneth**^{4} **Barlow** and **Rochelle** (———) were as follows:
272.   i. GEORGE^5.
273.   ii. LISA MARIE.
274.   iii. RASHEEDA.

112. THOMAS^4 **BARLOW** (*Mamie*^{3}*Carter, Virgil*^{2}*, Burrell*^{1}) was born in Georgia.

Children of **Thomas**^{4} **Barlow** and **Beatrice** (———) were:
275.   i. TONYA^5.

113. PHELMON^4 **BARLOW** (*Mamie*^{3}*Carter, Virgil*^{2}*, Burrell*^{1}) was born in Georgia.

Children of **Phelmon**^{4} **Barlow** and **Juanita** (———) were as follows:
276.   i. PHELMON^5 (JR.).
277.   ii. TIFFANY.
278.   iii. TIA.

114. ELSIE^4 **BARLOW** (*Mamie*^{3}*Carter, Virgil*^{2}*, Burrell*^{1}) was born in Georgia.

Children of **Elsie**^{4} **Barlow** and **W. Clark** were as follows:
279.   i. MELANIE^5.
280.   ii. PATRICIA.
281.   iii. ELSIE (JR.).
282.   iv. ELEANOR.
283.   v. DEMURIS.

115. DELORES^4 **BARLOW** (*Mamie*^{3}*Carter, Virgil*^{2}*, Burrell*^{1}) was born in Georgia.

Children of **Delores**^{4} **Barlow** and **Mr. West** were as follows:
284.   i. SYLVESTER^5.
285.   ii. KENNETH.
286.   iii. JACQUILINE.
287.   iv. MAMIE.

116. ERNESTINE^4 **BARLOW** (*Mamie*^{3}*Carter, Virgil*^{2}*, Burrell*^{1}) was born in Georgia.

Children of **Ernestine**^{4} **Barlow** include:
288.   i. TERRENCE^5.
289.   ii. SHARON.

117. CATHERINE^4 **BARLOW** (*Mamie*^{3}*Carter, Virgil*^{2}*, Burrell*^{1}) was born in Georgia.

Children of **Catherine**^{4} **Barlow** and **Leroy Johnson** were as follows:
290.   i. LEROY^5 (JR.).
291.   ii. MARCUS.
292.   iii. RHONDA.

118. **THELMA**^{4} **BARLOW** (*Mamie*^{3}*Carter, Virgil*^{2}*, Burrell*^{1}) was born in Georgia.

Children of **Thelma**^{4} **Barlow** and **E. Griffin** were:
293.   i. KAREN^5.

119. **JUANITA**^{4} **BARLOW** (*Mamie*^{3}*Carter, Virgil*^{2}*, Burrell*^{1}) was born in Georgia.

Children of **Juanita**^{4} **Barlow** include:
294.   i. DEFORIO^5.

120. **CONSTANCE**^{4} **BARLOW** (*Mamie*^{3}*Carter, Virgil*^{2}*, Burrell*^{1}) was born in Georgia.

Children of **Constance**^{4} **Barlow** and **S. Barr** were as follows:
295.   i. RAYMOND^5.
296.   ii. SHEILA.

121. **DIANE**^{4} **BARLOW** (*Mamie*^{3}*Carter, Virgil*^{2}*, Burrell*^{1}).

Children of **Diane**^{4} **Barlow** and **R. Williams** were as follows:
297.   i. CHRISTEL^5.
298.   ii. LATISHA.
299.   iii. MONIQUE.

124. **CHARLIE**^{4} **DIXON** (*Mary A.*^{3}*Cheeves, Susie*^{2}*Carter, Burrell*^{1}) was born circa 1916 in Georgia. He married **Elaine** (———).

Children of **Charlie**^{4} **Dixon** and **Elaine** (———) were:
300.   i. BRENDA^5 was born circa 1945.

127. **WILLIAM**^{4} **DIXON** (*Mary A.*^{3}*Cheeves, Susie*^{2}*Carter, Burrell*^{1}) married **Renee** (———).

Children of **William**^{4} **Dixon** and **Renee** (———) were:
301.   i. EARL^5.

128. **ROSALIE 'ROSE'**^{4} **DIXON** (*Mary A.*^{3}*Cheeves, Susie*^{2}*Carter, Burrell*^{1}) was born circa 1918 in Georgia.

Children of **Rosalie 'Rose'^{4} Dixon** include:
+ 302. i. ELAINE^5

131. ANNA JULIA^4 DIXON (*Mary A.^{3}Cheeves, Susie^{2}Carter, Burrell^1*).

Children of **Anna Julia^4 Dixon** include:
+ 303. i. LEWIS^5, married **Mary** (———).
+ 304. ii. MAJOR, married **Emma** (———).
+ 305. iii. JEROME, married **Rose** (———).
+ 306. iv. DAISY MAE
+ 307. v. MARLENE, married **Will Pearsall.**

132. HORACE^4 DIXON (*Sallie L.^{3}Cheeves, Susie^{2}Carter, Burrell^1*) was born on 13 March 1917 in Sandersville, Georgia. He married **Bertha McLemore.** He died in April 1979 in Philadelphia, Pennsylvania, at age 62.

Children of **Horace^4 Dixon** and **Bertha McLemore** were as follows:
+ 308. i. PHILIP (ALI SALAUDIN)^5, born 4 February 1947 in Philadelphia, Pennsylvania; married **Carol Haughton.**
+ 309. ii. RODNEY, born 8 March 1950 in Philadelphia, Pennsylvania; married **Beverly Diane Fisher.**

133. CHARLIE^4 DIXON (JR.) (*Sallie L.^{3}Cheeves, Susie^{2}Carter, Burrell^1*).

Children of **Charlie^4 Dixon (Jr.)** include:
  310. i. LONNIE^5.
  311. ii. CHARLIE (III).
  312. iii. STEVIE.
  313. iv. WAYNE.
  314. v. LINDA.
  315. vi. VALERIE.
  316. vii. ELIZABETH.

134. ED^4 DIXON (*Sallie L.^{3}Cheeves, Susie^{2}Carter, Burrell^1*).

Children of **Ed^4 Dixon** include:
  317. i. YVETTE^5.

135. MINNIE^4 DIXON (*Sallie L.^{3}Cheeves, Susie^{2}Carter, Burrell^1*) married **Mr. Woodard.**

Children of **Minnie^4 Dixon** and **Mr. Woodard** were:
+ 318. i. DELORES^5, married **Robert Handon.**

136. DORIS[4] DIXON (*Sallie L.[3] Cheeves, Susie[2] Carter, Burrell[1]*) married **Mr. Gates.**

Children of **Doris[4] Dixon** and **Mr. Gates** were:
+ 319.   i. BEVERLY ANN[5], married **Mr. Green.**

137. JANETTE[4] DIXON (*Sallie L.[3] Cheeves, Susie[2] Carter, Burrell[1]*) married **Mr. Beatha.**

Children of **Janette[4] Dixon** and **Mr. Beatha** were as follows:
320.   i. KLIM[5].
321.   ii. KALHI KAREEM.

138. REATHER[4] CHEEVES (*John[3], Susie[2] Carter, Burrell[1]*) was born on 16 February 1923 in Georgia. He married **Ella Dixon.** He married **Martha** (———) on 22 March 1948 in Philadelphia, Pennsylvania He died in September 1979 in Philadelphia, Pennsylvania, at age 56.

Children of **Reather[4] Cheeves** and **Ella Dixon** were:
322.   i. REATHER MARIE[5].

Children of **Reather[4] Cheeves** and **Martha** (———) were:
323.   i. DARLENE V.[5] was born on 29 October 1948 in Philadelphia, Pennsylvania

151. RUTH[4] MITCHELL (*Clyde[3] Cheeves, Susie[2] Carter, Burrell[1]*) was born circa 1940. She married **Lee Arthur Wright.**

Children of **Ruth[4] Mitchell** and **Lee Arthur Wright** were as follows:
324.   i. CAROLYN[5].
+ 325.   ii. ELAINE, married **William Wilkes.**
+ 326.   iii. DEBRA

154. WILLIE[4] MITCHELL (*Clyde[3] Cheeves, Susie[2] Carter, Burrell[1]*) married **Irene Flemmens.**

Children of **Willie[4] Mitchell** and **Irene Flemmens** were:
327.   i. NIKKEA[5].

155. MILEY[4] MITCHELL (*Clyde[3] Cheeves, Susie[2] Carter, Burrell[1]*) married **Timothy Kelsey.**
Children of **Miley[4] Mitchell** and **Timothy Kelsey** were as follows:
+ 328.   i. ARRON[5], married **Mary** (———).
+ 329.   ii. CECIL, married **Jackie** (———).
+ 330.   iii. DELORES, married **Calvin** (———).
+ 331.   iv. TIMOTHY (JR.), married **Amy** (———).

156. DORIS DOROTHY^4 MITCHELL (*Clyde^{3}Cheeves, Susie^{2}Carter, Burrell^1*).

Children of **Doris Dorothy^4 Mitchell** include:
+ 332. i. BETTY JEAN^5
+ 333. ii. ALTON

157. HAZEL^4 MITCHELL (*Clyde^{3}Cheeves, Susie^{2}Carter, Burrell^1*) was born in March 1937 in Washington County, Georgia She died in May 1980 in Milledgeville, Baldwin County, Georgia, at age 43.

Children of **Hazel^4 Mitchell** include:
+ 334. i. BERNICE^5, married **Mr. Woods.**
+ 335. ii. VICKIE, married **Joseph Williams.**

161. MARY L.^{4} LORD (*Burley^3, Susie^{2}Carter, Burrell^1*) was born on 5 November 1935. She married **Ronald Robinson.** She married **John Goodson.**

Children of **Mary L.^{4} Lord** and **Ronald Robinson** were as follows:
+ 336. i. MICHAEL^5, born 17 February 1953; married **Olivia Poole.**
+ 337. ii. CAROL LOVE, born 21 June 1954; married **Anthony Hailey.**

Children of **Mary L.^{4} Lord** and **John Goodson** were:
338. i. TRACEY JAVELLE^5 was born on 23 September 1968.

162. BURLEY 'SYTES'^{4} LORD (JR.) (*Burley^3, Susie^{2}Carter, Burrell^1*) was born on 6 July 1938. He married **Mary Edith Hall.** He married **Gloria 'Glo' Louise Trawick,** daughter of **Sam Trawick** and **Mary 'Ma-Mae' Ollie Cheeves.** He died on 25 June 1997 in Philadelphia, Pennsylvania, at age 58.

Children of **Burley 'Sytes'^{4} Lord (Jr.)** and **Mary Edith Hall** were:
339. i. BURLEY STEFAN^5 was born on 6 August 1960.

There were no children of **Burley 'Sytes'^{4} Lord (Jr.)** and **Gloria 'Glo' Louise Trawick.**

163. JEROME^4 LORD (*Burley^3, Susie^{2}Carter, Burrell^1*) was born on 1 April 1940. He married **Priscilla Miles.** He married **Patricia Pitts.**

Children of **Jerome^4 Lord** and **Priscilla Miles** were as follows:
+ 340. i. CHERYL ELIZABETH^5, born 13 January 1963; married **William Hacken;** married **Ronald Crosby.**
341. ii. JEFFREY was born on 18 December 1964.
342. iii. HOPE was born on 26 October 1965.

343.   iv. LISA was born on 27 October 1967.

344.   v. GERALD FONTAIN was born on 13 September 1969.

Children of Jerome⁴ **Lord** and **Patricia Pitts** were:

345.   i. JEROME⁵ (JR.) was born on 14 May 1958.

164. MELVIN⁴ LORD (*Burley³, Susie²Carter, Burrell¹*) was born on 1 October 1941. He married **Anita 'Cookie' Smith.** He married **Conchetta Brewer.** He married **Conchetta Brewer.** He married **Conchetta Brewer.** He married **Denise Johnson.**

Children of **Melvin⁴ Lord** and **Anita 'Cookie' Smith** were as follows:

346.   i. ALENCIA SMITH⁵ was born on 22 January 1965.

347.   ii. ALEX SMITH was born on 3 May 1967.

348.   iii. ARLEN SMITH was born on 19 April 1968.

349.   iv. ALLISON SMITH was born on 27 April 1969.

Children of **Melvin⁴ Lord** and **Conchetta Brewer** were as follows:

+ 350.   i. ALONDA⁵, born 28 September 1961; married **Martin Harris.**

351.   ii. MARQUETT was born on 13 August 1963.

352.   iii. TOWANDA.

Children of **Melvin⁴ Lord** and **Denise Johnson** were:

353.   i. ATRA LORD⁵ was born on 6 September 1984.

165. RONALD C.⁴ LORD (SR.) (*Burley³, Susie²Carter, Burrell¹*) was born on 4 February 1944. He married **Grace Corn.**

Children of **Ronald C.⁴ Lord (Sr.)** and **Grace Corn** were as follows:

+ 354.   i. TINA R.⁵, born 3 May 1963; married **Emory K. Copeland.**

+ 355.   ii. RONALD RODNEY, born 8 August 1965; married **Kisha Mapp;** married **Jucinta Bursch.**

+ 356.   iii. RONDA, born 8 August 1965; married **Harold E. Hall.**

+ 357.   iv. KAREN A., born 17 October 1967; married **Antoine Johnson.**

167. JACQUELINE 'JACKI'⁴ LORD (*Burley³, Susie²Carter, Burrell¹*) was born on 15 May 1948. She married **Edward English.**

Children of **Jacqueline 'Jacki'⁴ Lord** and **Edward English** were:

358.   i. LAVADA⁵ was born on 12 February 1970.

168. JOAN⁴ LORD (*Burley³, Susie²Carter, Burrell¹*) was born on 21 May 1949. She married **Charles Moore.**

Children of **Joan**^{4} **Lord** and **Charles Moore** were:
+ 359. i. KELLY S.^{5}, born 30 May 1969; married **Mark Stukes.**

Generation Five

172. JEAN^5 SMITH (*James Beryl 'Buddy'*^{4}, *Joseph 'Joe'*^{3}, *Milly*^{2}*Carter, Burrell*^{1}) was born on 7 August 1934 in Philadelphia, Pennsylvania. She married **Arnold Dixon Jackson Sr.** on 23 September 1961 in Philadelphia, Pennsylvania.

Children of **Jean**^{5} **Smith** and **Arnold Dixon Jackson Sr.** were as follows:
360. i. LISA^6 was born on 24 April 1962 in Philadelphia, Pennsylvania.
361. ii. ARNOLD JR. was born on 4 December 1963 in Philadelphia, Pennsylvania.
+ 362. iii. LAURIE, born 20 March 1965 in Philadelphia, Pennsylvania; married **Mark Darby.**
363. iv. LYNETTE was born on 21 November 1969 in Philadelphia, Pennsylvania.
364. v. LESLIE was born on 31 December 1970 in Philadelphia, Pennsylvania.

174. EVETTE^5 SMITH (*Kenneth Paul*^{4}, *Joseph 'Joe'*^{3}, *Milly*^{2}*Carter, Burrell*^{1}).

Children of **Evette**^{5} **Smith** include:
365. i. FALLON^6.
366. ii. PATRELL.

177. SANDRA CAROL^5 THOMAS (*Eva (Johnny)*^{4}*Trawick, Bertha*^{3}*Carter, Jeff*^{2}, *Burrell*^{1}) was born on 31 May 1946 in Philadelphia, Pennsylvania. She married **Herb Connelly** circa 1970 in Philadelphia, Pennsylvania.

Children of **Sandra Carol**^{5} **Thomas** and **Herb Connelly** were as follows:
367. i. KEISHA^6 was born on 13 March 1971 in Philadelphia, Pennsylvania.
+ 368. ii. KEIA, born 13 March 1971 in Philadelphia, Pennsylvania.

178. SIGRID ANN^5 THOMAS (*Eva (Johnny)*^{4}*Trawick, Bertha*^{3}*Carter, Jeff*^{2}, *Burrell*^{1}) was born on 10 March 1948 in Philadelphia, Pennsylvania. She was born on 10 March 1948 in Philadelphia, Pennsylvania. She married **Howard Edward McCall Jr.** on 30 January 1971 in Philadelphia, Pennsylvania.

Children of **Sigrid Ann**^{5} **Thomas** and **Howard Edward McCall Jr.** were as follows:
369. i. MARK ANTHONY^6 was born on 25 August 1971 in Philadelphia, Pennsylvania.
370. ii. KEITH HOWARD was born on 15 June 1974 in Philadelphia, Pennsylvania.

179. WANDA EILEEN^5 THOMAS (*Eva (Johnny)*^{4}*Trawick, Bertha*^{3}*Carter, Jeff*^{2}, *Burrell*^{1}) was born on 12 April 1950 in Philadelphia, Pennsylvania. She married **John 'Donald' Bird** in Philadelphia, Pennsylvania.

Children of **Wanda Eileen**^{5} **Thomas** and **John 'Donald' Bird** were:
371.   i. **HEATHER**^{6} was born on 27 December 1981 in Philadelphia, Pennsylvania.

186. ALTON^5 **BUTTS** (*Mary Julia*^{4}*Carter, Jeff*^{3}, *Jeff*^{2}, *Burrell*^{1}) was born on 28 October 1934 in Sandersville, Georgia. He married **Marlyn Farley.** He died on 19 May 2003 in Philadelphia, Pennsylvania, at age 68.

Children of **Alton**^{5} **Butts** and **Marlyn Farley** were as follows:
+ 372.   i. **VERONA**^{6}, born 3 December 1963 in Philadelphia, Pennsylvania
+ 373.   ii. **MARSHA,** born 20 October 1967 in Philadelphia, Pennsylvania
+ 374.   iii. **TERESE,** born 10 February 1970 in Philadelphia, Pennsylvania

188. MIRIAM^5 **CHEEVES** (*Lillian Arthur*^{4}*Carter, Jeff*^{3}, *Jeff*^{2}, *Burrell*^{1}) was born in Sandersville, Washington County, Georgia

Children of **Miriam**^{5} **Cheeves** include:
375.   i. **CLARA BELLE**^{6} was born on 2 February 1979 in Tacoma, Washington.

189. GLORIA^5 **CHEEVES** (*Lillian Arthur*^{4}*Carter, Jeff*^{3}, *Jeff*^{2}, *Burrell*^{1}) was born on 4 July 1941 in Sandersville, Washington County, Georgia. She married **Charles Graham.**

Children of **Gloria**^{5} **Cheeves** and **Charles Graham** were as follows:
+ 376.   i. **CHARLES DAVID**^{6}, born 20 May 1969 in Philadelphia, Pennsylvania; married **Lorrie Hatten.**
+ 377.   ii. **MELISSA AVA,** born 21 April 1970 in Philadelphia, Pennsylvania.
378.   iii. **JENNIFER ANNETTE** was born on 21 February 1979 in Philadelphia, Pennsylvania.

190. HORACE^5 **CHEEVES** (*Lillian Arthur*^{4}*Carter, Jeff*^{3}, *Jeff*^{2}, *Burrell*^{1}) was born on 4 September 1943 in Sandersville, Washington County, Georgia. He married **Fannie Pearl Williams,** daughter of **Coleman Williams** and **Florence Rogers,** on 6 July 1971 in Philadelphia, Pennsylvania.

Children of **Horace**^{5} **Cheeves** and **Fannie Pearl Williams** were:
379.   i. **DENISE NICOLE**^{6} was born on 20 February 1972 in Philadelphia, Pennsylvania.

191. FOREST^5 **CHEEVES** (*Lillian Arthur*^{4}*Carter, Jeff*^{3}, *Jeff*^{2}, *Burrell*^{1}) was born on 4 September 1943 in Sandersville, Washington County, Georgia. He married **Karen Kennedy** in Philadelphia, Pennsylvania. He died on 27 March 1987 in Detroit, Michigan, at age 43.

42

Children of **Forest**^{5} **Cheeves** and **Karen Kennedy** were as follows:
+ 380.   i. BARRY STEVEN^6, born 29 June 1960 in Philadelphia, Pennsylvania; married **Andrea Benita 'Nita' Hyden.**
+ 381.   ii. FORREST TROY, born 22 February 1962 in Philadelphia, Pennsylvania.
+ 382.   iii. DARNELL FRANK, born 17 February 1963 in Philadelphia, Pennsylvania; married **Diana 'Ann' Marie Johnson;** married **Pat Young.**
+ 383.   iv. BRUCE KENNETH, born 12 May 1964 in Philadelphia, Pennsylvania; married **Audrey Miree.**

195. MICHELLE^5 **COTTON** (*Ruby Clyde*^{4}*Carter, Jeff*^{3}*, Jeff*^{2}*, Burrell*^{1}) was born on 23 February 1958 in Detroit, Michigan. She died on 16 March 1993 in Philadelphia, Pennsylvania, at age 35.

Children of **Michelle**^{5} **Cotton** and **Stan Johnson** were:
+ 384.   i. VENICE GERVENIA^6, born 23 November 1982 in Philadelphia, Pennsylvania.

196. HERMAN^5 **NELSON** (*Ruby Clyde*^{4}*Carter, Jeff*^{3}*, Jeff*^{2}*, Burrell*^{1}) was born on 4 November 1943 in Philadelphia, Pennsylvania. He married **Dallay Yvonne Graham** on 14 March 1963 in Philadelphia, Pennsylvania.

Children of **Herman**^{5} **Nelson** and **Dallay Yvonne Graham** were as follows:
+ 385.   i. JAMES ANTHONY 'TONY'^{6}, born 1 March 1968 in Burlington County, New Jersey; married **Marsha Phillips.**
   386.   ii. HYMAN TERELL 'HYMIE' was born on 27 October 1979 in Philadelphia, Pennsylvania.

Children of **Herman**^{5} **Nelson** and **Dorothy Faraby** were:
   387.   i. KENISA^6 was born circa 1973 in Philadelphia, Pennsylvania.

Children of **Herman**^{5} **Nelson** and **Louise Bouche** were:
   388.   i. CHRISTOPHER 'CB'^{6} was born on 14 July 1982 in Philadelphia, Pennsylvania.

Children of **Herman**^{5} **Nelson** and **Joanne Jaworski** were:
   389.   i. TIFFANY ANNE^6 was born on 25 February 1989 in Philadelphia, Pennsylvania.

205. SHARON 'SHERRY'^{5} **CARTER** (*Jeff Raymond*^{4}*, Jeff*^{3}*, Jeff*^{2}*, Burrell*^{1}) was born on 18 April 1949 in Philadelphia, Pennsylvania.

Children of **Sharon 'Sherry'**^{5} **Carter** and **Arthur Malcolm Wright** were as follows:
+ 390.   i. ARTHUR MALCOLM 'SAM'^{6}, born 23 December 1967 in Philadelphia, Pennsylvania; married **Valerie Jean McMahon.**
+ 391.   ii. JUAN MALCOLM 'JOHNNY', born 12 January 1969 in Philadelphia, Pennsylvania.

+ 392. iii. APRIL DANEEN, born 8 June 1973 in Philadelphia, Pennsylvania; married **Shawn Tyrone Smith.**

Children of **Sharon 'Sherry'⁵ Carter** and **Willie 'Butch' Pannell** were:
393.   i. SHARON 'PIGGY'⁶ was born on 13 July 1987 in Philadelphia, Pennsylvania.

206. JEFF RAYMOND 'BROTHER'⁵ CARTER JR. (*Jeff Raymond⁴, Jeff³, Jeff², Burrell¹*) was born on 1 July 1950 in Philadelphia, Pennsylvania. He married **Sujuan Williams** on 4 May 1968 in Philadelphia, Pennsylvania.

Children of **Jeff Raymond 'Brother'⁵ Carter Jr.** and **Sujuan Williams** were as follows:
+ 394.   i. KIM PATRICE⁶, born 26 October 1968 in Philadelphia, Pennsylvania.
+ 395.   ii. CRYSTAL LARIN, born 4 July 1974 in Philadelphia, Pennsylvania.

Children of **Jeff Raymond 'Brother'⁵ Carter Jr.** and **Tia Councill** were as follows:
+ 396.   i. JEFF RAYMOND ISAAC COUNCILL⁶, born 16 September 1975 in Philadelphia, Pennsylvania.
+ 397.   ii. NATHANIEL IAN COUNCILL, born 15 March 1977 in Philadelphia, Pennsylvania.
398.   iii. JASON ADAM PERSON COUNCILL was born on 6 March 1986 in Philadelphia, Pennsylvania.

208. DENNIS⁵ CARTER (*Jeff Raymond⁴, Jeff³, Jeff², Burrell¹*) was born on 25 December 1952 in Philadelphia, Pennsylvania. He married **Marcia Earlene Jackson.**

Children of **Dennis⁵ Carter** and **Marcia Earlene Jackson** were as follows:
399.   i. ELI⁶ was born on 7 November 1978 in Philadelphia, Pennsylvania.
+ 400.   ii. EARL, born 7 November 1978 in Philadelphia, Pennsylvania.

Children of **Dennis⁵ Carter** and **Sonya Bernice Thompson** were:
401.   i. DENNIS⁶ JR. was born on 27 April 1973 in Philadelphia, Pennsylvania. He died on 12 October 1993 in Philadelphia, Pennsylvania, at age 20.

212. SHIRLEY⁵ FISHER (*Elizabeth⁴Dawson, Lora Ella 'Laura³Carter, Jeff², Burrell¹*) was born on 29 March. She married **Edward Brent.**

Children of **Shirley⁵ Fisher** and **Edward Brent** were:
+ 402.   i. ROBIN⁶, born 21 June 1962; married **Joseph Phelps.**

214. BRENDA⁵ DAWSON (*Timothy⁴, Lora Ella 'Laura³Carter, Jeff², Burrell¹*) was born on 18 September in Sandersville, Georgia. She married **Mark Scott.**

Children of **Brenda**[5] **Dawson** and **Mark Scott** were as follows:
403.   i. VALISE[6] was born on 25 July.
404.   ii. VALENE was born on 25 September 1986.

215. BENNIE LAWSON[5] **DAWSON** (*Timothy*[4], *Lora Ella 'Laura*[3] *Carter, Jeff*[2], *Burrell*[1]) was born on 6 July 1947 in Sandersville, Georgia. He married **Barbara Jones.**

Children of **Bennie Lawson**[5] **Dawson** and **Barbara Jones** were as follows:
405.   i. LIZ[6] was born on 23 June 1970.
406.   ii. PHILIP was born on 4 November 1982.

218. LORETTA[5] **DAWSON** (*Timothy*[4], *Lora Ella 'Laura*[3] *Carter, Jeff*[2], *Burrell*[1]) was born on 30 August 1952 in Sandersville, Georgia. She married **Aubrey Jones.**

Children of **Loretta**[5] **Dawson** and **Aubrey Jones** were as follows:
407.   i. AUBRINA[6].
408.   ii. GAYLA.
409.   iii. CRISTEN NOEL was born on 15 December 1981.

219. PAULINE[5] **DAWSON** (*Timothy*[4], *Lora Ella 'Laura*[3] *Carter, Jeff*[2], *Burrell*[1]) was born on 12 November 1954 in Sandersville, Georgia. She married **Alfred Ford.**

Children of **Pauline**[5] **Dawson** and **Alfred Ford** were:
410.   i. TORRANCE[6] was born on 2 November 1982.

222. GRACE HARRIS[5] **SPARKS** (*Deborah*[4] *Dawson, Lora Ella 'Laura*[3] *Carter, Jeff*[2], *Burrell*[1]) was born on 22 March 1944 in Sandersville, Georgia. She married **Hugh Bryant.**

Children of **Grace Harris**[5] **Sparks** and **Hugh Bryant** were as follows:
411.   i. HUGH JASON[6] was born on 5 December 1976.
412.   ii. KIRA LAUREN was born on 2 January 1979.

228. GWENDOLYN[5] **GORDY** (*Eloise 'Honey*[4] *Dawson, Lora Ella 'Laura*[3] *Carter, Jeff*[2], *Burrell*[1]) was born on 12 March 1947 in Utica, New York. She married **Julius Murphy.**

Children of **Gwendolyn**[5] **Gordy** and **Julius Murphy** were as follows:
413.   i. SONIA JOY[6] was born on 13 June 1976 in Albany, Georgia.
414.   ii. ASHLEY was born on 21 December 1984 in Macon, Georgia.

230. DAVID[5] GORDY (*Eloise 'Honey'[4]Dawson, Lora Ella 'Laura'[3]Carter, Jeff[2], Burrell[1]*) was born on 13 April 1952 in Sandersville, Georgia. He married **DeLois Turner.** He married **Darlene Robinson.**

Children of **David[5] Gordy** and **DeLois Turner** were as follows:
415.   i. DEBORAH[6] was born on 14 January 1971 in Augusta, Georgia.
416.   ii. DAVINA was born on 2 June 1972 in Augusta, Georgia.
417.   iii. DENISE was born on 13 June 1975 in Augusta, Georgia.
418.   iv. JOSHUA DAVID was born on 9 February 1987 in Augusta, Georgia.

Children of **David[5] Gordy** and **Darlene Robinson** were:
419.   i. DAYNA LYNN[6] was born on 14 August 1997 in Milledgeville, Georgia.

231. DEBORAH ANNE[5] GORDY (*Eloise 'Honey'[4]Dawson, Lora Ella 'Laura'[3]Carter, Jeff[2], Burrell[1]*) was born on 6 January 1954 in Sandersville, Georgia. She married **Samuel Duggan** on 9 June 1979.

Children of **Deborah Anne[5] Gordy** and **Samuel Duggan** were as follows:
420.   i. LORA ANNE[6] was born on 17 July 1982 in Milledgeville, Georgia.
421.   ii. LORETTA DENISE was born on 12 March 1985 in Milledgeville, Georgia.

232. MARY LUCY[5] GORDY (*Eloise 'Honey'[4]Dawson, Lora Ella 'Laura'[3]Carter, Jeff[2], Burrell[1]*) was born on 17 July 1956 in Sandersville, Georgia. She married **Tony Owen Hurt Sr.** on 7 July 1979.

Children of **Mary Lucy[5] Gordy** and **Tony Owen Hurt Sr.** were as follows:
422.   i. TONY OWEN[6] JR. was born on 19 April 1982 in Milledgeville, Georgia.
423.   ii. KARI LOUCYE was born on 17 February 1985 in Milledgeville, Georgia.
424.   iii. BRAXTON GORDY was born on 7 June 1992 in Macon, Georgia.

234. BERRY RENARD[5] GORDY (*Eloise 'Honey'[4]Dawson, Lora Ella 'Laura'[3]Carter, Jeff[2], Burrell[1]*) was born on 10 September 1958 in Sandersville, Georgia. He married **Brenda Lee Lord Barlow Cardy.**

Children of **Berry Renard[5] Gordy** and **Brenda Lee Lord Barlow Cardy** were:
425.   i. JALEN BERRY[6] was born on 19 October 1991 in Augusta, Georgia.

235. CATHERINE LORETTA[5] DAWSON (*Homer[4], Lora Ella 'Laura'[3]Carter, Jeff[2], Burrell[1]*) was born on 4 February 1951 in West Palm Beach, Florida. She married **Douglas Fulton.**

46

Children of **Catherine Loretta**^{5} **Dawson** and **Douglas Fulton** were as follows:
426.   i. LAURIE^6 was born on 14 August 1972.
427.   ii. ASHLEY was born on 30 September 1980.
428.   iii. WHITNEY BLAIR was born on 6 September 1987.

236. HOMER 'BILLY'^{5} **DAWSON III** (*Homer^4, Lora Ella 'Laura^3 Carter, Jeff^2, Burrell^1*) was born on 9 April 1953 in West Palm Beach, Florida. He married **Brenda McCullom.**

Children of **Homer 'Billy'**^{5} **Dawson III** and **Brenda McCullom** were as follows:
429.   i. HOMER^6.
430.   ii. TANYA was born on 25 June 1973.
431.   iii. ANTONIO was born on 7 August 1978.
432.   iv. ALBERT was born on 25 October 1980.

238. WENDELL^5 **DAWSON** (*Homer^4, Lora Ella 'Laura^3 Carter, Jeff^2, Burrell^1*) was born on 31 January 1957 in West Palm Beach, Florida. He married **Deborah Davis.**

Children of **Wendell**^{5} **Dawson** and **Deborah Davis** were:
433.   i. LESLIE CANELIA^6 was born on 24 November 1989 in Nashville, Tennessee.

239. NATALIE JEAN^5 **DAWSON** (*Homer^4, Lora Ella 'Laura^3 Carter, Jeff^2, Burrell^1*) was born on 6 April 1958 in West Palm Beach, Florida. She married **Robert Smith.**

Children of **Natalie Jean**^{5} **Dawson** and **Robert Smith** were as follows:
434.   i. NICOLE^6 was born on 29 September 1979.
435.   ii. NATALIE RENEE was born on 17 May 1987.
436.   iii. (FEMALE).

240. BEVERLY^5 **DAWSON** (*Cornelius^4, Lora Ella 'Laura^3 Carter, Jeff^2, Burrell^1*) was born on 5 February 1955 in East Palatka, Florida.

Children of **Beverly**^{5} **Dawson** include:
437.   i. HOPE^6 was born on 12 January 1975 in West Palm Beach, Florida.
438.   ii. ANTARIO.

241. WANDA^5 **DAWSON** (*Cornelius^4, Lora Ella 'Laura^3 Carter, Jeff^2, Burrell^1*) was born on 1 November 1959 in West Palm Beach, Florida. She married **Tim Hunt.**

Children of **Wanda**^{5} **Dawson** and **Tim Hunt** were as follows:
439.   i. JULIAN^6 was born on 17 August 1995 in Miami, Florida.
440.   ii. JUSTIN was born in February 1997 in Miami, Florida.

244. KAREN ' KAY' ELIZABETH^5 DAVIS ROSS (*Wilhelmina 'Candy'^{4}Dawson, Lora Ella 'Laura'^{3}Carter, Jeff^2, Burrell^1*) was born on 14 May 1956 in West Palm Beach, Florida. She married **Willie Neal.**

Children of **Karen ' Kay' Elizabeth^5 Davis Ross** and **Bernard Jackson** were:
+ 441.   i. KIMBERLY CORNELIA^6, born 19 June 1976 in Florida.

Children of **Karen ' Kay' Elizabeth^5 Davis Ross** and **Willie Neal** were:
442.   i. LINDSEY^6 was born on 1 August 1987 in Florida.

255. AVA DIANE^5 CARTER (*Ruth Mildred^4, Virgil 'Virge'^{3}, Jeff^2, Burrell^1*) was born on 28 June 1957 in Brooklyn, New York. She married **Ricky Holden.**

Children of **Ava Diane^5 Carter** and **Ricky Holden** were as follows:
443.   i. LESLIE NEVON^6 was born on 8 September 1986 in Colorado.
444.   ii. MALCOLM was born on 4 November 1988 in Colorado.

256. RICHARD CARTER^5 GREEN (*Anne^{4}Carter, Virgil 'Virge'^{3}, Jeff^2, Burrell^1*) was born on 28 October 1947 in Brooklyn, New York. He married **Elaine Parson** on 4 January 1968 in Brooklyn, New York.

Children of **Richard Carter^5 Green** and **Joy Bernard** were:
445.   i. ANTHONY^6 was born on 25 October 1967 in Brooklyn, New York.

Children of **Richard Carter^5 Green** and **Elaine Parson** were as follows:
+ 446.   i. DAMANI SAEED TALE'^{6}, born 18 February 1974 in Dayton, Ohio.
447.   ii. TAIESHA TENE' TALE' was born on 29 July 1976 in Dayton, Ohio.
448.   iii. KHALID ABDULLAH TALE' was born on 3 September 1980 in Dayton, Ohio.

258. BARI LYN^5 SNYDER (*Teresa^{4}Carter, Virgil 'Virge'^{3}, Jeff^2, Burrell^1*) was born on 6 February 1961 in Brooklyn, New York.

Children of **Bari Lyn^5 Snyder** and **Alvin White** were as follows:
449.   i. EVAN BRION^6 was born on 14 August 1993 in Brooklyn, New York.
450.   ii. DARNELL TYREE was born on 30 January 1996 in Brooklyn, New York.

259. DERON KEITH^5 SNYDER (*Teresa^{4}Carter, Virgil 'Virge'^{3}, Jeff^2, Burrell^1*) was born on 16 September 1962 in Brooklyn, New York.

Children of **Deron Keith^5 Snyder** and **Vanessa Williams** were:
451.   i. SIERRA NGOZI^6 was born on 9 July 1996 in Washington, D.C.

302. ELAINE^5 DIXON (*Rosalie 'Rose'^{4}, Mary A.^{3}Cheeves, Susie^{2}Carter, Burrell^1*).

Children of **Elaine^5 Dixon** include:
452. i. BRENDA^6.

303. LEWIS^5 DIXON (*Anna Julia^4, Mary A.^{3}Cheeves, Susie^{2}Carter, Burrell^1*) married
Mary (————-).
Children of **Lewis^5 Dixon** and **Mary** (————-) were as follows:
453. i. LEWIS^6 (JR.).
454. ii. CHARMINE.

304. MAJOR^5 DIXON (*Anna Julia^4, Mary A.^{3}Cheeves, Susie^{2}Carter, Burrell^1*) married
Emma (————-).

Children of **Major^5 Dixon** and **Emma** (————-) were as follows:
455. i. ANGELA^6.
456. ii. ANDREA.
457. iii. NICOLE.

305. JEROME^5 DIXON (*Anna Julia^4, Mary A.^{3}Cheeves, Susie^{2}Carter, Burrell^1*) married
Rose (————-).

Children of **Jerome^5 Dixon** and **Rose** (————-) were as follows:
458. i. CARMELLA^6.
459. ii. ALICIA.

306. DAISY MAE^5 DIXON (*Anna Julia^4, Mary A.^{3}Cheeves, Susie^{2}Carter, Burrell^1*).

Children of **Daisy Mae^5 Dixon** include:
460. i. MICHAEL^6.
461. ii. ADRINNE.

307. MARLENE^5 DIXON (*Anna Julia^4, Mary A.^{3}Cheeves, Susie^{2}Carter, Burrell^1*) married
Will Pearsall.

Children of **Marlene^5 Dixon** and **Will Pearsall** were as follows:
462. i. ANDREW^6.
463. ii. WANDA.

308. PHILIP (ALI SALAUDIN)^5 DIXON (*Horace^4, Sallie L.^{3}Cheeves, Susie^{2}Carter,
Burrell^1*) was born on 4 February 1947 in Philadelphia, Pennsylvania. He married
Carol Haughton.

Children of **Philip (Ali Salaudin)**[5] **Dixon** and **Carol Haughton** were as follows:
464.   i. JAMAL[6] was born on 2 April 1970 in Philadelphia, Pennsylvania.
465.   ii. SHARIAH K. was born on 23 February 1972 in Philadelphia, Pennsylvania.
466. iii. KAMILLAH 'MIMI' was born on 18 March 1974 in Philadelphia, Pennsylvania.

309. RODNEY[5] **DIXON** (*Horace*[4], *Sallie L.*[3]*Cheeves, Susie*[2]*Carter, Burrell*[1]) was born on
8 March 1950 in Philadelphia, Pennsylvania. He married **Beverly Diane Fisher.**

Children of **Rodney**[5] **Dixon** and **Beverly Diane Fisher** were as follows:
467.   i. KHALID[6] was born on 23 March 1976 in Philadelphia, Pennsylvania.
468.   ii. MURAD ALIM SALAUDIN was born on 12 August 1978 in Philadelphia,
        Pennsylvania.

318. DELORES[5] **WOODARD** (*Minnie*[4]*Dixon, Sallie L.*[3]*Cheeves, Susie*[2]*Carter, Burrell*[1])
married **Robert Handon.**

Children of **Delores**[5] **Woodard** and **Robert Handon** were as follows:
469.   i. DENISE[6].
470.   ii. JEANETTE.

319. BEVERLY ANN[5] **GATES** (*Doris*[4]*Dixon, Sallie L.*[3]*Cheeves, Susie*[2]*Carter, Burrell*[1])
married **Mr. Green.**

Children of **Beverly Ann**[5] **Gates** and **Mr. Green** were:
471.   i. STEPHANIE[6].

325. ELAINE[5] **WRIGHT** (*Ruth*[4]*Mitchell, Clyde*[3]*Cheeves, Susie*[2]*Carter, Burrell*[1]) married
William Wilkes.

Children of **Elaine**[5] **Wright** and **William Wilkes** were as follows:
472.   i. JASON[6].
473.   ii. MERCEDES.

326. DEBRA[5] **WRIGHT** (*Ruth*[4]*Mitchell, Clyde*[3]*Cheeves, Susie*[2]*Carter, Burrell*[1]).

Children of **Debra**[5] **Wright** include:
474.   i. DELISHA[6].

328. ARRON[5] **KELSEY** (*Miley*[4]*Mitchell, Clyde*[3]*Cheeves, Susie*[2]*Carter, Burrell*[1]) married
Mary (———).

Children of **Arron^5 Kelsey** and **Mary** (———) were as follows:
475.   i. ANGEL^6.
476.   ii. GREGG.
477.   iii. MELISSA.

329. CECIL^5 KELSEY (*Miley^4 Mitchell, Clyde^3 Cheeves, Susie^2 Carter, Burrell^1*) married **Jackie** (———).

Children of **Cecil^5 Kelsey** and **Jackie** (———) were as follows:
478.   i. CAMERON^6.
479.   ii. CECIL (JR.).
480.   iii. COURTNEY.

330. DELORES^5 KELSEY (*Miley^4 Mitchell, Clyde^3 Cheeves, Susie^2 Carter, Burrell^1*) married **Calvin** (———).

Children of **Delores^5 Kelsey** and **Calvin** (———) were:
481.   i. PAT^6.

331. TIMOTHY^5 KELSEY (JR.) (*Miley^4 Mitchell, Clyde^3 Cheeves, Susie^2 Carter, Burrell^1*) married **Amy** (———).

Children of **Timothy^5 Kelsey** (Jr.) and **Amy** (———) were:
482.   i. TAMMY^6.

332. BETTY JEAN^5 MITCHELL (*Doris Dorothy^4, Clyde^3 Cheeves, Susie^2 Carter, Burrell^1*).

Children of **Betty Jean^5 Mitchell** include:
483.   i. REMISHA^6.
484.   ii. PAUL.

333. ALTON^5 MITCHELL (*Doris Dorothy^4, Clyde^3 Cheeves, Susie^2 Carter, Burrell^1*).

Children of **Alton^5 Mitchell** include:
485.   i. STEPHANIE^6.
486.   ii. TIFFANEY.
487.   iii. ALTON (JR.).

334. BERNICE^5 MITCHELL (*Hazel^4, Clyde^3 Cheeves, Susie^2 Carter, Burrell^1*) married **Mr. Woods.**

Children of **Bernice^5 Mitchell** and **Mr. Woods** were as follows:
488.   i. CHELICE^6 was born on 27 May 1980.
489.   ii. KEITH was born on 23 August 1981.

335. VICKIE^5 MITCHELL (*Hazel^4, Clyde^{3}Cheeves, Susie^{2}Carter, Burrell^1*) married **Joseph Williams.**

Children of **Vickie^5 Mitchell** and **Joseph Williams** were as follows:
490.   i. DIONE^6.
491.   ii. TERRI.
492.   iii. JOESPH (JR.).

336. MICHAEL^5 ROBINSON (*Mary L.^{4}Lord, Burley^3, Susie^{2}Carter, Burrell^1*) was born on 17 February 1953. He married **Olivia Poole.**

Children of **Michael^5 Robinson** and **Olivia Poole** were:
493.   i. MELISSA^6 was born on 9 April 1976.

337. CAROL LOVE^5 ROBINSON (*Mary L.^{4}Lord, Burley^3, Susie^{2}Carter, Burrell^1*) was born on 21 June 1954. She married **Anthony Hailey.**

Children of **Carol Love^5 Robinson** and **Anthony Hailey** were:
494.   i. ANTIRA LOVE ROBINSON^6 was born on 4 February 1987.

340. CHERYL ELIZABETH^5 LORD (*Jerome^4, Burley^3, Susie^{2}Carter, Burrell^1*) was born on 13 January 1963. She married **William Hacken.** She married **Ronald Crosby** on 27 May 1989.

Children of **Cheryl Elizabeth^5 Lord** include:
495.   i. BRANDON S.^{6} was born on 3 May 1982.

There were no children of **Cheryl Elizabeth^5 Lord** and **William Hacken.**

There were no children of **Cheryl Elizabeth^5 Lord** and **Ronald Crosby.**

350. ALONDA^5 LORD (*Melvin^4, Burley^3, Susie^{2}Carter, Burrell^1*) was born on 28 September 1961. She married **Martin Harris.**

Children of **Alonda^5 Lord** and **Martin Harris** were:
496.   i. MARTIN^6 (JR.) was born on 2 September 1983.

354. TINA R.^{5} LORD (*Ronald C.^{4}, Burley^3, Susie^{2}Carter, Burrell^1*) was born on 3 May 1963. She married **Emory K. Copeland.**

Children of **Tina R.^{5} Lord** and **Emory K. Copeland** were:
497.   i. EMORY T. LORD^6 was born on 17 September 1984.

355. RONALD RODNEY^5 LORD (*Ronald C.^{4}, Burley^3, Susie^{2}Carter, Burrell^1*) was born on 8 August 1965. He married **Kisha Mapp.** He married **Jucinta Bursch.**

Children of **Ronald Rodney^5 Lord** and **Kisha Mapp** were:
498.   i. HAKIM LAMAR LORD^6 was born on 14 November 1986.

Children of **Ronald Rodney^5 Lord** and **Jucinta Bursch** were:
499.   i. JAHLIL^6 was born on 4 May 1988.

356. RONDA^5 LORD (*Ronald C.^{4}, Burley^3, Susie^{2}Carter, Burrell^1*) was born on 8 August 1965. She married **Harold E. Hall.**

Children of **Ronda^5 Lord** and **Harold E. Hall** were as follows:
500.   i. HAROLD M. LORD^6 was born on 8 June 1986.
501.   ii. MARQUES LORD was born on 2 October 1988.

357. KAREN A.^{5} LORD (*Ronald C.^{4}, Burley^3, Susie^{2}Carter, Burrell^1*) was born on 17 October 1967. She married **Antoine Johnson.**

Children of **Karen A.^{5} Lord** and **Antoine Johnson** were:
502.   i. SHERRIA A. LORD^6 was born on 4 August 1988.

359. KELLY S.^{5} MOORE (*Joan^{4}Lord, Burley^3, Susie^{2}Carter, Burrell^1*) was born on 30 May 1969. She married **Mark Stukes.**

Children of **Kelly S.^{5} Moore** include:
503.   i. BRYON TRACEY CHARLES^6 was born on 15 January 1986.

There were no children of **Kelly S.^{5} Moore** and **Mark Stukes.**

Generation Six

362. LAURIE^6 JACKSON (*Jean^{5}Smith, James Beryl 'Buddy'^{4}, Joseph 'Joe'^{3}, Milly^{2}Carter, Burrell^1*) was born on 20 March 1965 in Philadelphia, Pennsylvania. She married **Mark Darby.**

Children of **Laurie**^{6} **Jackson** and **Mark Darby** were as follows:
   504.   i. MYAH^7.
   505.   ii. DEENA.

368. KEIA^6 CONNELLY (*Sandra Carol*^{5} *Thomas, Eva (Johnny)*^{4} *Trawick, Bertha*^{3} *Carter, Jeff*^{2}*, Burrell*^{1}) was born on 13 March 1971 in Philadelphia, Pennsylvania.

Children of **Keia**^{6} **Connelly** and **Rob Baker** were:
   506.   i. HANNAH^7 was born on 5 January 1997 in Philadelphia, Pennsylvania.

372. VERONA^6 BUTTS (*Alton*^{5}*, Mary Julia*^{4} *Carter, Jeff*^{3}*, Jeff*^{2}*, Burrell*^{1}) was born on 3 December 1963 in Philadelphia, Pennsylvania.

Children of **Verona**^{6} **Butts** and **Craig Walker** were:
   507.   i. TERON BUTTS^7 was born on 21 July 1989 in Philadelphia, Pennsylvania.

373. MARSHA^6 BUTTS (*Alton*^{5}*, Mary Julia*^{4} *Carter, Jeff*^{3}*, Jeff*^{2}*, Burrell*^{1}) was born on 20 October 1967 in Philadelphia, Pennsylvania.

Children of **Marsha**^{6} **Butts** and **Bryan Ford** were:
   508.   i. NATASHA BUTTS^7 was born on 27 June 1984 in Philadelphia, Pennsylvania.

374. TERESE^6 BUTTS (*Alton*^{5}*, Mary Julia*^{4} *Carter, Jeff*^{3}*, Jeff*^{2}*, Burrell*^{1}) was born on 10 February 1970 in Philadelphia, Pennsylvania.

Children of **Terese**^{6} **Butts** and **Damont Heckstall** were:
   509.   i. ASHTON BUTTS^7 was born on 3 May 1989 in Fort Lauderdale, Florida.

376. CHARLES DAVID^6 GRAHAM (*Gloria*^{5} *Cheeves, Lillian Arthur*^{4} *Carter, Jeff*^{3}*, Jeff*^{2}*, Burrell*^{1}) was born on 20 May 1969 in Philadelphia, Pennsylvania. He married **Lorrie Hatten** on 5 September 1992 in Philadelphia, Pennsylvania.

Children of **Charles David**^{6} **Graham** include:
   510.   i. NOLAN LEWIS PAUL^7 was born on 29 May 1984 in Philadelphia, Pennsylvania.

There were no children of **Charles David**^{6} **Graham** and **Lorrie Hatten**.

377. MELISSA AVA^6 GRAHAM (*Gloria*^{5} *Cheeves, Lillian Arthur*^{4} *Carter, Jeff*^{3}*, Jeff*^{2}*, Burrell*^{1}) was born on 21 April 1970 in Philadelphia, Pennsylvania.

Children of **Melissa Ava**^{6} **Graham** and **Carlos Kinslow** were:
   511.   i. BRANDON ALEXANDER^7 was born on 28 March 1996 in Philadelphia, Pennsylvania.

380. BARRY STEVEN^6 **CHEEVES** (*Forest*^{5}, *Lillian Arthur*^{4}*Carter*, *Jeff*^{3}, *Jeff*^{2}, *Burrell*^{1}) was born on 29 June 1960 in Philadelphia, Pennsylvania. He married **Andrea Benita 'Nita' Hyden**, daughter of **Ronald Hyden** and **Judy Ryder**, on 30 April 1988 in Philadelphia, Pennsylvania.

Children of **Barry Steven**^{6} **Cheeves** and **Andrea Benita 'Nita' Hyden** were as follows:

+ 512.   i. RASETA NICOLE^7, born 7 May 1982 in Philadelphia, Pennsylvania.
  513.   ii. RANIKA MICHELLE was born on 2 February 1990 in Philadelphia, Pennsylvania.

Children of **Barry Steven**^{6} **Cheeves** and **Diane Johnson** were:
  514.   i. BARRY STEVEN^7 JR. was born on 25 August 1996 in Philadelphia, Pennsylvania.

381. FORREST TROY^6 **CHEEVES** (*Forest*^{5}, *Lillian Arthur*^{4}*Carter*, *Jeff*^{3}, *Jeff*^{2}, *Burrell*^{1}) was born on 22 February 1962 in Philadelphia, Pennsylvania.

Children of **Forrest Troy**^{6} **Cheeves** and **Sue Wilson** were as follows:
  515.   i. FORREST TROY^7 JR. was born on 30 March 1988 in Philadelphia, Pennsylvania.
  516.   ii. ALEXANDER DOMINIC was born on 19 May 1989 in Philadelphia, Pennsylvania.

382. DARNELL FRANK^6 **CHEEVES** (*Forest*^{5}, *Lillian Arthur*^{4}*Carter*, *Jeff*^{3}, *Jeff*^{2}, *Burrell*^{1}) was born on 17 February 1963 in Philadelphia, Pennsylvania. He married **Diana 'Ann' Marie Johnson**. He married **Pat Young** on 19 December 1997 in Philadelphia, Pennsylvania.

Children of **Darnell Frank**^{6} **Cheeves** and **Diana 'Ann' Marie Johnson** were as follows:
  517.   i. SHANAY LANELL^7 was born on 30 October 1985 in Philadelphia, Pennsylvania.
  518.   ii. SHEENA MONIQUE was born on 5 November 1989 in Philadelphia, Pennsylvania.

Children of **Darnell Frank**^{6} **Cheeves** and **Pat Young** were:
  519.   i. DARNELL FRANK^7 JR. was born on 20 March 1993 in Philadelphia, Pennsylvania.

383. BRUCE KENNETH^6 **CHEEVES** (*Forest*^{5}, *Lillian Arthur*^{4}*Carter*, *Jeff*^{3}, *Jeff*^{2}, *Burrell*^{1}) was born on 12 May 1964 in Philadelphia, Pennsylvania. He married **Audrey Miree** on 17 July 1998 in Philadelphia, Pennsylvania.

Children of **Bruce Kenneth**^{6} **Cheeves** and **Audrey Miree** were as follows:
  520.   i. BRUCE KENNETH^7 JR. was born on 24 October 1989 in Philadelphia, Pennsylvania.
  521.   ii. KAREN was born on 13 July 1991 in Philadelphia, Pennsylvania.

384. VENICE GERVENIA^6 **COTTON** (*Michelle*^{5}, *Ruby Clyde*^{4}*Carter*, *Jeff*^{3}, *Jeff*^{2}, *Burrell*^{1}) was born on 23 November 1982 in Philadelphia, Pennsylvania.

Children of **Venice Gervenia**[6] **Cotton** and **Ronald Terrell Mordecai** were:
522.   i. CYIR ISRAEL[7] was born on 28 July 2000 in Philadelphia, Pennsylvania.

385. **JAMES ANTHONY 'TONY'**[6] **NELSON** (*Herman*[5], *Ruby Clyde*[4]*Carter, Jeff*[3], *Jeff*[2], *Burrell*[1]) was born on 1 March 1968 in Burlington County, New Jersey. He married **Marsha Phillips** on 4 August 1991 in Enid, Oklahoma.

Children of **James Anthony 'Tony'**[6] **Nelson** and **Marsha Phillips** were:
523.   i. JASHA MIANA[7] was born on 23 May 1995 in Tokyo, Japan.

390. **ARTHUR MALCOLM 'SAM'**[6] **WRIGHT** (*Sharon 'Sherry'*[5]*Carter, Jeff Raymond*[4], *Jeff*[3], *Jeff*[2], *Burrell*[1]) was born on 23 December 1967 in Philadelphia, Pennsylvania. He married **Valerie Jean McMahon** on 3 November 1986 in Tampa, Florida.

Children of **Arthur Malcolm 'Sam'**[6] **Wright** and **Valerie Jean McMahon** were as follows:
524.   i. ALEXIS DANEEN[7] was born on 23 March 1991 in Clearwater, Florida.
525.   ii. DANIELLE MARIE was born on 4 July 1992 in Clearwater, Florida.
526.   iii. TIFFANY ELIZABETH was born on 4 April 1994 in Clearwater, Florida.

391. **JUAN MALCOLM 'JOHNNY'**[6] **WRIGHT** (*Sharon 'Sherry'*[5]*Carter, Jeff Raymond*[4], *Jeff*[3], *Jeff*[2], *Burrell*[1]) was born on 12 January 1969 in Philadelphia, Pennsylvania.

Children of **Juan Malcolm 'Johnny'**[6] **Wright** include:
527.   i. JUAN VALDEZ[7] was born on 28 July 1987.

392. **APRIL DANEEN**[6] **WRIGHT** (*Sharon 'Sherry'*[5]*Carter, Jeff Raymond*[4], *Jeff*[3], *Jeff*[2], *Burrell*[1]) was born on 8 June 1973 in Philadelphia, Pennsylvania. She married **Shawn Tyrone Smith** in February 2000 in Philadelphia, Pennsylvania.

Children of **April Daneen**[6] **Wright** and **Gary McCalla** were:
528.   i. LESHAUN DANEEN MCCALLA[7] was born on 14 September 1989 in Philadelphia, Pennsylvania.

Children of **April Daneen**[6] **Wright** and **Darryl Nesmith** were:
529.   i. DASHINA[7] was born on 12 July 1995 in Philadelphia, Pennsylvania.

Children of **April Daneen**[6] **Wright** and **Shawn Tyrone Smith** were:
530.   i. SHAWN TYRONE[7] JR. was born on 15 June 1997 in Philadelphia, Pennsylvania.

394. **KIM PATRICE**[6] **CARTER** (*Jeff Raymond 'Brother'*[5], *Jeff Raymond*[4], *Jeff*[3], *Jeff*[2], *Burrell*[1]) was born on 26 October 1968 in Philadelphia, Pennsylvania.

Children of **Kim Patrice**^{6} **Carter** and **Jujuan Falana** were as follows:
531.   i. SYEET^7 was born on 22 January 1988 in Philadelphia, Pennsylvania.
532.   ii. SUPREE was born on 27 April 1989 in Philadelphia, Pennsylvania.

395. **CRYSTAL LARIN**^{6} **CARTER** (*Jeff Raymond 'Brother'*^{5}, *Jeff Raymond*^{4}, *Jeff*^{3}, *Jeff*^{2}, *Burrell*^{1}) was born on 4 July 1974 in Philadelphia, Pennsylvania.

Children of **Crystal Larin**^{6} **Carter** and **Keemen Copeland** were:
533.   i. TAHIRAH KADIJAH^7 was born on 17 December 1996 in Philadelphia, Pennsylvania.

396. **JEFF RAYMOND ISAAC COUNCILL**^{6} **CARTER** (*Jeff Raymond 'Brother'*^{5}, *Jeff Raymond*^{4}, *Jeff*^{3}, *Jeff*^{2}, *Burrell*^{1}) was born on 16 September 1975 in Philadelphia, Pennsylvania.

Children of **Jeff Raymond Isaac Councill**^{6} **Carter** and **Tina Cole** were:
534.   i. DIAMOND JANETTE^7 was born on 12 June 1992 in Philadelphia, Pennsylvania.

Children of **Jeff Raymond Isaac Councill**^{6} **Carter** and **Sherisa Dennis** were:
535.   i. SHIANNA CHARLENE MALIKA^7 was born on 28 August 1993 in Philadelphia, Pennsylvania.

397. **NATHANIEL IAN COUNCILL**^{6} **CARTER** (*Jeff Raymond 'Brother'*^{5}, *Jeff Raymond*^{4}, *Jeff*^{3}, *Jeff*^{2}, *Burrell*^{1}) was born on 15 March 1977 in Philadelphia, Pennsylvania.

Children of **Nathaniel Ian Councill**^{6} **Carter** and **Dora Street** were:
536.   i. KOREY DERELL^7 was born on 17 May 1996 in Philadelphia, Pennsylvania.

Children of **Nathaniel Ian Councill**^{6} **Carter** and **Nikkia Thompson** were:
537.   i. NATHANIEL IAN JEFF^7 was born on 28 May 2001 in Philadelphia, Pennsylvania.

400. **EARL**^{6} **CARTER** (*Dennis*^{5}, *Jeff Raymond*^{4}, *Jeff*^{3}, *Jeff*^{2}, *Burrell*^{1}) was born on 7 November 1978 in Philadelphia, Pennsylvania.

Children of **Earl**^{6} **Carter** and **Myteesha Elaine Reynolds** were as follows:
538.   i. EARL^7 JR. was born on 7 May 2000 in Philadelphia, Pennsylvania.
539.   ii. ELI was born on 7 May 2000 in Philadelphia, Pennsylvania.

402. **ROBIN**^{6} **BRENT** (*Shirley*^{5}*Fisher, Elizabeth*^{4}*Dawson, Lora Ella 'Laura'*^{3}*Carter, Jeff*^{2}, *Burrell*^{1}) was born on 21 June 1962. She married **Joseph Phelps**.

Children of **Robin**[6] **Brent** and **Joseph Phelps** were as follows:
540.   i. JOEY[7].
541.   ii. ROMAN.

441. **KIMBERLY CORNELIA**[6] **JACKSON** (*Karen ' Kay' Elizabeth*[5]*Davis Ross, Wilhelmina 'Candy'*[4]*Dawson, Lora Ella 'Laura'*[3]*Carter, Jeff*[2]*, Burrell*[1]) was born on 19 June 1976 in Florida.

Children of **Kimberly Cornelia**[6] **Jackson** and **Adrian Davis** were:
542.   i. ALEXANDRIA MONIQUE[7] was born on 14 August 1998 in Fort Lauderdale, Florida.

446. **DAMANI SAEED TALE'**[6] **GREEN** (*Richard Carter*[5]*, Anne*[4]*Carter, Virgil 'Virge'*[3]*, Jeff*[2]*, Burrell*[1]) was born on 18 February 1974 in Dayton, Ohio.

Children of **Damani Saeed Tale'**[6] **Green** and **Katheryn Kirkland** were:
543.   i. KEVIN MICHAEL[7] was born on 2 December 1995 in Dayton, Ohio.

Generation Seven

512. **RASETA NICOLE**[7] **CHEEVES** (*Barry Steven*[6]*, Forest*[5]*, Lillian Arthur*[4]*Carter, Jeff*[3]*, Jeff*[2]*, Burrell*[1]) was born on 7 May 1982 in Philadelphia, Pennsylvania.

Children of **Raseta Nicole**[7] **Cheeves** and **James Kennedy** were:
544.   i. NICHOLAS SEMAJ[8] was born on 6 March 2001 in Philadelphia, Pennsylvania.

Descendants of Rita Strange
(Mother of Henry Cheeves)

Henry Cheeves, 1870 Census

Henry Cheeves, 1880 Census

U.S. Bureau of the Census 1880, Tenth Agriculture Census

Question No.	Column Heading	Entry
	ROW 1	
001	NAME: *Cheeves, Henry* Microfilm roll #: *T-1137, roll 20 Washington G. Ga* ED # *128* , Page *6* , Line *10*	
002	Owner	
003	Rent for fixed money rental	
004	Rent for shares of production	✓
	Acres of Land	
	Improved	
005	Tilled, including fallow and grass in rotation (whether pasture or meadow)	*75 acres*
006	Permenant meadows, permanent pastures, orchards, and vineyards	
	Unimproved	
007	Woodland and forest	
008	Other unimproved, including "old fields" not growing wood	
	Farm Values	
009	Of farm, including land, fences & buildings	$ 175
010	of farming implements and machinery	$ 15
011	of live stock on farm June 1, 1880	$ 175
	Fences	
012	Cost of building and repair	$ 50
013	Cost of Fertilizers pruchased, 1879	
014	**Labor** Amount paid for wages for farm labor 1879 including value of board	$75
	Weeks hired labor in 1879 upon farm (and dairy) excluding house work	
015	White *(no. f)*	
016	Colored *(no. f)*	40
	Estiamted value of all farm productions (sold, consumed, or on hand) for 1897	
017	(Dollars)	$500

Henry Cheeves, 1880 Agriculture Census, pg. 1

Question No.	Column Heading	Entry
	Grass Lands	
	Acreage 1879	
018	Mown	
019	Not Mown	
	Products Harvested in 1879	
020	Hay	
021	Clover Seed	
022	Grass Seed	
023	Horses of all ages on hand June 1, 1880	*1*
024	Mules and Asses all ages on hand June 1, 1880	*1*
	ROW 2	
	Meat Cattle and their Products	
	On hand June 1, 1880	
025	Working oxen	*1*
026	Milch cows	*2*
027	Other	*5*
	Movement, 1879	
028	Calves Dropped	
	Cattle of all ages	
029	Purchased	
030	Sold living	
031	Slaughtered	
032	Died	
	Dairy Products	
033	Milk sold or sent to butter and cheese factories in 1879	
034	Butter made on the farm in 1879	*20*
035	Cheese made on the farm in 1879	

Henry Cheeves, 1880 Agriculture Census, pg. 2

Question No.	Column Heading	Entry
	Sheep	
036	On hand June 1, 1880	
	Movement 1879	
037	Lambs Dropped	
038	Purchased	
039	Sold living	
040	Slaughtered	
041	Killed by dogs	
042	Died of disease	
043	Died of stress of weather	
	WOOL, spring clip of 1880	
044	Fleeces	
045	Weight	
046	Swine on hand June 1, 1880	*20*
	Poultry on hand June 1, 1880 exlusive of Spring Hatching	
047	Barn-Yard	*18*
048	Other	
049	Eggs produced in 1879	Doz. *16*
	Rice	
050	Acres	
051	Crop	lbs.

Row 3

	Cereal, 1879	
052	Barley - Acres	
053	Barley - Crop	Bu.
054	Buckwheat - Acres	
055	Buckwheat - Crop	Bu.
056	Indian Corn - Acres	*40*
057	Indian Corn - Crop	Bu. *280*
058	Oats - Acres	*6*
059	Oats - Crop	Bu. *30*

Henry Cheeves, 1880 Agriculture Census, pg. 3

Question No.	Column Heading	Entry
060	Rye - Acres	
061	Rye - Crop	Bu.
062	Wheat - Acres	
063	Wheat - Crop	Bu.

	Fiber, 1879	
064	Cotton - Acres	35
065	Cotton - Bales	10
066	Flax - Acres	
067	Flax - Seed	Bu.
068	Flax - straw	tons
069	Flax - Fiber	lbs.
070	Hemp - Acres	
071	Hemp - Crop	Tons

	Sugar and Molasses, 1879	
072	Cane - Acres in Crop	
073	Cane - Sugar	Hhds.
074	Cane - Molasses	gals.
075	Sorghum - Acres in Crop	
076	Sorghum - Sugar	lbs.
077	Sorghum - Molasses	gals.
078	Maple - Sugar	lbs.
079	Maple - Molasses	gals.

Row 4

	Pulse, 1879	
080	Pease	Bu.
081	Beans (Dry)	Bu.
082	Irish Potatoes - Acres	
083	Irish Potatoes - Crop	Bu.
084	Sweet Potatoes - Acres	1
085	Sweet Potatoes - Crop	Bu. 80
086	Tobacco - Acres	
087	Tobacco - Crop	lbs.

Henry Cheeves, 1880 Agriculture Census, pg. 4

Question No.	Column Heading	Entry
	Orchards, 1879	
088	Apples - Acres	
089	Apples - Bearing trees	
090	Apples - Bushels	
091	Peaches - Acres	
092	Peaches - Bearing trees	
093	Peaches - Bushels	
094	Total Value - Dollars	
	Nurseries, 1879	
095	Acres	
096	Value of products sold in 1879	
	Vineyards, 1879	
097	Acres	
098	Grapes sold in 1879	
099	Wine made in 1879	
100	Market garden - Value of Products sold - Dollars	
	Bees	
101	Honey	lbs.
102	Wax	lbs.
	Forest Products	
103	Amount of Wood cut in 1879	cords *30*
104	Value of all products sold or consumed in 1879	Dollars

Could not read

Henry Cheeves, 1880 Agriculture Census, pg. 5

66

"World War I Draft Card of Henry Cheeves, "12 September 1918; Georgia, Washington County; World War I Draft Registration Card, Selective Service System 1917-1918 (Record Group No.163). National Archives, Southeast Region, East Point, Georgia.

Mattie Cheeves Shenoster Johnson

Descendants of Rita Strange

Generation One

1. RITA^1 STRANGE was born in Sandersville, Washington County, Georgia.

Children of **Rita^1 Strange** include:
+   2.   i. HENRY^2 SR., born May 1834 in Georgia; married **Cenie** (————); married **Mary Ann Wise.**

Generation Two

2. HENRY^2 CHEEVES SR. (*Rita^1 Strange*) was born in May 1834 in Georgia. He married Cenie (————) in Georgia. He married **Mary Ann Wise** on 14 July 1880 in Washington County, Georgia. He died on 25 July 1908 in Georgia at age 74.

Children of **Henry^2 Cheeves Sr.** and **Cenie** (————) were as follows:
+   3.   i. JOE^3
     4.   ii. ABNER was born circa 1858 in Georgia.
     5.   iii. GUSSIE ANN.

Children of **Henry^2 Cheeves Sr.** and **Mary Ann Wise** were as follows:
     6.   i. HENRIETTA^3 was born circa 1864 in Georgia.
+   7.   ii. JOHN, born August 1867 in Georgia; married **Susie Carter.**
     8.   iii. MILLEDGE was born circa 1869 in Georgia.
+   9.   iv. DOVIE, born circa 1872 in Georgia; married **Randall Rogers.**
+   10.   v. DAVID 'COOT', born July 1873 in Washington County, Georgia; married **Hattie Johnson.**
     11.   vi. WILLIAM was born circa 1877 in Georgia.
     12.   vii. DAVIE was born circa 1879 in Georgia.
+   13.   viii. LOU, married **Sip Davis.**
     14.   ix. DANIEL was born circa 1870 in Georgia.
+   15.   x. HENRY JR., born 13 May 1884 in Sandersville, Washington County, Georgia; married **Clara Bell Trawick.**
+   16.   xi. LENNIE, married **William Hodges.**
+   17.   xii. CARRIE, born 22 December 1885 in Sandersville, Georgia; married **Samuel 'Sam' Gordy.**

Generation Three

3. JOE^3 CHEEVES (*Henry^2, Rita^1 Strange*).

Children of Joe[3] Cheeves include:

+ 18.   i. ANNIE[4], married **John Butler.**
  19.   ii. LILLIAN.
  20.   iii. LENA.
  21.   iv. JOE JR..
+ 22.   v. LEWIS ABNER 'BUSTER'
+ 23.   vi. OLLIE MAE
  24.   vii. LULA.
  25.   viii. ODIS.

7. JOHN[3] CHEEVES (*Henry[2], Rita[1] Strange*) was born in August 1867 in Georgia. He married **Susie Carter**, daughter of **Burrell Carter** and **Mary Ann Lane**, on 8 February 1894 in Washington County, Georgia. He died on 24 July 1908 at age 40.

Children of John[3] Cheeves and Susie Carter were as follows:

+ 26.   i. MARY A.[4], born February 1895 in Georgia; married **Major Dixon.**
+ 27.   ii. SALLIE L., born November 1897 in Georgia; married **Charlie Dixon.**
+ 28.   iii. JOHN JR., born March 1899 in Georgia; married **Pearl Jones.**
+ 29.   iv. JULIAN, born circa 1901 in Georgia; married **Marietta Harris.**
+ 30.   v. GRACE, born circa 1903 in Georgia; married **Willie Mosley.**
+ 31.   vi. LUELLA 'DERRA', born circa 1904 in Georgia; married **Jim Bivins.**
  32.   vii. ETHEL was born circa 1906 in Georgia. She married **Freddie Bullock.**
  33.   viii. BESSIE was born circa 1908 in Georgia. She married **James Wright.** She died on 30 October 1966.
+ 34.   ix. CLYDE, born circa 1909 in Georgia; married **Henry Mitchell.**

9. DOVIE[3] CHEEVES (*Henry[2], Rita[1] Strange*) was born circa 1872 in Georgia. She married **Randall Rogers**, son of **Eddie Rogers** and **Manerva (—?—)**, on 17 January 1897 in Washington County, Georgia. She died in 1956.

Children of Dovie[3] Cheeves and Randall Rogers were as follows:

+ 35.   i. LEOLA[4], born 19 September 1899 in Milledgeville, Baldwin County, Georgia; married **Cleveland Peeler.**
+ 36.   ii. MAE WILL, born 31 October 1899 in Milledgeville, Georgia; married **Lee Williams.**
+ 37.   iii. LINEN 'LENNIE', born circa 1920; married **Elton Turner.**
  38.   iv. RANDALL JR..
  39.   v. CLEOPHUS.
  40.   vi. ARNOLD LEE.
  41.   vii. HENRY EDWARD.
  42.   viii. JOSEPH B..
  43.   ix. OSCAR.

44. x. JOHN.
+ 45. xi. CLYDIE, born 22 April 1911 in Milledgeville, Georgia; married **Robert Hooks.**
46. xii. DOVIE LOU married **George Hooks.**

10. DAVID 'COOT'^{3} CHEEVES (*Henry^2, Rita^1 Strange*) was born in July 1873 in Washington County, Georgia. He married **Hattie Johnson** on 26 December 1893 in Washington County, Georgia. He died on 7 November 1932 in Washington County, Georgia, at age 59.

Children of **David 'Coot'^{3} Cheeves** and **Hattie Johnson** were as follows:
+ 47. i. LOLA^4, born January 1895 in Georgia; married **Willie Buckner.**
+ 48. ii. HENRY 'BUDDY', born November 1897 in Georgia; married **Gertrude Steele.**
49. iii. DAVID 'MUNCH' (JR.) was born in May 1898 in Georgia. He died in April 1934 at age 35.
+ 50. iv. MARY 'MA-MAE' OLLIE, born April 1900 in Georgia; married **Dock 'Whale' Trawick;** married **Sam Trawick.**
+ 51. v. SAMUEL 'SAMMIE', born circa 1903 in Georgia; married **Emily Hopkins.**
52. vi. ROSETTA 'ZETT' was born circa 1905 in Georgia. She married **Beryl Smith.** She married **Clarence Napier.** She died in 1977.
+ 53. vii. CLYDE 'BOB', born circa 1907 in Washington County, Georgia; married **Evelyn Veal.**
+ 54. viii. JOHN 'TOBE', born 18 October 1908 in Sandersville, Washington County, Georgia; married **Sarah Ella 'SC' Hopkins;** married **Lillian Ennis.**
+ 55. ix. LOUISE 'LOU', born circa 1912 in Georgia; married **Robert J. Hooks Jr.**
+ 56. x. LILLIAN LUCILLE 'SEAL', born circa 1914 in Washington County, Georgia; married **Rodell Carter.**

13. LOU^3 CHEEVES (*Henry^2, Rita^1 Strange*) married **Sip Davis** on 14 January 1888 in Washington County, Georgia

Children of **Lou^3 Cheeves** and **Sip Davis** were as follows:
57. i. ANNIE LOU^4 was born circa 1894 in Georgia.
58. ii. FANNIE BELL was born circa 1895 in Georgia.
59. iii. ZEFF was born circa 1904 in Georgia.
60. iv. HORACE was born circa 1907 in Georgia. He married **Eve** (—?—). He married **Angela** (—?—). He died in July 1971.
+ 61. v. GEORGIANNE, born 13 February 1908 in Georgia; married **Thomas Renfrow.**
62. vi. SIP was born circa 1910 in Georgia.
63. vii. ETHA was born after 1910 in Georgia. She married **Thomas Butts.** She died in May 1934.

15. HENRY³ CHEEVES JR. (*Henry², Rita¹ Strange*) was born on 13 May 1884 in Sandersville, Washington County, Georgia. He married **Clara Bell Trawick**, daughter of **Joseph 'Joe' Trawick** and **Mattie Young**, in Washington County, Georgia. He died on 23 September 1950 in Washington County, Georgia, at age 66.

Children of **Henry³ Cheeves Jr.** and **Clara Bell Trawick** were as follows:

64.   i. JOSEPH 'JOE'⁴ was born on 8 July 1905 in Sandersville, Georgia. He married **Beatrice Veal**. He married **Eva Mae Jordan**. He died in 1990 in Georgia.
+ 65.   ii. HENRIETTA, born 30 May 1907 in Sandersville, Georgia; married **Willie Smith**; married **Willie W. Hooks**.
+ 66.   iii. MATTIE LOU, born 24 June 1909 in Sandersville, Georgia; married **Bobby Lee Shenoster**; married **Oreain Johnson**.
+ 67.   iv. HENRY HOLMES, born 18 February 1918 in Sandersville, Washington County, Georgia; married **Lillian Arthur Carter**.
68.   v. CARRIE ANN was born on 6 November 1920 in Sandersville, Georgia. She died on 26 April 1921 in Sandersville, Washington County, Georgia.

16. LENNIE³ CHEEVES (*Henry², Rita¹ Strange*) married **William Hodges** on 21 January 1894 in Washington County, Georgia She died in 1905.

Children of **Lennie³ Cheeves** and **William Hodges** were as follows:
+ 69.   i. MARY LOU⁴, married **Johnny Lee Timmons**.
70.   ii. WILL OLA 'SISTER' married **Mr. Cary**.
71.   iii. LOU OLA 'MUNCH' married **Lee Woods**.
72.   iv. ELIZABETH married **Mr. Mathis**.
73.   v. CORNELIUS 'BUSTER'.

17. CARRIE³ CHEEVES (*Henry², Rita¹ Strange*) was born on 22 December 1885 in Sandersville, Georgia. She married **Samuel 'Sam' Gordy**, son of **Berry Gordy Sr.** and **Lucy Hellum**. She died in December 1970.

Children of **Carrie³ Cheeves** and **Samuel 'Sam' Gordy** were as follows:
+ 74.   i. HENRY BERRY⁴, born 3 May 1905 in Sandersville, Georgia; married **Hattie Mae Hooks**.
+ 75.   ii. MARY LUCY, born 10 November 1906 in Sandersville, Georgia; married **Robert Cawthon**.
+ 76.   iii. JOHN, born 3 December 1908 in Sandersville, Georgia; married **Georgia Belle Hodges**.
+ 77.   iv. SAMUEL 'SAM' JR., born 28 October 1910 in Sandersville, Georgia; married **Margaret Sheppard**.
78.   v. LENNIE RUTH was born on 28 June 1914 in Washington County, Georgia. She married **Robert J. Hooks Jr.**, son of **Robert Hooks Sr.** and **Clara Lane**.

79. vi. DAVID was born on 24 April 1919 in Sandersville, Georgia. He died in September 1950 at age 31.

+ 80. vii. ANN 'ANNIE' OWEN, born 30 December 1925 in Sandersville, Washington County, Georgia; married Herman Smith; married Maxel Hardy.

+ 81. viii. ROBERT DANIEL, born 21 June 1926 in Sandersville, Georgia; married Eloise 'Honey' Dawson.

Generation Four

18. ANNIE⁴ CHEEVES (*Joe³, Henry², Rita¹ Strange*) married John Butler.

Children of Annie⁴ Cheeves and John Butler were:
82. i. ANNIE LILLIAN⁵.

22. LEWIS ABNER 'BUSTER'⁴ CHEEVES (*Joe³, Henry², Rita¹ Strange*).

Children of Lewis Abner 'Buster'⁴ Cheeves include:
83. i. LEWIS ABNER⁵ (JR.).

23. OLLIE MAE⁴ CHEEVES (*Joe³, Henry², Rita¹ Strange*).

Children of Ollie Mae⁴ Cheeves include:
84. i. ULYSSES⁵.

26. MARY A.⁴ CHEEVES (*John³, Henry², Rita¹ Strange*) was born in February 1895 in Georgia. She married Major Dixon, son of Ransome Dixon and Betty (———). She died on 12 February 1942.

Children of Mary A.⁴ Cheeves and Major Dixon were as follows:
85. i. JOHNNIE⁵ was born circa 1913 in Georgia.
86. ii. LILLIAN was born circa 1914 in Georgia.
+ 87. iii. CHARLIE, born circa 1916 in Georgia; married Elaine (———).
88. iv. LOZELL.
89. v. BENJAMIN.
+ 90. vi. WILLIAM, married Renee (———).
+ 91. vii. ROSALIE 'ROSE', born circa 1918 in Georgia.
92. viii. ELAINE was born circa 1920.
93. ix. ANN PEARL.
+ 94. x. ANNA JULIA

27. SALLIE L.^{4} CHEEVES (*John^3, Henry^2, Rita^1 Strange*) was born in November 1897 in Georgia. She married **Charlie Dixon**, son of **Ransome Dixon** and **Betty** (———). She died in August 1959 at age 61.

Children of **Sallie L.^{4} Cheeves** and **Charlie Dixon** were as follows:

+ 95.   i. HORACE^5, born 13 March 1917 in Sandersville, Georgia; married **Bertha McLemore.**
+ 96.   ii. CHARLIE (JR.)
+ 97.   iii. ED
+ 98.   iv. MINNIE, married **Mr. Woodard.**
+ 99.   v. DORIS, married **Mr. Gates.**
+ 100.   vi. JANETTE, married **Mr. Beatha.**

28. JOHN^4 CHEEVES JR. (*John^3, Henry^2, Rita^1 Strange*) was born in March 1899 in Georgia. He married **Pearl Jones**. He died on 21 March 1928.

Children of **John^4 Cheeves Jr.** and **Pearl Jones** were as follows:

+ 101.   i. REATHER^5, born 16 February 1923 in Georgia; married **Ella Dixon;** married **Martha** (———).
102.   ii. JOHN III.
103.   iii. TOM.
104.   iv. BILL.
105.   v. MERIDETH.
106.   vi. ELIZABETH married **Mr. Tolston.**
107.   vii. BARBARA.

29. JULIAN^4 CHEEVES (*John^3, Henry^2, Rita^1 Strange*) was born circa 1901 in Georgia. He married **Marietta Harris**. He died in October 1943.

Children of **Julian^4 Cheeves** and **Marietta Harris** were as follows:
108.   i. BERNICE^5.
109.   ii. MARIE.

30. GRACE^4 CHEEVES (*John^3, Henry^2, Rita^1 Strange*) was born circa 1903 in Georgia. She married **Willie Mosley**. She died on 13 August 1945.

Children of **Grace^4 Cheeves** and **Willie Mosley** were:
110.   i. CARLTON^5 was born circa 1918 in Georgia.

31. LUELLA 'DERRA'^{4} CHEEVES (*John^3, Henry^2, Rita^1 Strange*) was born circa 1904 in Georgia. She married **Jim Bivins**.

Children of **Luella 'Derra'**[4] **Cheeves** and **Jim Bivins** were as follows:
- 111.   i. RUTH[5].
- 112.   ii. RUBY.
- 113.   iii. BUNCHIE.

34. CLYDE[4] **CHEEVES** (*John*[3], *Henry*[2], *Rita*[1] *Strange*) was born circa 1909 in Georgia. She married **Henry Mitchell.**

Children of **Clyde**[4] **Cheeves** and **Henry Mitchell** were as follows:
- + 114.   i. RUTH[5], born circa 1940; married **Lee Arthur Wright.**
- 115.   ii. HENRY (JR.).
- 116.   iii. BILL.
- + 117.   iv. WILLIE, married **Irene Flemmens.**
- + 118.   v. MILEY, married **Timothy Kelsey.**
- + 119.   vi. DORIS DOROTHY
- + 120.   vii. HAZEL, born March 1937 in Washington County, Georgia
- 121.   viii. MARY CLYDE.
- 122.   ix. ALMA JEAN.

35. LEOLA[4] **ROGERS** (*Dovie*[3] *Cheeves*, *Henry*[2], *Rita*[1] *Strange*) was born on 19 September 1899 in Milledgeville, Baldwin County, Georgia. She married **Cleveland Peeler**, son of **William 'Tump' Peeler** and **Susie Temple.**

Children of **Leola**[4] **Rogers** and **Cleveland Peeler** were as follows:
- + 123.   i. RUBY[5], born 28 December 1918 in Milledgeville, Georgia; married **William Jamison.**
- + 124.   ii. ROGERS, born 4 September 1920 in Milledgeville, Georgia; married **Mary Helen McBride.**
- 125.   iii. CLEVELAND JR. was born on 1 June 1922 in Milledgeville, Georgia. He died in December 1941 in Great Lake, Illinois, at age 19.
- + 126.   iv. SUSIE, born 7 April 1924 in Milledgeville, Georgia; married **Grady Jones.**
- + 127.   v. VERA, born 10 May 1926 in Milledgeville, Georgia; married **John Trawick.**
- 128.   vi. LEOLA was born on 24 May 1928 in Milledgeville, Georgia. She married **Mr. Banks.** She died in October 1986 in Detroit, Michigan, at age 58.
- + 129.   vii. DOVIE ONEAIN, born 19 April 1930 in Sandersville, Georgia; married **Frank Williams.**
- + 130.   viii. THOMAS JAMES 'TJ', born 22 May 1933 in Sandersville, Georgia.

36. MAE WILL[4] **ROGERS** (*Dovie*[3] *Cheeves*, *Henry*[2], *Rita*[1] *Strange*) was born on 31 October 1899 in Milledgeville, Georgia. She married **Lee Williams**, son of **Ed Williams** and **Nancy Boyer.** She died on 23 September 1982 in Milledgeville, Georgia, at age 82.

Children of **Mae Will**[4] **Rogers** and **Lee Williams** were as follows:
131.   i. ROBERT[5] was born on 12 November 1919 in Milledgeville, Georgia. He died in July 1955 in Milledgeville, Georgia, at age 35.
132.   ii. LEE ARTHUR was born on 18 April 1920 in Milledgeville, Georgia. He died in October 1985 in Detroit, Michigan, at age 65.
+ 133.   iii. MAE WILL, born 11 September 1922 in Milledgeville, Georgia; married **Johnnie Dark Renfroe.**
134.   iv. RANDALL was born on 5 February 1924 in Milledgeville, Georgia.
+ 135.   v. RUFUS, born 19 March 1925 in Milledgeville, Georgia; married **Francis Andrews.**
136.   vi. BLANCHE was born on 11 October 1927 in Milledgeville, Georgia.
137.   vii. DEVOLIA was born on 25 June 1928 in Milledgeville, Georgia.
138.   viii. ROHDELL was born on 5 February 1929 in Milledgeville, Georgia.
139.   ix. GLADYS was born on 4 August 1931 in Milledgeville, Georgia.

37. LINEN 'LENNIE'[4] **ROGERS** (*Dovie*[3] *Cheeves, Henry*[2], *Rita*[1] *Strange*) was born circa 1920. She married **Elton Turner**, son of **William 'Will' Turner** and **Rachel Hooks.**

Children of **Linen 'Lennie'**[4] **Rogers** and **Elton Turner** were as follows:
140.   i. ROGER[5].
141.   ii. EUGENE.
+ 142.   iii. JOHN RUBEN (SR.), born 26 September 1928; married **Mary** (———).
143.   iv. WILLIE DOUGLAS.
144.   v. ELTON (JR.).
145.   vi. WYMAN.

45. CLYDIE[4] **ROGERS** (*Dovie*[3] *Cheeves, Henry*[2], *Rita*[1] *Strange*) was born on 22 April 1911 in Milledgeville, Georgia. She married **Robert Hooks**, son of **Marshall Hooks** and **Claudie Stevens.**

Children of **Clydie**[4] **Rogers** and **Robert Hooks** were as follows:
146.   i. MARION[5].
147.   ii. RALPH.
148.   iii. ROBERT JR..
149.   iv. BARBARA JEAN.
150.   v. ROSALIE.
151.   vi. JOYCE.
152.   vii. EUNICE CLYDIE.
153.   viii. FRANKIE LOUISE.
154.   ix. HERBERT.

47. LOLA[4] **CHEEVES** (*David 'Coot'*[3], *Henry*[2], *Rita*[1] *Strange*) was born in January 1895 in Georgia. She married **Willie Buckner.** She died in 1919.

Children of **Lola**[4] **Cheeves** and **Willie Buckner** were:
+ 155.   i. ELMER CHEEVES[5], born 1919; married **Bertha Young**.

48. **HENRY 'BUDDY'**[4] **CHEEVES** (*David 'Coot*[3], *Henry*[2], *Rita*[1] *Strange*) was born in November 1897 in Georgia. He married **Gertrude Steele**. He died in 1944.

Children of **Henry 'Buddy'**[4] **Cheeves** and **Gertrude Steele** were as follows:
+ 156.   i. HENRY WILLIE 'SMOOK'[5], married **Hazel Jones**.
+ 157.   ii. LILLIAN MAE 'SANG', married **Wilbur Bond**.
+ 158.   iii. LOLA BELL 'JACK', married **Reginald** (—?—).
+ 159.   iv. ESTELLE 'STELL', married **Mr. Mills**.

50. **MARY 'MA-MAE' OLLIE**[4] **CHEEVES** (*David 'Coot*[3], *Henry*[2], *Rita*[1] *Strange*) was born in April 1900 in Georgia. She married **Dock 'Whale' Trawick**, son of **Dock Trawick** and **Violet Young**. She married **Sam Trawick**, son of **Dock Trawick** and **Violet Young**. She died in 1960.

Children of **Mary 'Ma-Mae' Ollie**[4] **Cheeves** and **Dock 'Whale' Trawick** were as follows:
+ 160.   i. JULIA INEZ[5], born 24 January 1920; married **Sidney C. Butts**.
  161.   ii. CLYDE 'BUDDY'.
+ 162.   iii. MAMYE DOROTHY 'MARY', born 16 January 1925; married **Bob Willis Butts**.
+ 163.   iv. JUANITA EASTER MAE, married **Cleophus Crumbly**; married **Mr. Elliott**.
  164.   v. JULIA married **Mr. Elliott**.

Children of **Mary 'Ma-Mae' Ollie**[4] **Cheeves** and **Sam Trawick** were as follows:
  165.   i. MYRIAN[5] married **Mr. Hall**.
  166.   ii. LAURTY.
  167.   iii. GLORIA 'GLO' LOUISE married **Burley 'Sytes' Lord (Jr.)**, son of **Burley Lord (Sr.)** and **Rosa Mae Butts**.

51. **SAMUEL 'SAMMIE'**[4] **CHEEVES** (*David 'Coot*[3], *Henry*[2], *Rita*[1] *Strange*) was born circa 1903 in Georgia. He married **Emily Hopkins**, daughter of **Edmond 'Buster' Hopkins** and **Georgeanne Hodges**. He died in 1973.

Children of **Samuel 'Sammie'**[4] **Cheeves** and **Emily Hopkins** were as follows:
  168.   i. ETHEL[5].
+ 169.   ii. CARLTON 'COLLIE', born 1 August 1938 in Philadelphia, Pennsylvania; married **Rosita Delores Talley**.

53. **CLYDE 'BOB'**[4] **CHEEVES** (*David 'Coot*[3], *Henry*[2], *Rita*[1] *Strange*) was born circa 1907 in Washington County, Georgia. He married **Evelyn Veal** in 1922. He died in 1943.

Children of **Clyde 'Bob'**[4] **Cheeves** and **Evelyn Veal** were:
170.　i. CURTIS[5].

54. JOHN 'TOBE'[4] **CHEEVES** (*David 'Coot*[3], *Henry*[2], *Rita*[1] *Strange*) was born on 18 October 1908 in Sandersville, Washington County, Georgia. He married **Sarah Ella 'SC' Hopkins**, daughter of **Tommy Boyer** and **Pearl Hopkins**. He married **Lillian Ennis**. He died in April 1974 in Sandersville, Georgia, at age 65.

Children of **John 'Tobe'**[4] **Cheeves** and **Sarah Ella 'SC' Hopkins** were:
+ 171.　i. ERNESTINE 'MOLLY'[5], born 22 December 1932 in Washington County, Georgia.

There were no children of **John 'Tobe'**[4] **Cheeves** and **Lillian Ennis**.

55. LOUISE 'LOU'[4] **CHEEVES** (*David 'Coot*[3], *Henry*[2], *Rita*[1] *Strange*) was born circa 1912 in Georgia. She married **Robert J. Hooks Jr.**, son of **Robert Hooks Sr.** and **Clara Lane**. She died in 1977.

Children of **Louise 'Lou'**[4] **Cheeves** and **Robert J. Hooks Jr.** were:
+ 172.　i. FLETA[5]

56. LILLIAN LUCILLE 'SEAL'[4] **CHEEVES** (*David 'Coot*[3], *Henry*[2], *Rita*[1] *Strange*) was born circa 1914 in Washington County, Georgia. She married **Rodell Carter**, son of **Jeff Carter Sr.** and **Easter Gordy**. She died on 2 November 1972.

Children of **Lillian Lucille 'Seal'**[4] **Cheeves** include:
173.　i. MARILYN SMITH[5].

There were no children of **Lillian Lucille 'Seal'**[4] **Cheeves** and **Rodell Carter**.

61. GEORGIANNE[4] **DAVIS** (*Lou*[3] *Cheeves*, *Henry*[2], *Rita*[1] *Strange*) was born on 13 February 1908 in Georgia. She married **Thomas Renfrow**. She died on 28 July.

Children of **Georgianne**[4] **Davis** and **Thomas Renfrow** were as follows:
+ 174.　i. CHARLIE[5], born 13 February 1908; married **Katie Butts**.
175.　ii. ANNIE married **Rhuber Miller**.
176.　iii. RUDOLPH married **Athalia** (———).
177.　iv. BERTHA.
178.　v. LOUISE 'LOU' married **Robinson Booz**.

65. HENRIETTA^4 **CHEEVES** (*Henry*^{3}, *Henry*^{2}, *Rita*^{1} *Strange*) was born on 30 May 1907 in Sandersville, Georgia. She married **Willie Smith**. She married **Willie W. Hooks**, son of **Mitchell Hooks** and **Love Andrews**. She died on 12 May 1969 in Augusta, Georgia, at age 61.

Children of **Henrietta**^{4} **Cheeves** and **Willie Smith** were:
179. i. **WILLIE C.**^{5} was born in Sandersville, Georgia. He married **Inez** (———).

Children of **Henrietta**^{4} **Cheeves** and **Willie W. Hooks** were as follows:
+ 180. i. **MITCHELL**^{5}, born 7 March 1933 in Sandersville, Georgia; married **Delores Hooks.**
+ 181. ii. **CHEEVES**, born 4 April 1935 in Washington County, Georgia; married **Myrtistine Cullens.**
182. iii. **WILLIE WALTER (JR.)** was born on 30 June 1937 in Washington County, Georgia. He married **Annie** (———). He married **Gussie** (———).
+ 183. iv. **MARION**, born 1 July 1940 in Sandersville, Georgia; married **Annie** (———); married **Christine** (—?—).
+ 184. v. **ORALENE**, born 4 April 1943 in Sandersville, Georgia; married **Frank Pierce.**

66. MATTIE LOU^4 **CHEEVES** (*Henry*^{3}, *Henry*^{2}, *Rita*^{1} *Strange*) was born on 24 June 1909 in Sandersville, Georgia. She married **Bobby Lee Shenoster**. She married **Oreain Johnson**. She died on 5 March 1995 in Philadelphia, Pennsylvania, at age 85.

Children of **Mattie Lou**^{4} **Cheeves** and **Bobby Lee Shenoster** were as follows:
+ 185. i. **ZELMA**^{5}, born 10 January 1932 in Sandersville, Georgia.
+ 186. ii. **KATHERINE**, born 19 April 1934 in Milledgeville, Georgia; married **John Benjamin Douglass (Sr.).**

There were no children of **Mattie Lou**^{4} **Cheeves** and **Oreain Johnson**.

67. HENRY HOLMES^4 **CHEEVES** (*Henry*^{3}, *Henry*^{2}, *Rita*^{1} *Strange*) was born on 18 February 1918 in Sandersville, Washington County, Georgia. He married **Lillian Arthur Carter**, daughter of **Jeff Carter Jr.** and **Gervenia Fisher**. He died on 15 September 2001 in Philadelphia, Pennsylvania, at age 83.

Children of **Henry Holmes**^{4} **Cheeves** and **Lillian Arthur Carter** were as follows:
+ 187. i. **MIRIAM**^{5}, born in Sandersville, Washington County, Georgia
+ 188. ii. **GLORIA,** born 4 July 1941 in Sandersville, Washington County, Georgia; married **Charles Graham.**
+ 189. iii. **HORACE,** born 4 September 1943 in Sandersville, Washington County, Georgia; married **Fannie Pearl Williams.**
+ 190. iv. **FOREST,** born 4 September 1943 in Sandersville, Washington County, Georgia; married **Karen Kennedy.**

191.   v. HENRY was born on 8 September 1948 in Sandersville, Washington County, Georgia
192.   vi. DAVID was born on 10 November 1954 in Philadelphia, Pennsylvania. He died
       on 17 August 1995 in Detroit, Mich, at age 40.
193.   vii. ANNETTE GAIL was born on 7 August 1958 in Philadelphia, Pennsylvania.

69. MARY LOU^4 HODGES (*Lennie^{3}Cheeves, Henry^2, Rita^{1}Strange*) married **Johnny Lee
    Timmons.**

Children of **Mary Lou^4 Hodges** and **Johnny Lee Timmons** were as follows:
+ 194.   i. LUCILLE 'LUCY'^{5}, married **Mr. Jones.**
  195.   ii. EULA married **Mr. Williams.**
  196.   iii. ROBERT.
  197.   iv. ISADORE.
  198.   v. A. SAMUEL.
  199.   vi. A.W. ANDREW.
  200.   vii. FRED.
  201.   viii. WILLIE MAE married **Mr. Diamond.**
  202.   ix. ARIZOLA married **Mr. Mobley.**

74. HENRY BERRY^4 GORDY (*Carrie^{3}Cheeves, Henry^2, Rita^{1}Strange*) was born on 3
    May 1905 in Sandersville, Georgia. He married **Hattie Mae Hooks,** daughter of
    Mack Hooks and **Judy Mason,** on 29 April 1928.

Children of **Henry Berry^4 Gordy** and **Hattie Mae Hooks** were as follows:
+ 203.   i. HENRY EDWARD^5, born 2 March 1929 in Sandersville, Georgia; married
          Jeanetta (—?—).
  204.   ii. SAM married **Mary Moses.**
+ 205.   iii. MARGARET JEWEL, married **Isaac King.**
+ 206.   iv. CLAUDETTE, born 9 February 1937; married **Alfred C. Johnson.**
+ 207.   v. CAROLYN, married **Leonard Kennedy.**
+ 208.   vi. LAWRENCE, married **Shirley Palmer.**
  209.   vii. GARY.
+ 210.   viii. JOYCE, born 1938 in Sandersville, Georgia; married **Welton Lawrence.**
+ 211.   ix. JAMES HAROLD, born 16 March 1942; married **Donna (———).**

75. MARY LUCY^4 GORDY (*Carrie^{3}Cheeves, Henry^2, Rita^{1}Strange*) was born on 10
    November 1906 in Sandersville, Georgia. She married **Robert Cawthon.** She
    died in October 1940 at age 33.

Children of **Mary Lucy^4 Gordy** and **Robert Cawthon** were as follows:
+ 212.   i. EVELYN BERNICE^5, born circa 1925 in Milledgeville, Georgia; married **William
          Turner.**

+ 213.   ii. MARY LOUVENIA 'BENIA', born 17 August 1928 in Milledgeville, Georgia; married **Ernest Butts.**

+ 214.   iii. ROBERT 'BOB' JR., born circa 1930 in Milledgeville, Georgia; married **Arlene (—?—).**

215.   iv. BARNEY was born circa 1935 in Milledgeville, Georgia. He died circa 1951.

+ 216.   v. BETTY JEAN, born circa 1940 in Milledgeville, Georgia; married **James Nelson.**

76. JOHN^4 GORDY (*Carrie^3 Cheeves, Henry^2, Rita^1 Strange*) was born on 3 December 1908 in Sandersville, Georgia. He married **Georgia Belle Hodges**, daughter of **Mitchell Hodges.** He died on 28 May 1969 at age 60.

Children of **John^4 Gordy** and **Georgia Belle Hodges** were as follows:
217.   i. LAVORA^5 was born in February 1932. He died in January 1995 at age 62.
218.   ii. HODGES BAY was born on 9 January 1935 in Sandersville, Georgia. He died in June 1996 at age 61.
219.   iii. JOHN 'JACK' JR. was born on 15 June 1937 in Sandersville, Georgia.
+ 220.   iv. EVELYN 'SIS', born 4 January 1939 in Sandersville, Georgia.

77. SAMUEL 'SAM'^{4} GORDY JR. (*Carrie^3 Cheeves, Henry^2, Rita^1 Strange*) was born on 28 October 1910 in Sandersville, Georgia. He married **Margaret Sheppard.** He died on 31 August 1985 in Sandersville, Georgia, at age 74.

Children of **Samuel 'Sam'^{4} Gordy Jr.** and **Margaret Sheppard** were as follows:
221.   i. BEVERLY^5 was born in Washington County, Georgia.
222.   ii. CLEAVIE was born in Washington County, Georgia.
223.   iii. SHEILA was born in Washington County, Georgia.
224.   iv. ROY SAMUEL was born circa 1935 in Washington County, Georgia.

Children of **Samuel 'Sam'^{4} Gordy Jr.** and **Sarah Ella 'SC' Hopkins** were:
+ 225.   i. MARY PEARL 'TOWN'^{5} CHEEVES, born 21 January 1930 in Sandersville, Georgia; married **Vernon 'Bud' Trawick.**

80. ANN 'ANNIE' OWEN^4 GORDY (*Carrie^3 Cheeves, Henry^2, Rita^1 Strange*) was born on 30 December 1925 in Sandersville, Washington County, Georgia. She married **Herman Smith.** She married **Maxel Hardy** on 11 August 1951 in Detroit, Michigan. She died on 12 July 1992 in Detroit, Michigan, at age 66.

There were no children of **Ann 'Annie' Owen^4 Gordy** and **Herman Smith.**

Children of **Ann 'Annie' Owen^4 Gordy** and **Maxel Hardy** were as follows:
+ 226.   i. MAXEL^5 JR., born 10 October 1952 in Detroit, Michigan.
227.   ii. LYNETTE was born on 5 May 1955 in Detroit, Michigan.

+ 228. iii. CHERYL DENISE, born 20 September 1958 in Detroit, Michigan.

81. ROBERT DANIEL[4] GORDY (*Carrie[3] Cheeves, Henry[2], Rita[1] Strange*) was born on 21 June 1926 in Sandersville, Georgia. He married Eloise 'Honey' Dawson, daughter of Homer Dawson and Lora Ella 'Laura' Carter, on 6 March 1950 in Sandersville, Washington County, Georgia.

Children of Robert Daniel[4] Gordy and Eloise 'Honey' Dawson were as follows:
+ 229. i. GWENDOLYN[5], born 12 March 1947 in Utica, New York; married Julius Murphy.
  230. ii. ROBERT DANIEL JR. was born on 27 July 1950 in Sandersville, Georgia.
+ 231. iii. DAVID, born 13 April 1952 in Sandersville, Georgia; married DeLois Turner; married Darlene Robinson.
+ 232. iv. DEBORAH ANNE, born 6 January 1954 in Sandersville, Georgia; married Samuel Duggan.
+ 233. v. MARY LUCY, born 17 July 1956 in Sandersville, Georgia; married Tony Owen Hurt Sr.
  234. vi. REGINALD CORNELIUS was born on 5 September 1957 in Sandersville, Georgia. He married Yvette (—?—).
+ 235. vii. BERRY RENARD, born 10 September 1958 in Sandersville, Georgia; married Brenda Lee Lord Barlow Cardy.

Generation Five

87. CHARLIE[5] DIXON (*Mary A.[4] Cheeves, John[3], Henry[2], Rita[1] Strange*) was born circa 1916 in Georgia. He married Elaine (———).

Children of Charlie[5] Dixon and Elaine (———) were:
  236. i. BRENDA[6] was born circa 1945.

90. WILLIAM[5] DIXON (*Mary A.[4] Cheeves, John[3], Henry[2], Rita[1] Strange*) married Renee (———).

Children of William[5] Dixon and Renee (———) were:
  237. i. EARL[6].

91. ROSALIE 'ROSE'[5] DIXON (*Mary A.[4] Cheeves, John[3], Henry[2], Rita[1] Strange*) was born circa 1918 in Georgia.

Children of Rosalie 'Rose'[5] Dixon include:
+ 238. i. ELAINE[6]

94. ANNA JULIA[5] DIXON (*Mary A.[4] Cheeves, John[3], Henry[2], Rita[1] Strange*).

Children of **Anna Julia**[5] **Dixon** include:
+ 239.   i. LEWIS[6], married **Mary** (———).
+ 240.   ii. MAJOR, married **Emma** (———).
+ 241.   iii. JEROME, married **Rose** (———).
+ 242.   iv. DAISY MAE
+ 243.   v. MARLENE, married **Will Pearsall.**

95. HORACE[5] **DIXON** (*Sallie L.*[4]*Cheeves, John*[3], *Henry*[2], *Rita*[1]*Strange*) was born on 13 March 1917 in Sandersville, Georgia. He married **Bertha McLemore.** He died in April 1979 in Philadelphia, Pennsylvania, at age 62.

Children of **Horace**[5] **Dixon** and **Bertha McLemore** were as follows:
+ 244.   i. PHILIP (ALI SALAUDIN)[6], born 4 February 1947 in Philadelphia, Pennsylvania; married **Carol Haughton.**
+ 245.   ii. RODNEY, born 8 March 1950 in Philadelphia, Pennsylvania; married **Beverly Diane Fisher.**

96. CHARLIE[5] **DIXON (JR.)** (*Sallie L.*[4]*Cheeves, John*[3], *Henry*[2], *Rita*[1]*Strange*).

Children of **Charlie**[5] **Dixon (Jr.)** include:
 246.   i. LONNIE[6].
 247.   ii. CHARLIE (III).
 248.   iii. STEVIE.
 249.   iv. WAYNE.
 250.   v. LINDA.
 251.   vi. VALERIE.
 252.   vii. ELIZABETH.

97. ED[5] **DIXON** (*Sallie L.*[4]*Cheeves, John*[3], *Henry*[2], *Rita*[1]*Strange*).

Children of **Ed**[5] **Dixon** include:
 253.   i. YVETTE[6].

98. MINNIE[5] **DIXON** (*Sallie L.*[4]*Cheeves, John*[3], *Henry*[2], *Rita*[1]*Strange*) married **Mr. Woodard.**

Children of **Minnie**[5] **Dixon** and **Mr. Woodard** were:
+ 254.   i. DELORES[6], married **Robert Handon.**

99. DORIS[5] **DIXON** (*Sallie L.*[4]*Cheeves, John*[3], *Henry*[2], *Rita*[1]*Strange*) married **Mr. Gates.**

Children of **Doris**[5] **Dixon** and **Mr. Gates** were:
+ 255.   i. BEVERLY ANN[6], married **Mr. Green.**

100. JANETTE^5 DIXON (*Sallie L.^{4}Cheeves, John^3, Henry^2, Rita^1 Strange*) married **Mr. Beatha.**

Children of **Janette^5 Dixon** and **Mr. Beatha** were as follows:
  256.   i. KLIM^6.
  257. ii. KALHI KAREEM.

101. REATHER^5 CHEEVES (*John^4, John^3, Henry^2, Rita^1 Strange*) was born on 16 February 1923 in Georgia. He married **Ella Dixon.** He married **Martha** (——) on 22 March 1948 in Philadelphia, Pennsylvania. He died in September 1979 in Philadelphia, Pennsylvania, at age 56.

Children of **Reather^5 Cheeves** and **Ella Dixon** were:
  258.   i. REATHER MARIE^6.

Children of **Reather^5 Cheeves** and **Martha** (——) were:
  259.   i. DARLENE V.^{6} was born on 29 October 1948 in Philadelphia, Pennsylvania.

114. RUTH^5 MITCHELL (*Clyde^{4}Cheeves, John^3, Henry^2, Rita^1 Strange*) was born circa 1940. She married **Lee Arthur Wright.**

Children of **Ruth^5 Mitchell** and **Lee Arthur Wright** were as follows:
    260.   i. CAROLYN^6.
+ 261. ii. ELAINE, married **William Wilkes.**
+ 262. iii. DEBRA

117. WILLIE^5 MITCHELL (*Clyde^{4}Cheeves, John^3, Henry^2, Rita^1 Strange*) married **Irene Flemmens.**

Children of **Willie^5 Mitchell** and **Irene Flemmens** were:
  263.   i. NIKKEA^6.

118. MILEY^5 MITCHELL (*Clyde^{4}Cheeves, John^3, Henry^2, Rita^1 Strange*) married **Timothy Kelsey.**

Children of **Miley^5 Mitchell** and **Timothy Kelsey** were as follows:
+ 264.   i. ARRON^6, married **Mary** (——).
+ 265. ii. CECIL, married **Jackie** (——).
+ 266. iii. DELORES, married **Calvin** (——).
+ 267. iv. TIMOTHY (JR.), married **Amy** (——).

119. DORIS DOROTHY^5 MITCHELL (*Clyde^{4}Cheeves, John^3, Henry^2, Rita^1 Strange*).

84

Children of **Doris Dorothy⁵ Mitchell** include:
+ 268.   i. BETTY JEAN⁶
+ 269.   ii. ALTON

120. HAZEL⁵ MITCHELL (*Clyde⁴Cheeves, John³, Henry², Rita¹Strange*) was born in March 1937 in Washington County, Georgia She died in May 1980 in Milledgeville, Baldwin County, Georgia, at age 43.

Children of **Hazel⁵ Mitchell** include:
+ 270.   i. BERNICE⁶, married **Mr. Woods.**
+ 271.   ii. VICKIE, married **Joseph Williams.**

123. RUBY⁵ PEELER (*Leola⁴Rogers, Dovie³Cheeves, Henry², Rita¹Strange*) was born on 28 December 1918 in Milledgeville, Georgia. She married **William Jamison.** She died on 29 June 1963 in Detroit, Michigan, at age 44.

Children of **Ruby⁵ Peeler** include:
+ 272.   i. CYNTHIA⁶, born 2 December 1951 in Detroit, Michigan.

There were no children of **Ruby⁵** Peeler and **William Jamison.**

124. ROGERS⁵ PEELER (*Leola⁴Rogers, Dovie³Cheeves, Henry², Rita¹Strange*) was born on 4 September 1920 in Milledgeville, Georgia. He married **Mary Helen McBride.** He died on 6 August 1991 in Macon, Georgia, at age 70.

Children of **Rogers⁵ Peeler** and **Mary Helen McBride** were as follows:
273.   i. GARY⁶ was born on 30 December 1959 in Sandersville, Georgia.
274.   ii. TANGA ANN was born on 26 June 1963 in Sandersville, Georgia.

Children of **Rogers⁵ Peeler** and **Laura Jean Hopkins** were:
+ 275.   i. WANDA JEAN⁶, born 11 October 1957 in Washington, DC.

126. SUSIE⁵ PEELER (*Leola⁴Rogers, Dovie³Cheeves, Henry², Rita¹Strange*) was born on 7 April 1924 in Milledgeville, Georgia. She married **Grady Jones.**

Children of **Susie⁵ Peeler** and **Grady Jones** were as follows:
+ 276.   i. GRADY⁶ JR., born 9 December 1953 in Detroit, Michigan; married **Jacqueline Denise Major.**
+ 277.   ii. MICHAEL, born 26 September 1955 in Detroit, Michigan; married **Gertrude Hawthorn.**
+ 278.   iii. SHIRLEY JEAN, born 5 April 1957 in Detroit, Michigan; married **Alvin Brezzell.**

+ 279. iv. PAULA, born 27 July 1963 in Detroit, Michigan; married **Marco Henry.**

127. VERA[5] PEELER (*Leola[4] Rogers, Dovie[3] Cheeves, Henry[2], Rita[1] Strange*) was born on 10 May 1926 in Milledgeville, Georgia. She married **John Trawick,** son of **Elisha Trawick** and **Mary Lucy Ann Barlow,** on 22 June 1947 in Sandersville, Georgia.

Children of **Vera[5] Peeler** and **John Trawick** were as follows:
280. i. MALVIN[6] was born on 22 October 1947 in Sandersville, Georgia. He married **Jacqueline Parklin.**
+ 281. ii. ALTON, born 18 January 1949 in Sandersville, Georgia; married **Joanne Washington.**
282. iii. LINDA JOYCE was born on 15 May 1950 in Sandersville, Georgia. She married **Samual Chandle.**
283. iv. BEVERLY LAVERNE was born on 1 July 1953 in Sandersville, Georgia.
+ 284. v. CATHY ANN, born 3 January 1955 in Sandersville, Georgia; married **Leo Suggs.**
285. vi. JOHN RICKY was born on 19 September 1959 in Sandersville, Georgia. He died in December 1995 in St. Paul, Minnesota, at age 36.
+ 286. vii. LYDIA JEAN, born 3 February 1961 in Sandersville, Georgia; married **Willie James Woodard.**

129. DOVIE ONEAIN[5] PEELER (*Leola[4] Rogers, Dovie[3] Cheeves, Henry[2], Rita[1] Strange*) was born on 19 April 1930 in Sandersville, Georgia. She married **Frank Williams** on 14 May 1950 in Detroit, Michigan.

Children of **Dovie Oneain[5] Peeler** and **Frank Williams** were as follows:
+ 287. i. BELINDA[6], born 23 April 1949 in Detroit, Michigan.
+ 288. ii. ROCHELLE, born 13 December 1951 in Detroit, Michigan.
+ 289. iii. FRAUN, born 3 December 1954 in Detroit, Michigan; married **Bernard Delmas Foster Sr.**
+ 290. iv. VIVIAN, born 26 October 1957 in Detroit, Michigan; married **Wendel Burch.**
+ 291. v. WENDY, born 26 October 1959 in Detroit, Michigan; married **Scott Rose.**
+ 292. vi. FRANK JR., born 28 December 1964 in St. Paul, Minnesota; married **Titka** (—?—).
293. vii. RODNEY BOONE was born on 27 March 1967 in St. Paul, Minnesota.

130. THOMAS JAMES 'TJ'[5] PEELER (*Leola[4] Rogers, Dovie[3] Cheeves, Henry[2], Rita[1] Strange*) was born on 22 May 1933 in Sandersville, Georgia. He died on 16 July 2001 in Milledgeville, Georgia, at age 68.

Children of **Thomas James 'TJ'[5] Peeler** include:
294. i. CHRISTOPHER[6] was born in Milledgeville, Georgia.
295. ii. JON was born in Milledgeville, Georgia.
296. iii. CORNELIUS was born in Milledgeville, Georgia.

297.   iv. NEIL was born in Milledgeville, Georgia.

133. MAE WILL[5] WILLIAMS (*Mae Will[4]Rogers, Dovie[3]Cheeves, Henry[2], Rita[1]Strange*) was born on 11 September 1922 in Milledgeville, Georgia. She married **Johnnie Dark Renfroe**, son of **Oscar Renfroe** and **Laura Trawick,** on 31 December 1943 in Philadelphia, Pennsylvania.

Children of **Mae Will[5] Williams** and **Johnnie Dark Renfroe** were as follows:
+ 298.   i. CAROLINE[6], born 7 July 1943 in Detroit, Michigan; married **William Johnson.**
  299.   ii. JOHNNIE DARK JR. was born on 31 January 1945 in Detroit, Michigan.
+ 300.   iii. PEGGY, born 4 November 1946 in Detroit, Michigan; married **Bobby Walton.**
+ 301.   iv. HAROLD, born 28 August 1947 in Detroit, Michigan; married **Catherine Lynch.**
  302.   v. OSCAR LEE was born on 11 September 1966 in Detroit, Michigan.

135. RUFUS[5] WILLIAMS (*Mae Will[4]Rogers, Dovie[3]Cheeves, Henry[2], Rita[1]Strange*) was born on 19 March 1925 in Milledgeville, Georgia. He married **Francis Andrews.** He died in August 1995 in Detroit, Michigan, at age 70.

Children of **Rufus[5] Williams** and **Francis Andrews** were:
  303.   i. RALPH[6].

142. JOHN RUBEN[5] TURNER (SR.) (*Linen 'Lennie'[4]Rogers, Dovie[3]Cheeves, Henry[2], Rita[1]Strange*) was born on 26 September 1928. He married **Mary (———).**

Children of **John Ruben[5] Turner (Sr.)** and **Mary (———)** were as follows:
+ 304.   i. LINDA[6]
+ 305.   ii. BARBARA
  306.   iii. JOHN RUBEN (JR.).

155. ELMER CHEEVES[5] BUCKNER (*Lola[4]Cheeves, David 'Coot'[3], Henry[2], Rita[1]Strange*) was born in 1919. He married **Bertha Young.** He died in 1992.

Children of **Elmer Cheeves[5] Buckner** and **Bertha Young** were as follows:
  307.   i. MARY[6].
  308.   ii. VIVIAN.

156. HENRY WILLIE 'SMOOK'[5] CHEEVES (*Henry 'Buddy'[4], David 'Coot'[3], Henry[2], Rita[1]Strange*) married **Hazel Jones.**

Children of **Henry Willie 'Smook'[5] Cheeves** and **Hazel Jones** were as follows:
  309.   i. FRANK[6] was born circa 1960.
  310.   ii. HENRY WILLIE JR. was born circa 1960.

+ 311.   iii. STEPHANIE, born circa 1960.

157. LILLIAN MAE 'SANG'[5] **CHEEVES** (*Henry 'Buddy'*[4], *David 'Coot'*[3], *Henry*[2], *Rita*[1] *Strange*) married **Wilbur Bond.**

Children of **Lillian Mae 'Sang'**[5] **Cheeves** and **Wilbur Bond** were as follows:
+ 312.   i. ANITA[6], married **George McLauren.**
+ 313.   ii. BARBARA
+ 314.   iii. AARON

158. LOLA BELL 'JACK'[5] **CHEEVES** (*Henry 'Buddy'*[4], *David 'Coot'*[3], *Henry*[2], *Rita*[1] *Strange*) married **Reginald** (—?—).

Children of **Lola Bell 'Jack'**[5] **Cheeves** and **Reginald** (—?—) were:
315.   i. REGINALD[6] (JR.) was born circa 1940.

159. ESTELLE 'STELL'[5] **CHEEVES** (*Henry 'Buddy'*[4], *David 'Coot'*[3], *Henry*[2], *Rita*[1] *Strange*) married **Mr. Mills.**

Children of **Estelle 'Stell'**[5] **Cheeves** and **Mr. Mills** were as follows:
+ 316.   i. SANDRA[6]
+ 317.   ii. PATRICIA
318.   iii. SHEILA.
+ 319.   iv. CLAUDIA

160. JULIA INEZ[5] **TRAWICK** (*Mary 'Ma-Mae' Ollie*[4] *Cheeves, David 'Coot'*[3], *Henry*[2], *Rita*[1] *Strange*) was born on 24 January 1920. She married **Sidney C. Butts**, son of **Milas Butts (Sr.)** and **Roeanor Dawson.**

Children of **Julia Inez**[5] **Trawick** and **Sidney C. Butts** were as follows:
+ 320.   i. CHESTER[6], born 13 September 1938; married **Joan Holmes**; married **Anna Gray.**
+ 321.   ii. JANICE, born 18 October 1940; married **William Williams (Sr.)**; married **James Rogers**; married **Edward Davis.**
+ 322.   iii. ROZEINE, born 5 December 1942; married **Anthony Armstrong**; married **Robert Ruckey**; married **Walter Wyatt.**
+ 323.   iv. CURTIS, born 18 December 1943; married **Thelma Lamar.**
324.   v. KENNETH was born on 27 February 1950. He married **Rochelle McLaurin.**
325.   vi. SIDNEY ALLEN was born on 27 February 1955.

162. MAMYE DOROTHY 'MARY'[5] **TRAWICK** (*Mary 'Ma-Mae' Ollie*[4] *Cheeves, David 'Coot'*[3], *Henry*[2], *Rita*[1] *Strange*) was born on 16 January 1925. She married **Bob Willis Butts**, son of **Milas Butts (Sr.)** and **Roeanor Dawson.**

Children of **Mamye Dorothy 'Mary'**[5] **Trawick** and **Bob Willis Butts** were as follows:

+ 326.   i. **DELORES**[6], born 3 January 1942; married **Edward Smithwick.**

+ 327.   ii. **DORIS,** born 4 July 1944; married **John Alcorn.**

+ 328.   iii. **GWENDOLYN 'GWEN',** born 12 August 1945; married **Gene Holliway.**

+ 329.   iv. **OLIVIA,** born 21 May 1950; married **Bernard Hines.**

163. **JUANITA EASTER MAE**[5] **TRAWICK** (*Mary 'Ma-Mae' Ollie*[4]*Cheeves, David 'Coot*[3], *Henry*[2], *Rita*[1]*Strange*) married **Cleophus Crumbly.** She married **Mr. Elliott.**

Children of **Juanita Easter Mae**[5] **Trawick** and **Cleophus Crumbly** were:

330.   i. **EDGAR**[6].

There were no children of **Juanita Easter Mae**[5] **Trawick** and **Mr. Elliott.**

169. **CARLTON 'COLLIE'**[5] **CHEEVES** (*Samuel 'Sammie*[4], *David 'Coot*[3], *Henry*[2], *Rita*[1]*Strange*) was born on 1 August 1938 in Philadelphia, Pennsylvania. He married **Rosita Delores Talley** on 27 May 1960 in Philadelphia, Pennsylvania. He died on 26 January 1998 in Fremont, California, at age 59.

Children of **Carlton 'Collie'**[5] **Cheeves** and **Rosita Delores Talley** were as follows:

+ 331.   i. **CARLTON CHRISTOPHER**[6], born 26 February 1962 in Philadelphia, Pennsylvania.

332.   ii. **STEPHEN ARNOLD** was born on 15 March 1964 in Philadelphia, Pennsylvania.

+ 333.   iii. **CARLOS JOHN,** born 14 January 1970 in Philadelphia, Pennsylvania.

171. **ERNESTINE 'MOLLY'**[5] **CHEEVES** (*John 'Tobe*[4], *David 'Coot*[3], *Henry*[2], *Rita*[1]*Strange*) was born on 22 December 1932 in Washington County, Georgia.

Children of **Ernestine 'Molly'**[5] **Cheeves** include:

+ 334.   i. **DARRYL**[6], born 30 January 1951 in Washington County, Georgia.

+ 335.   ii. **MICHAEL,** born 11 July 1952 in Washington County, Georgia; married **Catherine 'Cat' Watkins.**

+ 336.   iii. **ANGELA J. WIGGINS,** born 15 October 1956 in Washington County, Georgia.

+ 337.   iv. **CONNIE,** born 16 February 1958 in Washington County, Georgia.

+ 338.   v. **KAY CHEEVES,** born 25 March 1959 in Washington County, Georgia.

+ 339.   vi. **SHERYL 'SHERRY' WIGGINS,** born 23 October 1961 in Washington County, Georgia.

+ 340.   vii. **REGINALD,** born 31 August 1963 in Sandersville, Georgia; married **Demetria Head.**

341.   viii. **TAMMI JOHNSON** was born on 4 August 1965 in Washington County, Georgia.

172. **FLETA**[5] **HOOKS** (*Louise 'Lou*[4]*Cheeves, David 'Coot*[3], *Henry*[2], *Rita*[1]*Strange*).

Children of **Fleta**^{5} **Hooks** include:
342.   i. DAVIDA^6.
343.   ii. DENNIS.
344.   iii. LISA.

174. CHARLIE^5 **RENFROW** (*Georgianne*^{4}*Davis, Lou*^{3}*Cheeves, Henry*^{2}, *Rita*^{1}*Strange*) was born on 13 February 1908. He married **Katie Butts,** daughter of **Milas Butts (Sr.)** and **Roeanor Dawson.** He died on 31 July 1984 at age 76.

Children of **Charlie**^{5} **Renfrow** and **Katie Butts** were as follows:
+ 345.   i. YVETTE^6, married **Wendell Harris.**
346.   ii. LORRAINE.
347.   iii. CHARMAINE.
348.   iv. LAMONT.
+ 349.   v. EDWARD, married **Donna** (———).
+ 350.   vi. DELIA, married **James Davis.**
351.   vii. CHARLES.
+ 352.   viii. GERALD WAYNE, born 10 October 1945; married **Diane** (———); married **Connie** (———).
+ 353.   ix. WILSON, born 10 March 1953.

180. MITCHELL^5 **HOOKS** (*Henrietta*^{4}*Cheeves, Henry*^{3}, *Henry*^{2}, *Rita*^{1}*Strange*) was born on 7 March 1933 in Sandersville, Georgia. He married **Delores Hooks,** daughter of **Robert J. Hooks Jr.** and **Carrie B. Lawson.**

Children of **Mitchell**^{5} **Hooks** include:
354.   i. SARAH D.^{6}

Children of **Mitchell**^{5} **Hooks** and **Delores Hooks** were as follows:
+ 355.   i. MICHAEL D.^{6}, born 25 December 1956; married **Carol Anderson.**
356.   ii. RHONDA was born on 17 January 1958. She married **George Ashison.**
357.   iii. MONICA was born on 26 August 1970.

181. CHEEVES^5 **HOOKS** (*Henrietta*^{4}*Cheeves, Henry*^{3}, *Henry*^{2}, *Rita*^{1}*Strange*) was born on 4 April 1935 in Washington County, Georgia. He married **Myrtistine Cullens** on 11 May 1958 in Washington County, Georgia. He died on 17 February 1997 in Milledgeville, Baldwin County, Georgia, at age 61.

Children of **Cheeves**^{5} **Hooks** and **Myrtistine Cullens** were as follows:
+ 358.   i. ROSALIND LINETTE^6, born 4 January 1959; married **Thomas Victor Brown.**
359.   ii. CHARLES ANDRIE was born on 16 November 1961.
360.   iii. TRACY CHEEVES was born on 14 November 1964.

183. MARION^5 HOOKS (*Henrietta^{4}Cheeves, Henry^3, Henry^2, Rita^{1}Strange*) was born on 1 July 1940 in Sandersville, Georgia. He married **Annie** (———). He married **Christine** (—?—).

Children of **Marion^5 Hooks** and **Annie** (———) were as follows:
361.   i. MAXINE^6.
362.   ii. MARVIN S..
363.   iii. QUILLIAN E..
364.   iv. CHARLES T..

There were no children of **Marion^5 Hooks** and **Christine** (—?—).

184. ORALENE^5 HOOKS (*Henrietta^{4}Cheeves, Henry^3, Henry^2, Rita^{1}Strange*) was born on 4 April 1943 in Sandersville, Georgia. She married **Frank Pierce** on 25 December 1962 in Sandersville, Georgia.

Children of **Oralene^5 Hooks** and **Frank Pierce** were as follows:
365.   i. RAYNELL TYSON^6 was born on 10 March 1963 in Sandersville, Georgia.
+ 366.   ii. PATRICE ISLENE, born 25 January 1966 in New Haven, Connecticut; married **Nathaniel Balkcom III.**
367.   iii. FRANK MYRON was born on 1 October 1973 in New Haven, Connecticut.

185. ZELMA^5 SHENOSTER (*Mattie Lou^{4}Cheeves, Henry^3, Henry^2, Rita^{1}Strange*) was born on 10 January 1932 in Sandersville, Georgia.

Children of **Zelma^5 Shenoster** and **Ennis Carter** were:
368.   i. DONALD 'DUCK'^{6} was born on 29 September 1948 in Philadelphia, Pennsylvania. He died on 29 June 2001 in Philadelphia, Pennsylvania, at age 52.

Children of **Zelma^5 Shenoster** and **Rufus Hall** were:
+ 369.   i. SAUNDRA ERICKA^6, born 30 June 1950 in Philadelphia, Pennsylvania.

Children of **Zelma^5 Shenoster** and **Jesse James McLean** were as follows:
+ 370.   i. ANTHONY^6, born 27 November 1958 in Philadelphia, Pennsylvania; married **Linda Star Woodson.**
+ 371.   ii. JESSE JAMES (JR.), born 5 October 1960 in Philadelphia, Pennsylvania; married **Antoinette Coto.**

186. KATHERINE^5 SHENOSTER (*Mattie Lou^{4}Cheeves, Henry^3, Henry^2, Rita^{1}Strange*) was born on 19 April 1934 in Milledgeville, Georgia. She married **John Benjamin Douglass (Sr.)** on 7 February 1959 in Maryland.

Children of **Katherine**[5] **Shenoster** and **John Benjamin Douglass** (Sr.) were as follows:

372. i. CAROL LYNNE[6] was born on 1 May 1962 in Philadelphia, Pennsylvania.

+ 373. ii. JOHN BENJAMIN (JR.), born 4 April 1965 in Philadelphia, Pennsylvania; married **Tykeia Giles.**

187. **MIRIAM**[5] **CHEEVES** (*Henry Holmes*[4], *Henry*[3], *Henry*[2], *Rita*[1] *Strange*) was born in Sandersville, Washington County, Georgia

Children of **Miriam**[5] **Cheeves** include:

374. i. CLARA BELLE[6] was born on 2 February 1979 in Tacoma, Washington.

188. **GLORIA**[5] **CHEEVES** (*Henry Holmes*[4], *Henry*[3], *Henry*[2], *Rita*[1] *Strange*) was born on 4 July 1941 in Sandersville, Washington County, Georgia. She married **Charles Graham.**

Children of **Gloria**[5] **Cheeves** and **Charles Graham** were as follows:

+ 375. i. CHARLES DAVID[6], born 20 May 1969 in Philadelphia, Pennsylvania; married **Lorrie Hatten.**

+ 376. ii. MELISSA AVA, born 21 April 1970 in Philadelphia, Pennsylvania.

377. iii. JENNIFER ANNETTE was born on 21 February 1979 in Philadelphia, Pennsylvania.

189. **HORACE**[5] **CHEEVES** (*Henry Holmes*[4], *Henry*[3], *Henry*[2], *Rita*[1] *Strange*) was born on 4 September 1943 in Sandersville, Washington County, Georgia. He married **Fannie Pearl Williams**, daughter of **Coleman Williams** and **Florence Rogers**, on 6 July 1971 in Philadelphia, Pennsylvania.

Children of **Horace**[5] **Cheeves** and **Fannie Pearl Williams** were:

378. i. DENISE NICOLE[6] was born on 20 February 1972 in Philadelphia, Pennsylvania.

190. **FOREST**[5] **CHEEVES** (*Henry Holmes*[4], *Henry*[3], *Henry*[2], *Rita*[1] *Strange*) was born on 4 September 1943 in Sandersville, Washington County, Georgia. He married **Karen Kennedy** in Philadelphia, Pennsylvania. He died on 27 March 1987 in Detroit, Michigan, at age 43.

Children of **Forest**[5] **Cheeves** and **Karen Kennedy** were as follows:

+ 379. i. BARRY STEVEN[6], born 29 June 1960 in Philadelphia, Pennsylvania; married **Andrea Benita 'Nita' Hyden.**

+ 380. ii. FORREST TROY, born 22 February 1962 in Philadelphia, Pennsylvania.

+ 381. iii. DARNELL FRANK, born 17 February 1963 in Philadelphia, Pennsylvania; married **Diana 'Ann' Marie Johnson;** married **Pat Young.**

+ 382. iv. BRUCE KENNETH, born 12 May 1964 in Philadelphia, Pennsylvania; married **Audrey Miree.**

194. LUCILLE 'LUCY'^{5} TIMMONS (*Mary Lou^{4}Hodges, Lennie^{3}Cheeves, Henry^2, Rita^{1}Strange*) married **Mr. Jones.**

Children of **Lucille 'Lucy'^{5} Timmons** and **Mr. Jones** were:
383. i. CAROLYN D.^{6}.

203. HENRY EDWARD^5 GORDY (*Henry Berry^4, Carrie^{3}Cheeves, Henry^2, Rita^{1}Strange*) was born on 2 March 1929 in Sandersville, Georgia. He married **Jeanetta** (—?—). He died in 1985.

Children of **Henry Edward^5 Gordy** and **Jeanetta** (—?—) were as follows:
+ 384. i. BRIAN^6, married **Yvonne** (———).
+ 385. ii. BYRON, married **Willette** (———).
+ 386. iii. BRUCE, married **Deborah** (———).
+ 387. iv. BRENT, married **Effie** (———).
+ 388. v. BRIDGETTE, married **Bernell Seal.**
  389. vi. BRENDA married **Anthony Berry.**

205. MARGARET JEWEL^5 GORDY (*Henry Berry^4, Carrie^{3}Cheeves, Henry^2, Rita^{1}Strange*) married **Isaac King.**

Children of **Margaret Jewel^5 Gordy** and **Isaac King** were as follows:
+ 390. i. KAREN^6, married **Elvin Brooks.**
+ 391. ii. KYRA, married **James Ridgell.**
  392. iii. KEVIN married **Lillie** (—?—).

206. CLAUDETTE^5 GORDY (*Henry Berry^4, Carrie^{3}Cheeves, Henry^2, Rita^{1}Strange*) was born on 9 February 1937. She married **Alfred C. Johnson.**

Children of **Claudette^5 Gordy** and **Alfred C. Johnson** were:
393. i. MARCUS LAVON^6.

207. CAROLYN^5 GORDY (*Henry Berry^4, Carrie^{3}Cheeves, Henry^2, Rita^{1}Strange*) married **Leonard Kennedy.**

Children of **Carolyn^5 Gordy** and **Leonard Kennedy** were as follows:
394. i. STEPHANIE^6 married **James C. Gardner.**
395. ii. SEAN.
396. iii. STEVEN.
397. iv. SHANNON.

208. LAWRENCE[5] GORDY (*Henry Berry[4], Carrie[3] Cheeves, Henry[2], Rita[1] Strange*) married **Shirley Palmer.**

Children of **Lawrence[5] Gordy** and **Shirley Palmer** were:
398.   i. DWAYNE[6].

210. JOYCE[5] GORDY (*Henry Berry[4], Carrie[3] Cheeves, Henry[2], Rita[1] Strange*) was born in 1938 in Sandersville, Georgia. She married **Welton Lawrence.**

Children of **Joyce[5] Gordy** and **Welton Lawrence** were as follows:
+ 399.   i. DEBORAH[6], married **Lamont McClain.**
+ 400.   ii. DOREEN, married **Sam Hughes.**
  401.   iii. DAVID.
+ 402.   iv. DARIN, married **Shirley (———).**

211. JAMES HAROLD[5] GORDY (*Henry Berry[4], Carrie[3] Cheeves, Henry[2], Rita[1] Strange*) was born on 16 March 1942. He married **Donna (———).**

Children of **James Harold[5] Gordy** and **Donna (———)** were as follows:
403.   i. SHAWN[6] was born circa 1965.
404.   ii. JA VON was born circa 1965.
405.   iii. NICOLE.
406.   iv. ROBIN married **Timothy Banks.**
407.   v. MARISA.

212. EVELYN BERNICE[5] CAWTHON (*Mary Lucy[4] Gordy, Carrie[3] Cheeves, Henry[2], Rita[1] Strange*) was born circa 1925 in Milledgeville, Georgia. She married **William Turner.**

Children of **Evelyn Bernice[5] Cawthon** and **William Turner** were:
408.   i. HEATH[6].

213. MARY LOUVENIA 'BENIA'[5] CAWTHON (*Mary Lucy[4] Gordy, Carrie[3] Cheeves, Henry[2], Rita[1] Strange*) was born on 17 August 1928 in Milledgeville, Georgia. She married **Ernest Butts.** She died in December 1956 in Hartford, Connecticut, at age 28.

Children of **Mary Louvenia 'Benia'[5] Cawthon** and **Ernest Butts** were as follows:
+ 409.   i. LINDA[6], born 27 February 1951 in Milledgeville, Georgia; married **Donald Edwin Brooks.**
  410.   ii. BRENDA was born on 27 February 1951 in Milledgeville, Georgia.
+ 411.   iii. EVELYN BERNICE 'EBBIE', born 12 April 1954 in Hartford, Connecticut.

+ 412. iv. CHRISTIE TURNER, born 18 December 1956 in Hartford, Connecticut; married **Joseph Hicks Sr.**

214. ROBERT 'BOB'^{5} CAWTHON JR. (*Mary Lucy^{4}Gordy, Carrie^{3}Cheeves, Henry^2, Rita^{1}Strange*) was born circa 1930 in Milledgeville, Georgia. He married **Arlene** (—).

Children of **Robert 'Bob'^{5} Cawthon Jr.** and **Arlene** (—?—) were as follows:
413. i. ROBERT^6 III.
414. ii. JULIE.
415. iii. LINDA.
416. iv. DAVID.
417. v. MICHAEL.

216. BETTY JEAN^5 CAWTHON (*Mary Lucy^{4}Gordy, Carrie^{3}Cheeves, Henry^2, Rita^{1}Strange*) was born circa 1940 in Milledgeville, Georgia. She married **James Nelson.**

Children of **Betty Jean^5 Cawthon** and **James Nelson** were as follows:
418. i. MARY DENISE 'NIECY'^{6} was born in Georgia.
419. ii. JAMES 'JIMMY' JR. was born in July 1958 in Georgia.

220. EVELYN 'SIS'^{5} GORDY (*John^4, Carrie^{3}Cheeves, Henry^2, Rita^{1}Strange*) was born on 4 January 1939 in Sandersville, Georgia.

Children of **Evelyn 'Sis'^{5} Gordy** include:
420. i. JOHN C.^{6}
421. ii. LINDA was born on 30 May 1955.

225. MARY PEARL 'TOWN'^{5} GORDY CHEEVES (*Samuel 'Sam'^{4}, Carrie^{3}Cheeves, Henry^2, Rita^{1}Strange*) was born on 21 January 1930 in Sandersville, Georgia. She married **Vernon 'Bud' Trawick**, son of **Tom Trawick** and **Melissa Williams**, on 19 November 1948 in Sandersville, Georgia.

Children of **Mary Pearl 'Town'^{5} Gordy Cheeves** and **Vernon 'Bud' Trawick** were as follows:
422. i. VERNON^6 JR. was born on 10 April 1950 in Sandersville, Washington County, Georgia
+ 423. ii. BERNARD, born 14 December 1951 in Philadelphia, Pennsylvania; married **Kenya Wilson.**
424. iii. MARVIN was born on 6 November 1954 in Philadelphia, Pennsylvania.
425. iv. VERONICA was born on 17 February 1957 in Philadelphia, Pennsylvania.

+ 426.   v. CYNTHIA, born 12 November 1958 in Philadelphia, Pennsylvania; married **William Boyer.**

226. MAXEL⁵ HARDY JR. (*Ann 'Annie' Owen⁴Gordy, Carrie³Cheeves, Henry², Rita¹Strange*) was born on 10 October 1952 in Detroit, Michigan.

Children of **Maxel⁵ Hardy Jr.** and **Laverne Arnette** were:
427.   i. MAXEL⁶ III was born on 5 December 1983 in Detroit, Michigan.

228. CHERYL DENISE⁵ HARDY (*Ann 'Annie' Owen⁴Gordy, Carrie³Cheeves, Henry², Rita¹Strange*) was born on 20 September 1958 in Detroit, Michigan.

Children of **Cheryl Denise⁵ Hardy** and **William Desi Richardson** were as follows:
428.   i. WILLIAM ARNAZ⁶ was born on 30 November 1988 in Detroit, Michigan.
429.   ii. MALCOLM JAWAN was born on 29 April 1992 in Detroit, Michigan.

229. GWENDOLYN⁵ GORDY (*Robert Daniel⁴, Carrie³Cheeves, Henry², Rita¹Strange*) was born on 12 March 1947 in Utica, New York. She married **Julius Murphy.**

Children of **Gwendolyn⁵ Gordy** and **Julius Murphy** were as follows:
430.   i. SONIA JOY⁶ was born on 13 June 1976 in Albany, Georgia.
431.   ii. ASHLEY was born on 21 December 1984 in Macon, Georgia.

231. DAVID⁵ GORDY (*Robert Daniel⁴, Carrie³Cheeves, Henry², Rita¹Strange*) was born on 13 April 1952 in Sandersville, Georgia. He married **DeLois Turner.** He married **Darlene Robinson.**

Children of **David⁵ Gordy** and **DeLois Turner** were as follows:
432.   i. DEBORAH⁶ was born on 14 January 1971 in Augusta, Georgia.
433.   ii. DAVINA was born on 2 June 1972 in Augusta, Georgia.
434.   iii. DENISE was born on 13 June 1975 in Augusta, Georgia.
435.   iv. JOSHUA DAVID was born on 9 February 1987 in Augusta, Georgia.

Children of **David⁵ Gordy** and **Darlene Robinson** were:
436.   i. DAYNA LYNN⁶ was born on 14 August 1997 in Milledgeville, Georgia.

232. DEBORAH ANNE⁵ GORDY (*Robert Daniel⁴, Carrie³Cheeves, Henry², Rita¹Strange*) was born on 6 January 1954 in Sandersville, Georgia. She married **Samuel Duggan** on 9 June 1979.

Children of **Deborah Anne⁵ Gordy** and **Samuel Duggan** were as follows:
437.   i. LORA ANNE⁶ was born on 17 July 1982 in Milledgeville, Georgia.

438. ii. LORETTA DENISE was born on 12 March 1985 in Milledgeville, Georgia.

233. MARY LUCY^5 GORDY (*Robert Daniel^4, Carrie^{3}Cheeves, Henry^2, Rita^{1}Strange*) was born on 17 July 1956 in Sandersville, Georgia. She married **Tony Owen Hurt Sr.** on 7 July 1979.

Children of **Mary Lucy^5 Gordy** and **Tony Owen Hurt Sr.** were as follows:
439. i. TONY OWEN^6 JR. was born on 19 April 1982 in Milledgeville, Georgia.
440. ii. KARI LOUCYE was born on 17 February 1985 in Milledgeville, Georgia.
441. iii. BRAXTON GORDY was born on 7 June 1992 in Macon, Georgia.

235. BERRY RENARD^5 GORDY (*Robert Daniel^4, Carrie^{3}Cheeves, Henry^2, Rita^{1}Strange*) was born on 10 September 1958 in Sandersville, Georgia. He married **Brenda Lee Lord Barlow Cardy.**

Children of **Berry Renard^5 Gordy** and **Brenda Lee Lord Barlow Cardy** were:
442. i. JALEN BERRY^6 was born on 19 October 1991 in Augusta, Georgia.

Generation Six

238. ELAINE^6 DIXON (*Rosalie 'Rose^5, Mary A.^{4}Cheeves, John^3, Henry^2, Rita^{1}Strange*).

Children of **Elaine^6 Dixon** include:
443. i. BRENDA^7.

239. LEWIS^6 DIXON (*Anna Julia^5, Mary A.^{4}Cheeves, John^3, Henry^2, Rita^{1}Strange*) married **Mary** (———).

Children of **Lewis^6 Dixon** and **Mary** (———) were as follows:
444. i. LEWIS^7 (JR.).
445. ii. CHARMINE.

240. MAJOR^6 DIXON (*Anna Julia^5, Mary A.^{4}Cheeves, John^3, Henry^2, Rita^{1}Strange*) married **Emma** (———).

Children of **Major^6 Dixon** and **Emma** (———) were as follows:
446. i. ANGELA^7.
447. ii. ANDREA.
448. iii. NICOLE.

241. JEROME^6 DIXON (*Anna Julia^5, Mary A.^{4}Cheeves, John^3, Henry^2, Rita^{1}Strange*) married **Rose** (———).

Children of **Jerome^6 Dixon** and **Rose** (———) were as follows:
449.   i. CARMELLA^7.
450.   ii. ALICIA.

242. **DAISY MAE^6 DIXON** (*Anna Julia^5, Mary A.^{4}Cheeves, John^3, Henry^2, Rita^{1}Strange*).

Children of **Daisy Mae^6 Dixon** include:
451.   i. MICHAEL^7.
452.   ii. ADRINNE.

243. **MARLENE^6 DIXON** (*Anna Julia^5, Mary A.^{4}Cheeves, John^3, Henry^2, Rita^{1}Strange*) married **Will Pearsall.**

Children of **Marlene^6 Dixon** and **Will Pearsall** were as follows:
453.   i. ANDREW^7.
454.   ii. WANDA.

244. **PHILIP (ALI SALAUDIN)^6 DIXON** (*Horace^5, Sallie L.^{4}Cheeves, John^3, Henry^2, Rita^{1}Strange*) was born on 4 February 1947 in Philadelphia, Pennsylvania. He married **Carol Haughton.**

Children of **Philip (Ali Salaudin)^6 Dixon** and **Carol Haughton** were as follows:
455.   i. JAMAL^7 was born on 2 April 1970 in Philadelphia, Pennsylvania.
456.   ii. SHARIAH K. was born on 23 February 1972 in Philadelphia, Pennsylvania.
457.   iii. KAMILLAH 'MIMI' was born on 18 March 1974 in Philadelphia, Pennsylvania.

245. **RODNEY^6 DIXON** (*Horace^5, Sallie L.^{4}Cheeves, John^3, Henry^2, Rita^{1}Strange*) was born on 8 March 1950 in Philadelphia, Pennsylvania. He married **Beverly Diane Fisher.**

Children of **Rodney^6 Dixon** and **Beverly Diane Fisher** were as follows:
458.   i. KHALID^7 was born on 23 March 1976 in Philadelphia, Pennsylvania.
459.   ii. MURAD ALIM SALAUDIN was born on 12 August 1978 in Philadelphia, Pennsylvania.

254. **DELORES^6 WOODARD** (*Minnie^{5}Dixon, Sallie L.^{4}Cheeves, John^3, Henry^2, Rita^{1}Strange*) married **Robert Handon.**

Children of **Delores^6 Woodard** and **Robert Handon** were as follows:
460.   i. DENISE^7.
461.   ii. JEANETTE.

255. BEVERLY ANN^6 GATES (*Doris^{5}Dixon, Sallie L.^{4}Cheeves, John^3, Henry^2, Rita^{1}Strange*) married **Mr. Green.**

Children of **Beverly Ann^6 Gates** and **Mr. Green** were:
462.   i. STEPHANIE^7.

261. ELAINE^6 WRIGHT (*Ruth^{5}Mitchell, Clyde^{4}Cheeves, John^3, Henry^2, Rita^{1}Strange*) married **William Wilkes.**

Children of **Elaine^6 Wright** and **William Wilkes** were as follows:
463.   i. JASON^7.
464.   ii. MERCEDES.

262. DEBRA^6 WRIGHT (*Ruth^{5}Mitchell, Clyde^{4}Cheeves, John^3, Henry^2, Rita^{1}Strange*).

Children of **Debra^6 Wright** include:
465.   i. DELISHA^7.

264. ARRON^6 KELSEY (*Miley^{5}Mitchell, Clyde^{4}Cheeves, John^3, Henry^2, Rita^{1}Strange*) married **Mary** (———).

Children of **Arron^6 Kelsey** and **Mary** (———) were as follows:
466.   i. ANGEL^7.
467.   ii. GREGG.
468.   iii. MELISSA.

265. CECIL^6 KELSEY (*Miley^{5}Mitchell, Clyde^{4}Cheeves, John^3, Henry^2, Rita^{1}Strange*) married **Jackie** (———).

Children of **Cecil^6 Kelsey** and **Jackie** (———) were as follows:
469.   i. CAMERON^7.
470.   ii. CECIL (JR.).
471.   iii. COURTNEY.

266. DELORES^6 KELSEY (*Miley^{5}Mitchell, Clyde^{4}Cheeves, John^3, Henry^2, Rita^{1}Strange*) married **Calvin** (———).

Children of **Delores^6 Kelsey** and **Calvin** (———) were:
472.   i. PAT^7.

267. TIMOTHY^6 KELSEY (JR.) (*Miley^{5}Mitchell, Clyde^{4}Cheeves, John^3, Henry^2, Rita^{1}Strange*) married **Amy** (———).

Children of **Timothy**[6] **Kelsey (Jr.)** and **Amy** (———) were:
    473.   i. TAMMY[7].

268. BETTY JEAN[6] **MITCHELL** (*Doris Dorothy*[5], *Clyde*[4] *Cheeves, John*[3], *Henry*[2], *Rita*[1] *Strange*).

Children of **Betty Jean**[6] **Mitchell** include:
    474.   i. REMISHA[7].
    475.   ii. PAUL.

269. ALTON[6] **MITCHELL** (*Doris Dorothy*[5], *Clyde*[4] *Cheeves, John*[3], *Henry*[2], *Rita*[1] *Strange*).

Children of **Alton**[6] **Mitchell** include:
    476.   i. STEPHANIE[7].
    477.   ii. TIFFANEY.
    478.   iii. ALTON (JR.).

270. BERNICE[6] **MITCHELL** (*Hazel*[5], *Clyde*[4] *Cheeves, John*[3], *Henry*[2], *Rita*[1] *Strange*) married **Mr. Woods.**

Children of **Bernice**[6] **Mitchell** and **Mr. Woods** were as follows:
    479.   i. CHELICE[7] was born on 27 May 1980.
    480.   ii. KEITH was born on 23 August 1981.

271. VICKIE[6] **MITCHELL** (*Hazel*[5], *Clyde*[4] *Cheeves, John*[3], *Henry*[2], *Rita*[1] *Strange*) married **Joseph Williams.**

Children of **Vickie**[6] **Mitchell** and **Joseph Williams** were as follows:
    481.   i. DIONE[7].
    482.   ii. TERRI.
    483.   iii. JOESPH (JR.).

272. CYNTHIA[6] **PEELER** (*Ruby*[5], *Leola*[4] *Rogers, Dovie*[3] *Cheeves, Henry*[2], *Rita*[1] *Strange*) was born on 2 December 1951 in Detroit, Michigan.

Children of **Cynthia**[6] **Peeler** include:
    484.   i. PAUL MICHAEL[7] was born on 29 September 1986.

275. WANDA JEAN[6] **THOMAS** (*Rogers*[5] *Peeler, Leola*[4] *Rogers, Dovie*[3] *Cheeves, Henry*[2], *Rita*[1] *Strange*) was born on 11 October 1957 in Washington, DC.

Children of **Wanda Jean**[6] **Thomas** include:

485.   i. ZACHARY ROGERS[7] was born on 31 October 1991.

276. **GRADY**[6] **JONES JR.** (*Susie*[5]*Peeler, Leola*[4]*Rogers, Dovie*[3]*Cheeves, Henry*[2], *Rita*[1]*Strange*) was born on 9 December 1953 in Detroit, Michigan. He married **Jacqueline Denise Major.**

Children of **Grady**[6] **Jones Jr.** and **Jacqueline Denise Major** were:

486.   i. EMERY EDMOND[7] was born on 15 April 1987.

277. **MICHAEL**[6] **JONES** (*Susie*[5]*Peeler, Leola*[4]*Rogers, Dovie*[3]*Cheeves, Henry*[2], *Rita*[1]*Strange*) was born on 26 September 1955 in Detroit, Michigan. He married **Gertrude Hawthorn.**

Children of **Michael**[6] **Jones** and **Gertrude Hawthorn** were:

487.   i. LEBREE SINCLAIR[7] was born on 7 January 1987.

278. **SHIRLEY JEAN**[6] **JONES** (*Susie*[5]*Peeler, Leola*[4]*Rogers, Dovie*[3]*Cheeves, Henry*[2], *Rita*[1]*Strange*) was born on 5 April 1957 in Detroit, Michigan. She married **Alvin Brezzell.**

Children of **Shirley Jean**[6] **Jones** and **Alvin Brezzell** were as follows:

488.   i. CLARISSA[7].
489.   ii. NICHOLS GRADY was born on 10 December 1980.

279. **PAULA**[6] **JONES** (*Susie*[5]*Peeler, Leola*[4]*Rogers, Dovie*[3]*Cheeves, Henry*[2], *Rita*[1]*Strange*) was born on 27 July 1963 in Detroit, Michigan. She married **Marco Henry.**

Children of **Paula**[6] **Jones** and **Marco Henry** were as follows:

490.   i. SYDNEY[7].
491.   ii. PAIGE.

281. **ALTON**[6] **TRAWICK** (*Vera*[5]*Peeler, Leola*[4]*Rogers, Dovie*[3]*Cheeves, Henry*[2], *Rita*[1]*Strange*) was born on 18 January 1949 in Sandersville, Georgia. He married **Joanne Washington** on 21 September 1974 in Atlanta, Georgia.

Children of **Alton**[6] **Trawick** and **Joanne Washington** were:

492.   i. BRANDON ALTUS[7] was born on 8 January 1978 in Rochester, New York.

284. **CATHY ANN**[6] **TRAWICK** (*Vera*[5]*Peeler, Leola*[4]*Rogers, Dovie*[3]*Cheeves, Henry*[2], *Rita*[1]*Strange*) was born on 3 January 1955 in Sandersville, Georgia. She married **Leo Suggs** on 29 June 1984 in Elkhart, Indiana.

Children of **Cathy Ann**^{6} **Trawick** and **Leo Suggs** were as follows:

493.   i. LEO DEON^7 was born on 16 October 1986 in Atlanta, Georgia.
494.   ii. INDIA SHARNAE was born on 9 June 1990 in South Bend, Indiana.

286. **LYDIA JEAN**^{6} **TRAWICK** (*Vera*^{5}*Peeler, Leola*^{4}*Rogers, Dovie*^{3}*Cheeves, Henry*^{2}, *Rita*^{1}*Strange*) was born on 3 February 1961 in Sandersville, Georgia. She married **Willie James Woodard.**

Children of **Lydia Jean**^{6} **Trawick** and **Willie James Woodard** were as follows:

495.   i. VICTORIA DANIELLE^7 was born on 25 March 1984 in Atlanta, Georgia.
496.   ii. ASHLEY NICOLE was born on 1 November 1987 in Atlanta, Georgia.
497.   iii. WILLIE JAMES JR. was born on 5 August 1991 in Atlanta, Georgia.

287. **BELINDA**^{6} **WILLIAMS** (*Dovie Oneain*^{5}*Peeler, Leola*^{4}*Rogers, Dovie*^{3}*Cheeves, Henry*^{2}, *Rita*^{1}*Strange*) was born on 23 April 1949 in Detroit, Michigan.

Children of **Belinda**^{6} **Williams** and **Larry Brown** were:

498.   i. BRETT^7 was born on 3 November 1979 in St. Paul, Minnesota.

288. **ROCHELLE**^{6} **WILLIAMS** (*Dovie Oneain*^{5}*Peeler, Leola*^{4}*Rogers, Dovie*^{3}*Cheeves, Henry*^{2}, *Rita*^{1}*Strange*) was born on 13 December 1951 in Detroit, Michigan.

Children of **Rochelle**^{6} **Williams** and **Mitchell Adams** were:

499.   i. ELLIETTE O'NEIL^7 was born on 20 February 1991 in St. Paul, Minnesota.

289. **FRAUN**^{6} **WILLIAMS** (*Dovie Oneain*^{5}*Peeler, Leola*^{4}*Rogers, Dovie*^{3}*Cheeves, Henry*^{2}, *Rita*^{1}*Strange*) was born on 3 December 1954 in Detroit, Michigan. She married **Bernard Delmas Foster Sr.** on 15 October 1972.

Children of **Fraun**^{6} **Williams** and **Bernard Delmas Foster Sr.** were as follows:

500.   i. BERNARD DELMAS^7 JR. was born on 25 November 1973 in St. Paul, Minnesota.
501.   ii. BRANDON DAMONE was born on 15 November 1978 in St. Paul, Minnesota.
502.   iii. BRENT DEMITRI was born on 22 July 1981 in St. Paul, Minnesota.

290. **VIVIAN**^{6} **WILLIAMS** (*Dovie Oneain*^{5}*Peeler, Leola*^{4}*Rogers, Dovie*^{3}*Cheeves, Henry*^{2}, *Rita*^{1}*Strange*) was born on 26 October 1957 in Detroit, Michigan. She married **Wendel Burch** on 9 March 1975 in St. Paul, Minnesota.

Children of **Vivian**^{6} **Williams** and **Wendel Burch** were as follows:

503.   i. TYLER ONEAIN^7 was born on 26 October 1977 in St. Paul, Minnesota.
504.   ii. KELLEN RYAN was born on 22 September 1981 in St. Paul, Minnesota.
505.   iii. KIRSTEN NICOLE was born on 22 December 1985 in St. Paul, Minnesota.

291. WENDY[6] WILLIAMS (*Dovie Oneain[5] Peeler, Leola[4] Rogers, Dovie[3] Cheeves, Henry[2], Rita[1] Strange*) was born on 26 October 1959 in Detroit, Michigan. She married **Scott Rose.**

Children of **Wendy[6] Williams** include:
  506. i. KYLE[7] was born on 31 May 1988 in St. Paul, Minnesota.
  507. ii. DANNY was born on 18 April 1995 in St. Paul, Minnesota.

There were no children of **Wendy[6] Williams** and **Scott Rose.**

292. FRANK[6] WILLIAMS JR. (*Dovie Oneain[5] Peeler, Leola[4] Rogers, Dovie[3] Cheeves, Henry[2], Rita[1] Strange*) was born on 28 December 1964 in St. Paul, Minnesota. He married **Titka** (—?—).

Children of **Frank[6] Williams Jr.** and **Titka** (—?—) were as follows:
  508. i. EMANUEL FRANTE[7] was born on 8 September 1992 in St. Paul, Minnesota.
  509. ii. PAYTON was born in October 1996 in St. Paul, Minnesota.

298. CAROLINE[6] RENFROE (*Mae Will[5] Williams, Mae Will[4] Rogers, Dovie[3] Cheeves, Henry[2], Rita[1] Strange*) was born on 7 July 1943 in Detroit, Michigan. She married **William Johnson.**

Children of **Caroline[6] Renfroe** and **William Johnson** were as follows:
  510. i. RENITA[7] was born on 18 July 1962 in Detroit, Michigan.
  511. ii. WILLIAM JR. was born on 4 August 1964 in Detroit, Michigan.

300. PEGGY[6] RENFROE (*Mae Will[5] Williams, Mae Will[4] Rogers, Dovie[3] Cheeves, Henry[2], Rita[1] Strange*) was born on 4 November 1946 in Detroit, Michigan. She married **Bobby Walton.**

Children of **Peggy[6] Renfroe** and **Bobby Walton** were as follows:
+ 512. i. LASHAY[7], born 30 April 1967 in Detroit, Michigan.
  513. ii. MARY LATRICE was born on 27 July 1972 in Detroit, Michigan.

301. HAROLD[6] RENFROE (*Mae Will[5] Williams, Mae Will[4] Rogers, Dovie[3] Cheeves, Henry[2], Rita[1] Strange*) was born on 28 August 1947 in Detroit, Michigan. He married **Catherine Lynch** on 11 March in Detroit, Michigan.

Children of **Harold[6] Renfroe** and **Catherine Lynch** were as follows:
  514. i. HAROLD[7] JR. was born on 7 July 1968 in Detroit, Michigan.
  515. ii. DION was born in 1981 in Detroit, Michigan.
  516. iii. NATHAN was born in December 1982 in Detroit, Michigan.

304. LINDA[6] **TURNER** (*John Ruben*[5], *Linen 'Lennie'*[4] *Rogers, Dovie*[3] *Cheeves, Henry*[2], *Rita*[1] *Strange*).

Children of **Linda**[6] **Turner** include:
517.   i. SHAYLA[7].
518.   ii. SHANNON.

305. BARBARA[6] **TURNER** (*John Ruben*[5], *Linen 'Lennie'*[4] *Rogers, Dovie*[3] *Cheeves, Henry*[2], *Rita*[1] *Strange*).

Children of **Barbara**[6] **Turner** include:
519.   i. BRANDON[7].
520.   ii. TIFFANY.

311. STEPHANIE[6] **CHEEVES** (*Henry Willie 'Smook*[5], *Henry 'Buddy'*[4], *David 'Coot'*[3], *Henry*[2], *Rita*[1] *Strange*) was born circa 1960.

Children of **Stephanie**[6] **Cheeves** include:
521.   i. TIBBLET[7].

312. ANITA[6] **BOND** (*Lillian Mae 'Sang'*[5] *Cheeves, Henry 'Buddy'*[4], *David 'Coot'*[3], *Henry*[2], *Rita*[1] *Strange*) married **George McLauren.**

Children of **Anita**[6] **Bond** and **George McLauren** were as follows:
522.   i. SHERRY[7] married **Kenneth Parker.**
523.   ii. DAWN.

313. BARBARA[6] **BOND** (*Lillian Mae 'Sang'*[5] *Cheeves, Henry 'Buddy'*[4], *David 'Coot'*[3], *Henry*[2], *Rita*[1] *Strange*).

Children of **Barbara**[6] **Bond** include:
524.   i. TRACY[7].
525.   ii. ELLIOT.

314. AARON[6] **BOND** (*Lillian Mae 'Sang'*[5] *Cheeves, Henry 'Buddy'*[4], *David 'Coot'*[3], *Henry*[2], *Rita*[1] *Strange*).

Children of **Aaron**[6] **Bond** include:
526.   i. (MALE)[7].

316. SANDRA[6] **MILLS** (*Estelle 'Stell'*[5] *Cheeves, Henry 'Buddy'*[4], *David 'Coot'*[3], *Henry*[2], *Rita*[1] *Strange*).

104

Children of **Sandra**[6] **Mills** include:
527. i. KEVIN[7] was born circa 1960.
528. ii. KENT was born circa 1960.

317. PATRICIA[6] **MILLS** (*Estelle 'Stell'*[5]*Cheeves, Henry 'Buddy'*[4], *David 'Coot'*[3], *Henry*[2], *Rita*[1] *Strange*).

Children of **Patricia**[6] **Mills** include:
529. i. TOWANDA[7] was born circa 1960.
530. ii. LISA was born circa 1960.

319. CLAUDIA[6] **MILLS** (*Estelle 'Stell'*[5]*Cheeves, Henry 'Buddy'*[4], *David 'Coot'*[3], *Henry*[2], *Rita*[1] *Strange*).

Children of **Claudia**[6] **Mills** include:
531. i. TAMIKA[7] was born circa 1960.
532. ii. KEISHA was born circa 1960.
533. iii. SHAWN was born circa 1960.
534. iv. CHAD was born circa 1960.
535. v. ISAAC was born circa 1960.

320. CHESTER[6] **BUTTS** (*Julia Inez*[5] *Trawick, Mary 'Ma-Mae' Ollie*[4]*Cheeves, David 'Coot'*[3], *Henry*[2], *Rita*[1] *Strange*) was born on 13 September 1938. He married **Joan Holmes**. He married **Anna Gray**.

Children of **Chester**[6] **Butts** and **Joan Holmes** were as follows:
+ 536. i. EDDIE HOLMES[7], born 4 October 1954; married **Shirley Holmes;** married **Zina Holmes.**
+ 537. ii. CURTIS, born 27 April 1966; married **Sheila** (———); married **Crystle** (———).
  538. iii. KEVIN was born on 4 April 1967.
+ 539. iv. DARYL, born 19 July 1968; married **Nichelle** (———).
  540. v. DARNELL was born on 3 March 1970.

Children of **Chester**[6] **Butts** and **Anna Gray** were:
541. i. YALONDA[7] was born on 16 April 1970.

321. JANICE[6] **BUTTS** (*Julia Inez*[5] *Trawick, Mary 'Ma-Mae' Ollie*[4]*Cheeves, David 'Coot'*[3], *Henry*[2], *Rita*[1] *Strange*) was born on 18 October 1940. She married **Edward Davis**. She married **William Williams (Sr.)**. She married **James Rogers**. She died on 10 September 1989 at age 48.

Children of Janice^6 Butts and **William Williams (Sr.)** were as follows:

+ 542.   i. WILLIAM^7 (JR.), born 19 January 1958.
+ 543.   ii. KENNETH 'HUCKY', born 13 July 1960; married **Sylvita Barbour;** married **Deborah Lynn** (———).
+ 544.   iii. HERRELL A., born 23 May 1967; married **Stephanie Y Anderson;** married **Nadine Jackson.**
+ 545.   iv. ALONZO LONNIE, born 2 August 1969.
  546.   v. TYNEEK was born on 23 April 1976.

There were no children of Janice^6 Butts and **James Rogers.**

There were no children of Janice^6 Butts and **Edward Davis.**

322. ROZEINE^6 BUTTS (*Julia Inez^5 Trawick, Mary 'Ma-Mae' Ollie^4 Cheeves, David 'Coot^3, Henry^2, Rita^1 Strange*) was born on 5 December 1942. She married **Anthony Armstrong.** She married **Robert Ruckey.** She married **Walter Wyatt.**

Children of **Rozeine^6 Butts** and **Anthony Armstrong** were:
  547.   i. SEAN^7 was born on 15 November 1967.

Children of **Rozeine^6 Butts** and **Robert Ruckey** were:
  548.   i. ROBERT^7 was born on 11 January 1969.

Children of **Rozeine^6 Butts** and **Walter Wyatt** were:
  549.   i. JUNITA^7 was born on 7 July 1975.

323. CURTIS^6 BUTTS (*Julia Inez^5 Trawick, Mary 'Ma-Mae' Ollie^4 Cheeves, David 'Coot^3, Henry^2, Rita^1 Strange*) was born on 18 December 1943. He married **Thelma Lamar.**

Children of **Curtis^6 Butts** and **Thelma Lamar** were as follows:
  550.   i. DANIELLE MARIE^7 was born on 31 May 1969.
  551.   ii. LAMAR CRAIGE was born on 1 October 1970.
  552.   iii. LAMONTE DAWSON was born on 2 May 1974.
  553.   iv. BRANDEN LAVAR was born on 2 July 1978.

326. DELORES^6 BUTTS (*Mamye Dorothy 'Mary'^{5} Trawick, Mary 'Ma-Mae' Ollie^4 Cheeves, David 'Coot^3, Henry^2, Rita^1 Strange*) was born on 3 January 1942. She married **Edward Smithwick.**

Children of **Delores^6 Butts** and **Edward Smithwick** were as follows:
  554.   i. DERON^7 was born on 19 July 1965.
  555.   ii. DEAN was born on 24 January 1968.

556. iii. DENENA was born on 14 September 1970.

327. DORIS[6] **BUTTS** (*Mamye Dorothy 'Mary*[5] *Trawick, Mary 'Ma-Mae' Ollie*[4] *Cheeves, David 'Coot*[3], *Henry*[2], *Rita*[1] *Strange*) was born on 4 July 1944. She married **John Alcorn.**

Children of **Doris**[6] **Butts** and **John Alcorn** were as follows:

+ 557. i. SABRINA LYNN[7], born 5 February 1967; married **Derrick Girard McCann (Sr.).**
558. ii. DARLA RAE was born on 13 March 1970.
559. iii. ROOSEVELT.

328. GWENDOLYN 'GWEN'[6] **BUTTS** (*Mamye Dorothy 'Mary*[5] *Trawick, Mary 'Ma-Mae' Ollie*[4] *Cheeves, David 'Coot*[3], *Henry*[2], *Rita*[1] *Strange*) was born on 12 August 1945. She married **Gene Holliway.**

Children of **Gwendolyn 'Gwen'**[6] **Butts** and **Gene Holliway** were as follows:

+ 560. i. TANYA[7], born 9 February 1964; married **Todd Bell.**
561. ii. TERRANCE 'TERRY' was born on 31 July 1968.

329. OLIVIA[6] **BUTTS** (*Mamye Dorothy 'Mary*[5] *Trawick, Mary 'Ma-Mae' Ollie*[4] *Cheeves, David 'Coot*[3], *Henry*[2], *Rita*[1] *Strange*) was born on 21 May 1950. She married **Bernard Hines.**

Children of **Olivia**[6] **Butts** and **Bernard Hines** were as follows:

562. i. COURTLAND[7] was born on 27 July 1970.
563. ii. ARIC was born on 2 January 1975.

331. CARLTON CHRISTOPHER[6] **CHEEVES** (*Carlton 'Collie*[5], *Samuel 'Sammie*[4], *David 'Coot*[3], *Henry*[2], *Rita*[1] *Strange*) was born on 26 February 1962 in Philadelphia, Pennsylvania.

Children of **Carlton Christopher**[6] **Cheeves** and **Regina** (—?—) were:

564. i. CONSTANCE[7] was born on 24 December 1983.

333. CARLOS JOHN[6] **CHEEVES** (*Carlton 'Collie*[5], *Samuel 'Sammie*[4], *David 'Coot*[3], *Henry*[2], *Rita*[1] *Strange*) was born on 14 January 1970 in Philadelphia, Pennsylvania.

Children of **Carlos John**[6] **Cheeves** and **Sheila Maria Rubia** were:

565. i. TOPANGA MARIE[7] was born on 13 May 1996 in Fremont, California.

334. DARRYL[6] **CHEEVES** (*Ernestine 'Molly*[5], *John 'Tobe*[4], *David 'Coot*[3], *Henry*[2], *Rita*[1] *Strange*) was born on 30 January 1951 in Washington County, Georgia.

Children of **Darryl[6] Cheeves** include:
566.   i. **Darryl[7] Jr.** was born on 19 April 1974 in Baldwin County, Georgia.

335. MICHAEL[6] CHEEVES (*Ernestine 'Molly'[5], John 'Tobe'[4], David 'Coot'[3], Henry[2], Rita[1] Strange*) was born on 11 July 1952 in Washington County, Georgia. He married **Catherine 'Cat' Watkins** on 8 March 1992 in Hancock County, Georgia.

Children of **Michael[6] Cheeves** and **Catherine 'Cat' Watkins** were:
567.   i. **Lashonda[7]** was born on 31 October 1978 in Georgia.

336. ANGELA J.[6] CHEEVES WIGGINS (*Ernestine 'Molly'[5], John 'Tobe'[4], David 'Coot'[3], Henry[2], Rita[1] Strange*) was born on 15 October 1956 in Washington County, Georgia.

Children of **Angela J.[6] Cheeves Wiggins** include:
568.   i. **Ayala K.[7]** was born on 17 May 1986 in Atlanta, Georgia.
569.   ii. **Benjamin J.** was born on 29 January 1993 in Atlanta, Georgia.
570.   iii. **Angelia** was born on 24 December 1998 in Atlanta, Georgia.

337. CONNIE[6] CHEEVES (*Ernestine 'Molly'[5], John 'Tobe'[4], David 'Coot'[3], Henry[2], Rita[1] Strange*) was born on 16 February 1958 in Washington County, Georgia.

Children of **Connie[6] Cheeves** include:
571.   i. **Kirsten[7]** was born on 7 July 1981 in Augusta, Georgia

338. KAY CHEEVES[6] WIGGINS (*Ernestine 'Molly'[5] Cheeves, John 'Tobe'[4], David 'Coot'[3], Henry[2], Rita[1] Strange*) was born on 25 March 1959 in Washington County, Georgia.

Children of **Kay Cheeves[6] Wiggins** and **Chester Roberson** were as follows:
+ 572.   i. **Kye C.[7]**, born 4 February 1980 in Dublin, Georgia.
573.   ii. **Tray** was born on 14 March 1984 in Augusta, Georgia

339. SHERYL 'SHERRY'[6] CHEEVES WIGGINS (*Ernestine 'Molly'[5], John 'Tobe'[4], David 'Coot'[3], Henry[2], Rita[1] Strange*) was born on 23 October 1961 in Washington County, Georgia.

Children of **Sheryl 'Sherry'[6] Cheeves Wiggins** include:
574.   i. **Toi Sera[7]** was born on 16 November 1990 in Atlanta, Georgia.
575.   ii. **Malik Jamal** was born on 3 October 2000 in Stockbridge, Georgia.

340. REGINALD[6] CHEEVES (*Ernestine 'Molly'[5], John 'Tobe'[4], David 'Coot'[3], Henry[2], Rita[1] Strange*) was born on 31 August 1963 in Sandersville, Georgia. He married **Demetria Head** on 22 October 1994 in Atlanta, Georgia.

Children of **Reginald**[6] **Cheeves** and **Demetria Head** were:

576.   i. N'NAMDI AMIRA[7] was born on 11 February 1993 in Decatur, Georgia.

345. YVETTE[6] **RENFROW** (*Charlie*[5], *Georgianne*[4]*Davis, Lou*[3]*Cheeves, Henry*[2], *Rita*[1]*Strange*) married **Wendell Harris.**

Children of **Yvette**[6] **Renfrow** include:

577.   i. KENYATTA[7].

There were no children of **Yvette**[6] **Renfrow** and **Wendell Harris.**

349. EDWARD[6] **RENFROW** (*Charlie*[5], *Georgianne*[4]*Davis, Lou*[3]*Cheeves, Henry*[2], *Rita*[1]*Strange*) married **Donna** (———).

Children of **Edward**[6] **Renfrow** and **Donna** (———) were:

578.   i. NICOLE[7].

350. DELIA[6] **RENFROW** (*Charlie*[5], *Georgianne*[4]*Davis, Lou*[3]*Cheeves, Henry*[2], *Rita*[1]*Strange*) married **James Davis.**

Children of **Delia**[6] **Renfrow** include:

579.   i. QUINZEL[7].

There were no children of **Delia**[6] **Renfrow** and **James Davis.**

352. GERALD WAYNE[6] **RENFROW** (*Charlie*[5], *Georgianne*[4]*Davis, Lou*[3]*Cheeves, Henry*[2], *Rita*[1]*Strange*) was born on 10 October 1945. He married **Diane** (———). He married **Connie** (———).

Children of **Gerald Wayne**[6] **Renfrow** and **Diane** (———) were:

580.   i. BOBATAYA[7] was born on 12 August 1969.

Children of **Gerald Wayne**[6] **Renfrow** and **Connie** (———) were as follows:

581.   i. NICOLE[7] was born on 14 February 1970.
582.   ii. AMIR was born on 17 November 1979.

353. WILSON[6] **RENFROW** (*Charlie*[5], *Georgianne*[4]*Davis, Lou*[3]*Cheeves, Henry*[2], *Rita*[1]*Strange*) was born on 10 March 1953.

Children of **Wilson**[6] **Renfrow** include:

583.   i. SENATE[7].

355. **MICHAEL D.**^{6} **HOOKS** (*Mitchell*^{5}, *Henrietta*^{4}*Cheeves*, *Henry*^{3}, *Henry*^{2}, *Rita*^{1}*Strange*) was born on 25 December 1956. He married **Carol Anderson.**

Children of **Michael D.**^{6} **Hooks** and **Carol Anderson** were:
584.   i. KIRA LYNN^7.

358. **ROSALIND LINETTE**^{6} **HOOKS** (*Cheeves*^{5}, *Henrietta*^{4}*Cheeves*, *Henry*^{3}, *Henry*^{2}, *Rita*^{1}*Strange*) was born on 4 January 1959. She married **Thomas Victor Brown.**

Children of **Rosalind Linette**^{6} **Hooks** and **Thomas Victor Brown** were:
585.   i. CAMILLE VICTORIA^7.

366. **PATRICE ISLENE**^{6} **PIERCE** (*Oralene*^{5}*Hooks*, *Henrietta*^{4}*Cheeves*, *Henry*^{3}, *Henry*^{2}, *Rita*^{1}*Strange*) was born on 25 January 1966 in New Haven, Connecticut. She married **Nathaniel Balkcom III** on 11 March 1988 in Sandersville, Georgia.

Children of **Patrice Islene**^{6} **Pierce** and **Teddy Butler** were:
586.   i. KRISTEN JANA'^{7} was born on 22 September 1986 in Augusta, Georgia.

Children of **Patrice Islene**^{6} **Pierce** and **Nathaniel Balkcom III** were:
587.   i. NICHOLAS NATHANIEL^7 was born on 13 March 1998 in Georgia.

369. **SAUNDRA ERICKA**^{6} **SHENOSTER** (*Zelma*^{5}, *Mattie Lou*^{4}*Cheeves*, *Henry*^{3}, *Henry*^{2}, *Rita*^{1}*Strange*) was born on 30 June 1950 in Philadelphia, Pennsylvania. She died in December 1985 in Philadelphia, Pennsylvania, at age 35.

Children of **Saundra Ericka**^{6} **Shenoster** include:
588.   i. DONALD DANTE'^{7} was born on 26 November 1967 in Philadelphia, Pennsylvania.
589.   ii. MICHAEL LAMONT was born on 9 July 1974 in Philadelphia, Pennsylvania.

Children of **Saundra Ericka**^{6} **Shenoster** and **Barry Hilton** were:
590.   i. BARRY ANTHONY^7 was born on 17 July 1969 in Philadelphia, Pennsylvania.

370. **ANTHONY**^{6} **MCLEAN** (*Zelma*^{5}*Shenoster*, *Mattie Lou*^{4}*Cheeves*, *Henry*^{3}, *Henry*^{2}, *Rita*^{1}*Strange*) was born on 27 November 1958 in Philadelphia, Pennsylvania. He married **Linda Star Woodson** on 18 June 1994 in Philadelphia, Pennsylvania.

Children of **Anthony**^{6} **McLean** and **Gwendolyn Carmella Bond** were:
591.   i. NACHE' ANTOINETTE^7 was born on 12 June 1988 in Philadelphia, Pennsylvania.

There were no children of **Anthony**^{6} **McLean** and **Linda Star Woodson.**

371. JESSE JAMES^6 MCLEAN (JR.) (*Zelma^{5}Shenoster, Mattie Lou^{4}Cheeves, Henry^3, Henry^2, Rita^{1}Strange*) was born on 5 October 1960 in Philadelphia, Pennsylvania. He married **Antoinette Coto** on 9 July 1988 in Philadelphia, Pennsylvania.

Children of **Jesse James^6 McLean (Jr.)** and **Antoinette Coto** were:

592.   i. JESSE JAMES^7 (III) was born on 30 March 1986 in Philadelphia, Pennsylvania.

373. JOHN BENJAMIN^6 DOUGLASS (JR.) (*Katherine^{5}Shenoster, Mattie Lou^{4}Cheeves, Henry^3, Henry^2, Rita^{1}Strange*) was born on 4 April 1965 in Philadelphia, Pennsylvania. He married **Tykeia Giles** in Philadelphia, Pennsylvania.

Children of **John Benjamin^6 Douglass (Jr.)** and **Tykeia Giles** were:

593.   i. SHAUN SHAQUOI^7 was born on 2 October 1992 in Philadelphia, Pennsylvania.

375. CHARLES DAVID^6 GRAHAM (*Gloria^{5}Cheeves, Henry Holmes^4, Henry^3, Henry^2, Rita^{1}Strange*) was born on 20 May 1969 in Philadelphia, Pennsylvania. He married **Lorrie Hatten** on 5 September 1992 in Philadelphia, Pennsylvania.

Children of **Charles David^6 Graham** include:

594.   i. NOLAN LEWIS PAUL^7 was born on 29 May 1984 in Philadelphia, Pennsylvania.

There were no children of **Charles David^6 Graham** and **Lorrie Hatten**.

376. MELISSA AVA^6 GRAHAM (*Gloria^{5}Cheeves, Henry Holmes^4, Henry^3, Henry^2, Rita^{1}Strange*) was born on 21 April 1970 in Philadelphia, Pennsylvania.

Children of **Melissa Ava^6 Graham** and **Carlos Kinslow** were:

595.   i. BRANDON ALEXANDER^7 was born on 28 March 1996 in Philadelphia, Pennsylvania.

379. BARRY STEVEN^6 CHEEVES (*Forest^5, Henry Holmes^4, Henry^3, Henry^2, Rita^{1}Strange*) was born on 29 June 1960 in Philadelphia, Pennsylvania. He married **Andrea Benita 'Nita' Hyden**, daughter of **Ronald Hyden** and **Judy Ryder,** on 30 April 1988 in Philadelphia, Pennsylvania.

Children of **Barry Steven^6 Cheeves** and **Andrea Benita 'Nita' Hyden** were as follows:

+ 596.   i. RASETA NICOLE^7, born 7 May 1982 in Philadelphia, Pennsylvania.

597.   ii. RANIKA MICHELLE was born on 2 February 1990 in Philadelphia, Pennsylvania.

Children of **Barry Steven^6 Cheeves** and **Diane Johnson** were:

598.   i. BARRY STEVEN^7 JR. was born on 25 August 1996 in Philadelphia, Pennsylvania.

380. FORREST TROY[6] CHEEVES (*Forest[5], Henry Holmes[4], Henry[3], Henry[2], Rita[1] Strange*) was born on 22 February 1962 in Philadelphia, Pennsylvania.

Children of Forrest Troy[6] Cheeves and Sue Wilson were as follows:
599.   i. FORREST TROY[7] JR. was born on 30 March 1988 in Philadelphia, Pennsylvania.
600.   ii. ALEXANDER DOMINIC was born on 19 May 1989 in Philadelphia, Pennsylvania.

381. DARNELL FRANK[6] CHEEVES (*Forest[5], Henry Holmes[4], Henry[3], Henry[2], Rita[1] Strange*) was born on 17 February 1963 in Philadelphia, Pennsylvania. He married Diana 'Ann' Marie Johnson. He married Pat Young on 19 December 1997 in Philadelphia, Pennsylvania.

Children of Darnell Frank[6] Cheeves and Diana 'Ann' Marie Johnson were as follows:
601.   i. SHANAY LANELL[7] was born on 30 October 1985 in Philadelphia, Pennsylvania.
602.   ii. SHEENA MONIQUE was born on 5 November 1989 in Philadelphia, Pennsylvania.

Children of Darnell Frank[6] Cheeves and Pat Young were:
603.   i. DARNELL FRANK[7] JR. was born on 20 March 1993 in Philadelphia, Pennsylvania.

382. BRUCE KENNETH[6] CHEEVES (*Forest[5], Henry Holmes[4], Henry[3], Henry[2], Rita[1] Strange*) was born on 12 May 1964 in Philadelphia, Pennsylvania. He married Audrey Miree on 17 July 1998 in Philadelphia, Pennsylvania.

Children of Bruce Kenneth[6] Cheeves and Audrey Miree were as follows:
604.   i. BRUCE KENNETH[7] JR. was born on 24 October 1989 in Philadelphia, Pennsylvania.
605.   ii. KAREN was born on 13 July 1991 in Philadelphia, Pennsylvania.

384. BRIAN[6] GORDY (*Henry Edward[5], Henry Berry[4], Carrie[3] Cheeves, Henry[2], Rita[1] Strange*) married Yvonne (———).

Children of Brian[6] Gordy and Yvonne (———) were as follows:
606.   i. LANITA[7].
607.   ii. BRIANA.

385. BYRON[6] GORDY (*Henry Edward[5], Henry Berry[4], Carrie[3] Cheeves, Henry[2], Rita[1] Strange*) married Willette (———).

Children of Byron[6] Gordy and Willette (———) were:
608.   i. CHRISTINE[7].

386. BRUCE[6] GORDY (*Henry Edward[5], Henry Berry[4], Carrie[3] Cheeves, Henry[2], Rita[1] Strange*) married Deborah (———).

Children of **Bruce**^{6} **Gordy** and **Deborah** (———) were as follows:
609.　i. MARQITA^7.
610.　ii. APRIL.

387. BRENT^6 **GORDY** (*Henry Edward*^{5}, *Henry Berry*^{4}, *Carrie*^{3} *Cheeves*, *Henry*^{2}, *Rita*^{1} *Strange*) married **Effie** (———).

Children of **Brent**^{6} **Gordy** and **Effie** (———) were:
611.　i. JASMINE^7.

388. BRIDGETTE^6 **GORDY** (*Henry Edward*^{5}, *Henry Berry*^{4}, *Carrie*^{3} *Cheeves*, *Henry*^{2}, *Rita*^{1} *Strange*) married **Bernell Seal.**

Children of **Bridgette**^{6} **Gordy** and **Bernell Seal** were as follows:
612.　i. ROBERT^7.
613.　ii. RAYNELL.
614.　iii. RAYNARD.

390. KAREN^6 **KING** (*Margaret Jewel*^{5} *Gordy*, *Henry Berry*^{4}, *Carrie*^{3} *Cheeves*, *Henry*^{2}, *Rita*^{1} *Strange*) married **Elvin Brooks.**

Children of **Karen**^{6} **King** and **Elvin Brooks** were as follows:
615.　i. KYLE^7.
616.　ii. KARLIS.
617.　iii. KELLUM.
618.　iv. KRISTOPHER.
619.　v. KENNETH.
620.　vi. KARY.
621.　vii. KARIS.

391. KYRA^6 **KING** (*Margaret Jewel*^{5} *Gordy*, *Henry Berry*^{4}, *Carrie*^{3} *Cheeves*, *Henry*^{2}, *Rita*^{1} *Strange*) married **James Ridgell.**

Children of **Kyra**^{6} **King** and **James Ridgell** were as follows:
622.　i. IAN^7.
623.　ii. ETHAN.
624.　iii. JULIAN.

399. DEBORAH^6 **LAWRENCE** (*Joyce*^{5} *Gordy*, *Henry Berry*^{4}, *Carrie*^{3} *Cheeves*, *Henry*^{2}, *Rita*^{1} *Strange*) married **Lamont McClain.**

Children of **Deborah**[6] **Lawrence** and **Lamont McClain** were as follows:
625.　　i. VANESSA[7].
626.　　ii. KRISTIN.
627.　　iii. TASHA.

400. DOREEN[6] **LAWRENCE** (*Joyce*[5] *Gordy, Henry Berry*[4]*, Carrie*[3] *Cheeves, Henry*[2]*, Rita*[1] *Strange*) married **Sam Hughes.**

Children of **Doreen**[6] **Lawrence** and **Sam Hughes** were:
628.　　i. DAVID[7].

402. DARIN[6] **LAWRENCE** (*Joyce*[5] *Gordy, Henry Berry*[4]*, Carrie*[3] *Cheeves, Henry*[2]*, Rita*[1] *Strange*) married **Shirley** (———).

Children of **Darin**[6] **Lawrence** and **Shirley** (———) were as follows:
629.　　i. BRANDON[7].
630.　　ii. KEITH.

409. LINDA[6] **BUTTS** (*Mary Louvenia 'Benia*[5] *Cawthon, Mary Lucy*[4] *Gordy, Carrie*[3] *Cheeves, Henry*[2]*, Rita*[1] *Strange*) was born on 27 February 1951 in Milledgeville, Georgia. She married **Donald Edwin Brooks**, son of **Donald Brooks** and **Ermine Steadman-Johnson.**

Children of **Linda**[6] **Butts** and **Donald Edwin Brooks** were as follows:
631.　　i. DAWN ERMINE[7] was born on 11 November 1972 in Meriden, Connecticut.
632.　　ii. ANITRA LOUVINE was born on 20 July 1975 in Meriden, Connecticut.
633.　　iii. KAHLIL was born on 28 March 1977 in Meriden, Connecticut.

411. EVELYN BERNICE 'EBBIE'[6] **BUTTS** (*Mary Louvenia 'Benia*[5] *Cawthon, Mary Lucy*[4] *Gordy, Carrie*[3] *Cheeves, Henry*[2]*, Rita*[1] *Strange*) was born in Hartford, Connecticut. She was born on 12 April 1954 in Hartford, Connecticut.

Children of **Evelyn Bernice 'Ebbie'**[6] **Butts** include:
+ 634.　　i. BRITTANY EUGENIA[7], born 5 March 1976 in Middletown, Connecticut; married **Edward Ray Jordan.**
635.　　ii. ENID JO MCKENZIE was born on 16 December 1984 in Hartford, Connecticut.

412. CHRISTIE[6] **BUTTS TURNER** (*Mary Louvenia 'Benia*[5] *Cawthon, Mary Lucy*[4] *Gordy, Carrie*[3] *Cheeves, Henry*[2]*, Rita*[1] *Strange*) was born on 18 December 1956 in Hartford, Connecticut. She married **Joseph Hicks Sr.** in Atlanta, Georgia.

Children of **Christie**[6] **Butts Turner** and **Joseph Hicks Sr.** were:
+ 636. i. JOSEPH 'JOE'[7] JR., born in Atlanta, Georgia.

423. BERNARD[6] **TRAWICK** (*Mary Pearl 'Town'*[5]*Gordy, Samuel 'Sam'*[4]*, Carrie*[3]*Cheeves, Henry*[2]*, Rita*[1]*Strange*) was born on 14 December 1951 in Philadelphia, Pennsylvania. He married **Kenya Wilson.**

Children of **Bernard**[6] **Trawick** and **Kenya Wilson** were as follows:
637. i. TAFT[7] was born on 25 April 1986 in Winston-Salem, North Carolina.
638. ii. JASON was born on 14 December 1987 in Philadelphia, Pennsylvania.

426. CYNTHIA[6] **TRAWICK** (*Mary Pearl 'Town'*[5]*Gordy, Samuel 'Sam'*[4]*, Carrie*[3]*Cheeves, Henry*[2]*, Rita*[1]*Strange*) was born on 12 November 1958 in Philadelphia, Pennsylvania. She married **William Boyer.**

Children of **Cynthia**[6] **Trawick** and **William Boyer** were as follows:
639. i. AJA MARIE[7] was born on 9 June 1982 in Philadelphia, Pennsylvania.
640. ii. TODD was born on 20 January 1984 in Philadelphia, Pennsylvania.
641. iii. JENNA DANIELLE was born on 14 August 1989 in Philadelphia, Pennsylvania.
642. iv. WILLIAM 'BJ' JR. was born on 16 December 1997 in Philadelphia, Pennsylvania.

Generation Seven

512. LASHAY[7] **WALTON** (*Peggy*[6]*Renfroe, Mae Will*[5]*Williams, Mae Will*[4]*Rogers, Dovie*[3]*Cheeves, Henry*[2]*, Rita*[1]*Strange*) was born on 30 April 1967 in Detroit, Michigan.

Children of **Lashay**[7] **Walton** and **Byron** (—?—) were:
643. i. BYRON[8] was born on 17 July 1985 in Detroit, Michigan.

536. EDDIE HOLMES[7] **BUTTS** (*Chester*[6]*, Julia Inez*[5]*Trawick, Mary 'Ma-Mae' Ollie*[4]*Cheeves, David 'Coot'*[3]*, Henry*[2]*, Rita*[1]*Strange*) was born on 4 October 1954. He married **Shirley Holmes.** He married **Zina Holmes.**

Children of **Eddie Holmes**[7] **Butts** and **Shirley Holmes** were:
644. i. TAMIKA[8] was born on 3 March 1974.

Children of **Eddie Holmes**[7] **Butts** and **Zina Holmes** were:
645. i. ASHLEY[8] was born on 13 June 1987.

537. CURTIS[7] **BUTTS** (*Chester*[6]*, Julia Inez*[5]*Trawick, Mary 'Ma-Mae' Ollie*[4]*Cheeves, David 'Coot'*[3]*, Henry*[2]*, Rita*[1]*Strange*) was born on 27 April 1966. He married **Sheila** (———). He married **Crystle** (———).

Children of **Curtis**[7] **Butts** and **Sheila** (———) were:
646.   i. BRYON[8] was born on 14 September 1987.

Children of **Curtis**[7] **Butts** and **Crystle** (———) were:
647.   i. CHRISTIA[8] was born on 31 October 1985.

539. DARYL[7] **BUTTS** (*Chester*[6], *Julia Inez*[5] *Trawick, Mary 'Ma-Mae' Ollie*[4] *Cheeves, David 'Coot*[3], *Henry*[2], *Rita*[1] *Strange*) was born on 19 July 1968. He married **Nichelle** (——).

Children of **Daryl**[7] **Butts** and **Nichelle** (———) were:
648.   i. SHAUNICE[8] was born on 24 August 1985.

542. WILLIAM[7] **WILLIAMS (JR.)** (*Janice*[6] *Butts, Julia Inez*[5] *Trawick, Mary 'Ma-Mae' Ollie*[4] *Cheeves, David 'Coot*[3], *Henry*[2], *Rita*[1] *Strange*) was born on 19 January 1958.

Children of **William**[7] **Williams (Jr.)** include:
649.   i. LATICHIA[8].

543. KENNETH 'HUCKY'[7] **WILLIAMS** (*Janice*[6] *Butts, Julia Inez*[5] *Trawick, Mary 'Ma-Mae' Ollie*[4] *Cheeves, David 'Coot*[3], *Henry*[2], *Rita*[1] *Strange*) was born on 13 July 1960. He married **Sylvita Barbour**. He married **Deborah Lynn** (———).

Children of **Kenneth 'Hucky'**[7] **Williams** and **Sylvita Barbour** were:
650.   i. KINETA[8] was born on 12 February 1977.

Children of **Kenneth 'Hucky'**[7] **Williams** and **Deborah Lynn** (———) were as follows:
651.   i. RAHEEM ANTHONY[8] was born on 13 July 1980.
652.   ii. LATOYA DENISE was born on 6 March 1981.
653.   iii. KENNETH JAMELL was born on 3 March 1982.

544. HERRELL A.[7] **WILLIAMS** (*Janice*[6] *Butts, Julia Inez*[5] *Trawick, Mary 'Ma-Mae' Ollie*[4] *Cheeves, David 'Coot*[3], *Henry*[2], *Rita*[1] *Strange*) was born on 23 May 1967. He married **Stephanie Y. Anderson**. He married **Nadine Jackson**.

Children of **Herrell A.**[7] **Williams** and **Stephanie Y. Anderson** were:
654.   i. KIAUNA YVONNE[8] was born on 28 May 1985.

Children of **Herrell A.**[7] **Williams** and **Nadine Jackson** were:
655.   i. SHERRELL VIOLA[8] was born on 4 April 1989.

545. ALONZO LONNIE^7 WILLIAMS (*Janice^6 Butts, Julia Inez^5 Trawick, Mary 'Ma-Mae' Ollie^4 Cheeves, David 'Coot^3, Henry^2, Rita^1 Strange*) was born on 2 August 1969.

Children of **Alonzo Lonnie^7 Williams** and **Trina Straike** were:
656.   i. TRANIKA^8 was born on 9 March 1987.

Children of **Alonzo Lonnie^7 Williams** and **Nicole King** were:
657.   i. NATASHA^8 was born on 20 November 1987.

Children of **Alonzo Lonnie^7 Williams** and **Barbara M. Rock** were:
658.   i. ALONZO ALLEN ROCK^8 was born on 21 April 1989.

557. SABRINA LYNN^7 ALCORN (*Doris^6 Butts, Mamye Dorothy 'Mary^5 Trawick, Mary 'Ma-Mae' Ollie^4 Cheeves, David 'Coot^3, Henry^2, Rita^1 Strange*) was born on 5 February 1967. She married **Derrick Girard McCann (Sr.)**.

Children of **Sabrina Lynn^7 Alcorn** and **Derrick Girard McCann (Sr.)** were:
659.   i. DERRICK GIRARD^8 (JR.) was born on 4 May 1990.

560. TANYA^7 HOLLIWAY (*Gwendolyn 'Gwen^6 Butts, Mamye Dorothy 'Mary^5 Trawick, Mary 'Ma-Mae' Ollie^4 Cheeves, David 'Coot^3, Henry^2, Rita^1 Strange*) was born on 9 February 1964. She married **Todd Bell**.

Children of **Tanya^7 Holliway** include:
660.   i. T J^8 was born circa 1990.
661.   ii. TIANA was born circa 1990.

Children of **Tanya^7 Holliway** and **Todd Bell** were as follows:
662.   i. TIFFANY^8 was born on 31 August 1983.
663.   ii. TODD (JR.) was born on 26 February 1985.

572. KYE C.^{7} ROBERSON (*Kay Cheeves^6 Wiggins, Ernestine 'Molly^5 Cheeves, John 'Tobe^4, David 'Coot^3, Henry^2, Rita^1 Strange*) was born on 4 February 1980 in Dublin, Georgia.

Children of **Kye C.^{7} Roberson** and **Ronnie Taylor** were:
664.   i. AMAYA^8 was born on 22 April 2002 in Dublin, Georgia.

596. RASETA NICOLE^7 CHEEVES (*Barry Steven^6, Forest^5, Henry Holmes^4, Henry^3, Henry^2, Rita^1 Strange*) was born on 7 May 1982 in Philadelphia, Pennsylvania.

Children of **Raseta Nicole[7] Cheeves** and **James Kennedy** were:

665.   i. NICHOLAS SEMAJ[8] was born on 6 March 2001 in Philadelphia, Pennsylvania.

634. **BRITTANY EUGENIA[7] BUTTS** (*Evelyn Bernice 'Ebbie*[6], *Mary Louvenia 'Benia*[5] *Cawthon, Mary Lucy*[4] *Gordy, Carrie*[3] *Cheeves, Henry*[2], *Rita*[1] *Strange*) was born on 5 March 1976 in Middletown, Connecticut. She married **Edward Ray Jordan** in September 1994 in Middletown, Connecticut.

Children of **Brittany Eugenia[7] Butts** and **Edward Ray Jordan** were:

666.   i. NATHANIAL RAY[8] was born on 13 August 1995.

636. **JOSEPH 'JOE'[7] HICKS JR.** (*Christie*[6] *Butts, Mary Louvenia 'Benia*[5] *Cawthon, Mary Lucy*[4] *Gordy, Carrie*[3] *Cheeves, Henry*[2], *Rita*[1] *Strange*) was born in Atlanta, Georgia.

Children of **Joseph 'Joe'[7] Hicks Jr.** include:

667.   i. SYDNEY[8] was born in Atlanta, Georgia.

668.   ii. TAJI was born in Atlanta, Georgia.

Descendants of Porter Boyer

Porter Boyer

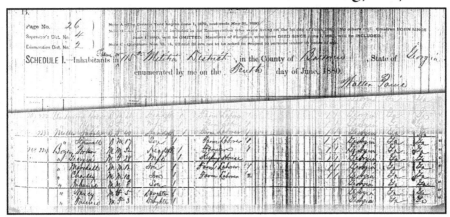

Porter Boyer, 1880 Census

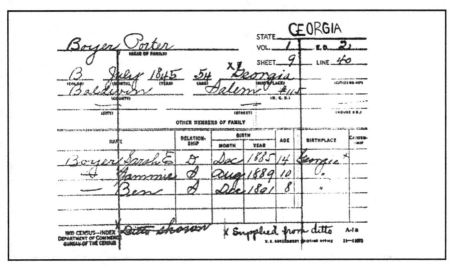

Porter Boyer, 1900 Census

Porter Boyer, 1900 Census

Will of
Georgean Boyer

Filed in Office
October 1st 1898.
W.R. Bell
County B.C.

Recorded in Book
of Wills page 238
October 10th 1898.
W.R. Bell
County B.C.

Georgean Boyer's Will, Filed October 1, 1898 and Recorded October 10, 1898

State of Georgia
Baldwin County } Last Will and Teasta
                } ment of Georgean
                } Boyer

I Georgean Boyer of Saide State and
County being of Sound and disposeing
minde and memrey do make this my last
Will and testament
Item first I Wish My Executor as soon
after my death to pay all of my just debts
If a Sale of property Shall be nessary
I Wish him to Select for Sale that which
can be most advantageous use for that
purpose and I authorize him to Sell the Same
at public or private Sale as he may See
fit
Item Second I Give to my 4 Yongist Children
mary Boyer Sarah Boyer Sam Boyer
Benney Boyer all of my property of Evrey
descruption that I may poses at the time
of my death
Item 3rd I do hereby appoint my husban
Poter Boyer Exec cutor of this my Will
In testimoney Whereof I have hereto Set my
hand this the 2 day of September 1898
Signed and publish by Georgean Boyer
as her last Will and testament in the presence
of the under Signed Who Subscribe our

Georgean Boyer's Will, September 2, 1898, pg. 1

124

Names hereto as witneses at the intance and request of Saide testator and in her presence and in the presence of Each other this the 2 day of September 1898

Georgean her + mark Boyer

Petent Dayfield.
John H. Thompson.
Miles D. Surrett.

Georgean Boyer's Will, September 2, 1898, pg. 2

Sworn Statement of Witness for Georgean Boyer, October 1, 1898

126

Warrant of Appraisement.

Estate of *Georgean Boyer*
deceased.

Porter Boyer, Executor
~~Administrator~~.

~~Administrator~~.

~~Administrator~~.

L. F. Palmer,
C. W. Ennis, Jr
J. A. Buck,
James Ennis, Jr
Uljrich Eames,

} *Appraisers*

Fillmore Office
March 6th 1899

Wm W Bell
Crerry

Recorded in Book of Inventory &
Appraisement Page 454,
June 9th 1899.
Wm W Bell Crerry

Georgean Boyer, Warrant of Appraisement

WARRANT TO APPRAISE ESTATE.   REVISED 1887.

State of Georgia, *Baldwin* County.

BY THE HONORABLE THE ORDINARY OF SAID COUNTY

To *L. F. Palmer, C. W. Ennis Jr. J. A. Rush, James Ennis. Myriah Ennis.*

.... *Greeting :*

These are to authorize and empower you, or any three of you, to make a just and true appraisement and valuation of all the personal property of...............................

Georgean Boyer late of said County, deceased. which shall be produced to you by *Porter Boyer*

the *Executor* of the Estate of the said...............................

Georgean Boyer and also of all the real estate of said

Georgean Boyer

lying in said County : You, and each of you, first taking the oath required by law, before some proper officer, or each other; and you will return the said Appraisement, certified under your hands, and also a certificate of your having taken the oath thereto annexed, unto the said *Porter Boyer Executor*

within the time prescribed by law.

In Witness Whereof, I have hereunto set my hand and affixed the seal of my office, this *three* day of *October* 189 *8*

M. R. Bell
                                                        Ordinary.

Georgean Boyer, Warrant of Appraisement, pg. 1

Returned in assets of
Peter Boyer the Executor
this 6th day of March 1899

M R Bell } his
Comy } Peter Boyer
mark Exr

Recorded in Book
of Inventory & Appraisement
Page 454 this
June 9th 1899

M R Bell
Comy [illegible]

march. 6. 1899

Capt. M. R. Bell

I find the property
that Poter Boyyer
Says is an will of his
wife to her Children

4 head cows & 4 calfs $45.00
1 Black horse mule name Rook 50.00
9 head hogs 25.00
1 Sewing machine 10.00
House & kitchen furniture 25.00

L. F. Palmer
G. W. Ennis Jr
J. T. [illegible] ([illegible])

Georgean Boyer, Warrant of Appraisement, pg. 2

No._____

Baldwin **Court of Ordinary,**

_October_____Term, *189 8*

PETITION FOR PROBATE OF WILL.

Porter Boyer

vs.

Georgean Boyer

deceased

Recorded in Book of Minutes, on page **396** October 3° 1898

M.R. Bell Ordinary B.C.

Filed in office, this____1st____day of

_October_____189 8.

M.R. Bell

Ordinary.

Porter Boyer's Petition for Probate of his Wife, Georgean's, Will

PETITION FOR PROBATE OF WILL.

GEORGIA, *Baldwin,* COUNTY.

To *McRee*   *Ordinary for said County:*

THE PETITION OF *Porter Boyer* shows that *Georgeen Boyer* late of said County, departed this life on the 6th day of *September* 189 8 after having made his last will and testament, wherein your petitioner is nominated the executor. Your petitioner produces said will in Court, and prays that the same may be admitted to record upon the proof thereof in common form, and that letters testamentary issue in terms of the law.

This *October 1st* 189 8.

McRee
Ordinary RC

Porter + Boyer
mark
Petitioner.

Baldwin Court of Ordinary, *October 3* Term, 189 8

Upon the foregoing petition of the nominated Executor and the affidavit of *Peter Loffield* one of the subscribing witnesses to the will of *Georgeen Boyer* deceased; it is ordered by the Court that the said will be admitted to record as satisfactorily proven in common form; and it is further ordered that letters testamentary issue to *Porter Boyer* the Executor named in said will upon his taking and subscribing the oath required by law.

This *third* day of *October* 189 8.

McRee Ordinary.

GEORGIA, *Baldwin* County.

I, *Porter Boyer* do solemnly swear that this writing contains the true last WILL of the within named *Georgeen Boyer* deceased, so far as I know or believe, and that I will well and truly execute the same in accordance with the laws of this State. So help me God.

Sworn to and subscribed before me, this _____ day of _____ 189—

_____ Ordinary.

Porter Boyer, Petition for Probate of Will, pg. 1

No. *6 28*

Baldwin Court of Ordinary,

At Chambers *March 9* 19*20*

EX PARTE.

Mrs Ida Boyer

APPLICATION FOR
TEMPORARY LETTERS OF ADMINISTRATION
ON THE ESTATE OF

Charles Boyer

DECEASED.

Filed in office *Mar 9* 19*22*

W H Stembridge Ordinary.

THE FRANKLIN PRINTING AND PUBLISHING CO., ATLANTA.

Recorded in Minutes "1919" p. 212.

Ida Boyer, Application for Temporary Letters of Administration

132

APPLICATION FOR TEMPORARY LETTERS OF ADMINISTRATION. The Franklin Prtg. & Pub. Co., Atlanta, Ga.

State of Georgia,

Baldwin COUNTY.

To the Ordinary of Said County.

The petition of __Mrs. Ida Boyer__ a citizen of the United States, residing in said State, showeth that __Charles Boyer__ departed this life on or about the __25th__ day of __March 1922.__, 19__ a resident of said county, intestate, leaving an estate __of real and personal property, of the probable value of __Two Hunderd__ Dollars, the realty worth about__ Dollars, and the personalty worth about__ Dollars; that said estate is unrepresented, and it is necessary for the purpose of collecting and taking care of the effects of said deceased, that Temporary Letters of Administration should be granted thereon; that Petitioner __Is the Mother of said Chales Boyer deceased,__

Wherefore, Petitioner prays an order appointing __her__ temporary administra__trix__ on said estate.

Mrs. Ida Boyer

Baldwin __Court of Ordinary,__

At Chambers __March 9th__ Term, 19__22.__

The petition of __Mrs. Ida Boyer__ for Temporary Letters of Administration on the estate of __Charles Boyer__ deceased, having been duly filed, and it appearing that said deceased died a resident of said County intestate; that said applicant is a citizen of this State, and lawfully qualified for said administration, and that it is necessary that such Letters should issue for the purpose of collecting and taking care of the effects of the said deceased until Permanent Letters are granted; it is, therefore, ordered that the said __Mrs. Ida Boyer__ be, and __she__ is hereby appointed Temporary Administra__trix__ on said estate, and that Letters as such issue to __her__ upon __her__ giving bond and security in the sum of __Four Hundred__ Dollars, and taking the oath as the law requires.

_____, Ordinary.

State of Georgia, Baldwin County.

You __Mrs Ida Boyer__ do solemnly swear that you will well and truly perform the duties of Temporary Administrator upon the estate of__ __Charles Boyer__ deceased, to the best of your ability.

So help you God.

Sworn to and subscribed before me this __9th__ day of __March 1922.__, 19__

Mrs. Ida Boyer

Ida Boyer, Application for Temporary Letters of Administration, pg. 1

Recorded 1922

H 628

BOND

TEMPORARY LETTERS

of Mrs. Ida Boyer e

Us,

Charles Boyer Est

Ida Boyer, Bond

GEORGIA, Baldwin County.

___

KNOW ALL MEN BY THESE PRESENTS:

THAT WE, _____Mrs Ida Boyer principal and Bennie Boyer as_

Security.

are held and firmly bound unto_____ W H Stembridge _____, Ordinary

of said County, and to his successors in office, in the sum of ___Four Hundred___

_____Dollars and_____Cents,

to the payment of which, well and truly to be made, we bind ourselves, our heirs, Executors and Administrators, of us and each of us, firmly by these presents.

Subscribed with our hands, and sealed with our seals, this___9th_____

day of ___March___1922.___191___

The Condition of the above Bond or Obligation is such, That whereas the above bound_____

_____Mrs Ida Boyer_____

ha___this day applied to the said___W H Stembridge_____

Ordinary, for, and ha__g___obtained Temporary Letters of Administration of the goods and chattels, rights

and credits of _____Charles Boyer_____ deceased.

Now if the above bound___Mrs Ida Boyer_____

shall carefully collect and preserve from waste or loss, all the goods or chattels and effects of the said

_____Charles Boyer_____deceased, and shall make

or cause to be made a true and perfect inventory of all such Estate, and the same being so preserved,

do surrender up such Estate and Effects, with the Inventory aforesaid, unto the legal and proper Administrator, on or by the first Monday in___June 1922,___next, or so soon thereafter as the Ordinary

shall direct, with all his other actings and doings therein, then this obligation to be void, otherwise to

remain in full force in law.

WH Stembridge
Ordinary

Mrs Ida Boyer (SEAL.)

Bennie Boyer (SEAL.)

_____ (SEAL.)

Ida Boyer, Bond, pg. 1

Marshall Boyer and Ida Amos, Marriage License

Charles Boyer and Mamie Adams, Marriage License

295

No.

MARRIAGE LICENSE.

State of Georgia, Baldwin County.

To any JUDGE, JUSTICE OF THE PEACE or MINISTER OF THE GOSPEL,

You are Hereby Authorized to Join

John Boyd & Annie Harper

In the Holy State of Matrimony, according to the Constitution and Laws of this State; and for so doing, this shall be your sufficient License.

And you are hereby required to return this License to me, with your Certificate hereon of the fact and date of the Marriage.

Given under my hand and seal, this 11 day of April 1881

M R Bell
Ordinary.

[L.S.]

GEORGIA, BALDWIN COUNTY.

I CERTIFY, that John Boyer and Annie Harper were joined in Matrimony by me, this 11 day of April Eighteen Hundred and Eighty one

Recorded: 11 day July 1891 Rev M J Dickson
M R Bell Ordinary.

John and Annie Boyer, Marriage License

GEORGIA, Baldwin County.

To any Minister of the Gospel, Judge, Justice of the Interior Court, or Justice of the Peace :

YOU are hereby authorized to join Joel C. Boyer

and Sophronia E. Garland in the holy state of Matrimony, according to the Constitution and Laws of this State; and for so doing, this shall be your sufficient license.

GIVEN under my hand and Seal of Office, this 12th day

of June 1856

John Hammond Ordinary.

GEORGIA, Hancock County.

I do certify that Joel C. Boyer and Sophronia E. Garland were duly joined in Matrimony by me, this 15th day of June 1857

Francis Minor J.P.

Joel C. Boyer, Marriage License

Descendants of Porter Boyer

Generation One

1. PORTER^1 **BOYER** was born in Georgia. He married **Georgeanne** (—?—) in Georgia.

Children of **Porter**^{1} **Boyer** and **Georgeanne** (—?—) were as follows:

+   2.   i. MARSHALL^2, born in Georgia; married **Ida Solomon**.
+   3.   ii. CHARLES 'CHARLIE', born in Georgia; married **Mamie Adams**.
    4.   iii. MAUD was born in Georgia. She married **Abe Wise** in Georgia. She married **Leonard Walker** in Georgia. She married **Burton Fuller** in Georgia.
+   5.   iv. JOHNNIE, born in Georgia; married **Mollie** (—?—).
+   6.   v. NANCY, born in Georgia; married **Ed Williams**.
+   7.   vi. FANNIE, born in Georgia; married **Julius Swint**.
+   8.   vii. MARY, born in Georgia; married **Tom Swint**.
    9.   viii. SARAH was born in Georgia. She married **Henry Allen**.
+   10.   ix. BENNIE, born in Georgia; married **Parrie Lee Adolphus**.
+   11.   x. MATTHEW, born in Georgia; married **Mamie** (—?—).
+   12.   xi. SAM 'SAMMIE', born 15 October 1892 in Milledgeville, Georgia; married **Lillian Hood**.

Generation Two

2. MARSHALL^2 **BOYER** (*Porter*^{1}) was born in Georgia. He married **Ida Solomon** in Georgia.

Children of **Marshall**^{2} **Boyer** and **Ida Solomon** were as follows:

  13.   i. TOMMIE^3 was born in Georgia.
  14.   ii. JOSEPH was born in Georgia.
  15.   iii. CHARLIE was born in Georgia.
  16.   iv. LUCY was born in Georgia. She married **Mr. Monroe** in Georgia.
  17.   v. MISSOURI was born in Georgia. She married **Mr. Andrews** in Georgia.
  18.   vi. JULIA was born in Georgia. She married **Mr. Hodge** in Georgia.
  19.   vii. PEARL was born in Georgia. She married **Mr. Gordy** in Georgia.
  20.   viii. BURENE was born in Georgia.
+   21.   ix. IDA, born in Georgia; married **Eugene Smith**.
  22.   x. JOHN 'BIT' was born in Georgia.
+   23.   xi. WILLIAM PORTER, born 30 July 1907 in Milledgeville, Georgia; married **Mozelle Hodges**.
+   24.   xii. MARSHALL 'NAY', born 11 August 1909 in Milledgeville, Georgia; married **Luola Mason**.

3. CHARLES 'CHARLIE'^{2} BOYER (*Porter^1*) was born in Georgia. He married **Mamie Adams** on 21 December 1892 in Baldwin County, Georgia.

Children of **Charles 'Charlie'^{2} Boyer** and **Mamie Adams** were as follows:

25. i. CALLIE^3 was born in Georgia.
26. ii. FLORENCE was born in Georgia.

5. JOHNNIE^2 BOYER (*Porter^1*) was born in Georgia. He married **Mollie** (—?—) in Georgia.

Children of **Johnnie^2 Boyer** and **Mollie** (—?—) were as follows:

27. i. JOHNNIE^3 JR. was born in Georgia.
28. ii. ADAM was born in Georgia.
29. iii. ERNEST was born in Georgia.
30. iv. MIRABEAU 'BE BE' was born in Georgia.
31. v. FOREST was born in Georgia.
32. vi. ELIZABETH was born in Georgia. She married **Mr. Collins**.
33. vii. SARAH was born in Georgia. She married **Mr. Riddenberry**.
34. viii. LUCILLE was born in Georgia. She married **Mr. Cannon**.

6. NANCY^2 BOYER (*Porter^1*) was born in Georgia. She married **Ed Williams** in Georgia.

Children of **Nancy^2 Boyer** and **Ed Williams** were as follows:

35. i. GEORGIANNE^3 was born in Milledgeville, Georgia.
36. ii. PORTER was born in Milledgeville, Georgia. He married **Nancy 'Dude' Turner**.
+ 37. iii. GUSSIE, born in Milledgeville, Georgia; married **Essie Hopkins**.
+ 38. iv. SIDNEY, born in Milledgeville, Georgia; married **Anna Lou Hill**.
+ 39. v. ED 'JUNE' JR., born in Milledgeville, Georgia; married **Catherine** (—?—).
40. vi. CLEMMIE was born in Milledgeville, Georgia.
+ 41. vii. LEE, born 11 March in Milledgeville, Georgia; married **Mae Will Rogers**.
+ 42. viii. FANNIE MAE, born 19 April in Milledgeville, Georgia; married **Addison Wiggins**.
+ 43. ix. JOHNNIE, born 16 December 1892 in Milledgeville, Georgia; married **Fannie Kitchens**.
+ 44. x. MELISSA, born 1900 in Baldwin County, Georgia; married **Tom Trawick**.
+ 45. xi. ROBERT SR., born 6 September 1900 in Milledgeville, Georgia; married **Eula Riddenberry**.
+ 46. xii. MARY 'MAE' ELLA, born 20 July 1912 in Milledgeville, Georgia; married **Arthur Liggins**.
+ 47. xiii. MINNIE, married **Willie Napier**.

7. FANNIE^2 BOYER (*Porter^1*) was born in Georgia. She married **Julius Swint** in Georgia.
Children of **Fannie^2 Boyer** and **Julius Swint** were as follows:

48.   i. MARSHALL^3 was born in Georgia.
49.   ii. EVA was born in Georgia.
50.   iii. JULIUS JR. was born in Georgia.
51.   iv. BENNIE was born in Georgia.
52.   v. ROSE was born in Georgia.
53.   vi. SARAH was born in Georgia.
54.   vii. NANCY was born in Georgia.
55.   viii. ANN was born in Georgia.
56.   ix. LONNIE LEWIS was born in Georgia.

8. MARY^2 BOYER (*Porter^1*) was born in Georgia. She married **Tom Swint.**

Children of **Mary^2 Boyer** and **Tom Swint** were as follows:
57.   i. SAM PORTER^3.
58.   ii. SYLVESTER.
59.   iii. TOM 'TOMMIE' JR..
60.   iv. BESSIE LOU.
61.   v. MARSHALL.

10. BENNIE^2 BOYER (*Porter^1*) was born in Georgia. He married **Parrie Lee Adolphus.**

Children of **Bennie^2 Boyer** and **Parrie Lee Adolphus** were as follows:
62.   i. SAMMIE^3.
63.   ii. JOHN was born in Detroit, Michigan.
64.   iii. MARY was born on 19 April in Detroit, Michigan. She married **Mr. Klugh.**
65.   iv. HARVEY OTTO was born on 19 April in Detroit, Michigan.
66.   v. BURENE was born on 10 May in Detroit, Michigan. She married **Mr. Highgate.**
67.   vi. MARIE was born on 2 June in Detroit, Michigan. She married **Mr. Brown.**
68.   vii. BENNIE JR. was born on 25 July.
+ 69.   viii. GEORGIANNA, born 24 July 1918 in Sandersville, Georgia; married **Mr. Hall.**
70.   ix. LEO was born on 3 July 1920.
+ 71.   x. ELIZA 'TRIXIE', born 8 February 1922 in Milledgeville, Georgia; married **Virgil Columbus Smith.**

11. MATTHEW^2 BOYER (*Porter^1*) was born in Georgia. He married **Mamie (—?—).**

Children of **Matthew^2 Boyer** and **Mamie (—?—)** were as follows:
72.   i. HAZEL^3 married **Mr. Goree.**
73.   ii. IDA married **Mr. Wilson.**

12. SAM 'SAMMIE'^{2} BOYER (*Porter^1*) was born on 15 October 1892 in Milledgeville, Georgia. He married **Lillian Hood** in 1915 in Milledgeville, Georgia. He died in April 1945 in Detroit, Michigan, at age 52.

Children of **Sam 'Sammie'^{2} Boyer** and **Lillian Hood** were as follows:

74. i. BENNIE^3 was born in Milledgeville, Georgia.

75. ii. JOSEPH was born in Milledgeville, Georgia.

76. iii. NAPOLEAN was born in Milledgeville, Georgia.

77. iv. KATHERINE was born in Detroit, Michigan. She died in August 1936 in Detroit, Michigan.

78. v. CALLIE MAUDE was born on 11 February 1918 in Milledgeville, Georgia. She married **Mr. Sharfner.**

79. vi. CLARA was born on 15 April 1921 in Milledgeville, Georgia. She married **Mr. Patton.** She died on 7 July 2003 in Detroit, Michigan, at age 82.

80. vii. SAM 'SAMMIE' JR. was born on 3 February 1924 in Detroit, Michigan.

81. viii. ELEAZAR was born on 10 February 1927 in Detroit, Michigan.

82. ix. REBECCA was born on 3 October 1928 in Detroit, Michigan. She married **Mr. Royser.**

+ 83. x. ALFRED, born 24 May 1930 in Detroit, Michigan; married **Celestine Ramirez.**

84. xi. JAMES was born on 30 July 1932 in Detroit, Michigan.

85. xii. ROBERT was born on 9 August 1934 in Detroit, Michigan.

+ 86. xiii. LILLIAN, born 23 September 1936 in Detroit, Michigan; married **Jesse Coulter.**

+ 87. xiv. EDWARD JAY, born 2 February 1939 in Detroit, Michigan; married **Jill Witherspoon.**

88. xv. CLEOPHAS was born on 13 February 1941 in Detroit, Michigan.

Generation Three

21. IDA^3 BOYER (*Marshall^2, Porter^1*) was born in Georgia. She married **Eugene Smith** in Georgia.

Children of **Ida^3 Boyer** and **Eugene Smith** were:

89. i. HERBERT DEAL^4.

23. WILLIAM PORTER^3 BOYER (*Marshall^2, Porter^1*) was born on 30 July 1907 in Milledgeville, Georgia. He married **Mozelle Hodges** in Milledgeville, Georgia.

Children of **William Porter^3 Boyer** and **Mozelle Hodges** were as follows:

+ 90. i. THELMA^4, born 12 May 1926 in Detroit, Michigan; married **Frank Ferguson.**

91. ii. PORTER DOUGLAS was born on 29 August 1927 in Detroit, Michigan. He married **Dorothy McKiever** on 7 June 1952 in Philadelphia, Pennsylvania. He married **Juanita McGhee** on 19 July 1992 in Philadelphia, Pennsylvania.

\+ 92.   iii. MARSHALL 'BEAU' DESHAUN, born 20 December 1930 in Detroit, Michigan; married **Agnes** (—?—).

24. MARSHALL 'NAY'^{3} BOYER (*Marshall^2, Porter^1*) was born on 11 August 1909 in Milledgeville, Georgia. He married **Luola Mason** on 28 October 1934 in Milledgeville, Georgia.

Children of **Marshall 'Nay'^{3} Boyer** and **Luola Mason** were as follows:

\+ 93.   i. WILLIAM 'TYRONE'^{4}, born 9 January 1944 in Detroit, Michigan; married **Dagmar Kanitz.**

\+ 94.   ii. VEDA AUDRA DEAN, born 29 December 1952 in Detroit, Michigan; married **Edmond Bryant.**

37. GUSSIE^3 WILLIAMS (*Nancy^2 Boyer, Porter^1*) was born in Milledgeville, Georgia. He married **Essie Hopkins**, daughter of **Arthur Hopkins** and **Emily Wiggins.**

Children of **Gussie^3 Williams** and **Essie Hopkins** were as follows:

95.   i. ARTHUR 'JAKE'^{4} was born in Milledgeville, Georgia.

96.   ii. ED was born on 16 April 1914 in Milledgeville, Georgia. He married **Reen Gordon.**

97.   iii. BELMOND was born in September 1919 in Milledgeville, Georgia.

38. SIDNEY^3 WILLIAMS (*Nancy^2 Boyer, Porter^1*) was born in Milledgeville, Georgia. He married **Anna Lou Hill.**

Children of **Sidney^3 Williams** and **Anna Lou Hill** were as follows:

\+ 98.   i. O' NEAL^4, born in Milledgeville, Georgia; married **Joel Shaw Jr.**

\+ 99.   ii. VIOLA, born in Milledgeville, Georgia.

\+ 100.   iii. CECILIA, born in Milledgeville, Georgia; married **Clawson Jones.**

\+ 101.   iv. EDSEL, born in Milledgeville, Georgia; married **Mildred** (—?—).

\+ 102.   v. SIDNEY JR., born 19 December 1916; married **Magdalene Cawthon.**

\+ 103.   vi. PERRY ALFRED, born 13 November 1919 in Milledgeville, Georgia; married **Gertrude Shaw.**

\+ 104.   vii. DOROTHY, born 12 October 1932 in Milledgeville, Georgia; married **Curtis Reynolds Stewart.**

39. ED 'JUNE'^{3} WILLIAMS JR. (*Nancy^2 Boyer, Porter^1*) was born in Milledgeville, Georgia. He married **Catherine** (—?—).

Children of **Ed 'June'^{3} Williams Jr.** and **Catherine** (—?—) were:

\+ 105.   i. GERALDINE^4

41. LEE³ WILLIAMS (*Nancy²Boyer, Porter¹*) was born on 11 March in Milledgeville, Georgia. He married **Mae Will Rogers**, daughter of **Randall Rogers** and **Dovie Cheeves.**

Children of **Lee³ Williams** and **Mae Will Rogers** were as follows:

106.   i. ROBERT⁴ was born on 12 November 1919 in Milledgeville, Georgia. He died in July 1955 in Milledgeville, Georgia, at age 35.

107.   ii. LEE ARTHUR was born on 18 April 1920 in Milledgeville, Georgia. He died in October 1985 in Detroit, Michigan, at age 65.

+ 108.   iii. MAE WILL, born 11 September 1922 in Milledgeville, Georgia; married **Johnnie Dark Renfroe.**

109.   iv. RANDALL was born on 5 February 1924 in Milledgeville, Georgia.

+ 110.   v. RUFUS, born 19 March 1925 in Milledgeville, Georgia; married **Francis Andrews.**

111.   vi. BLANCHE was born on 11 October 1927 in Milledgeville, Georgia.

112.   vii. DEVOLIA was born on 25 June 1928 in Milledgeville, Georgia.

113.   viii. ROHDELL was born on 5 February 1929 in Milledgeville, Georgia.

114.   ix. GLADYS was born on 4 August 1931 in Milledgeville, Georgia.

42. FANNIE MAE³ WILLIAMS (*Nancy²Boyer, Porter¹*) was born on 19 April in Milledgeville, Georgia. She married **Addison Wiggins.** She died on 1 April 1991 in Philadelphia, Pennsylvania.

Children of **Fannie Mae³ Williams** and **Addison Wiggins** were as follows:

115.   i. EDWARD STANLEY⁴ was born on 16 May 1946 in Philadelphia, Pennsylvania. He married **Shirley (—?—).**

+ 116.   ii. VALERIE ANN, born 16 April 1951 in Philadelphia, Pennsylvania; married **Kenneth C. Vanish.**

43. JOHNNIE³ WILLIAMS (*Nancy²Boyer, Porter¹*) was born on 16 December 1892 in Milledgeville, Georgia. He married **Fannie Kitchens** in Milledgeville, Georgia. He died on 14 August 1978 in Milledgeville, Georgia, at age 85.

Children of **Johnnie³ Williams** and **Fannie Kitchens** were as follows:

+ 117.   i. LUCY JANE⁴, born 9 February 1909 in Milledgeville, Georgia; married **John Clifford Arnold.**

118.   ii. EDDIE 'POOKUS' was born on 3 January 1910 in Milledgeville, Georgia. He died on 22 August 1992 in Milledgeville, Georgia, at age 82.

+ 119.   iii. COLEMAN, born 4 September 1911 in Milledgeville, Georgia; married **Florence Rogers.**

+ 120.   iv. JOHN HENRY, born 30 January 1914 in Milledgeville, Georgia.

+ 121.   v. VIOLA, born 10 March 1918 in Milledgeville, Georgia; married **John Temple.**

+ 122.   vi. MAMIE, born 11 February 1920 in Milledgeville, Georgia; married **Nemiah Hooks.**

+ 123. vii. LOUISE, born 16 July 1921 in Milledgeville, Georgia; married **James William Napier.**
+ 124. viii. FANNIE PEARL, born 23 November 1924 in Milledgeville, Georgia; married **Edward Allen.**
+ 125. ix. JOHNEVA, born 3 May 1926 in Milledgeville, Georgia; married **Eulysses Hitchcock;** married **Sam Hollingshed.**
+ 126. x. WILLIE, born 13 May 1927 in Milledgeville, Georgia; married **Minnie Kay Simmons.**
+ 127. xi. DAVID, born 27 October 1928 in Milledgeville, Georgia.
+ 128. xii. CLARA, born 20 May 1930 in Milledgeville, Georgia; married **Keptler 'Kep' Miller.**
+ 129. xiii. CATHERINE, born 23 October 1936 in Milledgeville, Georgia; married **Winston Travis.**

44. MELISSA^3 **WILLIAMS** (*Nancy*^{2}*Boyer, Porter*^{1}) was born in Milledgeville, Georgia. She was born in 1900 in Baldwin County, Georgia. She married **Tom Trawick,** son of **Dock Trawick** and **Violet Young,** in Georgia. She died on 15 December 1930 in Milledgeville, Baldwin County, Georgia.

Children of **Melissa**^{3} **Williams** and **Tom Trawick** were as follows:
+ 130. i. VERNON 'BUD'^{4}, born 29 September 1926 in Philadelphia, Pennsylvania; married **Mary Pearl 'Town' Gordy Cheeves.**
  131. ii. ORIAN.
+ 132. iii. NANCY
+ 133. iv. VIVIAN 'TUET', born 29 September 1926 in Philadelphia, Pennsylvania.
  134. v. LENWOOD.
+ 135. vi. THOMAS
  136. vii. SAMUEL.
  137. viii. DOCK.

45. ROBERT^3 **WILLIAMS SR.** (*Nancy*^{2}*Boyer, Porter*^{1}) was born on 6 September 1900 in Milledgeville, Georgia. He married **Eula Riddenberry.** He died on 29 July 1992 in Detroit, Michigan, at age 91.

Children of **Robert**^{3} **Williams Sr.** and **Eula Riddenberry** were as follows:
+ 138. i. VERA^4, born 19 August in Detroit, Michigan; married **James Brown.**
+ 139. ii. INEZ, born 17 April 1920 in Milledgeville, Georgia.
+ 140. iii. OTIS, born 25 August 1925; married **Thelma Davis.**
+ 141. iv. FRANK, born 12 May 1927 in Detroit, Michigan.
+ 142. v. ROBERTA, born 4 October 1933 in Detroit, Michigan; married **Al Smith.**
+ 143. vi. JOHN, born 1 January 1937 in Detroit, Michigan; married **Leona** (—?—).
+ 144. vii. RUDOLPH MORRIS 'RUDY', born 7 December 1939 in Detroit, Michigan; married **Janette** (—?—).

+ 145. viii. GLORIA DIANE, born 16 July 1944 in Detroit, Michigan; married **Charles North.**
+ 146. ix. ELAINE, born 28 September 1946 in Detroit, Michigan; married **Franklin Elzie 'Frank' Harris.**
  147. x. ROBERT JR..

46. MARY 'MAE' ELLA^3 WILLIAMS (*Nancy^{2}Boyer, Porter^1*) was born on 20 July 1912 in Milledgeville, Georgia. She married **Arthur Liggins.**

Children of **Mary 'Mae' Ella^3 Williams** and **Arthur Liggins** were:
+ 148. i. WILLIE MAE 'BELL'^{4}, born 30 October 1927 in Milledgeville, Georgia.

47. MINNIE^3 WILLIAMS (*Nancy^{2}Boyer, Porter^1*) was born on 19 January 1917 in Milledgeville, Georgia. She married **Willie Napier,** son of **Mr. Napier,** on 31 December 1933 in Milledgeville, Georgia. She died on 16 May 2003 in Los Angeles, California.

Children of **Minnie^3 Williams** and **Willie Napier** were as follows:
+ 149. i. NANCY^4, born 22 December 1935 in Detroit, Michigan; married **William Smith.**
+ 150. ii. WILLIAM EDWARD, born 30 September 1937 in Detroit, Michigan.
+ 151. iii. CATHERINE, born 5 October 1939 in Detroit, Michigan; married **William Burch.**
  152. iv. JERRY was born on 21 August 1941 in Detroit, Michigan.

69. GEORGIANNA^3 BOYER (*Bennie^2, Porter^1*) was born on 24 July 1918 in Sandersville, Georgia. She married **Mr. Hall.**

Children of **Georgianna^3 Boyer** and **Mr. Hall** were as follows:
+ 153. i. BRUCE LAMAR^4, born 26 May 1948 in Michigan; married **Sharon Diane LeGrand.**
  154. ii. BENNIE JAVON 'STARCHIE' was born on 10 June 1950.
  155. iii. GEORGIANNA MARIE 'JUDY' was born on 1 June 1952.
+ 156. iv. JOYCE ANITA, born 29 January 1956 in Michigan; married **Gregory Edward Wright.**
  157. v. PATRICIA LYNN 'GIGI' was born on 20 March 1958 in Michigan. She married **Lonnie Simpson.**

71. ELIZA 'TRIXIE'^{3} BOYER (*Bennie^2, Porter^1*) was born on 8 February 1922 in Milledgeville, Georgia. She married **Virgil Columbus Smith,** son of **David Columbus Smith** and **Georgia Bernice Clark,** on 6 March 1941 in Toledo, Ohio.

Children of **Eliza 'Trixie'**^{3} **Boyer** and **Virgil Columbus Smith** were as follows:

+ 158.   i.**BEVERLY JEAN**^{4}, born 3 August 1943 in Detroit, Michigan; married **Louis James Clark.**

159.   ii.**LAVERNE MARIE** was born on 8 October 1944 in Detroit, Michigan.

160.   iii.**VIRGIL** was born on 4 July 1947 in Detroit, Michigan.

83. ALFRED^3 **BOYER** (*Sam 'Sammie'*^{2}, *Porter*^{1}) was born on 24 May 1930 in Detroit, Michigan. He married **Celestine Ramirez** on 14 February 1953 in Philippines.

Children of **Alfred**^{3} **Boyer** and **Celestine Ramirez** were as follows:

+ 161.   i.**MARILYN CRISTINA**^{4}, born 10 January 1959 in Angeles Pam Panga, Philippines; married **Gregory Martin Clardy Jr.**

162.   ii.**ALFRED JR.** was born on 26 April 1962 in Wright Patterson, Ohio.

+ 163.   iii.**CATHERINE 'KATE'**, born 12 March 1964 in Wright Patterson, Ohio; married **Eric Eugene Wetzstein.**

164.   iv.**CHRISTINE 'CUWI'** was born on 23 March 1968 in Angeles Pam Panga, Philippines.

165.   v.**ROBERT CHRISTOPHER 'BOO'** was born on 19 January 1972 in Lancaster, California.

86. LILLIAN^3 **BOYER** (*Sam 'Sammie'*^{2}, *Porter*^{1}) was born on 23 September 1936 in Detroit, Michigan. She married **Jesse Coulter.**

Children of **Lillian**^{3} **Boyer** and **Jesse Coulter** were as follows:

166.   i.**LISA KAY**^{4} was born on 3 March 1959 in Detroit, Michigan.

+ 167.   ii.**KELLY JOE**, born April 1960 in Detroit, Michigan; married **Craig Coleman.**

87. EDWARD JAY^3 **BOYER** (*Sam 'Sammie'*^{2}, *Porter*^{1}) was born on 2 February 1939 in Detroit, Michigan. He married **Jill Witherspoon** on 13 May 1970 in Detroit, Michigan.

Children of **Edward Jay**^{3} **Boyer** and **Jill Witherspoon** were:

168.   i.**LILIANA MALAIKA**^{4} was born on 30 May 1975 in Southfield, Michigan.

Generation Four

90. THELMA^4 **BOYER** (*William Porter*^{3}, *Marshall*^{2}, *Porter*^{1}) was born on 12 May 1926 in Detroit, Michigan. She married **Frank Ferguson** in March 1948 in Wilmington, Delaware.

Children of **Thelma**^{4} **Boyer** and **Frank Ferguson** were:

+ 169.   i.**THEODORE 'TEDDY'**^{5}, born 6 January 1952 in Philadelphia, Pennsylvania.

92. MARSHALL 'BEAU' DESHAUN^4 BOYER (*William Porter^3, Marshall^2, Porter^1*) was born on 20 December 1930 in Detroit, Michigan. He married **Agnes** (—?—). He died on 13 January 1995 in Rancocus, New Jersey, at age 64.

Children of **Marshall 'Beau' Deshaun^4 Boyer** and **Agnes** (—?—) were as follows:
170. i. ANNIE^5.
171. ii. CODY.

93. WILLIAM 'TYRONE'^{4} BOYER (*Marshall 'Nay^3, Marshall^2, Porter^1*) was born on 9 January 1944 in Detroit, Michigan. He married **Dagmar Kanitz** on 16 July 1988 in Detroit, Michigan.

Children of **William 'Tyrone'^{4} Boyer** and **Dagmar Kanitz** were as follows:
172. i. ARMAND^5 was born on 10 April 1989 in Detroit, Michigan.
173. ii. ETIENNE was born on 18 February 1991 in Detroit, Michigan.
174. iii. ANN KATRINE was born on 30 May 1993 in Detroit, Michigan.
175. iv. SABASTIAN was born on 17 October 1994 in Detroit, Michigan.

94. VEDA AUDRA DEAN^4 BOYER (*Marshall 'Nay^3, Marshall^2, Porter^1*) was born on 29 December 1952 in Detroit, Michigan. She married **Edmond Bryant** on 25 March 1989 in Detroit, Michigan.

Children of **Veda Audra Dean^4 Boyer** include:
176. i. GERALD DUANE^5 was born on 23 December 1973 in Detroit, Michigan.

There were no children of **Veda Audra Dean^4 Boyer** and **Edmond Bryant**.

98. O' NEAL^4 WILLIAMS (*Sidney^3, Nancy^{2}Boyer, Porter^1*) was born in Milledgeville, Georgia. She married **Joel Shaw Jr.**, son of **Joel Shaw**.

Children of **O' Neal^4 Williams** and **Joel Shaw Jr.** were as follows:
177. i. THOMAS^5.
178. ii. CHERYL.
179. iii. AMOS.
180. iv. ARNOLD.
181. v. PATRICIA 'PATTY'.

99. VIOLA^4 WILLIAMS (*Sidney^3, Nancy^{2}Boyer, Porter^1*) was born in Milledgeville, Georgia.

Children of **Viola^4 Williams** include:
182. i. ALTHEA^5.

183.   ii. EARL.

100. CECILIA^4 WILLIAMS (*Sidney^3, Nancy^{2}Boyer, Porter^1*) was born in Milledgeville, Georgia. She married **Clawson Jones.**

Children of **Cecilia^4 Williams** and **Clawson Jones** were as follows:
184.   i. CLAWSON^5 JR.
185.   ii. WILLIAM ANTHONY.

101. EDSEL^4 WILLIAMS (*Sidney^3, Nancy^{2}Boyer, Porter^1*) was born in Milledgeville, Georgia. He married **Mildred** (—?—).

Children of **Edsel^4 Williams** and **Mildred** (—?—) were as follows:
186.   i. EDSEL^5 JR..
187.   ii. LAVINIA.
188.   iii. DEBORAH.

102. SIDNEY^4 WILLIAMS JR. (*Sidney^3, Nancy^{2}Boyer, Porter^1*) was born on 19 December 1916. He married **Magdalene Cawthon.** He died on 18 February 1973 at age 56.

Children of **Sidney^4 Williams Jr.** and **Magdalene Cawthon** were as follows:
+ 189.   i. JEWEL MARLENE^5, born 12 January; married **Joseph Ferrell Dillard.**
+ 190.   ii. KENNETH 'KENNY' ELTON, born 22 January; married **Gwendolyn** (—?—).
+ 191.   iii. CALVIN EVEREST, born 25 January; married **Michelle** (—?—).
+ 192.   iv. RILEY CORNELIUS, born 14 September; married **Antoneet Moon.**
+ 193.   v. GERALD IRVIN, born 21 December; married **Serderia Jean Butler.**
+ 194.   vi. ROBERT MARVIN, born 1 July 1938; married **Floretta Davis.**
195.   vii. SIDNEY LESTER was born on 29 July 1940.

103. PERRY ALFRED^4 WILLIAMS (*Sidney^3, Nancy^{2}Boyer, Porter^1*) was born on 13 November 1919 in Milledgeville, Georgia. He married **Gertrude Shaw,** daughter of **Joel Shaw,** on 15 November 1937. He died on 18 February 1976 in Detroit, Michigan, at age 56.

Children of **Perry Alfred^4 Williams** and **Gertrude Shaw** were as follows:
+ 196.   i. VIVIAN LUCILLE^5, born 15 September 1938 in Detroit, Michigan; married **Calvin Murphy McDuffie Jr.**
197.   ii. PERRY ALFRED JR. was born on 7 February 1940 in Detroit, Michigan. He married **Easter Williams** on 3 September 1960 in Detroit, Michigan.
+ 198.   iii. BARBARA JEAN, born 4 October 1942 in Detroit, Michigan; married **Theotus Melvin Nunlee Jr.**

+ 199.   iv. DONALD LEYONDER, born 27 April 1943 in Detroit, Michigan; married
Sharon Yvonne Williams.

104. DOROTHY[4] WILLIAMS (*Sidney*[3], *Nancy*[2]*Boyer, Porter*[1]) was born on 12 October
1932 in Milledgeville, Georgia. She married **Curtis Reynolds Stewart** on 12
September 1948.

Children of **Dorothy**[4] **Williams** include:
200.   i. CHRISTINE 'CHRIS'[5] was born on 14 January 1947.
201.   ii. REGINA ANNIE was born on 31 March 1951. She married **John Alvin Hall** on
16 May 1981.
+ 202.   iii. CECILIA 'CIL' LAVERN, born 1 March 1952.

Children of **Dorothy**[4] **Williams** and **Curtis Reynolds Stewart** were as follows:
+ 203.   i. LINDA JOYCE[5], born 30 January 1950; married **Johnny B. Burge**.
204.   ii. MONTY.
205.   iii. CURTIS LAMONT was born on 26 April 1953.
+ 206.   iv. VALERIE ZACTORIA, born 20 June 1954; married (—?—) **Dickerson**.
+ 207.   v. BRENDA DIANE, born 5 August 1955; married **Jessie James Johnson Jr.**
208.   vi. EMMITT REGINALD was born on 12 October 1956.
209.   vii. KAREN BETH was born on 31 May 1958.
+ 210.   viii. CLIFTON ODAL, born 6 April 1961; married **Anita Dyer**.
+ 211.   ix. IRIS YVETTE, born 17 January 1962.
+ 212.   x. SYDNEY, born 5 November 1964; married **Lori** (—?—).

105. GERALDINE[4] WILLIAMS (*Ed 'June*[3], *Nancy*[2]*Boyer, Porter*[1]).

Children of **Geraldine**[4] **Williams** include:
213.   i. VANESSA[5].
214.   ii. TONY.

108. MAE WILL[4] WILLIAMS (*Lee*[3], *Nancy*[2]*Boyer, Porter*[1]) was born on 11 September 1922
in Milledgeville, Georgia. She married **Johnnie Dark Renfroe**, son of **Oscar
Renfroe** and **Laura Trawick**, on 31 December 1943 in Philadelphia, Pennsylvania.

Children of **Mae Will**[4] **Williams** and **Johnnie Dark Renfroe** were as follows:
+ 215.   i. CAROLINE[5], born 7 July 1943 in Detroit, Michigan; married **William Johnson**.
216.   ii. JOHNNIE DARK JR. was born on 31 January 1945 in Detroit, Michigan.
+ 217.   iii. PEGGY, born 4 November 1946 in Detroit, Michigan; married **Bobby Walton**.
+ 218.   iv. HAROLD, born 28 August 1947 in Detroit, Michigan; married **Catherine Lynch**.
219.   v. OSCAR LEE was born on 11 September 1966 in Detroit, Michigan.

110. RUFUS^4 WILLIAMS (*Lee^3*, *Nancy^{2}Boyer*, *Porter^1*) was born on 19 March 1925 in Milledgeville, Georgia. He married **Francis Andrews.** He died in August 1995 in Detroit, Michigan, at age 70.

Children of **Rufus^4 Williams** and **Francis Andrews** were:
   220.   i. RALPH^5.

116. VALERIE ANN^4 WIGGINS (*Fannie Mae^{3}Williams*, *Nancy^{2}Boyer*, *Porter^1*) was born on 16 April 1951 in Philadelphia, Pennsylvania. She married **Kenneth C. Vanish** on 2 July 1972 in Philadelphia, Pennsylvania.

Children of **Valerie Ann^4 Wiggins** and **Kenneth C. Vanish** were as follows:
   221.   i. JACOB 'JAY' CHARLES^5 was born on 17 October 1979 in Philadelphia, Pennsylvania.
   222.   ii. RICHARD ADDISON was born on 8 November 1985 in Philadelphia, Pennsylvania.

117. LUCY JANE^4 WILLIAMS (*Johnnie^3*, *Nancy^{2}Boyer*, *Porter^1*) was born on 9 February 1909 in Milledgeville, Georgia. She married **John Clifford Arnold.**

Children of **Lucy Jane^4 Williams** and **John Clifford Arnold** were as follows:
   223.   i. OTHON^5 was born on 11 February in Newark, New Jersey. She married **Kirk Allen.**
 + 224.   ii. CLAUDIA, born 10 March.
   225.   iii. FREDDIE BRUCE was born on 26 June in Newark, New Jersey. He married **Serene Green.**
   226.   iv. MARY ANNE was born on 1 September.
 + 227.   v. JOHN CLIFFORD 'JC' JR., born 10 October; married **Joan** (—?—).
 + 228.   vi. ERNESTINE, born 28 August 1941 in Newark, New Jersey; married **Algernon Davis;** married **Donald White.**

119. COLEMAN^4 WILLIAMS (*Johnnie^3*, *Nancy^{2}Boyer*, *Porter^1*) was born on 4 September 1911 in Milledgeville, Georgia. He married **Florence Rogers,** daughter of **Thomas Rogers** and **Murial** (—?—), in Milledgeville, Georgia.

Children of **Coleman^4 Williams** and **Florence Rogers** were as follows:
 + 229.   i. MAUDE LIZABETH^5, born 6 April 1934 in Milledgeville, Georgia; married **Harry David Michael Jackson.**
 + 230.   ii. MILDRED, born 31 August 1935 in Milledgeville, Georgia; married **John Arthur Cox Jr.**
   231.   iii. BERNICE was born in May 1938 in Milledgeville, Georgia. She died in June 1942 in Philadelphia, Pennsylvania, at age 4.

+ 232. iv. FANNIE PEARL, born 10 December 1939 in Milledgeville, Georgia; married Willie Howard Glover; married Horace Cheeves.

+ 233. v. CHARLES, born 3 December 1941 in Philadelphia, Pennsylvania; married Dahlia Beatrice Scott.

234. vi. COLEMAN 'JUNIE' JR. was born on 30 April 1943 in Philadelphia, Pennsylvania. He died on 27 April 1975 in Philadelphia, Pennsylvania, at age 31.

+ 235. vii. JANET, born 28 August 1944 in Philadelphia, Pennsylvania; married Richard Bland Jasper.

+ 236. viii. ROGER, born 25 April 1946 in Philadelphia, Pennsylvania; married Cynthia Simmons.

+ 237. ix. JOYCE CHERYL, born 22 December 1948 in Philadelphia, Pennsylvania.

+ 238. x. DONALD 'HOPE', born 28 August 1950 in Philadelphia, Pennsylvania.

+ 239. xi. ALAN, born 1 May 1955 in Philadelphia, Pennsylvania; married Kim Louise Sorapuru.

+ 240. xii. TIMOTHY, born 27 June 1958 in Philadelphia, Pennsylvania; married Andrea Johnson.

120. JOHN HENRY^4 WILLIAMS (*Johnnie^3, Nancy^{2}Boyer, Porter^1*) was born on 30 January 1914 in Milledgeville, Georgia. He died on 21 February 1992 in Philadelphia, Pennsylvania, at age 78.

Children of John Henry^4 Williams include:
241. i. DIANE^5.
242. ii. JOHN HENRY JR..

121. VIOLA^4 WILLIAMS (*Johnnie^3, Nancy^{2}Boyer, Porter^1*) was born on 10 March 1918 in Milledgeville, Georgia. She married John Temple on 9 February 1936 in Milledgeville, Georgia. She died on 10 July 2002 in Detroit, Michigan, at age 84.

Children of Viola^4 Williams and John Temple were as follows:
+ 243. i. ELLA MAE^5, born 13 March 1937 in Atlanta, Georgia; married Samuel Clark.

+ 244. ii. EDDIE HENRY, born 19 July 1938 in Atlanta, Georgia; married Pearl Louise Anderson.

+ 245. iii. EVA MAE, born 16 June 1940 in Atlanta, Georgia; married Agustus Davis.

+ 246. iv. SHERRY, born 7 October 1944 in Detroit, Michigan; married Earl Johnson.

+ 247. v. HAROLD, born 30 April 1948 in Detroit, Michigan.

+ 248. vi. HERBERT, born 30 April 1948 in Detroit, Michigan; married Sylvia (—?—).

249. vii. FRED was born on 2 March 1949 in Detroit, Michigan. He died on 26 July 1967 in Detroit, Michigan, at age 18.

122. MAMIE^4 WILLIAMS (*Johnnie^3, Nancy^2 Boyer, Porter^1*) was born on 11 February 1920 in Milledgeville, Georgia. She married **Nemiah Hooks.** She died on 18 July 1997 in Detroit, Michigan, at age 77.

Children of **Mamie^4 Williams** and **Nemiah Hooks** were as follows:

+ 250. i. NEMIAH 'SONNY'^{5} JR., born 8 March 1940 in Milledgeville, Georgia; married **Linda Dennis.**
  251. ii. LARRY DARNELL was born on 6 November 1941 in Milledgeville, Georgia.
+ 252. iii. VERONICA 'RONNIE', born 19 February 1943 in Detroit, Michigan; married **Lowell Massey Jr.**
+ 253. iv. MAMIE SHARON, born 4 October 1944 in Detroit, Michigan; married **Lester Marvin Dennis.**
  254. v. SYLVIA was born on 23 August 1946 in Detroit, Michigan.
+ 255. vi. MARSHALL DENNIS, born 13 December 1947 in Detroit, Michigan.
  256. vii. VAN WILLIAM was born on 2 November 1949 in Detroit, Michigan.
  257. viii. GAIL PATRICIA was born in May 1952 in Detroit, Michigan. She died in 1957 in Detroit, Michigan.
+ 258. ix. DONNA MARIE, born 11 November 1954 in Detroit, Michigan; married **Smart Onuigbo.**

123. LOUISE^4 WILLIAMS (*Johnnie^3, Nancy^2 Boyer, Porter^1*) was born on 16 July 1921 in Milledgeville, Georgia. She married **James William Napier,** son of **Mr. Napier,** on 25 October 1941 in Detroit, Michigan.

Children of **Louise^4 Williams** and **James William Napier** were as follows:

  259. i. BEATRICE JEAN^5 was born on 1 February 1943 in Detroit, Michigan. She died on 1 July 1961 in Detroit, Michigan, at age 18.
+ 260. ii. JAMES 'JABO' WILLIAM JR., born 22 September 1945 in Detroit, Michigan.
+ 261. iii. PHYLLIS, born 13 January 1946 in Detroit, Michigan; married **Albert Green.**
+ 262. iv. GARY, born 6 March 1947 in Detroit, Michigan; married **Shirley Gumby;** married **Deborah Fisher.**
+ 263. v. JOYCE 'PERK', born 3 January 1950 in Detroit, Michigan; married **Kenneth Johnson.**

124. FANNIE PEARL^4 WILLIAMS (*Johnnie^3, Nancy^2 Boyer, Porter^1*) was born on 23 November 1924 in Milledgeville, Georgia. She married **Edward Allen** in Detroit, Michigan.

Children of **Fannie Pearl^4 Williams** and **Edward Allen** were as follows:

+ 264. i. LLOYD^5, born 21 April in Detroit, Michigan; married **Patricia Hatwood.**
+ 265. ii. KENNETH 'KENNY', born 30 May in Detroit, Michigan.
+ 266. iii. MORRIS, born 21 June in Detroit, Michigan; married **Joyce** (—?—).

+ 267.   iv. JOHN 'JOHNNY' RAY, born 15 September in Detroit, Michigan; married
         Lajanda Ford.
+ 268.   v. DONALD, born 23 June 1957 in Detroit, Michigan; married Robin (—?—);
         married Carol (—?—).
+ 269.   vi. ERIC, born 15 March 1959 in Detroit, Michigan; married Kim (—?—);
         married Deborah (—?—).

125. JOHNEVA[4] WILLIAMS (*Johnnie[3]*, *Nancy[2]Boyer*, *Porter[1]*) was born on 3 May 1926
in Milledgeville, Georgia. She married Eulysses Hitchcock. She married Sam
Hollingshed.

Children of Johneva[4] Williams and Eulysses Hitchcock were as follows:
270.   i. EARL[5].
271.   ii. EULYSSES 'SPODY' JR..

Children of Johneva[4] Williams and Sam Hollingshed were as follows:
272.   i. DEBORAH[5].
273.   ii. SHEILA.
274.   iii. SAM JR..

126. WILLIE[4] WILLIAMS (*Johnnie[3]*, *Nancy[2]Boyer*, *Porter[1]*) was born on 13 May 1927 in
Milledgeville, Georgia. He married Minnie Kay Simmons on 2 September 1950
in Detroit, Michigan. He died on 7 March 1995 in Detroit, Michigan, at age 67.

Children of Willie[4] Williams and Louise Clark were:
+ 275.   i. FREDDIE[5], born 19 January 1947 in Milledgeville, Georgia; married Sheila
          Yarborough.

Children of Willie[4] Williams and Minnie Kay Simmons were as follows:
+ 276.   i. MARION GAY[5], born 21 May 1951 in Detroit, Michigan.
277.   ii. BERNARD was born on 16 August 1952 in Detroit, Michigan.
+ 278.   iii. ANNE ADELE, born 13 November 1956 in Detroit, Michigan; married James
          Stubbs.
279.   iv. FREDDIE CLARK.

127. DAVID[4] WILLIAMS (*Johnnie[3]*, *Nancy[2]Boyer*, *Porter[1]*) was born on 27 October 1928
in Milledgeville, Georgia. He died in April 1971 in Detroit, Michigan, at age 42.

Children of David[4] Williams and Sally Mason were:
+ 280.   i. NANCY[5], born 22 August 1949 in Milledgeville, Georgia; married Willie
          Williams.

Children of **David**^{4} **Williams** and **Carrie Butts** were:
281.   i. DIANA^5 was born on 18 September 1949 in Milledgeville, Georgia. She married **Wilburt John Williams** on 15 July 1978 in Detroit, Michigan.

128. CLARA^4 **WILLIAMS** (*Johnnie*^{3}, *Nancy*^{2}*Boyer*, *Porter*^{1}) was born on 20 May 1930 in Milledgeville, Georgia. She married **Keptler 'Kep' Miller** on 17 December 1948 in Detroit, Michigan.

Children of **Clara**^{4} **Williams** and **Keptler 'Kep' Miller** were as follows:
282.   i. CORLISS LAVERNE^5 was born on 30 November 1949 in Detroit, Michigan. She married **Robert 'Bob' Pickron** in June 1986 in Detroit, Michigan.
+ 283.   ii. BRENDA SUSAN, born 26 April 1951 in Detroit, Michigan; married **Howard William McElrath II.**
+ 284.   iii. DWIGHT KEPTLER, born 17 September 1952 in Detroit, Michigan; married **JoAnn Whitley.**
+ 285.   iv. ROSALYN, born 14 June 1954 in Detroit, Michigan; married **Mark Bennett.**

129. CATHERINE^4 **WILLIAMS** (*Johnnie*^{3}, *Nancy*^{2}*Boyer*, *Porter*^{1}) was born on 23 October 1936 in Milledgeville, Georgia. She married **Winston Travis.**

Children of **Catherine**^{4} **Williams** and **Winston Travis** were as follows:
286.   i. KEITH ALEXANDER^5 was born on 5 July 1958 in Detroit, Michigan.
287.   ii. BARRY PIERRE was born on 1 September 1961 in Detroit, Michigan.

130. VERNON 'BUD'^{4} **TRAWICK** (*Melissa*^{3}*Williams*, *Nancy*^{2}*Boyer*, *Porter*^{1}) was born on 29 September 1926 in Philadelphia, Pennsylvania. He married **Mary Pearl 'Town' Gordy Cheeves,** daughter of **Samuel 'Sam' Gordy Jr.** and **Sarah Ella 'SC' Hopkins,** on 19 November 1948 in Sandersville, Georgia. He died on 26 March 2001 in Philadelphia, Pennsylvania, at age 74.

Children of **Vernon 'Bud'**^{4} **Trawick** and **Mary Pearl 'Town' Gordy Cheeves** were as follows:
288.   i. VERNON^5 JR. was born on 10 April 1950 in Sandersville, Georgia.
+ 289.   ii. BERNARD, born 14 December 1951 in Philadelphia, Pennsylvania; married **Kenya Wilson.**
290.   iii. MARVIN was born on 6 November 1954 in Philadelphia, Pennsylvania.
291.   iv. VERONICA was born on 17 February 1957 in Philadelphia, Pennsylvania.
+ 292.   v. CYNTHIA, born 12 November 1958 in Philadelphia, Pennsylvania; married **William Boyer.**

132. NANCY^4 **TRAWICK** (*Melissa*^{3}*Williams*, *Nancy*^{2}*Boyer*, *Porter*^{1}).

Children of **Nancy**[4] **Trawick** include:
+ 293.   i. RHONDA[5]

133. **VIVIAN 'TUET'**[4] **TRAWICK** (*Melissa*[3] *Williams, Nancy*[2] *Boyer, Porter*[1]) was born on
29 September 1926 in Philadelphia, Pennsylvania.

Children of **Vivian 'Tuet'**[4] **Trawick** include:
294.   i. VIVIAN[5].
295.   ii. GREGORY.
296.   iii. ANTHONY.
297.   iv. GAIL.
298.   v. GERALDINE.
299.   vi. NANCY.

135. **THOMAS**[4] **TRAWICK** (*Melissa*[3] *Williams, Nancy*[2] *Boyer, Porter*[1]).

Children of **Thomas**[4] **Trawick** include:
300.   i. RALPH[5].

138. **VERA**[4] **WILLIAMS** (*Robert*[3], *Nancy*[2] *Boyer, Porter*[1]) was born on 19 August in
Detroit, Michigan. She married **James Brown.**

Children of **Vera**[4] **Williams** and **James Brown** were as follows:
301.   i. JANICE[5].
302.   ii. REBECCA.
303.   iii. KEITH.
+ 304.   iv. KEVIN

139. **INEZ**[4] **WILLIAMS** (*Robert*[3], *Nancy*[2] *Boyer, Porter*[1]) was born on 17 April 1920 in
Milledgeville, Georgia.

Children of **Inez**[4] **Williams** include:
+ 305.   i. PHYLLIS ALLEN[5], born 9 November 1946; married **William Edward Banks.**

140. **OTIS**[4] **WILLIAMS** (*Robert*[3], *Nancy*[2] *Boyer, Porter*[1]) was born on 25 August 1925. He
married **Thelma Davis.** He died on 3 March 2003 in Detroit, Michigan, at age 77.

Children of **Otis**[4] **Williams** and **Thelma Davis** were as follows:
306.   i. LINDA[5].
307.   ii. CARL.
308.   iii. MICHELLE.
309.   iv. MARK.

141. FRANK⁴ WILLIAMS (*Robert³, Nancy²Boyer, Porter¹*) was born on 12 May 1927 in Detroit, Michigan. He died on 4 March 1996 in Detroit, Michigan, at age 68.

Children of **Frank⁴ Williams** include:
310.   i. SONYA⁵.
311.   ii. FELICIA.
312.   iii. DAVID.
313.   iv. CRAIG.

142. ROBERTA⁴ WILLIAMS (*Robert³, Nancy²Boyer, Porter¹*) was born on 4 October 1933 in Detroit, Michigan. She married **Al Smith**. She died on 22 August 2001 in Detroit, Michigan, at age 67.

Children of **Roberta⁴ Williams** and **Al Smith** were as follows:
314.   i. DARRYL⁵.
315.   ii. GAIL.
316.   iii. MARSHALL.

143. JOHN⁴ WILLIAMS (*Robert³, Nancy²Boyer, Porter¹*) was born on 1 January 1937 in Detroit, Michigan. He married **Leona** (—?—).

Children of **John⁴ Williams** and **Leona** (—?—) were as follows:
317.   i. JOYA⁵.
318.   ii. RON.

144. RUDOLPH MORRIS 'RUDY'⁴ WILLIAMS (*Robert³, Nancy²Boyer, Porter¹*) was born on 7 December 1939 in Detroit, Michigan. He married **Janette** (—?—).

Children of **Rudolph Morris 'Rudy'⁴ Williams** and **Janette** (—?—) were as follows:
319.   i. KEITH⁵.
320.   ii. TONY.

145. GLORIA DIANE⁴ WILLIAMS (*Robert³, Nancy²Boyer, Porter¹*) was born on 16 July 1944 in Detroit, Michigan. She married **Charles North**.

Children of **Gloria Diane⁴ Williams** and **Charles North** were:
321.   i. CHARLES⁵ JR..

146. ELAINE⁴ WILLIAMS (*Robert³, Nancy²Boyer, Porter¹*) was born on 28 September 1946 in Detroit, Michigan. She married **Franklin Elzie 'Frank' Harris**.

Children of **Elaine**[4] **Williams** and **Franklin Elzie 'Frank' Harris** were:

322.   i. LAEKI DYAN[5] was born on 31 March 1974 in Detroit, Michigan.

148. WILLIE MAE 'BELL'[4] **LIGGINS** (*Mary 'Mae' Ella*[3] *Williams, Nancy*[2] *Boyer, Porter*[1]) was born on 30 October 1927 in Milledgeville, Georgia.

Children of **Willie Mae 'Bell'**[4] **Liggins** and **Archie Winston** were:

+ 323.   i. KENNETH[5], born 7 April 1941 in Philadelphia, Pennsylvania; married **Avon Charles.**

149. NANCY[4] **NAPIER** (*Minnie*[3] *Williams, Nancy*[2] *Boyer, Porter*[1]) was born on 22 December 1935 in Detroit, Michigan. She married **William Smith.**

Children of **Nancy**[4] **Napier** and **William Smith** were as follows:

324.   i. CRYSTAL[5] was born on 15 January 1955 in Detroit, Michigan.

+ 325.   ii. ROBIN, born 2 December 1956 in Detroit, Michigan; married **Joseph Beasley.**

326.   iii. CAROL was born on 9 March 1961 in Detroit, Michigan.

+ 327.   iv. KEVIN, born 12 June 1965 in Los Angeles, California; married **Terry (—?—).**

328.   v. LAVERNE was born on 16 April 1968 in Los Angeles, California.

150. WILLIAM EDWARD[4] **NAPIER** (*Minnie*[3] *Williams, Nancy*[2] *Boyer, Porter*[1]) was born on 30 September 1937 in Detroit, Michigan.

Children of **William Edward**[4] **Napier** include:

+ 329.   i. SHARON[5], born 16 December 1960 in Los Angeles, California; married **Harold Johnson.**

+ 330.   ii. JUNIE, born 22 June 1962 in Los Angeles, California; married **Leslie Bowman.**

331.   iii. NANCY was born on 4 June 1963 in Los Angeles, California.

332.   iv. CATHY was born on 25 August 1964 in Los Angeles, California.

333.   v. WILLIAM was born on 13 November 1965 in Los Angeles, California.

334.   vi. VICTORIA was born on 9 August 1970 in Los Angeles, California.

151. CATHERINE[4] **NAPIER** (*Minnie*[3] *Williams, Nancy*[2] *Boyer, Porter*[1]) was born on 5 October 1939 in Detroit, Michigan. She married **William Burch.**

Children of **Catherine**[4] **Napier** and **William Burch** were as follows:

335.   i. DENNIS[5] was born on 27 July 1961.

336.   ii. GLENNIE was born on 5 February 1963.

337.   iii. DIONNE was born on 11 December 1965.

153. BRUCE LAMAR[4] **HALL** (*Georgianna*[3] *Boyer, Bennie*[2], *Porter*[1]) was born on 26 May 1948 in Michigan. He married **Sharon Diane LeGrand.**

Children of **Bruce Lamar**^{4} **Hall** and **Sharon Diane LeGrand** were:
338.   i. JAVON LAMAR^5 was born on 13 January 1969.

156. JOYCE ANITA^4 HALL (*Georgianna*^{3} *Boyer, Bennie*^{2}, *Porter*^{1}) was born on 29 January 1956 in Michigan. She married **Gregory Edward Wright** on 23 July 1982 in Ohio.

Children of **Joyce Anita**^{4} **Hall** and **Gregory Edward Wright** were as follows:
339.   i. GREGORY EDWIN^5 was born on 1 October 1986 in Michigan.
340.   ii. ANTONIO EDWARD was born on 2 September 1988 in Michigan.

158. BEVERLY JEAN^4 SMITH (*Eliza 'Trixie'*^{3} *Boyer, Bennie*^{2}, *Porter*^{1}) was born on 3 August 1943 in Detroit, Michigan. She married **Louis James Clark.**

Children of **Beverly Jean**^{4} **Smith** and **Louis James Clark** were:
341.   i. MARCIA ANN^5 was born on 12 April.

161. MARILYN CRISTINA^4 BOYER (*Alfred*^{3}, *Sam 'Sammie'*^{2}, *Porter*^{1}) was born on 10 January 1959 in Angeles Pam Panga, Philippines. She married **Gregory Martin Clardy Jr.** in May 1977 in Riverside, California.

Children of **Marilyn Cristina**^{4} **Boyer** and **Gregory Martin Clardy Jr.** were as follows:
+ 342.   i. GREGORY MARTIN 'GOOGOO'^{5} III, born 11 May 1977 in Los Angeles, California.
+ 343.   ii. CRISTINA 'KIZZY', born 15 March 1979 in Loma Linda, California.

163. CATHERINE 'KATE'^{4} BOYER (*Alfred*^{3}, *Sam 'Sammie'*^{2}, *Porter*^{1}) was born on 12 March 1964 in Wright Patterson, Ohio. She married **Eric Eugene Wetzstein** on 10 June 1989 in Riverside, California.

Children of **Catherine 'Kate'**^{4} **Boyer** and **Eric Eugene Wetzstein** were as follows:
344.   i. FOREST BOYER^5 was born on 15 August 1994 in San Diego, California.
345.   ii. MALCOLM XAVIER was born on 27 January 1996 in San Diego, California.
346.   iii. DEKKER GIDION was born on 20 October 1998 in San Diego, California.

167. KELLY JOE^4 COULTER (*Lillian*^{3} *Boyer, Sam 'Sammie'*^{2}, *Porter*^{1}) was born in April 1960 in Detroit, Michigan. She married **Craig Coleman.**

Children of **Kelly Joe**^{4} **Coulter** and **Craig Coleman** were as follows:
347.   i. STEVEN^5.
348.   ii. JOHNATHON.
349.   iii. CATHERINE 'KATIE'.

Generation Five

169. THEODORE 'TEDDY'^{5} FERGUSON (*Thelma^{4}Boyer, William Porter^3, Marshall^2, Porter^1*) was born on 6 January 1952 in Philadelphia, Pennsylvania.

Children of **Theodore 'Teddy'^{5} Ferguson** and **Elizabeth Johnson** were:
+ 350.   i. DOUGLAS^6, born 27 March 1969 in Philadelphia, Pennsylvania; married **Sherry** (—?—).

189. JEWEL MARLENE^5 WILLIAMS (*Sidney^4, Sidney^3, Nancy^{2}Boyer, Porter^1*) was born on 12 January. She married **Joseph Ferrell Dillard.**

Children of **Jewel Marlene^5 Williams** and **Joseph Ferrell Dillard** were as follows:
351.   i. BRITTANAY CHERISE^6 was born on 22 March.
352.   ii. TIFFANY JEWEL JOVAN was born on 11 December.

190. KENNETH 'KENNY' ELTON^5 WILLIAMS (*Sidney^4, Sidney^3, Nancy^{2}Boyer, Porter^1*) was born on 22 January. He married **Gwendolyn** (—?—).

Children of **Kenneth 'Kenny' Elton^5 Williams** and **Gwendolyn** (—?—) were as follows:
353.   i. TINA MARZETTE^6 was born on 3 June.
354.   ii. GWENDOLYN MONIQUE was born on 10 June.

191. CALVIN EVEREST^5 WILLIAMS (*Sidney^4, Sidney^3, Nancy^{2}Boyer, Porter^1*) was born on 25 January. He married **Michelle** (—?—).

Children of **Calvin Everest^5 Williams** and **Michelle** (—?—) were as follows:
355.   i. DANA MICHELLE^6 was born on 27 June.
356.   ii. CALVIN ERIC was born on 13 December.

192. RILEY CORNELIUS^5 WILLIAMS (*Sidney^4, Sidney^3, Nancy^{2}Boyer, Porter^1*) was born on 14 September. He married **Antoneet Moon.**

Children of **Riley Cornelius^5 Williams** and **Antoneet Moon** were as follows:
+ 357.   i. MICHAEL DAVID^6, born 13 April 1965; married **Amiesha** (—?—).
+ 358.   ii. ANTHONY JOSEPH, born 16 September 1968.

193. GERALD IRVIN^5 WILLIAMS (*Sidney^4, Sidney^3, Nancy^{2}Boyer, Porter^1*) was born on 21 December. He married **Serderia Jean Butler** on 8 June 1991.

Children of **Gerald Irvin^5 Williams** and **Serderia Jean Butler** were as follows:
359.   i. DANIEL JOHN^6 was born on 21 March 1979.

360.   ii. STAISHA JONAE' was born on 29 January 1993.

194. ROBERT MARVIN^5 WILLIAMS (*Sidney^4, Sidney^3, Nancy^{2}Boyer, Porter^1*) was born on 1 July 1938. He married **Floretta Davis.**

Children of **Robert Marvin^5 Williams** and **Floretta Davis** were:

361.   i. ROBERT JAMES^6 was born on 11 April.

196. VIVIAN LUCILLE^5 WILLIAMS (*Perry Alfred^4, Sidney^3, Nancy^{2}Boyer, Porter^1*) was born on 15 September 1938 in Detroit, Michigan. She married **Calvin Murphy McDuffie Jr.** on 17 August 1963.

Children of **Vivian Lucille^5 Williams** and **Calvin Murphy McDuffie Jr.** were as follows:

362.   i. KELLY MARIA^6 was born on 6 November 1961. She died on 6 November 1961.
+ 363.   ii. KIMBERLY ANN, born 7 August 1962; married **Derrick Christopher Bunch.**
+ 364.   iii. CALVIN MURPHY III, born 24 September 1965 in Detroit, Michigan; married **Sharon 'Sherrie' Cross.**
+ 365.   iv. NIKOL GERTRUDE, born 3 August 1967 in Detroit, Michigan; married **Terrell Constantine Brooks Jr.**
+ 366.   v. TIERA PATRICE, born 31 May 1975 in Detroit, Michigan; married **Clifford Melvin Wilson Jr.**

198. BARBARA JEAN^5 WILLIAMS (*Perry Alfred^4, Sidney^3, Nancy^{2}Boyer, Porter^1*) was born on 4 October 1942 in Detroit, Michigan. She married **Theotus Melvin Nunlee Jr.** on 1 July 1961 in Detroit, Michigan. She died on 24 August 1985 in Detroit, Michigan, at age 42.

Children of **Barbara Jean^5 Williams** and **Theotus Melvin Nunlee Jr.** were as follows:
+ 367.   i. LAJUDE 'JUDY'^{6}, born 13 March 1962 in Detroit, Michigan; married **Orrin Richardo Josey.**
+ 368.   ii. THEOTUS MELVIN III, born 19 April 1963 in Detroit, Michigan; married **Alma Grace Westbrook.**
+ 369.   iii. PERRY ALLEN, born 16 November 1969 in Detroit, Michigan; married **Latina Latrease McCray.**
+ 370.   iv. TERESA DONNA, born 25 October 1970 in Detroit, Michigan; married **Ernest Gass Jr.**
371.   v. TERENCE DONALD was born on 25 October 1970 in Detroit, Michigan. He died in January 1971 in Detroit, Michigan.

199. DONALD LEYONDER^5 WILLIAMS (*Perry Alfred^4, Sidney^3, Nancy^{2}Boyer, Porter^1*) was born on 27 April 1943 in Detroit, Michigan. He married **Sharon Yvonne Williams** on 24 July 1964 in Detroit, Michigan. He died on 5 October 1998 in Detroit, Michigan, at age 55.

Children of **Donald Leyonder^5 Williams** and **Sharon Yvonne Williams** were as follows:

+ 372.   i. DONALD LEYONDER^6 JR., born 9 January 1965 in Detroit, Michigan; married **Geraldine 'Gerry' Maria** (—?—).

+ 373.   ii. DARRYL ALEX, born 27 July 1967 in Detroit, Michigan; married **Kewanna 'Kiki' Wilder.**

+ 374.   iii. QWANA SHANTA 'POOH', born 2 December 1980 in Detroit, Michigan.

202. CECILIA 'CIL' LAVERN^5 STEWART (*Dorothy^{4}Williams, Sidney^3, Nancy^{2}Boyer, Porter^1*) was born on 1 March 1952.

Children of **Cecilia 'Cil' Lavern^5 Stewart** include:

375.   i. THERESA ANN^6 was born on 10 March 1968. She married **Jose Moore** on 6 October 1990.

+ 376.   ii. FELISA IVY, born 6 March 1969; married **Alvin Boyd.**

+ 377.   iii. LINDA BERNADETTE, born 3 September 1970; married **Paul Denardi Johnson.**

+ 378.   iv. RICHARD ODAL, born 7 January 1972; married **Holly Fletcher.**

+ 379.   v. MICHAEL SYDNEY, born 22 February 1973.

203. LINDA JOYCE^5 STEWART (*Dorothy^{4}Williams, Sidney^3, Nancy^{2}Boyer, Porter^1*) was born on 30 January 1950. She married **Johnny B. Burge** on 22 June 1968 in Detroit, Michigan.

Children of **Linda Joyce^5 Stewart** and **Johnny B. Burge** were as follows:

+ 380.   i. JOHNNY B.^{6} JR., born 22 October 1969 in Detroit, Michigan; married **Sharon Jenkins.**

381.   ii. ANTONIO SHONTELL was born on 14 June 1971 in Detroit, Michigan.

382.   iii. LATAUSHA LYNN was born on 7 April 1973 in Detroit, Michigan. She married **Brian Kos** on 15 July 2000.

383.   iv. CHRISTINE was born on 11 October 1975 in Detroit, Michigan.

206. VALERIE ZACTORIA^5 STEWART (*Dorothy^{4}Williams, Sidney^3, Nancy^{2}Boyer, Porter^1*) was born on 20 June 1954. She married (—?—) **Dickerson.**

Children of **Valerie Zactoria^5 Stewart** and (—?—) **Dickerson** were:

+ 384.   i. REGINA^6, born 15 March 1971.

207. BRENDA DIANE^5 STEWART (*Dorothy^4 Williams, Sidney^3, Nancy^2 Boyer, Porter^1*) was born on 5 August 1955. She married **Jessie James Johnson Jr** on 30 July 1976.

Children of **Brenda Diane^5 Stewart** and **Jessie James Johnson Jr** were as follows:
385.   i. DOROTHY ANGELA^6 was born on 15 June 1972.
+ 386.   ii. CHRISTOPHER JAMES, born 29 October 1975; married **Sealicka Brown**.
+ 387.   iii. CASANDRA DIANE, born 30 May 1977.

210. CLIFTON ODAL^5 STEWART (*Dorothy^4 Williams, Sidney^3, Nancy^2 Boyer, Porter^1*) was born on 6 April 1961. He married **Anita Dyer** in August 1986.

Children of **Clifton Odal^5 Stewart** and **Anita Dyer** were as follows:
388.   i. CLIFTON ODAL^6 JR. was born on 3 August 1985.
389.   ii. ANITRA RENEE was born on 17 June 1987.
390.   iii. AYISHIA RESHAWN was born on 17 June 1987.

211. IRIS YVETTE^5 STEWART (*Dorothy^4 Williams, Sidney^3, Nancy^2 Boyer, Porter^1*) was born on 17 January 1962.

Children of **Iris Yvette^5 Stewart** include:
+ 391.   i. DARRYL ALLAN^6, born 29 January 1980.

212. SYDNEY^5 STEWART (*Dorothy^4 Williams, Sidney^3, Nancy^2 Boyer, Porter^1*) was born on 5 November 1964. He married **Lori (—?—)**.

Children of **Sydney^5 Stewart** and **Lori (—?—)** were as follows:
392.   i. DAVID PERKINS^6 was born on 13 September 1983.
393.   ii. LASHANDA ROBINSON was born on 26 November 1984.
394.   iii. SYDNEY JR. was born on 11 February 1987.
395.   iv. JAMES CURTIS was born on 30 April 1990.
396.   v. KAYLON was born on 27 June 1995.

215. CAROLINE^5 RENFROE (*Mae Will^4 Williams, Lee^3, Nancy^2 Boyer, Porter^1*) was born on 7 July 1943 in Detroit, Michigan. She married **William Johnson**.

Children of **Caroline^5 Renfroe** and **William Johnson** were as follows:
397.   i. RENITA^6 was born on 18 July 1962 in Detroit, Michigan.
398.   ii. WILLIAM JR. was born on 4 August 1964 in Detroit, Michigan.

217. PEGGY^5 RENFROE (*Mae Will^4 Williams, Lee^3, Nancy^2 Boyer, Porter^1*) was born on 4 November 1946 in Detroit, Michigan. She married **Bobby Walton**.

Children of **Peggy⁵ Renfroe** and **Bobby Walton** were as follows:
+ 399.   i. LASHAY⁶, born 30 April 1967 in Detroit, Michigan.
    400.   ii. MARY LATRICE was born on 27 July 1972 in Detroit, Michigan.

218. HAROLD⁵ RENFROE (*Mae Will⁴ Williams, Lee³, Nancy² Boyer, Porter¹*) was born
    on 28 August 1947 in Detroit, Michigan. He married **Catherine Lynch** on 11
    March in Detroit, Michigan.

Children of **Harold⁵ Renfroe** and **Catherine Lynch** were as follows:
    401.   i. HAROLD⁶ JR. was born on 7 July 1968 in Detroit, Michigan.
    402.   ii. DION was born in 1981 in Detroit, Michigan.
    403.   iii. NATHAN was born in December 1982 in Detroit, Michigan.

224. CLAUDIA⁵ ARNOLD (*Lucy Jane⁴ Williams, Johnnie³, Nancy² Boyer, Porter¹*) was
    born on 10 March.

Children of **Claudia⁵ Arnold** include:
    404.   i. SHARON⁶.
+ 405.   ii. DENISE

227. JOHN CLIFFORD 'JC'⁵ ARNOLD JR. (*Lucy Jane⁴ Williams, Johnnie³,
    Nancy² Boyer, Porter¹*) was born on 10 October. He married **Joan** (—?—).

Children of **John Clifford 'JC'⁵ Arnold Jr.** and **Joan** (—?—) were as follows:
    406.   i. LAUREN⁶.
    407.   ii. VICTORIA 'VICKY'.
    408.   iii. ANITA.
    409.   iv. JOHN CLIFFORD III.
    410.   v. MARNIE.

228. ERNESTINE⁵ ARNOLD (*Lucy Jane⁴ Williams, Johnnie³, Nancy² Boyer, Porter¹*) was
    born on 28 August 1941 in Newark, New Jersey. She married **Algernon Davis**
    on 13 April 1958 in Newark, New Jersey. She married **Donald White** on 15
    August 1987 in Edison, New Jersey.

Children of **Ernestine⁵ Arnold** and **Algernon Davis** were as follows:
+ 411.   i. DARLENE⁶, born 13 October 1958 in Newark, New Jersey; married **Alexander
    Hamilton**.
+ 412.   ii. ALGERNON JR., born 13 September 1959 in Newark, New Jersey.

There were no children of **Ernestine⁵ Arnold** and **Donald White**.

229. MAUDE LIZABETH^5 WILLIAMS (*Coleman^4, Johnnie^3, Nancy^2 Boyer, Porter^1*)
was born on 6 April 1934 in Milledgeville, Georgia. She married **Harry David
Michael Jackson** in Philadelphia, Pennsylvania.

Children of **Maude Lizabeth^5 Williams** and **Harry David Michael Jackson** were as follows:
+ 413.   i. MICHELE BERNICE^6, born 27 July 1953 in Philadelphia, Pennsylvania; married
         Wayne Dewitt McNight.
+ 414.   ii. VERONICA 'RONNIE' LYNN, born 23 January 1956 in Philadelphia,
         Pennsylvania; married **Gerald Lamont Steele.**
+ 415. iii. HARRY MICHAEL DAVID 'MIKE', born 27 October 1957 in Philadelphia,
         Pennsylvania; married **Charmaine Little.**
+ 416.   iv. STEPHEN MARK, born 2 February 1961 in Philadelphia, Pennsylvania; married
         Terri Holliman; married **Cynthia Kurtz.**
+ 417.   v. BRUCE KEVIN, born 6 September 1963 in Philadelphia, Pennsylvania; married
         Cynthia Lee Piner.

230. MILDRED^5 WILLIAMS (*Coleman^4, Johnnie^3, Nancy^2 Boyer, Porter^1*) was born on
31 August 1935 in Milledgeville, Georgia. She married **John Arthur Cox Jr.** on
13 August 1953 in Philadelphia, Pennsylvania.

Children of **Mildred^5 Williams** and **John Arthur Cox Jr.** were as follows:
+ 418.   i. PAMELA^6, born 26 March 1954 in Anchorage, Alaska; married **Joseph Bryant.**
+ 419.   ii. JOHN ARTHUR 'CHUBBY' III, born 29 December 1955 in Philadelphia,
         Pennsylvania; married **Vicki Renee Bransford.**

232. FANNIE PEARL^5 WILLIAMS (*Coleman^4, Johnnie^3, Nancy^2 Boyer, Porter^1*) was
born on 10 December 1939 in Milledgeville, Georgia. She married **Willie
Howard Glover** in Philadelphia, Pennsylvania. She married **Horace Cheeves,**
son of **Henry Holmes Cheeves** and **Lillian Arthur Carter,** on 6 July 1971 in
Philadelphia, Pennsylvania.

Children of **Fannie Pearl^5 Williams** and **Willie Howard Glover** were:
420.   i. HOWARD ANTHONY^6 was born on 6 July 1959 in Philadelphia, Pennsylvania.
        He died on 29 December 1980 in Philadelphia, Pennsylvania, at age 21.

Children of **Fannie Pearl^5 Williams** and **Horace Cheeves** were:
421.   i. DENISE NICOLE^6 was born on 20 February 1972 in Philadelphia, Pennsylvania.

233. CHARLES^5 WILLIAMS (*Coleman^4, Johnnie^3, Nancy^2 Boyer, Porter^1*) was born on 3
December 1941 in Philadelphia, Pennsylvania. He married **Dahlia Beatrice
Scott** on 9 March 1963 in Philadelphia, Pennsylvania.

Children of **Charles**[5] **Williams** and **Dahlia Beatrice Scott** were as follows:

+ 422.   i. CHARLES 'CHUCK'[6] JR., born 16 September 1963 in Philadelphia, Pennsylvania; married **Donna Johnson**; married **Debbie Turnage**.

+ 423.   ii. L'TANYA DAHLIA 'TAMMY', born 2 March 1965 in Philadelphia, Pennsylvania; married **Terry Pittman**.

424.   iii. SHARON BERNICE was born on 10 May 1969 in Philadelphia, Pennsylvania.

235. JANET[5] WILLIAMS (*Coleman*[4], *Johnnie*[3], *Nancy*[2]*Boyer*, *Porter*[1]) was born on 28 August 1944 in Philadelphia, Pennsylvania. She married **Richard Bland Jasper** in June 1965 in New Jersey.

Children of **Janet**[5] **Williams** and **Richard Bland Jasper** were:

+ 425.   i. DONNA ROCHELLE[6], born 3 January 1966 in Mount Holly, New Jersey; married **George Childs Petagrew**.

236. ROGER[5] WILLIAMS (*Coleman*[4], *Johnnie*[3], *Nancy*[2]*Boyer*, *Porter*[1]) was born on 25 April 1946 in Philadelphia, Pennsylvania. He married **Cynthia Simmons**, daughter of **William Griffin 'Bill' Simmons** and **Lula Elizabeth Dix**, on 6 November 1965 in Philadelphia, Pennsylvania. He died on 14 August 1983 in Philadelphia, Pennsylvania, at age 37.

Children of **Roger**[5] **Williams** and **Cynthia Simmons** were as follows:

426.   i. GAIL BERNICE[6] was born on 15 November 1966 in Philadelphia, Pennsylvania.

+ 427.   ii. ANGELA RENEA, born 4 January 1971 in Philadelphia, Pennsylvania; married **Rudolph Frederick Valentine Jr.**

237. JOYCE CHERYL[5] WILLIAMS (*Coleman*[4], *Johnnie*[3], *Nancy*[2]*Boyer*, *Porter*[1]) was born on 22 December 1948 in Philadelphia, Pennsylvania.

Children of **Joyce Cheryl**[5] **Williams** and **George Bailey** were:

+ 428.   i. GERMAINE DAPHNE[6], born 30 March 1974 in Philadelphia, Pennsylvania.

238. DONALD 'HOPE'[5] WILLIAMS (*Coleman*[4], *Johnnie*[3], *Nancy*[2]*Boyer*, *Porter*[1]) was born on 28 August 1950 in Philadelphia, Pennsylvania. He died on 29 August 1998 in Philadelphia, Pennsylvania, at age 48.

Children of **Donald 'Hope'**[5] **Williams** and **Peggy Pitchford** were:

429.   i. LAWRENCE[6] was born on 22 May 1975 in Philadelphia, Pennsylvania.

239. ALAN[5] WILLIAMS (*Coleman*[4], *Johnnie*[3], *Nancy*[2]*Boyer*, *Porter*[1]) was born on 1 May 1955 in Philadelphia, Pennsylvania. He married **Kim Louise Sorapuru** on 2 May 1981 in Philadelphia, Pennsylvania.

Children of **Alan**[5] **Williams** and **Kim Louise Sorapuru** were as follows:

430. i. CHRISTOPHER ALAN[6] was born on 17 August 1981 in Gaithersburg, Maryland.
431. ii. MATTHEW COLEMAN was born on 11 May 1986 in Germantown, Maryland.
432. iii. JORDAN ISAIAH was born on 3 July 1997 in Frederick, Maryland.

240. TIMOTHY[5] **WILLIAMS** (*Coleman*[4], *Johnnie*[3], *Nancy*[2]*Boyer, Porter*[1]) was born on 27 June 1958 in Philadelphia, Pennsylvania. He married **Andrea Johnson.**

Children of **Timothy**[5] **Williams** and **Andrea Johnson** were:

433. i. JASMINE TENILLE[6] was born on 8 December 1990 in Marlton, New Jersey.

Children of **Timothy**[5] **Williams** and **Lorraine Clark** were:

434. i. MIYA LAKISHA[6] was born on 29 December 1979 in Philadelphia, Pennsylvania.

243. ELLA MAE[5] **TEMPLE** (*Viola*[4]*Williams, Johnnie*[3], *Nancy*[2]*Boyer, Porter*[1]) was born on 13 March 1937 in Atlanta, Georgia. She married **Samuel Clark.**

Children of **Ella Mae**[5] **Temple** and **Samuel Clark** were:

435. i. PHILLIP[6] was born on 26 December 1954 in Detroit, Michigan. He died on 14 May 1990 in Desert Sands, California, at age 35.

244. EDDIE HENRY[5] **TEMPLE** (*Viola*[4]*Williams, Johnnie*[3], *Nancy*[2]*Boyer, Porter*[1]) was born on 19 July 1938 in Atlanta, Georgia. He married **Pearl Louise Anderson.**

Children of **Eddie Henry**[5] **Temple** and **Pearl Louise Anderson** were as follows:

436. i. ANDREA CHERYL[6] was born on 20 March 1960 in Detroit, Michigan.
437. ii. TYRONE EDDIE was born on 19 August 1961 in Detroit, Michigan.
438. iii. ERIK TODD was born on 9 December 1970 in Detroit, Michigan. He married **Patricia Ann Moss.**
439. iv. RAMIA KAULETTE was born on 3 June 1974 in Southfield, Michigan.

245. EVA MAE[5] **TEMPLE** (*Viola*[4]*Williams, Johnnie*[3], *Nancy*[2]*Boyer, Porter*[1]) was born on 16 June 1940 in Atlanta, Georgia. She married **Agustus Davis** in 1957 in Cleveland, Ohio.

Children of **Eva Mae**[5] **Temple** and **Agustus Davis** were as follows:

440. i. ENA MARIE[6] was born on 16 August 1958 in Cleveland, Ohio.
441. ii. DWAYNE was born on 29 September 1965 in Cleveland, Ohio.

246. SHERRY[5] **TEMPLE** (*Viola*[4]*Williams, Johnnie*[3], *Nancy*[2]*Boyer, Porter*[1]) was born on 7 October 1944 in Detroit, Michigan. She married **Earl Johnson** on 15 May 1965 in Detroit, Michigan.

Children of **Sherry**[5] **Temple** and **Earl Johnson** were as follows:

+ 442.   i. JOHN ANDREW[6], born 4 June 1942 in Atlanta, Georgia; married **Geraldine** (—?—).

443.   ii. EARL DERRICK was born on 4 February 1967 in Detroit, Michigan.

444.   iii. RAYNARD JEMAL was born on 8 October 1969 in Detroit, Michigan.

247. HAROLD[5] **TEMPLE** (*Viola*[4] *Williams, Johnnie*[3], *Nancy*[2] *Boyer, Porter*[1]) was born on 30 April 1948 in Detroit, Michigan.

Children of **Harold**[5] **Temple** and **Veronica** (—?—) were:

445.   i. BRANDON TERRELL[6] was born on 21 September 1986 in Detroit, Michigan.

248. HERBERT[5] **TEMPLE** (*Viola*[4] *Williams, Johnnie*[3], *Nancy*[2] *Boyer, Porter*[1]) was born on 30 April 1948 in Detroit, Michigan. He married **Sylvia** (—?—). He died in 2002 in Detroit, Michigan.

Children of **Herbert**[5] **Temple** and **Sylvia** (—?—) were as follows:

446.   i. DAWN[6] was born on 30 May 1979 in Detroit, Michigan.

447.   ii. DIONNE was born on 30 May 1979 in Detroit, Michigan.

448.   iii. LILLIAN ELMIRA COLE died on 26 November 1989 in Detroit, Michigan.

250. NEMIAH 'SONNY'[5] **HOOKS JR.** (*Mamie*[4] *Williams, Johnnie*[3], *Nancy*[2] *Boyer, Porter*[1]) was born on 8 March 1940 in Milledgeville, Georgia. He married **Linda Dennis.**

Children of **Nemiah 'Sonny'**[5] **Hooks Jr.** and **Linda Dennis** were as follows:

449.   i. KEVIN KEITH[6].

450.   ii. GENA.

451.   iii. RICO.

252. VERONICA 'RONNIE'[5] **HOOKS** (*Mamie*[4] *Williams, Johnnie*[3], *Nancy*[2] *Boyer, Porter*[1]) was born on 19 February 1943 in Detroit, Michigan. She married **Lowell Massey Jr.** on 14 March 1966 in Detroit, Michigan.

Children of **Veronica 'Ronnie'**[5] **Hooks** and **Lowell Massey Jr.** were as follows:

+ 452.   i. LOWELL[6] III, born 22 April 1967 in Detroit, Michigan; married **Classie Legardy.**

453.   ii. MICHELE RENEE was born on 14 January 1969 in Detroit, Michigan.

454.   iii. TIFFANY NICOLE was born on 18 March 1982 in Detroit, Michigan.

253. MAMIE SHARON[5] **HOOKS** (*Mamie*[4] *Williams, Johnnie*[3], *Nancy*[2] *Boyer, Porter*[1]) was born on 4 October 1944 in Detroit, Michigan. She married **Lester Marvin Dennis.**

Children of **Mamie Sharon**^{5} **Hooks** and **Lester Marvin Dennis** were as follows:
+ 455.   i. CHRISONDRA 'CHRIS' LYNN^6, born 3 June 1967 in Highland Park, Michigan; married **Ronald Austin.**
+ 456.   ii. LESTER 'MAN' MARVIN II, born 26 October 1969 in Royal Oaks, Michigan; married **Susan Ford.**

255. MARSHALL DENNIS^5 HOOKS (*Mamie^4 Williams, Johnnie^3, Nancy^2 Boyer, Porter^1*) was born on 13 December 1947 in Detroit, Michigan.

Children of **Marshall Dennis^5 Hooks** and **Myra** (—?—) were as follows:
457.   i. CHANTELLE^6 was born in Detroit, Michigan.
458.   ii. MARSHELLE was born in Detroit, Michigan.

Children of **Marshall Dennis^5 Hooks** and **Mona** (—?—) were as follows:
459.   i. BRANDY^6 was born in Detroit, Michigan.
460.   ii. MARSHALL DENNIS II was born in Detroit, Michigan.

258. DONNA MARIE^5 HOOKS (*Mamie^4 Williams, Johnnie^3, Nancy^2 Boyer, Porter^1*) was born on 11 November 1954 in Detroit, Michigan. She married **Smart Onuigbo** on 7 April 2001 in Detroit, Michigan.

Children of **Donna Marie^5 Hooks** include:
461.   i. DAWN LYNETTE^6 was born on 21 June 1973 in Detroit, Michigan.

There were no children of **Donna Marie^5 Hooks** and **Smart Onuigbo.**

260. JAMES 'JABO' WILLIAM^5 NAPIER JR. (*Louise^4 Williams, Johnnie^3, Nancy^2 Boyer, Porter^1*) was born on 22 September 1945 in Detroit, Michigan. He died in September 1972 in Detroit, Michigan.

Children of **James 'Jabo' William^5 Napier Jr.** and **Ollevette 'Ollie' Gant** were:
+ 462.   i. STEPHANIE^6, born 17 June 1964 in Detroit, Michigan.

261. PHYLLIS^5 NAPIER (*Louise^4 Williams, Johnnie^3, Nancy^2 Boyer, Porter^1*) was born on 13 January 1946 in Detroit, Michigan. She married **Albert Green** on 5 July 1969 in Detroit, Michigan.

Children of **Phyllis^5 Napier** and **Albert Green** were:
+ 463.   i. ADRIAN ANTHONY^6, born 11 July 1971 in Detroit, Michigan.

262. GARY^5 NAPIER (*Louise^{4}Williams, Johnnie^3, Nancy^{2}Boyer, Porter^1*) was born on 6 March 1947 in Detroit, Michigan. He married **Shirley Gumby.** He married **Deborah Fisher.**

Children of **Gary^5 Napier** and **Shirley Gumby** were:
464.   i. GARY^6 JR. was born on 17 March 1969 in Detroit, Michigan.

Children of **Gary^5 Napier** and **Deborah Fisher** were as follows:
465.   i. DAWN MARIE^6 was born on 24 July 1975 in Detroit, Michigan.
466.   ii. JAMES SAMUEL was born on 27 October 1980 in Detroit, Michigan.

263. JOYCE 'PERK'^{5} NAPIER (*Louise^{4}Williams, Johnnie^3, Nancy^{2}Boyer, Porter^1*) was born on 3 January 1950 in Detroit, Michigan. She married **Kenneth Johnson.**

Children of **Joyce 'Perk'^{5} Napier** and **Kenneth Johnson** were as follows:
467.   i. DARYL^6 was born on 27 September 1967 in Detroit, Michigan.
468.   ii. MICKEY DIONNE was born on 6 July 1969 in Detroit, Michigan.

264. LLOYD^5 ALLEN (*Fannie Pearl^{4}Williams, Johnnie^3, Nancy^{2}Boyer, Porter^1*) was born on 21 April in Detroit, Michigan. He married **Patricia Hatwood.**

Children of **Lloyd^5 Allen** and **Patricia Hatwood** were as follows:
469.   i. LISA^6.
470.   ii. MARK.

265. KENNETH 'KENNY'^{5} ALLEN (*Fannie Pearl^{4}Williams, Johnnie^3, Nancy^{2}Boyer, Porter^1*) was born on 30 May in Detroit, Michigan.

Children of **Kenneth 'Kenny'^{5} Allen** and **Brenda** (—?—) were:
471.   i. LISA^6.

266. MORRIS^5 ALLEN (*Fannie Pearl^{4}Williams, Johnnie^3, Nancy^{2}Boyer, Porter^1*) was born on 21 June in Detroit, Michigan. He married **Joyce** (—?—).

Children of **Morris^5 Allen** and **Joyce** (—?—) were:
472.   i. DAVID^6.

267. JOHN 'JOHNNY' RAY^5 ALLEN (*Fannie Pearl^{4}Williams, Johnnie^3, Nancy^{2}Boyer, Porter^1*) was born on 15 September in Detroit, Michigan. He married **Lajanda Ford.**

Children of **John 'Johnny' Ray^5 Allen** and **Lajanda Ford** were:
+ 473.   i. MECHA BETTINA^6, born 2 July 1979 in Detroit, Michigan.

268. **DONALD**^{5} **ALLEN** (*Fannie Pearl*^{4} *Williams, Johnnie*^{3}*, Nancy*^{2}*Boyer, Porter*^{1}) was born on 23 June 1957 in Detroit, Michigan. He married **Robin** (—?—). He married **Carol** (—?—).

Children of **Donald**^{5} **Allen** and **Robin** (—?—) were:
474. i. LUCIANA 'POOH'^{6} was born on 18 June 1976 in Detroit, Michigan.

Children of **Donald**^{5} **Allen** and **Carol** (—?—) were:
475. i. BIANCA^6 was born on 30 June 1990 in Detroit, Michigan.

269. **ERIC**^{5} **ALLEN** (*Fannie Pearl*^{4} *Williams, Johnnie*^{3}*, Nancy*^{2}*Boyer, Porter*^{1}) was born on 15 March 1959 in Detroit, Michigan. He married **Kim** (—?—). He married **Deborah** (—?—).

Children of **Eric**^{5} **Allen** and **Kim** (—?—) were:
476. i. TAKIMA^6 was born in Detroit, Michigan.

Children of **Eric**^{5} **Allen** and **Deborah** (—?—) were:
477. i. ERICA^6 was born in November 1994 in Detroit, Michigan.

Children of **Eric**^{5} **Allen** and **Denise** (—?—) were:
478. i. GEORGIA^6 was born on 19 September 1977 in Detroit, Michigan.

275. **FREDDIE**^{5} **CLARK** (*Willie*^{4} *Williams, Johnnie*^{3}*, Nancy*^{2}*Boyer, Porter*^{1}) was born on 19 January 1947 in Milledgeville, Georgia. He married **Sheila Yarborough** on 12 October 1968 in Cleveland, Ohio.

Children of **Freddie**^{5} **Clark** and **Sheila Yarborough** were as follows:
479. i. ANGELA LEVINE^6 was born on 18 April 1969 in Cleveland, Ohio.
480. ii. REGINALD LAMAR was born on 17 May 1974 in Cleveland, Ohio.

276. **MARION GAY**^{5} **WILLIAMS** (*Willie*^{4}*, Johnnie*^{3}*, Nancy*^{2}*Boyer, Porter*^{1}) was born on 21 May 1951 in Detroit, Michigan.

Children of **Marion Gay**^{5} **Williams** include:
481. i. OMARI ZUBIRA^6 was born on 2 December 1972 in Detroit, Michigan.

278. **ANNE ADELE**^{5} **WILLIAMS** (*Willie*^{4}*, Johnnie*^{3}*, Nancy*^{2}*Boyer, Porter*^{1}) was born on 13 November 1956 in Detroit, Michigan. She married **James Stubbs** on 23 December 1976 in Detroit, Michigan.

Children of **Anne Adele⁵ Williams** and **James Stubbs** were as follows:
- 482.   i. LEONA MICHELLE⁶ was born on 11 September 1977 in Detroit, Michigan.
- 483.   ii. VERONICA DIANE was born on 21 February 1981 in Detroit, Michigan.
- 484. iii. KIMBERLY NICOLE was born on 14 April 1984 in Fort Ord, California.

280. NANCY⁵ WILLIAMS (*David⁴, Johnnie³, Nancy²Boyer, Porter¹*) was born on 22 August 1949 in Milledgeville, Georgia. She married **Willie Williams** on 12 May 1965 in Philadelphia, Pennsylvania. She died on 2 May 2003 in Philadelphia, Pennsylvania, at age 53.

Children of **Nancy⁵ Williams** and **Willie Williams** were as follows:
- 485.   i. DERRICK⁶ was born on 26 August 1965 in Philadelphia, Pennsylvania.
- + 486.   ii. DAVID, born 11 September 1968 in Philadelphia, Pennsylvania.

283. BRENDA SUSAN⁵ MILLER (*Clara⁴Williams, Johnnie³, Nancy²Boyer, Porter¹*) was born on 26 April 1951 in Detroit, Michigan. She married **Howard William McElrath II**.

Children of **Brenda Susan⁵ Miller** and **Howard William McElrath II** were as follows:
- + 487.   i. JENELLE KIMBERLY⁶, born 9 August 1971 in Detroit, Michigan; married **Antonio Mitchell**.
- 488.   ii. HOWARD WILLIAM III was born on 24 July 1972 in Detroit, Michigan. He died on 1 July 1993 at age 20.
- 489.   iii. KEVIN THOMAS was born on 19 June 1974 in Detroit, Michigan.
- 490.   iv. ANGELA SUSAN was born on 27 March 1976 in Detroit, Michigan. She married **William White** on 22 June 2002 in Detroit, Michigan.

284. DWIGHT KEPTLER⁵ MILLER (*Clara⁴Williams, Johnnie³, Nancy²Boyer, Porter¹*) was born on 17 September 1952 in Detroit, Michigan. He married **JoAnn Whitley** on 15 September 1973 in Detroit, Michigan.

Children of **Dwight Keptler⁵ Miller** and **JoAnn Whitley** were:
- + 491.   i. DWIGHT KEPTLER⁶ JR., born 9 May 1976 in Detroit, Michigan; married **Renee (—?—)**.

285. ROSALYN⁵ MILLER (*Clara⁴Williams, Johnnie³, Nancy²Boyer, Porter¹*) was born on 14 June 1954 in Detroit, Michigan. She married **Mark Bennett** in Detroit, Michigan.

Children of **Rosalyn⁵ Miller** and **Mark Bennett** were:
- 492.   i. ALISA CLAIRE⁶ was born on 20 December 1972 in Detroit, Michigan.

289. BERNARD^5 **TRAWICK** (*Vernon 'Bud'*^{4}, *Melissa*^{3}*Williams, Nancy*^{2}*Boyer, Porter*^{1})
was born on 14 December 1951 in Philadelphia, Pennsylvania. He married
Kenya Wilson.

Children of **Bernard**^{5} **Trawick** and **Kenya Wilson** were as follows:
493.   i. TAFT^6 was born on 25 April 1986 in Winston-Salem, North Carolina.
494.   ii. JASON was born on 14 December 1987 in Philadelphia, Pennsylvania.

292. CYNTHIA^5 **TRAWICK** (*Vernon 'Bud'*^{4}, *Melissa*^{3}*Williams, Nancy*^{2}*Boyer, Porter*^{1}) was born
on 12 November 1958 in Philadelphia, Pennsylvania. She married **William Boyer.**

Children of **Cynthia**^{5} **Trawick** and **William Boyer** were as follows:
495.   i. AJA MARIE^6 was born on 9 June 1982 in Philadelphia, Pennsylvania.
496.   ii. TODD was born on 20 January 1984 in Philadelphia, Pennsylvania.
497.   iii. JENNA DANIELLE was born on 14 August 1989 in Philadelphia, Pennsylvania.
498.   iv. WILLIAM 'BJ' JR. was born on 16 December 1997 in Philadelphia, Pennsylvania.

293. RHONDA^5 **TRAWICK** (*Nancy*^{4}, *Melissa*^{3}*Williams, Nancy*^{2}*Boyer, Porter*^{1}).

Children of **Rhonda**^{5} **Trawick** include:
499.   i. ROBBIE^6 was born circa 1965.

304. KEVIN^5 **BROWN** (*Vera*^{4}*Williams, Robert*^{3}, *Nancy*^{2}*Boyer, Porter*^{1}).

Children of **Kevin**^{5} **Brown** include:
500.   i. MARTISSA^6.

305. PHYLLIS ALLEN^5 **WILLIAMS** (*Inez*^{4}, *Robert*^{3}, *Nancy*^{2}*Boyer, Porter*^{1}) was born on
9 November 1946. She married **William Edward Banks.**

Children of **Phyllis Allen**^{5} **Williams** and **William Edward Banks** were as follows:
+ 501.   i. JAMILA DANIELLE^6, born 15 December 1972 in Los Angeles, California.
+ 502.   ii. CANYON KASAI, born 4 September 1975 in Los Angeles, California.

323. KENNETH^5 **LIGGINS** (*Willie Mae 'Bell'*^{4}, *Mary 'Mae' Ella*^{3}*Williams, Nancy*^{2}*Boyer,
Porter*^{1}) was born on 7 April 1941 in Philadelphia, Pennsylvania. He married
Avon Charles on 24 June 1964 in Philadelphia, Pennsylvania. He died on 4
January 2000 in Philadelphia, Pennsylvania, at age 58.

Children of **Kenneth**^{5} **Liggins** include:
503.   i. A'NAYA^6 was born in Philadelphia, Pennsylvania.
504.   ii. KATHY was born in Philadelphia, Pennsylvania.

505. iii. TRACY was born in Philadelphia, Pennsylvania.

Children of **Kenneth**[5] **Liggins** and **Nancy Lee** (—?—) were:
506. i. KAREN[6] was born on 18 August 1963 in Philadelphia, Pennsylvania.

Children of **Kenneth**[5] **Liggins** and **Avon Charles** were as follows:
507. i. APRIL[6] was born on 30 September 1966 in Philadelphia, Pennsylvania.
+ 508. ii. ANGEL, born 7 November 1968 in Philadelphia, Pennsylvania.
+ 509. iii. KENNETH 'KENNY' JR., born 2 February 1970 in Philadelphia, Pennsylvania.

325. ROBIN[5] **SMITH** (*Nancy*[4]*Napier, Minnie*[3]*Williams, Nancy*[2]*Boyer, Porter*[1]) was born on 2 December 1956 in Detroit, Michigan. She married **Joseph Beasley.**

Children of **Robin**[5] **Smith** and **Joseph Beasley** were as follows:
510. i. FRANCESCA[6] was born on 28 January 1978 in Los Angeles, California.
511. ii. ANDREIA was born on 20 November 1999 in Houston, Texas.

327. KEVIN[5] **SMITH** (*Nancy*[4]*Napier, Minnie*[3]*Williams, Nancy*[2]*Boyer, Porter*[1]) was born on 12 June 1965 in Los Angeles, California. He married **Terry** (—?—).

Children of **Kevin**[5] **Smith** and **Terry** (—?—) were:
512. i. JUSTIN[6] was born on 9 April 1998 in Los Angeles, California.

329. SHARON[5] **NAPIER** (*William Edward*[4], *Minnie*[3]*Williams, Nancy*[2]*Boyer, Porter*[1]) was born on 16 December 1960 in Los Angeles, California. She married **Harold Johnson** in Los Angeles, California.

Children of **Sharon**[5] **Napier** and **Harold Johnson** were as follows:
513. i. ROBERT[6] was born in Los Angeles, California.
514. ii. JASON was born on 12 June 1983 in Los Angeles, California.

330. JUNIE[5] **NAPIER** (*William Edward*[4], *Minnie*[3]*Williams, Nancy*[2]*Boyer, Porter*[1]) was born on 22 June 1962 in Los Angeles, California. He married **Leslie Bowman** in Los Angeles, California.

Children of **Junie**[5] **Napier** and **Leslie Bowman** were as follows:
515. i. LESLIE[6] was born on 18 January 1981 in Los Angeles, California.
516. ii. VICTORIA was born on 20 February 1983 in Los Angeles, California.

342. GREGORY MARTIN 'GOOGOO'[5] **CLARDY III** (*Marilyn Cristina*[4]*Boyer, Alfred*[3], *Sam 'Sammie'*[2], *Porter*[1]) was born on 11 May 1977 in Los Angeles, California.

Children of **Gregory Martin 'Googoo'**[5] **Clardy III** and **Amy Chapouris** were:
517. i. SYRUS GREGORY[6] was born on 5 July 1998 in Orange County, California.

343. CRISTINA 'KIZZY'[5] **CLARDY** (*Marilyn Cristina*[4]*Boyer, Alfred*[3]*, Sam 'Sammie'*[2]*, Porter*[1]) was born on 15 March 1979 in Loma Linda, California.

Children of **Cristina 'Kizzy'**[5] **Clardy** and **Antwang Karem Brown** were:
518. i. RYANNE CELESTE[6] was born on 27 February 2003 in Riverside, California.

Generation Six

350. DOUGLAS[6] **JOHNSON** (*Theodore 'Teddy'*[5]*Ferguson, Thelma*[4]*Boyer, William Porter*[3]*, Marshall*[2]*, Porter*[1]) was born on 27 March 1969 in Philadelphia, Pennsylvania. He married **Sherry** (—?—).

Children of **Douglas**[6] **Johnson** and **Sherry** (—?—) were:
519. i. MAYORCA 'MAYA'[7] was born in 1989 in Philadelphia, Pennsylvania.

357. MICHAEL DAVID[6] **WILLIAMS** (*Riley Cornelius*[5]*, Sidney*[4]*, Sidney*[3]*, Nancy*[2]*Boyer, Porter*[1]) was born on 13 April 1965. He married **Amiesha** (—?—) on 12 September 1998.

Children of **Michael David**[6] **Williams** and **Amiesha** (—?—) were as follows:
520. i. MARCELLOUS[7] was born on 25 March 1988.
521. ii. ASHLEY was born on 28 July 1989.
522. iii. MATTHEW was born on 25 March 1992.
523. iv. CAMERON was born on 7 November 1999.
524. v. CALEB MICHAEL was born on 11 January 2002.

358. ANTHONY JOSEPH[6] **WILLIAMS** (*Riley Cornelius*[5]*, Sidney*[4]*, Sidney*[3]*, Nancy*[2]*Boyer, Porter*[1]) was born on 16 September 1968.

Children of **Anthony Joseph**[6] **Williams** include:
525. i. RACHEL[7].

363. KIMBERLY ANN[6] **MCDUFFIE** (*Vivian Lucille*[5]*Williams, Perry Alfred*[4]*, Sidney*[3]*, Nancy*[2]*Boyer, Porter*[1]) was born on 7 August 1962. She married **Derrick Christopher Bunch** on 10 April 1987 in Detroit, Michigan.

Children of **Kimberly Ann**[6] **McDuffie** and **Derrick Christopher Bunch** were as follows:
526. i. KRISTIN RENEE[7] was born on 2 February 1987 in Detroit, Michigan.
527. ii. DERRICK CHRISTOPHER JR. was born on 10 November 1992 in Detroit, Michigan.

364. CALVIN MURPHY^6 MCDUFFIE III (*Vivian Lucille^{5}Williams, Perry Alfred^4, Sidney^3, Nancy^{2}Boyer, Porter^1*) was born on 24 September 1965 in Detroit, Michigan. He married **Sharon 'Sherrie' Cross** on 20 April 1984 in Lansing, Michigan.

Children of **Calvin Murphy^6 McDuffie III** and **Sharon 'Sherrie' Cross** were as follows:

528. i. CALVIN 'CUBBY'^{7} IV was born on 17 April 1984 in Detroit, Michigan.

529. ii. CAPRICE GABRIELLE was born on 4 April 1989 in Detroit, Michigan.

530. iii. CONNER JEFFREY was born on 3 June 2001 in Detroit, Michigan.

365. NIKOL GERTRUDE^6 MCDUFFIE (*Vivian Lucille^{5}Williams, Perry Alfred^4, Sidney^3, Nancy^{2}Boyer, Porter^1*) was born on 3 August 1967 in Detroit, Michigan. She married **Terrell Constantine Brooks Jr.** on 7 November 1988 in Detroit, Michigan.

Children of **Nikol Gertrude^6 McDuffie** and **Terrell Constantine Brooks Jr.** were as follows:

531. i. TERRELL CONSTANTINE^7 III was born on 29 November 1990 in Detroit, Michigan.

532. ii. N' DIA VIVIAN was born on 24 November 1992 in Detroit, Michigan.

533. iii. MURPHY CALVIN MCDUFFIE was born on 1 September 1994 in Detroit, Michigan. He died on 1 September 1994 in Detroit, Michigan.

534. iv. PARADISE KELLY was born on 22 August 1997 in Detroit, Michigan.

366. TIERA PATRICE^6 MCDUFFIE (*Vivian Lucille^{5}Williams, Perry Alfred^4, Sidney^3, Nancy^{2}Boyer, Porter^1*) was born on 31 May 1975 in Detroit, Michigan. She married **Clifford Melvin Wilson Jr.** on 3 December 1994 in Detroit, Michigan.

Children of **Tiera Patrice^6 McDuffie** and **Clifford Melvin Wilson Jr.** were:

535. i. CLIFFORD MELVIN^7 III was born on 19 March 1996 in Detroit, Michigan.

367. LAJUDE 'JUDY'^{6} NUNLEE (*Barbara Jean^{5}Williams, Perry Alfred^4, Sidney^3, Nancy^{2}Boyer, Porter^1*) was born on 13 March 1962 in Detroit, Michigan. She married **Orrin Richardo Josey** on 22 August 1992 in Detroit, Michigan.

Children of **LaJude 'Judy'^{6} Nunlee** and **Orrin Richardo Josey** were as follows:

536. i. JANAE' BARBARA^7 was born on 8 June 1993 in Detroit, Michigan.

537. ii. ORIANA LAJUDE was born on 12 November 1994 in Detroit, Michigan.

538. iii. PARIS NICOLE was born on 27 August 1995 in North Carolina.

368. THEOTUS MELVIN^6 NUNLEE III (*Barbara Jean^{5}Williams, Perry Alfred^4, Sidney^3, Nancy^{2}Boyer, Porter^1*) was born on 19 April 1963 in Detroit, Michigan. He married **Alma Grace Westbrook** on 31 August 1986 in Detroit, Michigan.

Children of **Theotus Melvin^6 Nunlee III** and **Alma Grace Westbrook** were as follows:

539.   i. THEOTUS 'TODD' MELVIN^7 IV was born on 30 September 1988 in Detroit, Michigan.

540.   ii. JADE TANAE was born on 11 November 1991 in Detroit, Michigan.

541.   iii. TREY CHRISTIAN JAMES was born on 7 May 1999 in Detroit, Michigan.

542.   iv. JANA PATRICE was born on 19 July 2001 in Detroit, Michigan.

369. PERRY ALLEN^6 NUNLEE (*Barbara Jean^{5}Williams, Perry Alfred^4, Sidney^3, Nancy^{2}Boyer, Porter^1*) was born on 16 November 1969 in Detroit, Michigan. He married **Latina Latrease McCray** on 1 July 1995 in Detroit, Michigan.

Children of **Perry Allen^6 Nunlee** and **Latina Latrease McCray** were as follows:

543.   i. JASMINE^7 was born on 17 March 1993 in Detroit, Michigan.

544.   ii. PERRY ALLAN JR. was born on 10 April 1997 in Detroit, Michigan.

545.   iii. BLAKE TERENCE was born on 22 August 2002 in Detroit, Michigan.

370. TERESA DONNA^6 NUNLEE (*Barbara Jean^{5}Williams, Perry Alfred^4, Sidney^3, Nancy^{2}Boyer, Porter^1*) was born on 25 October 1970 in Detroit, Michigan. She married **Ernest Gass Jr.** on 17 January 1999 in Detroit, Michigan.

Children of **Teresa Donna^6 Nunlee** and **Ernest Gass Jr.** were as follows:

546.   i. ANGELIQUE EASTER-JEAN^7 was born on 21 February 1998 in Detroit, Michigan.

547.   ii. TRINITY ELISE was born on 6 July 1999 in Detroit, Michigan.

372. DONALD LEYONDER^6 WILLIAMS JR. (*Donald Leyonder^5, Perry Alfred^4, Sidney^3, Nancy^{2}Boyer, Porter^1*) was born on 9 January 1965 in Detroit, Michigan. He married **Geraldine 'Gerry' Maria** (—?—) on 30 December 1988 in Detroit, Michigan.

Children of **Donald Leyonder^6 Williams Jr.** and **Geraldine 'Gerry' Maria** (—?—) were:

548.   i. DONALD LEYONDER^7 III was born on 17 October 1989 in Detroit, Michigan.

Children of **Donald Leyonder^6 Williams Jr.** and **Chi Chi** (—?—) were:

549.   i. DOMINIQUE YVONNE^7 was born on 24 July 1998 in Detroit, Michigan.

373. DARRYL ALEX^6 WILLIAMS (*Donald Leyonder^5, Perry Alfred^4, Sidney^3, Nancy^{2}Boyer, Porter^1*) was born on 27 July 1967 in Detroit, Michigan. He married **Kewanna 'Kiki' Wilder** in August 1992 in Detroit, Michigan.

Children of **Darryl Alex^6 Williams** and **Kewanna 'Kiki' Wilder** were as follows:
550.   i. DARRYL ALEX^7 JR. was born on 3 October 1991 in Detroit, Michigan.
551.   ii. KORAN was born on 7 February 1994 in Detroit, Michigan.
552.   iii. KIERA was born on 31 December 1995 in Detroit, Michigan.
553.   iv. DALLAS was born on 26 July 1997 in Detroit, Michigan.

374. QWANA SHANTA 'POOH'^{6} WILLIAMS (*Donald Leyonder^5, Perry Alfred^4, Sidney^3, Nancy^2 Boyer, Porter^1*) was born on 2 December 1980 in Detroit, Michigan.

Children of **Qwana Shanta 'Pooh'^{6} Williams** include:
554.   i. TIANA MARIA^7 was born on 11 June 1998 in Detroit, Michigan.

376. FELISA IVY^6 STEWART (*Cecilia 'Cil' Lavern^5, Dorothy^4 Williams, Sidney^3, Nancy^2 Boyer, Porter^1*) was born on 6 March 1969. She married **Alvin Boyd** on 2 September 1989.

Children of **Felisa Ivy^6 Stewart** and **Alvin Boyd** were as follows:
555.   i. RICHARD^7 was born on 4 September 1992.
556.   ii. SENKINA EAST was born on 8 October 1997.

377. LINDA BERNADETTE^6 STEWART (*Cecilia 'Cil' Lavern^5, Dorothy^4 Williams, Sidney^3, Nancy^2 Boyer, Porter^1*) was born on 3 September 1970. She married **Paul Denardi Johnson** on 24 February 1996.

Children of **Linda Bernadette^6 Stewart** and **Paul Denardi Johnson** were as follows:
557.   i. ASHLEY PAULETTE^7 was born on 2 November 1992.
558.   ii. PAUL DENARDI JR. was born on 7 November 1995.
559.   iii. JOHN JEROME was born on 27 February 1999.

378. RICHARD ODAL^6 STEWART (*Cecilia 'Cil' Lavern^5, Dorothy^4 Williams, Sidney^3, Nancy^2 Boyer, Porter^1*) was born on 7 January 1972. He married **Holly Fletcher** on 9 July 2002.

Children of **Richard Odal^6 Stewart** and **Holly Fletcher** were as follows:
560.   i. BROOK FLETCHER^7 was born on 20 May 1993.
561.   ii. BRANDON was born on 7 March 1996.
562.   iii. BREENA was born on 20 January 2002.

379. MICHAEL SYDNEY^6 STEWART (*Cecilia 'Cil' Lavern^5, Dorothy^4 Williams, Sidney^3, Nancy^2 Boyer, Porter^1*) was born on 22 February 1973.

Children of **Michael Sydney^6 Stewart** include:

563.　i. MICHAEL SYDNEY^7 JR. was born on 22 November 1992.

380. JOHNNY B.^{6} BURGE JR. (*Linda Joyce^{5}Stewart, Dorothy^{4}Williams, Sidney^3, Nancy^{2}Boyer, Porter^1*) was born on 22 October 1969 in Detroit, Michigan. He married **Sharon Jenkins** on 19 July 1995 in Detroit, Michigan.

Children of **Johnny B.^{6} Burge Jr.** and **Sharon Jenkins** were:

564.　i. ANTONIO JULIAN^7 was born on 18 December 1992 in Detroit, Michigan.

384. REGINA^6 DICKERSON (*Valerie Zactoria^{5}Stewart, Dorothy^{4}Williams, Sidney^3, Nancy^{2}Boyer, Porter^1*) was born on 15 March 1971.

Children of **Regina^6 Dickerson** include:

565.　i. DOMINIQUE^7 was born on 8 March 1991.
566.　ii. RAKEISHA GORDON was born on 1 April 1992.
567.　iii. JALAUGHN LINDSEY was born on 3 September 1993.

386. CHRISTOPHER JAMES^6 JOHNSON (*Brenda Diane^{5}Stewart, Dorothy^{4}Williams, Sidney^3, Nancy^{2}Boyer, Porter^1*) was born on 29 October 1975. He married **Sealicka Brown.**

Children of **Christopher James^6 Johnson** and **Sealicka Brown** were:

568.　i. NIRA^7 was born on 30 May 2001.

387. CASANDRA DIANE^6 JOHNSON (*Brenda Diane^{5}Stewart, Dorothy^{4}Williams, Sidney^3, Nancy^{2}Boyer, Porter^1*) was born on 30 May 1977.

Children of **Casandra Diane^6 Johnson** include:

569.　i. CHRISTOPHER COY^7 was born on 2 February 1996.
570.　ii. ERIC TURNER was born on 20 April 2000.

391. DARRYL ALLAN^6 STEWART (*Iris Yvette^5, Dorothy^{4}Williams, Sidney^3, Nancy^{2}Boyer, Porter^1*) was born on 29 January 1980.

Children of **Darryl Allan^6 Stewart** include:

571.　i. DARRYL ALLAN^7 JR. was born on 2 July 2000.

399. LASHAY^6 WALTON (*Peggy^{5}Renfroe, Mae Will^{4}Williams, Lee^3, Nancy^{2}Boyer, Porter^1*) was born on 30 April 1967 in Detroit, Michigan.

Children of **Lashay**^{6} **Walton** and **Byron** (—?—) were:
572.   i. BYRON^7 was born on 17 July 1985 in Detroit, Michigan.

405. DENISE^6 **EPPS** (*Claudia*^{5}*Arnold, Lucy Jane*^{4}*Williams, Johnnie*^{3}*, Nancy*^{2}*Boyer, Porter*^{1}).

Children of **Denise**^{6} **Epps** include:
573.   i. SAKENNAH^7 was born on 5 September.

411. DARLENE^6 **DAVIS** (*Ernestine*^{5}*Arnold, Lucy Jane*^{4}*Williams, Johnnie*^{3}*, Nancy*^{2}*Boyer, Porter*^{1}) was born on 13 October 1958 in Newark, New Jersey. She married **Alexander Hamilton.**

Children of **Darlene**^{6} **Davis** and **Alexander Hamilton** were as follows:
574.   i. JERMEL^7 was born on 27 October 1981 in Savannah, Georgia.
575.   ii. JADE LEWIS.
576.   iii. NILES was born on 7 December 1994 in Atlanta, Georgia.

412. ALGERNON^6 **DAVIS JR.** (*Ernestine*^{5}*Arnold, Lucy Jane*^{4}*Williams, Johnnie*^{3}*, Nancy*^{2}*Boyer, Porter*^{1}) was born on 13 September 1959 in Newark, New Jersey.

Children of **Algernon**^{6} **Davis Jr.** and **Cathy Ismael** were:
577.   i. AALIYAH KEYONA^7.

Children of **Algernon**^{6} **Davis Jr.** and **Gina Brown** were:
578.   i. ASHLEY BROWN^7 was born on 28 August 1985 in East Orange, New Jersey.

413. MICHELE BERNICE^6 **JACKSON** (*Maude Lizabeth*^{5}*Williams, Coleman*^{4}*, Johnnie*^{3}*, Nancy*^{2}*Boyer, Porter*^{1}) was born on 27 July 1953 in Philadelphia, Pennsylvania. She married **Wayne Dewitt McNight** on 4 June 1977 in Magnolia, New Jersey.

Children of **Michele Bernice**^{6} **Jackson** and **Wayne Dewitt McNight** were:
579.   i. SELENA BERNICE^7 was born on 21 July 1979 in Cherry Hill, New Jersey.

414. VERONICA 'RONNIE' LYNN^6 **JACKSON** (*Maude Lizabeth*^{5}*Williams, Coleman*^{4}*, Johnnie*^{3}*, Nancy*^{2}*Boyer, Porter*^{1}) was born on 23 January 1956 in Philadelphia, Pennsylvania. She married **Gerald Lamont Steele** on 21 January 1977 in New Jersey. She died on 2 April 2001 in Camden, New Jersey, at age 45.

Children of **Veronica 'Ronnie' Lynn**^{6} **Jackson** and **Gerald Lamont Steele** were:
580.   i. GERALD LAMONT^7 JR. was born on 8 December 1978 in Cherry Hill, New Jersey.

415. HARRY MICHAEL DAVID 'MIKE'^{6} JACKSON (*Maude Lizabeth^5 Williams, Coleman^4, Johnnie^3, Nancy^2 Boyer, Porter^1*) was born on 27 October 1957 in Philadelphia, Pennsylvania. He married **Charmaine Little** on 15 August 1987 in Trenton, New Jersey.

Children of **Harry Michael David 'Mike'^{6} Jackson** and **Charmaine Little** were as follows:
581.   i. KARONE^7 was born on 24 March 1988 in Trenton, New Jersey.
582.   ii. CHAQUANA was born on 14 January 1989 in Trenton, New Jersey.
583.   iii. THOMAS MICHAEL was born on 8 July 1990 in Camden, New Jersey.
584.   iv. SASHA was born on 8 August 1999 in Trenton, New Jersey.
585.   v. ISAIAH DAVID was born on 2 July 2000 in Camden, New Jersey.

416. STEPHEN MARK^6 JACKSON (*Maude Lizabeth^5 Williams, Coleman^4, Johnnie^3, Nancy^2 Boyer, Porter^1*) was born on 2 February 1961 in Philadelphia, Pennsylvania. He married **Terri Holliman** on 15 February 1985 in Tyler, Texas. He married **Cynthia Kurtz** in May 1991 in Raleigh, North Carolina.

Children of **Stephen Mark^6 Jackson** and **Terri Holliman** were:
586.   i. SIERRA MARIE^7 was born on 29 December 1987 in San Francisco, California.

There were no children of **Stephen Mark^6 Jackson** and **Cynthia Kurtz**.

417. BRUCE KEVIN^6 JACKSON (*Maude Lizabeth^5 Williams, Coleman^4, Johnnie^3, Nancy^2 Boyer, Porter^1*) was born on 6 September 1963 in Philadelphia, Pennsylvania. He married **Cynthia Lee Piner**, daughter of **Romero H. Piner** and **Juanita F. Cason**, on 1 July 1989 in Haddonfield, New Jersey.

Children of **Bruce Kevin^6 Jackson** and **Melissa Gonzales** were as follows:
587.   i. BRUCE KEVIN^7 JR. was born on 29 May 1985 in Camden, New Jersey.
588.   ii. MELANIE was born in October 1986 in Camden, New Jersey.

Children of **Bruce Kevin^6 Jackson** and **Cynthia Lee Piner** were:
589.   i. MARK ANTHONY^7 was born on 16 January 1998 in Camden, New Jersey.

418. PAMELA^6 COX (*Mildred^5 Williams, Coleman^4, Johnnie^3, Nancy^2 Boyer, Porter^1*) was born on 26 March 1954 in Anchorage, Alaska. She married **Joseph Bryant** on 1 June 1974 in Philadelphia, Pennsylvania.

Children of **Pamela^6 Cox** and **Joseph Bryant** were as follows:
+ 590.   i. SHARIA DANIELLE^7, born 19 March 1976 in Los Angeles, California; married **Jerrod Erwin Washington**.
591.   ii. SHAYA MONIQUE was born on 30 July 1977 in Los Angeles, California.

+ 592.   iii. KOBE BEAN, born 23 August 1978 in Los Angeles, California; married Vanessa Laine.

419. JOHN ARTHUR 'CHUBBY'^{6} COX III (*Mildred*^{5}*Williams, Coleman*^{4}*, Johnnie*^{3}*, Nancy*^{2}*Boyer, Porter*^{1}) was born on 29 December 1955 in Philadelphia, Pennsylvania. He married Vicki Renee Bransford.

Children of John Arthur 'Chubby'^{6} Cox III and Vicki Renee Bransford were as follows:
593.   i. JOHN ARTHUR^7 IV was born on 6 July 1981 in Caracas, Venezuela.
594.   ii. SEAN LEE was born on 9 January 1987 in San Diego, California.

Children of John Arthur 'Chubby'^{6} Cox III and Del-Rita Sharmette Butler were:
595.   i. SHARIF DAVID^7 was born on 21 July 1975 in Philadelphia, Pennsylvania.

422. CHARLES 'CHUCK'^{6} WILLIAMS JR. (*Charles*^{5}*, Coleman*^{4}*, Johnnie*^{3}*, Nancy*^{2}*Boyer, Porter*^{1}) was born on 16 September 1963 in Philadelphia, Pennsylvania. He married Donna Johnson in Philadelphia, Pennsylvania. He married Debbie Turnage.

Children of Charles 'Chuck'^{6} Williams Jr. and Donna Johnson were:
596.   i. BLAIR^7 was born on 7 April 1989 in Philadelphia, Pennsylvania.

Children of Charles 'Chuck'^{6} Williams Jr. and Debbie Turnage were:
597.   i. RAYNOR JAMAL^7 was born on 29 March 1994 in Philadelphia, Pennsylvania.

423. L'TANYA DAHLIA 'TAMMY'^{6} WILLIAMS (*Charles*^{5}*, Coleman*^{4}*, Johnnie*^{3}*, Nancy*^{2}*Boyer, Porter*^{1}) was born on 2 March 1965 in Philadelphia, Pennsylvania. She married Terry Pittman in 1990 in Philadelphia, Pennsylvania.

Children of L'Tanya Dahlia 'Tammy'^{6} Williams and Terry Pittman were as follows:
598.   i. TERRY MYLES^7 was born on 27 November 1995 in Philadelphia, Pennsylvania.
599.   ii. TROY DAHLIA was born on 1 May 2000 in Philadelphia, Pennsylvania.

425. DONNA ROCHELLE^6 JASPER (*Janet*^{5}*Williams, Coleman*^{4}*, Johnnie*^{3}*, Nancy*^{2}*Boyer, Porter*^{1}) was born on 3 January 1966 in Mount Holly, New Jersey. She married George Childs Petagrew on 14 September 1991 in Philadelphia, Pennsylvania.

Children of Donna Rochelle^6 Jasper and George Childs Petagrew were as follows:
600.   i. ALLISON JANETTE^7 was born on 29 August 1993 in Newark, New Jersey.
601.   ii. GEORGE EARNEST was born on 1 December 1996 in Newark, New Jersey.

427. ANGELA RENEA^6 **WILLIAMS** (*Roger*^{5}, *Coleman*^{4}, *Johnnie*^{3}, *Nancy*^{2}*Boyer*, *Porter*^{1}) was born on 4 January 1971 in Philadelphia, Pennsylvania. She married **Rudolph Frederick Valentine Jr.**, son of **Rudolph Frederick Valentine** and **Jacqueline Williams,** on 21 July 2001 in Philadelphia, Pennsylvania.

Children of **Angela Renea**^{6} **Williams** and **Kenneth 'Kenny' Liggins Jr.** were:
602.   i. ASHLEY GAIL^7 was born on 30 March 1993 in Philadelphia, Pennsylvania.

Children of **Angela Renea**^{6} **Williams** and **Rudolph Frederick Valentine Jr.** were:
603.   i. SUMMER CHRISTINE^7 was born on 27 December 2002 in Philadelphia, Pennsylvania.

428. GERMAINE DAPHNE^6 **WILLIAMS** (*Joyce Cheryl*^{5}, *Coleman*^{4}, *Johnnie*^{3}, *Nancy*^{2}*Boyer*, *Porter*^{1}) was born on 30 March 1974 in Philadelphia, Pennsylvania.

Children of **Germaine Daphne**^{6} **Williams** and **Alfred Harrison** were:
604.   i. JAI SABIR^7 was born on 11 June 1995 in Philadelphia, Pennsylvania.

442. JOHN ANDREW^6 **JOHNSON** (*Sherry*^{5}*Temple*, *Viola*^{4}*Williams*, *Johnnie*^{3}, *Nancy*^{2}*Boyer*, *Porter*^{1}) was born on 4 June 1942 in Atlanta, Georgia. He married **Geraldine** (—?—). He died on 8 October 1974 in Detroit, Michigan, at age 32.

Children of **John Andrew**^{6} **Johnson** and **Geraldine** (—?—) were as follows:
605.   i. DAVID^7 was born on 15 July in Detroit, Michigan. He died on 22 February 1983 in Detroit, Michigan.
606.   ii. JOHN ANDREW JR. was born on 7 September in Detroit, Michigan.

452. LOWELL^6 **MASSEY III** (*Veronica 'Ronnie'*^{5}*Hooks*, *Mamie*^{4}*Williams*, *Johnnie*^{3}, *Nancy*^{2}*Boyer*, *Porter*^{1}) was born on 22 April 1967 in Detroit, Michigan. He married **Classie Legardy** on 15 September 1998 in Detroit, Michigan.

Children of **Lowell**^{6} **Massey III** and **Lezlie Robinson** were as follows:
607.   i. JOYCE DENISE^7 was born on 24 January 1986 in Detroit, Michigan.
608.   ii. JOSALYN was born on 5 May 1994 in Detroit, Michigan.

Children of **Lowell**^{6} **Massey III** and **Classie Legardy** were as follows:
609.   i. LOWELL^7 IV was born on 19 May 1998 in Detroit, Michigan.
610.   ii. LAVELL JOSEPH was born on 25 May 1999 in Detroit, Michigan.

455. CHRISONDRA 'CHRIS' LYNN^6 DENNIS (*Mamie Sharon^{5}Hooks, Mamie^{4}Williams, Johnnie^3, Nancy^{2}Boyer, Porter^1*) was born on 3 June 1967 in Highland Park, Michigan. She married **Ronald Austin** on 19 June 1993 in Detroit, Michigan.

Children of **Chrisondra 'Chris' Lynn^6 Dennis** and **Ronald Austin** were as follows:
611.   i. JOURDAN LAMAR^7 was born on 3 June 1996 in Detroit, Michigan.
612.   ii. JESSICA LYNN was born on 3 June 1996 in Detroit, Michigan.

456. LESTER 'MAN' MARVIN^6 DENNIS II (*Mamie Sharon^{5}Hooks, Mamie^{4}Williams, Johnnie^3, Nancy^{2}Boyer, Porter^1*) was born on 26 October 1969 in Royal Oaks, Michigan. He married **Susan Ford** in Detroit, Michigan.

Children of **Lester 'Man' Marvin^6 Dennis II** and **Susan Ford** were as follows:
613.   i. JUSTIN^7 was born on 24 February 1996 in Southfield, Michigan.
614.   ii. BRALEN was born on 2 October 1998 in Southfield, Michigan.

462. STEPHANIE^6 GANT (*James 'Jabo' William^{5}Napier, Louise^{4}Williams, Johnnie^3, Nancy^{2}Boyer, Porter^1*) was born on 17 June 1964 in Detroit, Michigan.

Children of **Stephanie^6 Gant** include:
615.   i. SHARIA^7 was born on 19 April 1983 in Detroit, Michigan.

463. ADRIAN ANTHONY^6 GREEN (*Phyllis^{5}Napier, Louise^{4}Williams, Johnnie^3, Nancy^{2}Boyer, Porter^1*) was born on 11 July 1971 in Detroit, Michigan.

Children of **Adrian Anthony^6 Green** and **Akika Pitts** were:
616.   i. ADRIAN ANTHONY^7 JR. was born on 16 April 1997 in Detroit, Michigan.

473. MECHA BETTINA^6 ALLEN (*John 'Johnny' Ray^5, Fannie Pearl^{4}Williams, Johnnie^3, Nancy^{2}Boyer, Porter^1*) was born on 2 July 1979 in Detroit, Michigan.

Children of **Mecha Bettina^6 Allen** and **Clarence Love** were:
617.   i. JOHNNY D'SEAN^7 was born on 24 February 1999 in Ventura, California.

486. DAVID^6 WILLIAMS (*Nancy^5, David^4, Johnnie^3, Nancy^{2}Boyer, Porter^1*) was born on 11 September 1968 in Philadelphia, Pennsylvania.

Children of **David^6 Williams** include:
618.   i. DAVINA^7 was born on 22 December 1991 in Philadelphia, Pennsylvania.

487. JENELLE KIMBERLY^6 MCELRATH (*Brenda Susan^{5}Miller, Clara^{4}Williams, Johnnie^3, Nancy^{2}Boyer, Porter^1*) was born on 9 August 1971 in Detroit, Michigan. She married **Antonio Mitchell** on 30 September 1994 in Detroit, Michigan.

Children of **Jenelle Kimberly^6 McElrath** and **Antonio Mitchell** were as follows:
619.   i. TAYLOR MONET^7 was born on 28 June 1996 in Detroit, Michigan.
620.   ii. TYRA BRIANNA was born on 20 June 1997 in Detroit, Michigan.

491. DWIGHT KEPTLER^6 MILLER JR. (*Dwight Keptler^5, Clara^{4}Williams, Johnnie^3, Nancy^{2}Boyer, Porter^1*) was born on 9 May 1976 in Detroit, Michigan. He married **Renee** (—?—) on 7 September 2002 in Detroit, Michigan.

Children of **Dwight Keptler^6 Miller Jr.** and **Renee** (—?—) were:
621.   i. JUSTIN DWIGHT^7 was born on 19 February 2003 in Detroit, Michigan.

501. JAMILA DANIELLE^6 BANKS (*Phyllis Allen^{5}Williams, Inez^4, Robert^3, Nancy^{2}Boyer, Porter^1*) was born on 15 December 1972 in Los Angeles, California.

Children of **Jamila Danielle^6 Banks** include:
622.   i. XAVIER KASAI^7 was born on 19 August 2000 in Los Angeles, California.

502. CANYON KASAI^6 BANKS (*Phyllis Allen^{5}Williams, Inez^4, Robert^3, Nancy^{2}Boyer, Porter^1*) was born on 4 September 1975 in Los Angeles, California.

Children of **Canyon Kasai^6 Banks** include:
623.   i. MAYA DANIELLE^7 was born on 17 July 2000 in Los Angeles, California.

508. ANGEL^6 LIGGINS (*Kenneth^5, Willie Mae 'Bell'^{4}, Mary 'Mae' Ella^{3}Williams, Nancy^{2}Boyer, Porter^1*) was born on 7 November 1968 in Philadelphia, Pennsylvania.

Children of **Angel^6 Liggins** and **Tyrone Tidwell** were:
624.   i. AMBER MICHELLE^7 was born on 30 September 1989 in Philadelphia, Pennsylvania.

509. KENNETH 'KENNY'^{6} LIGGINS JR. (*Kenneth^5, Willie Mae 'Bell'^{4}, Mary 'Mae' Ella^{3}Williams, Nancy^{2}Boyer, Porter^1*) was born on 2 February 1970 in Philadelphia, Pennsylvania.

Children of **Kenneth 'Kenny'^{6} Liggins Jr.** and **Angela Renea Williams** were:
625.   i. ASHLEY GAIL^7, born 30 March 1993 in Philadelphia, Pennsylvania.

184

Generation Seven

590. **SHARIA DANIELLE**[7] **BRYANT** (*Pamela*[6]*Cox, Mildred*[5]*Williams, Coleman*[4], *Johnnie*[3], *Nancy*[2]*Boyer, Porter*[1]) was born on 19 March 1976 in Los Angeles, California. She married **Jerrod Erwin Washington**, son of **Erwin Washington** and **Philena** (—?—), on 17 May 1998 in Los Angeles, California.

Children of **Sharia Danielle**[7] **Bryant** and **Jerrod Erwin Washington** were as follows:
    626.   i. TAYA LEE[8] was born on 5 January 1999 in Los Angeles, California.
    627.   ii. SYDNEY TAYLOR was born on 22 April 2000 in Los Angeles, California.

592. **KOBE BEAN**[7] **BRYANT** (*Pamela*[6]*Cox, Mildred*[5]*Williams, Coleman*[4], *Johnnie*[3], *Nancy*[2]*Boyer, Porter*[1]) was born on 23 August 1978 in Los Angeles, California. He married **Vanessa Laine** in April 2001 in California.

Children of **Kobe Bean**[7] **Bryant** and **Vanessa Laine** were:
    628.   i. NATALIA DIAMANTE[8] was born in January 2003 in Los Angeles, California.

Descendants of James Hooks

	The name of every person whose place of abode on the first day of June, 1870, was in this family.	Age	Sex	Color	Profession, Occupation, or Trade of each person, male or female.	Value of Real Estate	Value of Personal Estate	Place of Birth, naming State or Territory of U.S., or the Country, if of foreign birth.										
	3	4	5	6	7	8	9	10	11	12	13	14	15	16	17	18	19	20
7	Hooks James	30	M	B	Farm Laborer			Georgia					1	1			1	
	Mary	29	F	B	Keeping House			"					1					
	Jordan	10	M	B	Work on farm			"					1	1				
	Meackie	8	M	B	"	"			"					1				
	Lee	6	M	B				"										
	Cella	4	F	B				"										
	Anna	9/12	F	B						at								
8	Kelsie Elijah	22	M	B	Farm Laborer			Georgia					1	1			1	
	Dinah	30	F	B	Keeping House			"					1					
	Lilla	4	F	B				"										
	Isaac	7/12	M	B				"		At								
9	Kelsie Shepard	30	M	B	Farm Laborer			Georgia					1	1			1	
	Jane	29	F	B	Keeping House			"					1					
	Mitchell	6	M	B				"										
	Henry	4	M	B				"										
	Anna	7/12	F	B				"		Feb								
10	Young Ceasar	40	M	B	Farm Laborer			Georgia					1	1			1	
	Tellie	20	M	B	Work on farm			"					1	1				
	Anna	17	F	B	House Keeper			"					1	1				
	Martha	14	F	B	Attending School			"				1						
	James	12	M	B				"				1						
	Mary	10	F	B	"	"			"				1					
	Rachel	6	F	B				"										
11	King Moses	53	M	B	Farm Laborer			Georgia					1	1			1	
	Jane	50	F	B	Keeping House			"					1					
	Cicero	17	M	B	Farm Laborer			"						1				
	Fannie	12	F	B	Attending School			"										

James Hooks, 1870 Census

GRANTEE - GRANTOR INDEX

Date _23 Nov, 1992_

Researcher _L. Geiger_   Ancestor _Hooks_

File No. _____

Circle one: ORIGINAL / MICROFILM / BOOK / EXTRACT   Call number

Library/courthouse _Superior Court, Washington Co._

Legible _____   Publisher _____

Date recorded	GRANTOR OR GRANTEE (Circle one)	GRANTOR OR GRANTEE (Circle one)	INSTRA-MENT	TOWN	BOOK No.	PAGE No.
9 June 1866	E J Langmode	Hook, James J	Deed	*	A	2-
23 Jan 1869	John A Emerson & wife	Hooks, BA & Gabriel J	Deed		A	43.
19 Feb 1869	Thomas M Harris	Hook, James J	Deed & plat	*	A	51.
19 Oct 1869	James H Jackson	Hooks, James J	Mtg	*	A	60-
7 Jan 1873	Hillary Hooks (By Sherif)	Hooks, Elisha	Deed		C	9
22 Jan 1876	Benj Churchwell Harris	Hooks, Mr North J etal	Agreement		D	17
28 Feb 1880	Gabriel W Stubbs	Hooks, Hopewell	Deed & Plat		E	63
1 Dec 1880	Jacob G Fulghum	Hooks, Nathaniel	Deed		F	30
20 Jan 1881	R. T. Pounds	Hooks, James	Mtg	*	A	9-
3 Nov 1881	James Fulghum (By Adm.)	Hooks, Bennett A	Deed		F	10-
27 June 1881	Mary J & Frank Harris	Hooks, N.H.	Deed		F	18-
17 Oct 1881	Wm J Brantley	Hooks James J etal	Deed	*	F	215
24 Feb 1882	Sarah J Hooks	Hooks, N.H. et al.	Deed		F	375
22 Apr 1882	Ivey H W Duggan	Hooks James	Deed	*	F	437
4 Dec 1883	T. Warthen & Co	Hooks, Nathaniel H.	Deed		G	148
24 Dec 1883	G J Hooks	Hooks, N.H.	Deed		G	178
13 Jan 1887	Mary Harris	Hooks N.H.	Deed		H	68
12 Jan 1887	Nancy Jordan	Hooks, N.H.	Deed		H	615
16 Apr 1887	J C Duggan	Hooks M.J. et.al.	Deed		I	29
12 Sep 1887	Sarah Jane Kelly	Hooks, NH	Deed		I	13.
17 Nov 1887	Lo H Dorsett	Hooks, NH	Deed		I	19
11 Dec 1887	W S Lozier	Hooks, Martha Olivia, Lucinda	Mtg		F	675
11 Dec 1887	W S Lozier	Hooks NH	Mtg		F	67-
	Many more transactions for Hooks, NH. did not copy					
10 Jul 1900	Plat	Hooks, James	Division	*	O	72

Topic No. 6

James Hooks, Recorded Deed

188

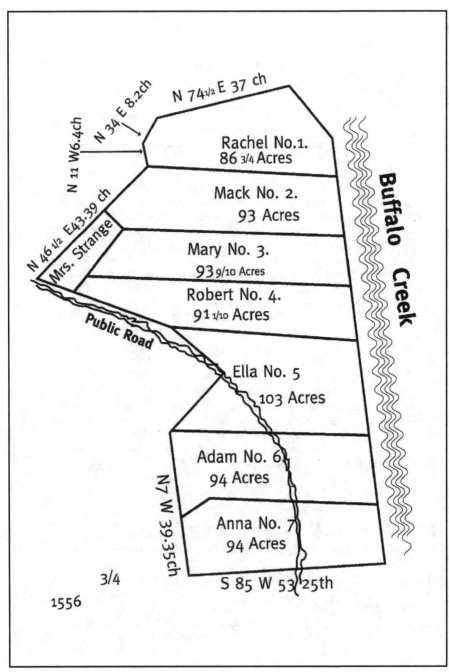

Plat of James Hooks' Estate

U.S. Bureau of the Census 1880, Tenth Agriculture Census

Question No.	Column Heading	Entry
	ROW 1	
001	NAME: *Hooks, James* Microfilm roll #: *T1137, roll 20 Washington Co., Ga* ED # *128*, Page *16*, Line *6*	
002	Owner	
003	Rent for fixed money rental	
004	Rent for shares of production	✓
	Acres of Land	
	Improved	
005	Tilled, including fallow and grass in rotation (whether pasture or meadow)	*22 acres*
006	Permanent meadows, permanent pastures, orchards, and vineyards	
	Unimproved	
007	Woodland and forest	
008	Other unimproved, including "old fields" not growing wood	
	Farm Values	
009	Of farm, including land, fences & buildings	*$410*
010	of farming implements and machinery	*3 40*
011	of live stock on farm June 1, 1880	*$300*
	Fences	
012	Cost of building and repair	
013	Cost of Fertilizers pruchased, 1879	*$50*
014	**Labor** Amount paid for wages for farm labor 1879 including value of board	*$60*
	Weeks hired labor in 1879 upon farm (and dairy) excluding house work	
015	White *(No.)*	
016	Colored *(No.)*	6
	Estiamted value of all farm productions (sold, consumed, or on hand) for 1897	
017	(Dollars)	*$1000*

James Hooks, 1880 Agriculture Census, pg. 1

190

1880 Agriculture Census

Question No.	Column Heading	Entry
	Grass Lands	
	Acreage 1879	
018	Mown	
019	Not Mown	
	Products Harvested in 1879	
020	Hay	
021	Clover Seed	
022	Grass Seed	
023	Horses of all ages on hand June 1, 1880	
024	Mules and Asses all ages on hand June 1, 1880	2
	ROW 2	
	Meat Cattle and their Products	
	On hand June 1, 1880	
025	Working oxen	1
026	Milch cows	2
027	Other	10
	Movement, 1879	
028	Calves Dropped	
	Cattle of all ages	
029	Purchased	
030	Sold living	
031	Slaughtered	
032	Died	
	Dairy Products	
033	Milk sold or sent to butter and cheese factories in 1879	
034	Butter made on the farm in 1879	25 lb
035	Cheese made on the farm in 1879	

James Hooks, 1880 Agriculture Census, pg. 2

Question No.	Column Heading	Entry
	Sheep	
036	On hand June 1, 1880	
	Movement 1879	
037	Lambs Dropped	
038	Purchased	
039	Sold living	
040	Slaughtered	
041	Killed by dogs	
042	Died of disease	
043	Died of stress of weather	
	WOOL, spring clip of 1880	
044	Fleeces	
045	Weight	
046	Swine on hand June 1, 1880	*18*
	Poultry on hand June 1, 1880 exlusive of Spring Hatching	
047	Barn-Yard	*20*
048	Other	*11*
049	Eggs produced in 1879	Doz. *42*
	Rice	
050	Acres	
051	Crop	lbs.
	Row 3	
	Cereal, 1879	
052	Barley - Acres	
053	Barley - Crop	Bu.
054	Buckwheat - Acres	
055	Buckwheat - Crop	Bu.
056	Indian Corn - Acres	*40*
057	Indian Corn - Crop	Bu. *240*
058	Oats - Acres	*5*
059	Oats - Crop	Bu. *30*

James Hooks, 1880 Agriculture Census, pg. 3

192

Question No.	Column Heading	Entry
060	Rye - Acres	
061	Rye - Crop	Bu.
062	Wheat - Acres	
063	Wheat - Crop	Bu.
	Fiber, 1879	
064	Cotton - Acres	*40*
065	Cotton - Bales	*15*
066	Flax - Acres	
067	Flax - Seed	Bu.
068	Flax - straw	tons
069	Flax - Fiber	lbs.
070	Hemp - Acres	
071	Hemp - Crop	Tons
	Sugar and Molasses, 1879	
072	Cane - Acres in Crop	*1*
073	Cane - Sugar	Hhds.
074	Cane - Molasses	gals. *40*
075	Sorghum - Acres in Crop	
076	Sorghum - Sugar	lbs.
077	Sorghum - Molasses	gals.
078	Maple - Sugar	lbs.
079	Maple - Molasses	gals.

Row 4

	Pulse, 1879	
080	Pease	Bu.
081	Beans (Dry)	Bu.
082	Irish Potatoes - Acres	
083	Irish Potatoes - Crop	Bu.
084	Sweet Potatoes - Acres	*1*
085	Sweet Potatoes - Crop	Bu. *45*
086	Tobacco - Acres	
087	Tobacco - Crop	lbs.

10, 40, 80 ? could not read ←

James Hooks, 1880 Agriculture Census, pg. 4

Question No.	Column Heading	Entry
	Orchards, 1879	
088	Apples - Acres	
089	Apples - Bearing trees	
090	Apples - Bushels	
091	Peaches - Acres	
092	Peaches - Bearing trees	
093	Peaches - Bushels	
094	Total Value - Dollars	
	Nurseries, 1879	
095	Acres	
096	Value of products sold in 1879	
	Vineyards, 1879	
097	Acres	
098	Grapes sold in 1879	
099	Wine made in 1879	
100	Market garden - Value of Products sold - Dollars	
	Bees	
101	Honey	lbs.
102	Wax	lbs.
	Forest Products	
103	Amount of Wood cut in 1879	cords 40
104	Value of all products sold or consumed in 1879	Dollars

Could not read

James Hooks, 1880 Agriculture Census, pg. 5

DEPARTMENT OF COMMERCE—BUREAU OF THE CENSUS   165
FOURTEENTH CENSUS OF THE UNITED STATES: 1920—POPULATION

	111	114	Hooks Mack	Head		O F	M	B	58	Wd
			— Mack Jr	Son			M	B	24	S
			— Robert	Son			M	B	19	S
			— Joe	Son			M	B	17	S
			— Samuel	Son			M	B	15	S
			— Hattie May	Daughter			F	B	12	S
			— Laura Ann	Daughter			F	B	10	S
			— Bessie Cleve	Daughter			F	B	5	S
			Hooks Joe	Head			M	B	16	S

Mack Hooks, 1920 Census

Descendants of James Hooks

Generation One

1. JAMES^1 HOOKS was born circa 1833 in Georgia. He married **Ella Kelsey**. He married **Mary (———)**. He died circa 1891.

Children of James^1 Hooks and Ella Kelsey were as follows:
+   2.   i. ROBERT^2 SR., born 6 June 1869; married **Clara Lane**.
+   3.   ii. ADAM 'ADD', born circa 1875 in Washington County, Georgia; married **Kizzie Trawick**.
+   4.   iii. RACHEL, born March 1876 in Washington County, Georgia; married **William 'Will' Turner**.
     5.   iv. REUBEN was born circa 1878 in Georgia.

Children of James^1 Hooks and Mary (———) were as follows:
     6.   i. JORDAN^2 was born circa 1859 in Georgia.
+   7.   ii. MACK, born December 1861 in Washington County, Georgia; married **Judy Mason**.
     8.   iii. LEE was born circa 1863 in Georgia.
+   9.   iv. ANNA, born circa 1866 in Washington County, Georgia; married **Doss Dixon**.
+   10.   v. MARY, born 1866 in Washington County, Georgia; married **Western Wiggins**.
+   11.   vi. ELLA, born September 1870 in Washington County, Georgia; married **Jeff Carter Sr.**

Generation Two

2. ROBERT^2 HOOKS SR. (*James^1*) was born on 6 June 1869. He married **Clara Lane** in Georgia. He died on 5 September 1946 at age 77.

Children of Robert^2 Hooks Sr. and Clara Lane were as follows:
+   12.   i. PEARL L.^{3}, born December 1894 in Georgia; married **Dessie Canty**.
     13.   ii. GIRLY was born in June 1899 in Georgia.
+   14.   iii. MAMIE, married **John Gaudy**.
+   15.   iv. CLIFFORD SR., born 3 February 1896 in Georgia; married **Beatrice Butts**.
     16.   v. IZOLA was born circa 1901 in Washington County, Georgia.
     17.   vi. ANNIE was born circa 1903 in Georgia. She married **Al Chester**. She married **William Taylor**.
+   18.   vii. JAMES, born 9 December 1905; married **Mozella Matthew**.
+   19.   viii. ROBERT J. JR., born 20 April 1908 in Washington County, Georgia; married **Sarah Dixon**; married **Carrie B. Lawson**; married **Louise 'Lou' Cheeves**; married **Lennie Ruth Gordy**.

20. ix. JOHN was born after 1910.
21. x. DICK was born circa 1911 in Washington County, Georgia.

3. ADAM 'ADD'^{2} HOOKS (*James*^{1}) was born circa 1875 in Washington County, Georgia. He married **Kizzie Trawick**, daughter of **Dock Trawick** and **Violet Young**, on 26 December 1894 in Washington County, Georgia.

Children of **Adam 'Add'**^{2} **Hooks** and **Kizzie Trawick** were as follows:
22. i. LEE^3 was born in September 1895 in Georgia. He married **Eunice O'Neal**.
23. ii. SYLVESTER was born on 2 September 1899 in Georgia. He married **Lucille Smith**.
+ 24. iii. JOE, married **Fannie Smith**.
25. iv. INEZ married **Mr. Garcia**.

4. RACHEL^2 HOOKS (*James*^{1}) was born in March 1876 in Washington County, Georgia. She married **William 'Will' Turner**. She died in 1907.

Children of **Rachel**^{2} **Hooks** and **William 'Will' Turner** were as follows:
+ 26. i. ALBERTA^3, born October 1898 in Georgia; married **Snap Bridges**.
+ 27. ii. ELTON, born 20 April 1900 in Georgia; married **Linen 'Lennie' Rogers**.
28. iii. ARTHUR was born circa 1902 in Georgia.
+ 29. iv. MATTIE, born circa 1904 in Georgia; married **Joe Taylor**.
30. v. MCKINLEY.
31. vi. RACHEL.
32. vii. WILLIAM 'WILLIE' JR. was born circa 1906 in Washington County, Georgia.

7. MACK^2 HOOKS (*James*^{1}) was born in December 1861 in Washington County, Georgia. He married **Judy Mason** in Georgia. He died in 1940.

Children of **Mack**^{2} **Hooks** and **Judy Mason** were as follows:
+ 33. i. JENNIE^3, born May 1889 in Georgia; married **Frank Hall**.
34. ii. MACK (JR.) was born on 28 February 1895 in Washington County, Georgia.
+ 35. iii. ROBERT, born circa 1901 in Washington County, Georgia; married **Marie Bivens**; married **Sarah White**.
36. iv. SALLY.
+ 37. v. WILLIAM, born January 1897 in Georgia; married **Julia Walker**.
+ 38. vi. LUCY FRANCES, born March 1899 in Georgia; married **Eldridge Barlow Jr.**
39. vii. JOE was born circa 1903 in Georgia.
40. viii. SAM was born circa 1905 in Georgia.
+ 41. ix. HATTIE MAE, born 8 May 1907 in Georgia; married **Henry Berry Gordy**.
42. x. LAURA ANN was born on 20 April 1909. She married **Moses Harper**. She married **Mr. Wilkin**.
+ 43. xi. BESSIE, born 4 November 1914; married **Jessie Pitts**.

9. ANNA[2] HOOKS (*James[1]*) was born circa 1866 in Washington County, Georgia. She married **Doss Dixon.**

Children of **Anna[2] Hooks** and **Doss Dixon** were as follows:
- 44. i. ANNIE[3].
- 45. ii. OTIS.
- 46. iii. LEDONIA.

10. MARY[2] HOOKS (*James[1]*) was born in 1866 in Washington County, Georgia. She married **Western Wiggins.**

Children of **Mary[2] Hooks** and **Western Wiggins** were:
- 47. i. GERTRUDE[3].

11. ELLA[2] HOOKS (*James[1]*) was born in September 1870 in Washington County, Georgia. She married **Jeff Carter Sr.**, son of **Burrell Carter** and **Mary Ann Lane**, on 19 January 1887 in Washington County, Georgia. She died before 1910 in Georgia.

Children of **Ella[2] Hooks** and **Jeff Carter Sr.** were as follows:
- + 48.   i. BERTHA[3], married **Thomas Renfrow;** married **Johnnie Trawick.**
- + 49.   ii. MARY ETHEL, born December 1887 in Georgia; married **Bert Lundy;** married **Charlie Young.**
- 50.   iii. LUCY was born circa 1889 in Sandersville, Washington County, Georgia.
- 51.   iv. ANNIE B. was born in March 1890 in Georgia.
- + 52.   v. JEFF JR., born 10 September 1894 in Oconee, Washington County, Georgia; married **Gervenia Fisher.**
- + 53.   vi. LORA ELLA 'LAURA', born 2 June 1895 in Sandersville, Washington County, Georgia; married **Homer Dawson.**
- + 54.   vii. LILLIE RUTH, born February 1897 in Georgia; married **Samuel Turner.**
- 55.   viii. BOYSIE was born in August 1899 in Georgia.
- + 56.   ix. VIRGIL 'VIRGE', born 15 August 1900 in Sandersville, Washington County, Georgia; married **Mamie Ethridge.**
- 57.   x. CRAWFORD was born in 1905 in Sandersville, Washington County, Georgia. He married **Susie (—?—)**. He married **Mary (—?—)**.
- 58.   xi. MINNIE was born circa 1907 in Sandersville, Washington County, Georgia. She married **Jesse Butts.**

Generation Three

12. PEARL L.*3* HOOKS (*Robert2, James1*) was born in December 1894 in Georgia. She married **Dessie Canty.**

Children of **Pearl L.*3* Hooks** and **Dessie Canty** were:
+ 59. i. MAMIE*4*, born 30 September 1913.

14. MAMIE*3* HOOKS (*Robert2, James1*) was born on 19 October 1900 in Washington County, Georgia. She married **John Gaudy,** son of **Berry Gordy Sr.** and **Lucy Hellum.** She died on 19 February 1991.

Children of **Mamie*3* Hooks** and **John Gaudy** were as follows:
  60.   i. BENJAMIN*4* was born in Sandersville, Georgia. He married **Barbara** (—?—).
+ 61.   ii. CLARA, born in Sandersville, Georgia.
+ 62. iii. MAMIE, born in Sandersville, Georgia; married **Alfred Lawson.**
+ 63. iv. JOHN JR., born in Sandersville, Georgia; married **Florine** (———).
+ 64.   v. NAOMIE, born in Sandersville, Georgia; married **Joe Johnson.**
+ 65. vi. BRENDA, born in Sandersville, Georgia; married **Hezekiah McDonald.**
+ 66. vii. THELMA, born in Sandersville, Georgia.
+ 67. viii. RAYMOND, born in Sandersville, Georgia; married **Florence** (———).
  68. ix. ROBERT was born in Sandersville, Washington County, Georgia.
+ 69.   x. JOHNNIE LOU, born circa 1918 in Washington County, Georgia; married **William Carithers.**
+ 70. xi. LULA MAE, born 22 November 1919 in Washington County, Georgia; married **William Johnson;** married **David James Lemon Sr.**
+ 71. xii. PORTER, born 2 February 1929 in Sandersville, Washington County, Georgia; married **Frances** (———).

15. CLIFFORD*3* HOOKS SR. (*Robert2, James1*) was born on 3 February 1896 in Georgia. He married **Beatrice Butts.** He died in 1963.

Children of **Clifford*3* Hooks Sr.** and **Beatrice Butts** were as follows:
  72.   i. MARY LOU*4* was born circa 1918 in Washington County, Georgia. She died in 1920 in Georgia.
  73.   ii. MAZOLA was born in November 1919 in Oconee, Washington County, Georgia. She married **Edward Taylor.**
+ 74. iii. CLARA, married **C. Williams;** married **James Liston.**
+ 75. iv. CLIFFORD JR., born 13 November 1925 in Philadelphia, Pennsylvania; married **Alice Lindsey.**
  76.   v. DANIEL ROBERT was born on 6 February 1928 in Steubenville, Ohio. He married **Ida Bell Stewart.**

+ 77. vi. BEATRICE, married **Willie Greenlee**; married **Carl Johnson.**

18. **JAMES**^{3} **HOOKS** (*Robert*^{2}, *James*^{1}) was born on 9 December 1905. He married **Mozella Matthew.**

Children of **James**^{3} **Hooks** and **Mozella Matthew** were as follows:
+ 78. i. MARACELLA^4, married **Herman David Young.**
+ 79. ii. VIOLA, born 8 June 1933; married **Benjamin Lacey**; married **Mr. Jones.**
+ 80. iii. JANETTA, married **Alvin Thomas (Jr.).**
+ 81. iv. ELEANOR, married **Winston Edwards.**

19. **ROBERT J.**^{3} **HOOKS JR.** (*Robert*^{2}, *James*^{1}) was born on 20 April 1908 in Washington County, Georgia. He married **Louise 'Lou' Cheeves**, daughter of **David 'Coot' Cheeves** and **Hattie Johnson.** He married **Sarah Dixon.** He married **Carrie B. Lawson.** He married **Lennie Ruth Gordy**, daughter of **Samuel 'Sam' Gordy** and **Carrie Cheeves.** He died in 1993.

Children of **Robert J.**^{3} **Hooks Jr.** and **Sarah Dixon** were as follows:
82. i. ROBERT^4 III.
+ 83. ii. OSCAR HOOKS, married **Delores (—?—).**
84. iii. BRENDA.

Children of **Robert J.**^{3} **Hooks Jr.** and **Carrie B. Lawson** were:
+ 85. i. DELORES^4, born 20 March 1939; married **Mitchell Hooks.**

Children of **Robert J.**^{3} **Hooks Jr.** and **Louise 'Lou' Cheeves** were:
+ 86. i. FLETA^4

There were no children of **Robert J.**^{3} **Hooks Jr.** and **Lennie Ruth Gordy.**

24. **JOE**^{3} **HOOKS** (*Adam 'Add'*^{2}, *James*^{1}) married **Fannie Smith.**

Children of **Joe**^{3} **Hooks** and **Fannie Smith** were as follows:
+ 87. i. FRANK^4, married **Bertha (———).**
88. ii. HAROLD.

26. **ALBERTA**^{3} **TURNER** (*Rachel*^{2}*Hooks, James*^{1}) was born in October 1898 in Georgia. She married **Snap Bridges.**

Children of **Alberta**^{3} **Turner** and **Snap Bridges** were as follows:
89. i. MACK^4.
90. ii. TOBIE.

91.   iii. ANNIE.
92.   iv. JOY.
93.   v. MAZOLA.
94.   vi. ARTHUR.
95.   vii. VIOLA.
96.   viii. LONNIE.
97.   ix. ULYSSES.

27. ELTON[3] TURNER (*Rachel[2] Hooks, James[1]*) was born on 20 April 1900 in Georgia. He married **Linen 'Lennie' Rogers**, daughter of **Randall Rogers** and **Dovie Cheeves**. He died on 7 December 1978 in Macon, Bibb County, Georgia, at age 78.

Children of **Elton[3] Turner** and **Linen 'Lennie' Rogers** were as follows:
98.   i. ROGER[4].
99.   ii. EUGENE.
+ 100.   iii. JOHN RUBEN (SR.), born 26 September 1928; married **Mary** (———).
101.   iv. WILLIE DOUGLAS.
102.   v. ELTON (JR.).
103.   vi. WYMAN.

29. MATTIE[3] TURNER (*Rachel[2] Hooks, James[1]*) was born circa 1904 in Georgia. She married **Joe Taylor**.

Children of **Mattie[3] Turner** and **Joe Taylor** were as follows:
104.   i. WILLIE MAE[4].
105.   ii. RALPH.
106.   iii. THELMA.
107.   iv. WALTER.
108.   v. ROY.
109.   vi. MARGIE.
110.   vii. SHIRLEY.
111.   viii. ARTHUR.

33. JENNIE[3] HOOKS (*Mack[2], James[1]*) was born in May 1889 in Georgia. She married **Frank Hall**.

Children of **Jennie[3] Hooks** and **Frank Hall** were as follows:
+ 112.   i. MARY[4], born 21 April 1921; married **Joseph Wright**.
+ 113.   ii. FRANK (JR.), married **Fannie Walker**.
+ 114.   iii. JULIA P., married **Adam M. Adolphus**.
+ 115.   iv. JOHN, born 20 July 1923; married **Eunice Terry**.
+ 116.   v. JOSEPH, married **Sarah Greenwood**.

+ 117.   vi. MACK T., married **Marion Trawick.**
+ 118.   vii. RUFUS, married **Gladys Williams.**

35. ROBERT³ HOOKS (*Mack²*, *James¹*) was born circa 1901 in Washington County, Georgia. He married **Marie Bivens.** He married **Sarah White.**

Children of **Robert³ Hooks** and **Marie Bivens** were as follows:
+ 119.   i. EDDIE LEE⁴, born 8 January 1925.
  120.   ii. JULIA.
+ 121.   iii. ROBERT
+ 122.   iv. EARL
  123.   v. CARL.
  124.   vi. MARIE.
  125.   vii. INEZ.

Children of **Robert³ Hooks** and **Sarah White** were:
+ 126.   i. KARIE⁴

37. WILLIAM³ HOOKS (*Mack²*, *James¹*) was born in January 1897 in Georgia. He married **Julia Walker.**

Children of **William³ Hooks** and **Julia Walker** were as follows:
  127.   i. ADDIE JULIA⁴ was born in 1919 in Washington County, Georgia. She married **Lee Crenshaw.**
  128.   ii. ROGERS.
  129.   iii. GENEVA married **Henry Trawick.**
  130.   iv. SYLVESTER.
  131.   v. RUTH married **Clinton Davidson.**
  132.   vi. HOWARD.

38. LUCY FRANCES³ HOOKS (*Mack²*, *James¹*) was born in March 1899 in Georgia. She married **Eldridge Barlow Jr.**, son of **Eldridge Barlow** and **Elsie Canty.**

Children of **Lucy Frances³ Hooks** and **Eldridge Barlow Jr.** were as follows:
+ 133.   i. ROOSEVELT⁴, born circa 1917 in Georgia; married **Virginia** (———).
+ 134.   ii. ROBERT, born circa 1919 in Georgia; married **Eddie Mae** (———).
  135.   iii. SONNY.
+ 136.   iv. LOUIS, married **Eleanor** (———).
  137.   v. ADOLPH.
+ 138.   vi. OTIS, married **Delores** (———).
+ 139.   vii. ARTHUR
  140.   viii. ELDRIDGE.

+ 141.   ix. LUCY MAE, married **Joseph Lee.**
+ 142.   x. BERNICE, married **Frederick Lee.**
+ 143.   xi. MARGARET, married **Earl Manley.**
+ 144.   xii. SHIRLEY, married **Rendell Brooks.**

41. **HATTIE MAE^3 HOOKS** (*Mack^2, James^1*) was born on 8 May 1907 in Georgia. She married **Henry Berry Gordy**, son of **Samuel 'Sam' Gordy** and **Carrie Cheeves**, on 29 April 1928. She died in 1989.

Children of **Hattie Mae^3 Hooks** and **Henry Berry Gordy** were as follows:
+ 145.   i. HENRY EDWARD^4, born 2 March 1929 in Sandersville, Georgia; married **Jeanetta** (—?—).
  146.   ii. SAM married **Mary Moses.**
+ 147.   iii. MARGARET JEWEL, married **Isaac King.**
+ 148.   iv. CLAUDETTE, born 9 February 1937; married **Alfred C. Johnson.**
+ 149.   v. CAROLYN, married **Leonard Kennedy.**
+ 150.   vi. LAWRENCE, married **Shirley Palmer.**
  151.   vii. GARY.
+ 152.   viii. JOYCE, born 1938 in Sandersville, Georgia; married **Welton Lawrence.**
+ 153.   ix. JAMES HAROLD, born 16 March 1942; married **Donna** (———).

43. **BESSIE^3 HOOKS** (*Mack^2, James^1*) was born on 4 November 1914. She married **Jessie Pitts.**

Children of **Bessie^3 Hooks** and **Jessie Pitts** were as follows:
  154.   i. ESTHER^4.
  155.   ii. JUDITH C.
  156.   iii. JAMES A.
  157.   iv. GENTRY J.
  158.   v. MICHAEL D.

48. **BERTHA^3 CARTER** (*Ella^{2}Hooks, James^1*) married **Thomas Renfrow.** She married **Johnnie Trawick**, son of **Dock Trawick** and **Violet Young.**

Children of **Bertha^3 Carter** and **Thomas Renfrow** were as follows:
  159.   i. EDWARD 'BUDDY'^{4} married **Ella** (—?—).
  160.   ii. THOMAS (JR.).
+ 161.   iii. LUCIOUS, married **Gladys Spann.**

Children of **Bertha^3 Carter** and **Johnnie Trawick** were:
+ 162.   i. EVA (JOHNNY)^4, born 31 January 1920 in Sandersville, Washington County, Georgia; married **Matthew Thomas.**

49. MARY ETHEL^3 **CARTER** (*Ella*^{2}*Hooks, James*^{1}) was born in December 1887 in Georgia. She married **Bert Lundy** in Georgia. She married **Charlie Young.**

Children of **Mary Ethel**^{3} **Carter** and **Bert Lundy** were as follows:
+ 163. i. WILLIE BELL^4, born circa 1909 in Georgia; married **K. Jenkins.**
+ 164. ii. ELLA MAE, born circa 1911 in Milledgeville, Baldwin County, Georgia.

Children of **Mary Ethel**^{3} **Carter** and **Charlie Young** were as follows:
  165. i. CHARLIE^4 (JR.).
  166. ii. CORENE was born circa 1916 in Georgia. She married **H. Harris.**
+ 167. iii. BERTHA, born 1919 in Georgia; married **Elmer Cheeves.**
  168. iv. LILLIE married **W. Glenn.**
  169. v. LOU DESSA.

52. JEFF^3 **CARTER JR.** (*Ella*^{2}*Hooks, James*^{1}) was born on 10 September 1894 in Oconee, Washington County, Georgia. He married **Gervenia Fisher**, adopted daughter of **Robert Fisher** and **Rachel** (———), on 17 October 1915 in Washington County, Georgia. He died in 1930 in Washington County, Georgia.

Children of **Jeff**^{3} **Carter Jr.** and **Gervenia Fisher** were as follows:
+ 170. i. MARY JULIA^4, born 6 October 1916 in Sandersville, Washington County, Georgia; married **Milas Butts (Jr.).**
+ 171. ii. LILLIAN ARTHUR, born 19 September 1918 in Sandersville, Washington County, Georgia; married **Henry Holmes Cheeves.**
+ 172. iii. RUBY CLYDE, born 20 February 1921 in Sandersville, Washington County, Georgia; married **James Nelson.**
+ 173. iv. ENNIS, born 7 April 1925 in Sandersville, Washington County, Georgia; married **Alvonia** (———).
+ 174. v. JEFF RAYMOND, born 19 November 1932 in Sandersville, Washington County, Georgia; married **Leonia 'Lumpy' Adams.**

53. LORA ELLA 'LAURA'^{3} **CARTER** (*Ella*^{2}*Hooks, James*^{1}) was born on 2 June 1895 in Sandersville, Washington County, Georgia. She married **Homer Dawson**, son of **Sampson Dawson** and **Mamie Robinson.** She died in October 1966 in West Palm Beach, Florida, at age 71.

Children of **Lora Ella 'Laura'**^{3} **Carter** and **Homer Dawson** were as follows:
  175. i. SAM^4 was born in Sandersville, Washington County, Georgia.
+ 176. ii. ROBERTA, born circa 5 November 1916 in Sandersville, Washington County, Georgia; married **Wesley Pettis.**
+ 177. iii. ELIZABETH, born 20 August 1921 in Sandersville, Washington County, Georgia; married **Lucious 'Lewis' Fisher**; married **Booker T. Whitehead.**

+ 178.   iv. TIMOTHY, born 31 August 1924 in Sandersville, Washington County, Georgia; married **Lillie Ruth Wiley.**

+ 179.   v. DEBORAH, born 29 June 1927 in Sandersville, Washington County, Georgia; married **Edward Sparks.**

+ 180.   vi. ELOISE 'HONEY', born 27 September 1929 in Sandersville, Washington County, Georgia; married **Robert Daniel Gordy.**

+ 181.   vii. HOMER (JR.), born 4 January 1932 in Sandersville, Washington County, Georgia; married **Bettye Tanner.**

+ 182.   viii. CORNELIUS, born 5 November 1933 in Sandersville, Washington County, Georgia; married **Delores Pinkston.**

+ 183.   ix. WILHELMINA 'CANDY', born 29 September 1936 in Sandersville, Washington County, Georgia; married **Amos Ross;** married **Frank Davis.**

54. LILLIE RUTH^3 CARTER (*Ella^{2}Hooks, James^1*) was born in February 1897 in Georgia. She married **Samuel Turner.**

Children of **Lillie Ruth^3 Carter** and **Samuel Turner** were as follows:

+ 184.   i. SAMUEL^4 (JR.), married **Odessa Boiling.**
185.   ii. O'NEAL.
+ 186.   iii. BLANCHE, married **Dabney Holley.**
+ 187.   iv. MILDRED, married **James Moore.**

56. VIRGIL 'VIRGE'^{3} CARTER (*Ella^{2}Hooks, James^1*) was born on 15 August 1900 in Sandersville, Washington County, Georgia. He married **Mamie Ethridge** on 24 December 1918 in Baldwin County, Georgia. He died on 1 June 1936 in Sandersville, Washington County, Georgia, at age 35.

Children of **Virgil 'Virge'^{3} Carter** and **Mamie Ethridge** were as follows:

+ 188.   i. RUTH MILDRED^4, born 30 July 1920 in Sandersville, Georgia; married **Kenneth Rawlins.**

+ 189.   ii. ANNE, born 21 March 1923 in Sandersville, Georgia; married **David Green.**

190.   iii. DOROTHY LUCILLE was born on 29 June 1925 in Sandersville, Georgia. She married **Alfred Peachy.** She died on 26 June 1981 in Brooklyn, New York, at age 55.

191.   iv. VIRGIL (JR.) was born on 6 October 1928 in Sandersville, Georgia.

192.   v. MARY LILLIAN was born on 30 November 1931 in Sandersville, Georgia. She married **Timothy Vincent.** She died on 27 February 2000 in Brooklyn, New York, at age 68.

+ 193.   vi. TERESA, born 4 September 1933 in Sandersville, Georgia; married **Stanley Snyder.**

Generation Four

59. MAMIE^4 CANTY (*Pearl L.^{3}Hooks, Robert^2, James^1*) was born on 30 September 1913.

Children of **Mamie**[4] **Canty** and **John Garrison** were as follows:
+ 194.   i. JOHN DESSIE[5], married **Dolly** (———).
+ 195.   ii. YVONNE AUDREY, born 20 December 1945; married **William Q. Frazier.**
+ 196.   iii. MARCELLA, married **Douglas Scott Bowmen**; married **Al Edmonds (Jr.).**
  197.   iv. GARY RICHARD.
  198.   v. RONALD DEXTER married **Brenda** (—?—).
  199.   vi. ANTHONY LEE.
+ 200.   vii. TYRONE K., born 19 October 1952.

61. CLARA[4] **GAUDY** (*Mamie*[3]*Hooks, Robert*[2]*, James*[1]) was born in Sandersville, Georgia.

Children of **Clara**[4] **Gaudy** and **Leonard Eston** were as follows:
+ 201.   i. LEONARD[5] JR.
+ 202.   ii. DIANE, married **Lamar Riddle.**
  203.   iii. ARMON.

62. MAMIE[4] **GAUDY** (*Mamie*[3]*Hooks, Robert*[2]*, James*[1]) was born in Sandersville, Georgia. She married **Alfred Lawson.**

Children of **Mamie**[4] **Gaudy** and **Alfred Lawson** were as follows:
+ 204.   i. JOYCE[5], married **Joseph Moore.**
+ 205.   ii. SHARON, married **James E. Garrett.**

63. JOHN[4] **GAUDY JR.** (*Mamie*[3]*Hooks, Robert*[2]*, James*[1]) was born in Sandersville, Georgia. He married **Florine** (———).

Children of **John**[4] **Gaudy Jr.** and **Florine** (———) were as follows:
+ 206.   i. BERNADETTE[5], married **David Anderson.**
+ 207.   ii. FLORENCE, married **Eugene Anderson.**
  208.   iii. JOHN III.
+ 209.   iv. JANICE, married **Dwight McCarter.**
+ 210.   v. VALERIE, married **Keith Martin**; married **Columbus Sykes.**
+ 211.   vi. JOCELYN, married **Jerry Flowers.**
  212.   vii. ROBERT.

64. NAOMIE[4] **GORDY** (*Mamie*[3]*Hooks, Robert*[2]*, James*[1]) was born in Sandersville, Georgia. She married **Joe Johnson.**

Children of **Naomie**[4] **Gordy** and **Joe Johnson** were as follows:
  213.   i. DENISE[5].
+ 214.   ii. CYNTHIA
+ 215.   iii. CHERYL, married **Robert Marshall.**

65. BRENDA^4 **GORDY** (*Mamie*^{3}*Hooks, Robert*^{2}*, James*^{1}) was born in Sandersville, Georgia. She married **Hezekiah McDonald.**

Children of **Brenda**^{4} **Gordy** and **Hezekiah McDonald** were as follows:
216.   i. MICHELLE^5.
217.   ii. HEZEKIAH TROY.

66. THELMA^4 **GORDY** (*Mamie*^{3}*Hooks, Robert*^{2}*, James*^{1}) was born in Sandersville, Georgia.

Children of **Thelma**^{4} **Gordy** and **James Brooks** were as follows:
+ 218.   i. JAMES^5 (JR.)
+ 219.   ii. KARLA
+ 220.   iii. SEDARA, married **Darryl Stroud.**
+ 221.   iv. SHARRENA, married **Frank Johnson.**
+ 222.   v. LINDA, married **Ken Wells.**

67. RAYMOND^4 **GORDY** (*Mamie*^{3}*Hooks, Robert*^{2}*, James*^{1}) was born in Sandersville, Georgia. He married **Florence** (———).

Children of **Raymond**^{4} **Gordy** and **Florence** (———) were as follows:
+ 223.   i. BARBARA^5
224.   ii. RAYMOND (JR.).
225.   iii. TRACY.
+ 226.   iv. NICOLE

69. JOHNNIE LOU^4 **GORDY** (*Mamie*^{3}*Hooks, Robert*^{2}*, James*^{1}) was born circa 1918 in Washington County, Georgia. She married **William Carithers.**

Children of **Johnnie Lou**^{4} **Gordy** and **William Carithers** were:
+ 227.   i. GARY^5

70. LULA MAE^4 **GAUDY** (*Mamie*^{3}*Hooks, Robert*^{2}*, James*^{1}) was born on 22 November 1919 in Washington County, Georgia. She married **William Johnson.** She married **David James Lemon Sr.** in January 1940 in Detroit, Michigan.

There were no children of **Lula Mae**^{4} **Gaudy** and **William Johnson.**

Children of **Lula Mae**^{4} **Gaudy** and **David James Lemon Sr.** were as follows:
+ 228.   i. HOWARD LOVELL^5, born 26 October 1940 in Detroit, Michigan; married **Sandra Lynn Powell.**
+ 229.   ii. PATRICIA M., born 2 April 1942 in Detroit, Mich; married **Phil Green.**

+ 230.   iii. DAVID JAMES JR., born 21 November 1944 in Detroit, Michigan; married
          Merilyn Ann Bradley.
+ 231.   iv. RICHARD, born 26 December 1947 in Detroit, Michigan; married **Lorraine** (——
          ——); married **Shirley Boyd.**
+ 232.   v. DEBRA, born 6 March 1954 in Detroit, Michigan; married **Jimmy Forrest;**
          married **Felton Wright.**
+ 233.   vi. SONIA DARLENE, born 22 July 1958 in Detroit, Michigan; married **Cassell
          Mathews.**

71. **PORTER**^{4} **GORDY** (*Mamie*^{3}*Hooks, Robert*^{2}*, James*^{1}) was born on 2 February 1929 in
    Sandersville, Washington County, Georgia. He married **Frances** (————).

Children of **Porter**^{4} **Gordy** and **Frances** (————) were as follows:
   234.   i. ABBIE GAIL^5.
+ 235.   ii. CLARENCE
+ 236.   iii. PORTIA
+ 237.   iv. CAROL

74. **CLARA**^{4} **HOOKS** (*Clifford*^{3}*, Robert*^{2}*, James*^{1}) married **C. Williams.** She married
    James Liston.

Children of **Clara**^{4} **Hooks** and **C. Williams** were as follows:
   238.   i. CHERYL^5.
+ 239.   ii. JENNIFER

There were no children of **Clara**^{4} **Hooks** and **James Liston.**

75. **CLIFFORD**^{4} **HOOKS JR.** (*Clifford*^{3}*, Robert*^{2}*, James*^{1}) was born on 13 November 1925
    in Philadelphia, Pennsylvania. He married **Alice Lindsey** on 2 September 1962.

Children of **Clifford**^{4} **Hooks Jr.** and **Alice Lindsey** were as follows:
   240.   i. CLIFFORD LEMUEL^5.
   241.   ii. DANIEL.

77. **BEATRICE**^{4} **HOOKS** (*Clifford*^{3}*, Robert*^{2}*, James*^{1}) married **Willie Greenlee.** She
    married **Carl Johnson.**

Children of **Beatrice**^{4} **Hooks** and **Willie Greenlee** were as follows:
+ 242.   i. WILLIAM^5, married **Sandra** (————).
   243.   ii. RICHARD married **June Fanning.**
+ 244.   iii. EMMA JEAN, married **William Dunson.**

208

There were no children of **Beatrice**[4] **Hooks** and **Carl Johnson.**

78. **MARACELLA**[4] **HOOKS** (*James*[3], *Robert*[2], *James*[1]) married **Herman David Young.**

Children of **Maracella**[4] **Hooks** and **Herman David Young** were:
245.   i. MARITA DENISE[5].

79. **VIOLA**[4] **HOOKS** (*James*[3], *Robert*[2], *James*[1]) was born on 8 June 1933. She married **Benjamin Lacey.** She married **Mr. Jones** on 8 June 1984.

Children of **Viola**[4] **Hooks** and **Benjamin Lacey** were:
246.   i. SUSAN DENISE[5].

There were no children of **Viola**[4] **Hooks** and **Mr. Jones.**

80. **JANETTA**[4] **HOOKS** (*James*[3], *Robert*[2], *James*[1]) married **Alvin Thomas (Jr.).**

Children of **Janetta**[4] **Hooks** and **Alvin Thomas (Jr.)** were as follows:
+ 247.   i. STEPHANIE[5]
+ 248.   ii. LISA, married **Mr. Hendley.**
249.   iii. CYNTHIA.
+ 250.   iv. GREGORY

81. **ELEANOR**[4] **HOOKS** (*James*[3], *Robert*[2], *James*[1]) married **Winston Edwards.**

Children of **Eleanor**[4] **Hooks** and **Winston Edwards** were:
+ 251.   i. MELODIE[5], married **Michael Frances Cooper.**

83. **OSCAR HOOKS**[4] **KELSEY** (*Robert J.*[3] *Hooks*, *Robert*[2], *James*[1]) married **Delores (—?—).**

Children of **Oscar Hooks**[4] **Kelsey** and **Delores (—?—)** were as follows:
252.   i. WILLARD[5].
253.   ii. DONALD.
254.   iii. BETTY.
255.   iv. JULIE.
256.   v. LAMONT.
257.   vi. ROBERT RYAN.
258.   vii. WENDALL.

85. **DELORES**[4] **HOOKS** (*Robert J.*[3], *Robert*[2], *James*[1]) was born on 20 March 1939. She married **Mitchell Hooks**, son of **Willie W. Hooks** and **Henrietta Cheeves.**

Children of **Delores**[4] **Hooks** and **Mitchell Hooks** were as follows:

+ 259. i. MICHAEL D.[5], born 25 December 1956; married **Carol Anderson**.
  260. ii. RHONDA was born on 17 January 1958. She married **George Ashison**.
  261. iii. MONICA was born on 26 August 1970.

86. **FLETA**[4] **HOOKS** (*Robert J.*[3], *Robert*[2], *James*[1]).

Children of **Fleta**[4] **Hooks** include:
  262. i. DAVIDA[5].
  263. ii. DENNIS.
  264. iii. LISA.

87. **FRANK**[4] **HOOKS** (*Joe*[3], *Adam 'Add'*[2], *James*[1]) married **Bertha** (———).

Children of **Frank**[4] **Hooks** and **Bertha** (———) were as follows:
  265. i. GERALD[5].
  266. ii. JOSEPH.
  267. iii. CHARLIE.

100. **JOHN RUBEN**[4] **TURNER (SR.)** (*Elton*[3], *Rachel*[2] *Hooks*, *James*[1]) was born on 26
September 1928. He married **Mary** (———).

Children of **John Ruben**[4] **Turner (Sr.)** and **Mary** (———) were as follows:
+ 268. i. LINDA[5]
+ 269. ii. BARBARA
  270. iii. JOHN RUBEN (JR.).

112. **MARY**[4] **HALL** (*Jennie*[3] *Hooks*, *Mack*[2], *James*[1]) was born on 21 April 1921. She
married **Joseph Wright**.

Children of **Mary**[4] **Hall** and **Joseph Wright** were as follows:
  271. i. ANNIE R.[5].
  272. ii. PHYLLIS.

113. **FRANK**[4] **HALL (JR.)** (*Jennie*[3] *Hooks*, *Mack*[2], *James*[1]) married **Fannie Walker**.

Children of **Frank**[4] **Hall (Jr.)** and **Fannie Walker** were:
  273. i. KEITH[5].

114. **JULIA P.**[4] **HALL** (*Jennie*[3] *Hooks*, *Mack*[2], *James*[1]) married **Adam M. Adolphus**.

Children of **Julia P.**[4] **Hall** and **Adam M. Adolphus** were as follows:
274. i. MARY J. COOK[5].
275. ii. LINDSEY.
276. iii. ADAM LEE.

115. JOHN[4] **HALL** (*Jennie*[3]*Hooks, Mack*[2]*, James*[1]) was born on 20 July 1923. He married **Eunice Terry** in 1953.

Children of **John**[4] **Hall** and **Eunice Terry** were as follows:
277. i. CLEVELAND RHODES[5].
278. ii. DONALD L.

116. JOSEPH[4] **HALL** (*Jennie*[3]*Hooks, Mack*[2]*, James*[1]) married **Sarah Greenwood.**

Children of **Joseph**[4] **Hall** and **Sarah Greenwood** were as follows:
279. i. ANTHONY[5].
280. ii. RAYMOND.
281. iii. STEPHEN.

117. MACK T.[4] **HALL** (*Jennie*[3]*Hooks, Mack*[2]*, James*[1]) married **Marion Trawick.**

Children of **Mack T.**[4] **Hall** and **Marion Trawick** were as follows:
+ 282. i. BRENDA[5], married **Dennis Staten.**
283. ii. MAXINE.
284. iii. GRACE.
285. iv. ANITA.
286. v. ELBERT.
287. vi. ELLEON.
288. vii. SEITH.

118. RUFUS[4] **HALL** (*Jennie*[3]*Hooks, Mack*[2]*, James*[1]) married **Gladys Williams.**

Children of **Rufus**[4] **Hall** and **Gladys Williams** were as follows:
289. i. RUFUS[5] (JR.).
290. ii. RALPH.
291. iii. JOHNNIE.
292. iv. MELINDA.
293. v. DANIEL.
294. vi. GERALD.

119. EDDIE LEE[4] **HOOKS** (*Robert*[3]*, Mack*[2]*, James*[1]) was born on 8 January 1925.

Children of **Eddie Lee**^{4} **Hooks** include:
+ 295.   i. TYRONE LEE^5
+ 296.   ii. ERIC EDWARD
   297.   iii. CARLA MARIA.

121. **ROBERT**^{4} **HOOKS** (*Robert*^{3}, *Mack*^{2}, *James*^{1}).

Children of **Robert**^{4} **Hooks** include:
   298.   i. VALERIE^5.

122. **EARL**^{4} **HOOKS** (*Robert*^{3}, *Mack*^{2}, *James*^{1}).

Children of **Earl**^{4} **Hooks** include:
   299.   i. EARL^5 (JR.).
   300.   ii. PAMELA.
+ 301.   iii. SHARON
   302.   iv. KEITH.

126. **KARIE**^{4} **HOOKS** (*Robert*^{3}, *Mack*^{2}, *James*^{1}).

Children of **Karie**^{4} **Hooks** include:
+ 303.   i. IRENE^5
   304.   ii. BRUCE.

133. **ROOSEVELT**^{4} **BARLOW** (*Lucy Frances*^{3}*Hooks, Mack*^{2}, *James*^{1}) was born circa 1917 in Georgia. He married **Virginia** (———).

Children of **Roosevelt**^{4} **Barlow** and **Virginia** (———) were:
   305.   i. RAYMOND^5.

134. **ROBERT**^{4} **BARLOW** (*Lucy Frances*^{3}*Hooks, Mack*^{2}, *James*^{1}) was born circa 1919 in Georgia. He married **Eddie Mae** (———).

Children of **Robert**^{4} **Barlow** and **Eddie Mae** (———) were as follows:
   306.   i. ROBERT^5 (JR.).
   307.   ii. LINDA.
   308.   iii. PAULA.

136. **LOUIS**^{4} **BARLOW** (*Lucy Frances*^{3}*Hooks, Mack*^{2}, *James*^{1}) married **Eleanor** (———).

Children of **Louis**^{4} **Barlow** and **Eleanor** (———) were as follows:
   309.   i. DENISE^5.

310.   ii. ELEANOR.

138. OTIS^4 BARLOW (*Lucy Frances^{3}Hooks, Mack^2, James^1*) married Delores (———).

Children of Otis^4 Barlow and Delores (———) were as follows:
311.   i. OTIS^5 (JR.).
312.   ii. DELORES.
313.   iii. GAYLE.

139. ARTHUR^4 BARLOW (*Lucy Frances^{3}Hooks, Mack^2, James^1*).

Children of Arthur^4 Barlow include:
314.   i. SANDRA^5.

141. LUCY MAE^4 BARLOW (*Lucy Frances^{3}Hooks, Mack^2, James^1*) married Joseph Lee.

Children of Lucy Mae^4 Barlow and Joseph Lee were as follows:
315.   i. JOSEPH^5 (JR.).
316.   ii. EMMANUEL.
317.   iii. DOROTHY.
318.   iv. FRANCES.
319.   v. JOAN.
320.   vi. JUDITH.

142. BERNICE^4 BARLOW (*Lucy Frances^{3}Hooks, Mack^2, James^1*) married Frederick Lee.

Children of Bernice^4 Barlow and Frederick Lee were as follows:
321.   i. AURTHUR^5.
322.   ii. JOHN.
323.   iii. ANTHONY.
324.   iv. BELINDA.

143. MARGARET^4 BARLOW (*Lucy Frances^{3}Hooks, Mack^2, James^1*) married Earl Manley.

Children of Margaret^4 Barlow and Earl Manley were as follows:
325.   i. EARL^5 (JR.).
326.   ii. MARILYN.

144. SHIRLEY^4 BARLOW (*Lucy Frances^{3}Hooks, Mack^2, James^1*) married Rendell Brooks.

Children of Shirley^4 Barlow and Rendell Brooks were:
327.   i. CHRISTEL^5.

145. HENRY EDWARD[4] GORDY (*Hattie Mae[3] Hooks, Mack[2], James[1]*) was born on 2
March 1929 in Sandersville, Georgia. He married Jeanetta (———). He died in 1985.

Children of Henry Edward[4] Gordy and Jeanetta (—?—) were as follows:

+ 328.   i. BRIAN[5], married Yvonne (———).
+ 329.   ii. BYRON, married Willette (———).
+ 330.   iii. BRUCE, married Deborah (———).
+ 331.   iv. BRENT, married Effie (———).
+ 332.   v. BRIDGETTE, married Bernell Seal.
  333.   vi. BRENDA married Anthony Berry.

147. MARGARET JEWEL[4] GORDY (*Hattie Mae[3] Hooks, Mack[2], James[1]*) married Isaac
    King.

Children of Margaret Jewel[4] Gordy and Isaac King were as follows:

+ 334.   i. KAREN[5], married Elvin Brooks.
+ 335.   ii. KYRA, married James Ridgell.
  336.   iii. KEVIN married Lillie (—?—).

148. CLAUDETTE[4] GORDY (*Hattie Mae[3] Hooks, Mack[2], James[1]*) was born on 9
February 1937. She married Alfred C. Johnson.

Children of Claudette[4] Gordy and Alfred C. Johnson were:

  337.   i. MARCUS LAVON[5].

149. CAROLYN[4] GORDY (*Hattie Mae[3] Hooks, Mack[2], James[1]*) married Leonard Kennedy.

Children of Carolyn[4] Gordy and Leonard Kennedy were as follows:

  338.   i. STEPHANIE[5] married James C. Gardner.
  339.   ii. SEAN.
  340.   iii. STEVEN.
  341.   iv. SHANNON.

150. LAWRENCE[4] GORDY (*Hattie Mae[3] Hooks, Mack[2], James[1]*) married Shirley Palmer.

Children of Lawrence[4] Gordy and Shirley Palmer were:

  342.   i. DWAYNE[5].

152. JOYCE[4] GORDY (*Hattie Mae[3] Hooks, Mack[2], James[1]*) was born in 1938 in
Sandersville, Georgia. She married Welton Lawrence.

Children of **Joyce**^{4} **Gordy** and **Welton Lawrence** were as follows:

+ 343.   i. DEBORAH^5, married **Lamont McClain.**
+ 344.   ii. DOREEN, married **Sam Hughes.**
  345.   iii. DAVID.
+ 346.   iv. DARIN, married **Shirley (———).**

153. JAMES HAROLD^4 **GORDY** (*Hattie Mae*^{3}*Hooks, Mack*^{2}*, James*^{1}) was born on 16 March 1942. He married **Donna (———).**

Children of **James Harold**^{4} **Gordy** and **Donna (———)** were as follows:
  347.   i. SHAWN^5 was born circa 1965.
  348.   ii. JA VON was born circa 1965.
  349.   iii. NICOLE.
  350.   iv. ROBIN married **Timothy Banks.**
  351.   v. MARISA.

161. LUCIOUS^4 **RENFROW** (*Bertha*^{3}*Carter, Ella*^{2}*Hooks, James*^{1}) married **Gladys Spann.**

Children of **Lucious**^{4} **Renfrow** and **Gladys Spann** were as follows:
  352.   i. CRAIG^5.
  353.   ii. BEVERLY married **Robert Anderson.**

162. EVA (JOHNNY)^4 **TRAWICK** (*Bertha*^{3}*Carter, Ella*^{2}*Hooks, James*^{1}) was born on 31 January 1920 in Sandersville, Washington County, Georgia. She married **Matthew Thomas.**

Children of **Eva (Johnny)**^{4} **Trawick** and **Matthew Thomas** were as follows:
+ 354.   i. SANDRA CAROL^5, born 31 May 1946 in Philadelphia, Pennsylvania; married **Herb Connelly.**
+ 355.   ii. SIGRID ANN, born 10 March 1948 in Philadelphia, Pennsylvania; married **Howard Edward McCall Jr.**
+ 356.   iii. WANDA EILEEN, born 12 April 1950 in Philadelphia, Pennsylvania; married **John 'Donald' Bird.**

163. WILLIE BELL^4 **LUNDY** (*Mary Ethel*^{3}*Carter, Ella*^{2}*Hooks, James*^{1}) was born circa 1909 in Georgia. He married **K. Jenkins.**

Children of **Willie Bell**^{4} **Lundy** and **K. Jenkins** were as follows:
  357.   i. CHARLES^5.
  358.   ii. JEROME.
  359.   iii. JUDY.

164. ELLA MAE^4 LUNDY (*Mary Ethel^{3}Carter, Ella^{2}Hooks, James^1*) was born circa 1911 in Milledgeville, Baldwin County, Georgia.

Children of Ella Mae^4 Lundy include:
360. i. WILLIE^5.

167. BERTHA^4 YOUNG (*Mary Ethel^{3}Carter, Ella^{2}Hooks, James^1*) was born in 1919 in Georgia. She married Elmer Cheeves.

Children of Bertha^4 Young and Elmer Cheeves were as follows:
361. i. MARY^5.
362. ii. VIVIAN.

170. MARY JULIA^4 CARTER (*Jeff^3, Ella^{2}Hooks, James^1*) was born on 6 October 1916 in Sandersville, Washington County, Georgia. She married Milas Butts (Jr.), son of Milas Butts (Sr.) and Roeanor Dawson. She died on 16 October 1943 in Philadelphia, Pennsylvania, at age 27.

Children of Mary Julia^4 Carter and Milas Butts (Jr.) were as follows:
+ 363. i. ALTON^5, born 28 October 1934 in Sandersville, Georgia; married Marlyn Farley.
364. ii. VIVIAN.

171. LILLIAN ARTHUR^4 CARTER (*Jeff^3, Ella^{2}Hooks, James^1*) was born on 19 September 1918 in Sandersville, Washington County, Georgia. She married Henry Holmes Cheeves, son of Henry Cheeves Jr. and Clara Bell Trawick. She died on 2 February 1966 at age 47.

Children of Lillian Arthur^4 Carter and Henry Holmes Cheeves were as follows:
+ 365. i. MIRIAM^5, born in Sandersville, Washington County, Georgia.
+ 366. ii. GLORIA, born 4 July 1941 in Sandersville, Washington County, Georgia; married Charles Graham.
+ 367. iii. HORACE, born 4 September 1943 in Sandersville, Washington County, Georgia; married Fannie Pearl Williams.
+ 368. iv. FOREST, born 4 September 1943 in Sandersville, Washington County, Georgia; married Karen Kennedy.
369. v. HENRY was born on 8 September 1948 in Sandersville, Washington County, Georgia.
370. vi. DAVID was born on 10 November 1954 in Philadelphia, Pennsylvania. He died on 17 August 1995 in Detroit, Michigan, at age 40.
371. vii. ANNETTE GAIL was born on 7 August 1958 in Philadelphia, Pennsylvania.

172. **RUBY CLYDE**^{4} **CARTER** (*Jeff*^{3}, *Ella*^{2}*Hooks, James*^{1}) was born on 20 February 1921 in Sandersville, Washington County, Georgia. She married **James Nelson.** She died on 13 April 2002 in Philadelphia, Pennsylvania, at age 81.

Children of **Ruby Clyde**^{4} **Carter** and **Jack Cotton** were:
+ 372.   i. MICHELLE^5, born 23 February 1958 in Detroit, Michigan.

Children of **Ruby Clyde**^{4} **Carter** and **James Nelson** were:
+ 373.   i. HERMAN^5, born 4 November 1943 in Philadelphia, Pennsylvania; married **Dallay Yvonne Graham.**

173. **ENNIS**^{4} **CARTER** (*Jeff*^{3}, *Ella*^{2}*Hooks, James*^{1}) was born on 7 April 1925 in Sandersville, Washington County, Georgia. He married **Alvonia** (———) on 12 December 1970 in Detroit, Michigan.

Children of **Ennis**^{4} **Carter** include:
374.   i. BERNICE^5 was born in 1942 in Sandersville, Washington County, Georgia.
375.   ii. HARVEY was born in November 1942 in Newnan, Georgia. He died in November 1984 in Sandersville, Washington County, Georgia.
376.   iii. LEWIS was born on 7 July 1943 in Sandersville, Washington County, Georgia.
377.   iv. LOIS was born on 7 July 1943 in Sandersville, Washington County, Georgia.
378.   v. DELRA was born on 17 August 1949 in Detroit, Michigan.
379.   vi. DENISE was born on 26 July 1952 in Detroit, Michigan.
380.   vii. DONNA was born on 2 February 1956 in Detroit, Michigan.

Children of **Ennis**^{4} **Carter** and **Zelma Shenoster** were:
381.   i. DONALD 'DUCK'^{5} was born on 29 September 1948 in Philadelphia, Pennsylvania. He died on 29 June 2001 in Philadelphia, Pennsylvania, at age 52.

There were no children of **Ennis**^{4} **Carter** and **Alvonia** (———).

174. **JEFF RAYMOND**^{4} **CARTER** (*Jeff*^{3}, *Ella*^{2}*Hooks, James*^{1}) was born on 19 November 1932 in Sandersville, Washington County, Georgia. He married **Leonia 'Lumpy' Adams.** He died on 1 December 1990 in Philadelphia, Pennsylvania, at age 58.

Children of **Jeff Raymond**^{4} **Carter** and **Leonia 'Lumpy' Adams** were as follows:
+ 382.   i. SHARON 'SHERRY'^{5}, born 18 April 1949 in Philadelphia, Pennsylvania.
+ 383.   ii. JEFF RAYMOND 'BROTHER' JR., born 1 July 1950 in Philadelphia, Pennsylvania; married **Sujuan Williams.**
384.   iii. DENISE.
+ 385.   iv. DENNIS, born 25 December 1952 in Philadelphia, Pennsylvania; married **Marcia Earlene Jackson.**

386.   v. RAYMOND was born in September 1959.

176. ROBERTA[4] DAWSON (*Lora Ella 'Laura*[3] *Carter, Ella*[2] *Hooks, James*[1]) was born circa
5 November 1916 in Sandersville, Washington County, Georgia. She married
Wesley Pettis. She died in December 1954 in West Palm Beach, Florida.

Children of **Roberta**[4] **Dawson** and **Wesley Pettis** were as follows:
387.   i. CALVIN[5].
388.   ii. JOYCE.

177. ELIZABETH[4] DAWSON (*Lora Ella 'Laura*[3] *Carter, Ella*[2] *Hooks, James*[1]) was born
on 20 August 1921 in Sandersville, Washington County, Georgia. She married
Lucious 'Lewis' Fisher. She married **Booker T. Whitehead.**

Children of **Elizabeth**[4] **Dawson** include:
+ 389.   i. SHIRLEY[5], born 29 March; married **Edward Brent.**

There were no children of **Elizabeth**[4] **Dawson** and Lucious 'Lewis' Fisher.

There were no children of **Elizabeth**[4] **Dawson** and Booker T. Whitehead.

178. TIMOTHY[4] DAWSON (*Lora Ella 'Laura*[3] *Carter, Ella*[2] *Hooks, James*[1]) was born on 31
August 1924 in Sandersville, Washington County, Georgia. He married **Lillie Ruth
Wiley** in 1949. He died on 26 April 1995 in Philadelphia, Pennsylvania, at age 70.

Children of **Timothy**[4] **Dawson** and **Lillie Ruth Wiley** were as follows:
390.   i. JEFFREY[5] was born on 6 August in Sandersville, Georgia.
+ 391.   ii. BRENDA, born 18 September in Sandersville, Georgia; married **Mark Scott.**
+ 392.   iii. BENNIE LAWSON, born 6 July 1947 in Sandersville, Georgia; married **Barbara
Jones.**
393.   iv. TIMOTHY (JR.) was born on 11 November 1950 in Sandersville, Georgia. He
married **Volanda (—?—).**
394.   v. EMORY was born on 21 June 1951 in Sandersville, Georgia. He married **Patricia
Pates.**
+ 395.   vi. LORETTA, born 30 August 1952 in Sandersville, Georgia; married **Aubrey Jones.**
+ 396.   vii. PAULINE, born 12 November 1954 in Sandersville, Georgia; married **Alfred Ford.**
397.   viii. ROBERTA was born on 19 April 1956 in Sandersville, Georgia.
398.   ix. LILLIAN was born on 6 August 1957 in Sandersville, Georgia. She married **Eddie
Pulliam.**

179. DEBORAH[4] DAWSON (*Lora Ella 'Laura'[3] Carter, Ella[2] Hooks, James[1]*) was born on 29 June 1927 in Sandersville, Washington County, Georgia. She married **Edward Sparks.**

Children of **Deborah[4] Dawson** and **Edward Sparks** were as follows:

+ 399.   i. GRACE HARRIS[5], born 22 March 1944 in Sandersville, Georgia; married **Hugh Bryant.**
  400.   ii. EDWARD TRACY was born on 28 September 1958 in Syracuse, New York.
  401. iii. MICHAEL was born on 31 October 1959 in Syracuse, New York.
  402.   iv. GARY was born on 13 October 1960 in Syracuse, New York.
  403.   v. WILLIAM 'BILLY' KENNETH was born on 29 January 1962 in Syracuse, New York.
  404.   vi. RICHARD was born on 17 July 1965 in Syracuse, New York.

180. ELOISE 'HONEY'[4] DAWSON (*Lora Ella 'Laura'[3] Carter, Ella[2] Hooks, James[1]*) was born on 27 September 1929 in Sandersville, Washington County, Georgia. She married **Robert Daniel Gordy**, son of **Samuel 'Sam' Gordy** and **Carrie Cheeves**, on 6 March 1950 in Sandersville, Washington County, Georgia.

Children of **Eloise 'Honey'[4] Dawson** and **Robert Daniel Gordy** were as follows:

+ 405.   i. GWENDOLYN[5], born 12 March 1947 in Utica, New York; married **Julius Murphy.**
  406.   ii. ROBERT DANIEL JR. was born on 27 July 1950 in Sandersville, Georgia.
+ 407. iii. DAVID, born 13 April 1952 in Sandersville, Georgia; married **DeLois Turner**; married **Darlene Robinson.**
+ 408.   iv. DEBORAH ANNE, born 6 January 1954 in Sandersville, Georgia; married **Samuel Duggan.**
+ 409.   v. MARY LUCY, born 17 July 1956 in Sandersville, Georgia; married **Tony Owen Hurt Sr.**
  410.   vi. REGINALD CORNELIUS was born on 5 September 1957 in Sandersville, Georgia. He married **Yvette (—?—).**
+ 411. vii. BERRY RENARD, born 10 September 1958 in Sandersville, Georgia; married **Brenda Lee Lord Barlow Cardy.**

181. HOMER[4] DAWSON (JR.) (*Lora Ella 'Laura'[3] Carter, Ella[2] Hooks, James[1]*) was born on 4 January 1932 in Sandersville, Washington County, Georgia. He married **Bettye Tanner.**

Children of **Homer[4] Dawson (Jr.)** and **Bettye Tanner** were as follows:

+ 412.   i. CATHERINE LORETTA[5], born 4 February 1951 in West Palm Beach, Florida; married **Douglas Fulton.**
+ 413.   ii. HOMER 'BILLY' III, born 9 April 1953 in West Palm Beach, Florida; married **Brenda McCullom.**

414. iii. JEFFREY was born on 4 June 1954 in West Palm Beach, Florida. He married **Bernice (—?—)**.
+ 415. iv. WENDELL, born 31 January 1957 in West Palm Beach, Florida; married **Deborah Davis**.
+ 416. v. NATALIE JEAN, born 6 April 1958 in West Palm Beach, Florida; married **Robert Smith**.

182. CORNELIUS^4 DAWSON (*Lora Ella 'Laura^{3}Carter, Ella^{2}Hooks, James^1*) was born on 5 November 1933 in Sandersville, Washington County, Georgia. He married **Delores Pinkston**.

Children of **Cornelius^4 Dawson** and **Delores Pinkston** were as follows:
+ 417. i. BEVERLY^5, born 5 February 1955 in East Palatka, Florida.
+ 418. ii. WANDA, born 1 November 1959 in West Palm Beach, Florida; married **Tim Hunt**.
419. iii. ROBBYN was born on 2 November 1961 in West Palm Beach, Florida.
420. iv. ERIC was born on 25 November 1967 in West Palm Beach, Florida.

183. WILHELMINA 'CANDY'^{4} DAWSON (*Lora Ella 'Laura^{3}Carter, Ella^{2}Hooks, James^1*) was born on 29 September 1936 in Sandersville, Washington County, Georgia. She married **Amos Ross**. She married **Frank Davis**.

There were no children of **Wilhelmina 'Candy'^{4} Dawson** and **Amos Ross**.

Children of **Wilhelmina 'Candy'^{4} Dawson** and **Frank Davis** were as follows:
+ 421. i. KAREN ' KAY' ELIZABETH^5, born 14 May 1956 in West Palm Beach, Florida; married **Willie Neal**.
422. ii. GWENETH 'RUTHIE' was born on 29 September 1957.

184. SAMUEL^4 TURNER (JR.) (*Lillie Ruth^{3}Carter, Ella^{2}Hooks, James^1*) married **Odessa Boiling**.

Children of **Samuel^4 Turner (Jr.)** and **Odessa (———)** were:
423. i. DORICE^5.

Children of **Samuel^4 Turner (Jr.)** and **Odessa Boiling** were as follows:
424. i. MICHAEL^5.
425. ii. CAROLYN.

186. BLANCHE^4 TURNER (*Lillie Ruth^{3}Carter, Ella^{2}Hooks, James^1*) married **Dabney Holley**.

Children of **Blanche**[4] **Turner** and **Dabney Holley** were:
426.   i. NADINE[5].

187. **MILDRED**[4] **TURNER** (*Lillie Ruth*[3] *Carter, Ella*[2] *Hooks, James*[1]) married **James Moore**.

Children of **Mildred**[4] **Turner** and **James Moore** were as follows:
427.   i. DONALD[5].
428.   ii. JAMES.
429.   iii. LILLIAN.
430.   iv. SANDRA.

188. **RUTH MILDRED**[4] **CARTER** (*Virgil 'Virge*[3], *Ella*[2] *Hooks, James*[1]) was born on 30 July 1920 in Sandersville, Georgia. She married **Kenneth Rawlins**. She died on 13 August 1993 in Brooklyn, New York, at age 73.

Children of **Ruth Mildred**[4] **Carter** include:
431.   i. JOSEPH EDWARD ALEXANDER[5] was born on 5 October 1950 in Brooklyn, New York. He died on 3 June 1992 at age 41.
+ 432.   ii. AVA DIANE, born 28 June 1957 in Brooklyn, New York; married **Ricky Holden**.

There were no children of **Ruth Mildred**[4] **Carter** and **Kenneth Rawlins**.

189. **ANNE**[4] **CARTER** (*Virgil 'Virge*[3], *Ella*[2] *Hooks, James*[1]) was born on 21 March 1923 in Sandersville, Georgia. She married **David Green** on 21 July 1945 in Brooklyn, New York.

Children of **Anne**[4] **Carter** and **David Green** were as follows:
+ 433.   i. RICHARD CARTER[5], born 28 October 1947 in Brooklyn, New York; married **Elaine Parson**.
434.   ii. MICHAEL DAVID was born on 23 November 1950 in Brooklyn, New York. He died on 18 December 1981 in Hawaii at age 31.

193. **TERESA**[4] **CARTER** (*Virgil 'Virge*[3], *Ella*[2] *Hooks, James*[1]) was born on 4 September 1933 in Sandersville, Georgia. She married **Stanley Snyder**.

Children of **Teresa**[4] **Carter** and **Stanley Snyder** were as follows:
+ 435.   i. BARI LYN[5], born 6 February 1961 in Brooklyn, New York.
+ 436.   ii. DERON KEITH, born 16 September 1962 in Brooklyn, New York.

Generation Five

194. JOHN DESSIE^5 GARRISON (*Mamie^{4}Canty, Pearl L.^{3}Hooks, Robert^2, James^1*) married Dolly (——).

Children of John Dessie^5 Garrison and Dolly (——) were as follows:
437.   i. LINDA^6.
438.   ii. JOHNNIE.
439.   iii. MAMIE.
440.   iv. SCHERYL.
441.   v. SHIRLEY.

195. YVONNE AUDREY^5 GARRISON (*Mamie^{4}Canty, Pearl L.^{3}Hooks, Robert^2, James^1*) was born on 20 December 1945. She married William Q. Frazier.

Children of Yvonne Audrey^5 Garrison and William Q. Frazier were:
442.   i. KEITH AARON^6.

196. MARCELLA^5 GARRISON (*Mamie^{4}Canty, Pearl L.^{3}Hooks, Robert^2, James^1*) married Douglas Scott Bowmen. She married Al Edmonds (Jr.).

Children of Marcella^5 Garrison and Douglas Scott Bowmen were as follows:
443.   i. DOUGLAS SCOTT^6 (JR.).
444.   ii. DANA SUZETTA.

Children of Marcella^5 Garrison and Al Edmonds (Jr.) were:
445.   i. DALLAS ALEXIS-RANDOLPH^6.

200. TYRONE K.^{5} GARRISON (*Mamie^{4}Canty, Pearl L.^{3}Hooks, Robert^2, James^1*) was born on 19 October 1952.

Children of Tyrone K.^{5} Garrison include:
446.   i. ERIC WILLIAM^6.
447.   ii. AARON TYRONE.
448.   iii. TYMIA.

201. LEONARD^5 ESTON JR. (*Clara^{4}Gaudy, Mamie^{3}Hooks, Robert^2, James^1*).

Children of Leonard^5 Eston Jr. include:
449.   i. OSCAR^6.

202. DIANE^5 **ESTON** (*Clara*^{4}*Gaudy, Mamie*^{3}*Hooks, Robert*^{2}*, James*^{1}) married **Lamar Riddle.**

Children of **Diane**^{5} **Eston** and **Lamar Riddle** were as follows:
450.　i. LaTonya^6.
451.　ii. LaVelle.

204. JOYCE^5 **LAWSON** (*Mamie*^{4}*Gaudy, Mamie*^{3}*Hooks, Robert*^{2}*, James*^{1}) married **Joseph Moore.**

Children of **Joyce**^{5} **Lawson** and **Joseph Moore** were:
+ 452.　i. Karen^6, born 11 February 1967.

205. SHARON^5 **LAWSON** (*Mamie*^{4}*Gaudy, Mamie*^{3}*Hooks, Robert*^{2}*, James*^{1}) married **James E. Garrett.**

Children of **Sharon**^{5} **Lawson** and **James E. Garrett** were as follows:
453.　i. James E.^{6} Jr.
454.　ii. Joi.

206. BERNADETTE^5 **GAUDY** (*John*^{4}*, Mamie*^{3}*Hooks, Robert*^{2}*, James*^{1}) married **David Anderson.**

Children of **Bernadette**^{5} **Gaudy** and **David Anderson** were as follows:
455.　i. David^6 (Jr.).
456.　ii. Eugene.
457.　iii. Camile.
458.　iv. Simeon.
459.　v. LaTrisha.
460.　vi. Cindy.

207. FLORENCE^5 **GAUDY** (*John*^{4}*, Mamie*^{3}*Hooks, Robert*^{2}*, James*^{1}) married **Eugene Anderson.**

Children of **Florence**^{5} **Gaudy** and **Eugene Anderson** were as follows:
461.　i. Yolanda^6.
+ 462.　ii. Eugene (IV), married **Kimberly** (———).

209. JANICE^5 **GAUDY** (*John*^{4}*, Mamie*^{3}*Hooks, Robert*^{2}*, James*^{1}) married **Dwight McCarter.**

Children of **Janice**^{5} **Gaudy** and **Dwight McCarter** were as follows:
463.　i. Jennifer^6.
464.　ii. Janelle.

465.   iii. DWIGHT (JR.).

210. VALERIE^5 GAUDY (*John^4, Mamie^{3}Hooks, Robert^2, James^1*) married **Keith Martin.** She married **Columbus Sykes.**

Children of **Valerie^5 Gaudy** and **Keith Martin** were as follows:
+ 466.   i. KENDRA^6
467.   ii. KEITH.
468.   iii. VALENTE.
469.   iv. ANTWON.
470.   v. VINCENT.

There were no children of **Valerie^5 Gaudy** and **Columbus Sykes.**

211. JOCELYN^5 GAUDY (*John^4, Mamie^{3}Hooks, Robert^2, James^1*) married **Jerry Flowers.**

Children of **Jocelyn^5 Gaudy** and **Jerry Flowers** were as follows:
471.   i. CRYSTAL^6.
472.   ii. NATHANIEL JEROME.
473.   iii. JACQUELINE.
474.   iv. ROBERT.

214. CYNTHIA^5 JOHNSON (*Naomie^{4}Gordy, Mamie^{3}Hooks, Robert^2, James^1*).

Children of **Cynthia^5 Johnson** include:
475.   i. JESSICA^6.

215. CHERYL^5 JOHNSON (*Naomie^{4}Gordy, Mamie^{3}Hooks, Robert^2, James^1*) married **Robert Marshall.**

Children of **Cheryl^5 Johnson** and **Robert Marshall** were as follows:
476.   i. TABITHA^6.
477.   ii. ANTHONY.
478.   iii. ROBERT.
479.   iv. JOE.

218. JAMES^5 BROOKS (JR.) (*Thelma^{4}Gordy, Mamie^{3}Hooks, Robert^2, James^1*).

Children of **James^5 Brooks (Jr.)** include:
480.   i. CHRISTINA^6.
481.   ii. KAI.

219. KARLA^5 BROOKS (*Thelma^{4}Gordy, Mamie^{3}Hooks, Robert^2, James^1*).

Children of **Karla^5 Brooks** include:
    482.   i. KYLE^6.

220. SEDARA^5 BROOKS (*Thelma^{4}Gordy, Mamie^{3}Hooks, Robert^2, James^1*) married **Darryl Stroud.**

Children of **Sedara^5 Brooks** and **Darryl Stroud** were as follows:
    483.   i. MELANIE^6.
    484.   ii. MELISSA.

221. SHARRENA^5 BROOKS (*Thelma^{4}Gordy, Mamie^{3}Hooks, Robert^2, James^1*) married **Frank Johnson.**

Children of **Sharrena^5 Brooks** and **Frank Johnson** were as follows:
    485.   i. BENJAMIN^6.
    486.   ii. SONYA.
    487.   iii. KALEB.

222. LINDA^5 BROOKS (*Thelma^{4}Gordy, Mamie^{3}Hooks, Robert^2, James^1*) married **Ken Wells.**

Children of **Linda^5 Brooks** and **Ken Wells** were as follows:
    488.   i. MONICA^6.
    489.   ii. JAMES.

223. BARBARA^5 GORDY (*Raymond^4, Mamie^{3}Hooks, Robert^2, James^1*).

Children of **Barbara^5 Gordy** include:
    490.   i. DIONNE^6.

226. NICOLE^5 GORDY (*Raymond^4, Mamie^{3}Hooks, Robert^2, James^1*).

Children of **Nicole^5 Gordy** include:
    491.   i. JASON^6.

227. GARY^5 CARITHERS (*Johnnie Lou^{4}Gordy, Mamie^{3}Hooks, Robert^2, James^1*).

Children of **Gary^5 Carithers** include:
    492.   i. CLAUDETTE^6.
    493.   ii. AMANI.

228. HOWARD LOVELL^5 LEMON (*Lula Mae^{4}Gaudy, Mamie^{3}Hooks, Robert^2, James^1*) was born on 26 October 1940 in Detroit, Michigan. He married **Sandra Lynn Powell** on 16 May 1970 in Detroit, Michigan.

Children of **Howard Lovell^5 Lemon** and **Sandra Lynn Powell** were as follows:
494.   i. MYRON LOVELL^6 was born on 3 October 1971 in Detroit, Michigan. He married **Yolanda** (—?—) in Detroit, Michigan.
495.   ii. ERICA LYNN was born on 24 August 1974 in Detroit, Michigan. She married **Stacy Gordon** in September 1997 in Detroit, Michigan.
+ 496.   iii. LATOYA MERTRICE, born 20 October 1976 in Detroit, Michigan; married **Henry James.**

229. PATRICIA M.^{5} LEMON (*Lula Mae^{4}Gaudy, Mamie^{3}Hooks, Robert^2, James^1*) was born on 2 April 1942 in Detroit, Michigan. She married **Phil Green.**

Children of **Patricia M.^{5} Lemon** and **Phil Green** were as follows:
+ 497.   i. SHEILA RENE^6
498.   ii. CARL ANTHONY.
499.   iii. KEVIN LOUIS.
+ 500.   iv. SONJA DENISE
501.   v. CHRISTOPHER C.

230. DAVID JAMES^5 LEMON JR. (*Lula Mae^{4}Gaudy, Mamie^{3}Hooks, Robert^2, James^1*) was born on 21 November 1944 in Detroit, Michigan. He married **Merilyn Ann Bradley.**

Children of **David James^5 Lemon Jr.** and **Merilyn Ann Bradley** were as follows:
502.   i. DEMARCO^6.
503.   ii. KAMRON.
504.   iii. TUAN.

231. RICHARD^5 LEMON (*Lula Mae^{4}Gaudy, Mamie^{3}Hooks, Robert^2, James^1*) was born on 26 December 1947 in Detroit, Michigan. He married **Lorraine** (———). He married **Shirley Boyd** in 1970 in Detroit, Michigan.

There were no children of **Richard^5 Lemon** and **Lorraine** (———).

Children of **Richard^5 Lemon** and **Shirley Boyd** were as follows:
505.   i. NAKEMA^6.
506.   ii. LAQUAN.

232. DEBRA[5] **LEMON** (*Lula Mae*[4]*Gaudy, Mamie*[3]*Hooks, Robert*[2]*, James*[1]) was born on 6 March 1954 in Detroit, Michigan. She married **Jimmy Forrest** in Detroit, Michigan. She married **Felton Wright** on 14 February 1998 in Detroit, Michigan.

Children of **Debra**[5] **Lemon** and **Jimmy Forrest** were as follows:
507.   i. JIMMY QUATRELL[6] was born in September 1977 in Detroit, Michigan.
508.   ii. LOUIS was born in October 1978 in Detroit, Michigan.

There were no children of **Debra**[5] **Lemon** and **Felton Wright**.

233. SONIA DARLENE[5] **LEMON** (*Lula Mae*[4]*Gaudy, Mamie*[3]*Hooks, Robert*[2]*, James*[1]) was born on 22 July 1958 in Detroit, Michigan. She married **Cassell Mathews** on 3 August 2002 in Detroit, Michigan.

Children of **Sonia Darlene**[5] **Lemon** and **Dennis Hall** were:
509.   i. LAMAR[6] was born on 19 October 1976 in Detroit, Michigan.

Children of **Sonia Darlene**[5] **Lemon** and **Kevin Stevenson** were:
510.   i. SONIA[6] was born on 3 October 1990 in Detroit, Michigan.

Children of **Sonia Darlene**[5] **Lemon** and **Cassell Mathews** were:
511.   i. SHARROD[6] was born on 11 December 1986 in Detroit, Michigan.

235. CLARENCE[5] **GAUDY** (*Porter*[4]*Gordy, Mamie*[3]*Hooks, Robert*[2]*, James*[1]).

Children of **Clarence**[5] **Gaudy** include:
512.   i. FELICIA FRANCIS[6].
513.   ii. JENNIFER LEE.
514.   iii. JASON.
515.   iv. JAMAR.

236. PORTIA[5] **GAUDY** (*Porter*[4]*Gordy, Mamie*[3]*Hooks, Robert*[2]*, James*[1]).

Children of **Portia**[5] **Gaudy** include:
516.   i. STACY[6].

237. CAROL[5] **GAUDY** (*Porter*[4]*Gordy, Mamie*[3]*Hooks, Robert*[2]*, James*[1]).

Children of **Carol**[5] **Gaudy** include:
517.   i. ASHLEY[6].

239. JENNIFER[5] **WILLIAMS** (*Clara*[4]*Hooks, Clifford*[3]*, Robert*[2]*, James*[1]).

Children of **Jennifer**[5] **Williams** include:
> 518.   i. DAVID[6].
> 519.   ii. GENEVIEVE.

242. WILLIAM[5] **GREENLEE** (*Beatrice*[4]*Hooks, Clifford*[3]*, Robert*[2]*, James*[1]) married **Sandra** (———).

Children of **William**[5] **Greenlee** and **Sandra** (———) were:
> 520.   i. SANDRA[6].

244. EMMA JEAN[5] **GREENLEE** (*Beatrice*[4]*Hooks, Clifford*[3]*, Robert*[2]*, James*[1]) married **William Dunson.**

Children of **Emma Jean**[5] **Greenlee** and **William Dunson** were as follows:
> 521.   i. LISA MARIE[6].
> 522.   ii. WENDY ANDRE.
> 523.   iii. EDWAMA JANINE.

247. STEPHANIE[5] **THOMAS** (*Janetta*[4]*Hooks, James*[3]*, Robert*[2]*, James*[1]).

Children of **Stephanie**[5] **Thomas** include:
> 524.   i. EVAN[6].

248. LISA[5] **THOMAS** (*Janetta*[4]*Hooks, James*[3]*, Robert*[2]*, James*[1]) married **Mr. Hendley.**

Children of **Lisa**[5] **Thomas** and **Mr. Hendley** were as follows:
> 525.   i. JANET[6].
> 526.   ii. JOCELYN.

250. GREGORY[5] **THOMAS** (*Janetta*[4]*Hooks, James*[3]*, Robert*[2]*, James*[1]).

Children of **Gregory**[5] **Thomas** include:
> 527.   i. KIA JOHNSON[6].
> 528.   ii. KAMANE JOHNSON.

251. MELODIE[5] **EDWARDS** (*Eleanor*[4]*Hooks, James*[3]*, Robert*[2]*, James*[1]) married **Michael Frances Cooper.**

Children of **Melodie**[5] **Edwards** and **Michael Frances Cooper** were:
> 529.   i. MICHAEL JAMES[6].

259. MICHAEL D.^{5} HOOKS (*Delores^4, Robert J.^{3}, Robert^2, James^1*) was born on 25 December 1956. He married **Carol Anderson.**

Children of **Michael D.**^{5} **Hooks** and **Carol Anderson** were:
530.   i. KIRA LYNN^6.

268. LINDA^5 TURNER (*John Ruben^4, Elton^3, Rachel^2 Hooks, James^1*).

Children of **Linda**^{5} **Turner** include:
531.   i. SHAYLA^6.
532.   ii. SHANNON.

269. BARBARA^5 TURNER (*John Ruben^4, Elton^3, Rachel^2 Hooks, James^1*).

Children of **Barbara**^{5} **Turner** include:
533.   i. BRANDON^6.
534.   ii. TIFFANY.

282. BRENDA^5 HALL (*Mack T.^{4}, Jennie^3 Hooks, Mack^2, James^1*) married **Dennis Staten.**

Children of **Brenda**^{5} **Hall** and **Dennis Staten** were as follows:
535.   i. AMBER^6.
536.   ii. MALLORY.

295. TYRONE LEE^5 HOOKS (*Eddie Lee^4, Robert^3, Mack^2, James^1*).

Children of **Tyrone Lee**^{5} **Hooks** include:
537.   i. VALERIE^6.

296. ERIC EDWARD^5 HOOKS (*Eddie Lee^4, Robert^3, Mack^2, James^1*).

Children of **Eric Edward**^{5} **Hooks** include:
538.   i. ERIC^6 (JR.).

301. SHARON^5 HOOKS (*Earl^4, Robert^3, Mack^2, James^1*).

Children of **Sharon**^{5} **Hooks** include:
539.   i. TERRANCE^6.

303. IRENE^5 HOOKS (*Karie^4, Robert^3, Mack^2, James^1*).

Children of **Irene**[5] **Hooks** include:
540. i. AMBER[6].

328. BRIAN[5] **GORDY** (*Henry Edward*[4], *Hattie Mae*[3] *Hooks, Mack*[2], *James*[1]) married Yvonne (———).

Children of **Brian**[5] **Gordy** and **Yvonne** (———) were as follows:
541. i. LANITA[6].
542. ii. BRIANA.

329. BYRON[5] **GORDY** (*Henry Edward*[4], *Hattie Mae*[3] *Hooks, Mack*[2], *James*[1]) married Willette (———).

Children of **Byron**[5] **Gordy** and **Willette** (———) were:
543. i. CHRISTINE[6].

330. BRUCE[5] **GORDY** (*Henry Edward*[4], *Hattie Mae*[3] *Hooks, Mack*[2], *James*[1]) married Deborah (———).

Children of **Bruce**[5] **Gordy** and **Deborah** (———) were as follows:
544. i. MARQITA[6].
545. ii. APRIL.

331. BRENT[5] **GORDY** (*Henry Edward*[4], *Hattie Mae*[3] *Hooks, Mack*[2], *James*[1]) married Effie (———).

Children of **Brent**[5] **Gordy** and **Effie** (———) were:
546. i. JASMINE[6].

332. BRIDGETTE[5] **GORDY** (*Henry Edward*[4], *Hattie Mae*[3] *Hooks, Mack*[2], *James*[1]) married **Bernell Seal.**

Children of **Bridgette**[5] **Gordy** and **Bernell Seal** were as follows:
547. i. ROBERT[6].
548. ii. RAYNELL.
549. iii. RAYNARD.

334. KAREN[5] **KING** (*Margaret Jewel*[4] *Gordy, Hattie Mae*[3] *Hooks, Mack*[2], *James*[1]) married **Elvin Brooks.**

Children of **Karen**[5] **King** and **Elvin Brooks** were as follows:
550. i. KYLE[6].

551. ii. KARLIS.
552. iii. KELLUM.
553. iv. KRISTOPHER.
554. v. KENNETH.
555. vi. KARY.
556. vii. KARIS.

335. KYRA^5 **KING** (*Marret Jewel*^{4}*Gordy, Hattie Mae*^{3}*Hooks, Mack*^{2}*, James*^{1}) married **James Ridgell.**

Children of **Kyra**^{5} **King** and **James Ridgell** were as follows:
557. i. IAN^6.
558. ii. ETHAN.
559. iii. JULIAN.

343. DEBORAH^5 **LAWRENCE** (*Joyce*^{4}*Gordy, Hattie Mae*^{3}*Hooks, Mack*^{2}*, James*^{1}) married **Lamont McClain.**

Children of **Deborah**^{5} **Lawrence** and **Lamont McClain** were as follows:
560. i. VANESSA^6.
561. ii. KRISTIN.
562. iii. TASHA.

344. DOREEN^5 **LAWRENCE** (*Joyce*^{4}*Gordy, Hattie Mae*^{3}*Hooks, Mack*^{2}*, James*^{1}) married **Sam Hughes.**

Children of **Doreen**^{5} **Lawrence** and **Sam Hughes** were:
563. i. DAVID^6.

346. DARIN^5 **LAWRENCE** (*Joyce*^{4}*Gordy, Hattie Mae*^{3}*Hooks, Mack*^{2}*, James*^{1}) married **Shirley** (———).

Children of **Darin**^{5} **Lawrence** and **Shirley** (———) were as follows:
564. i. BRANDON^6.
565. ii. KEITH.

354. SANDRA CAROL^5 **THOMAS** (*Eva (Johnny)*^{4}*Trawick, Bertha*^{3}*Carter, Ella*^{2}*Hooks, James*^{1}) was born on 31 May 1946 in Philadelphia, Pennsylvania. She married **Herb Connelly** circa 1970 in Philadelphia, Pennsylvania.

Children of **Sandra Carol**^{5} **Thomas** and **Herb Connelly** were as follows:
566. i. KEISHA^6 was born on 13 March 1971 in Philadelphia, Pennsylvania.

+ 567.   ii. KEIA, born 13 March 1971 in Philadelphia, Pennsylvania.

355. SIGRID ANN^5 THOMAS (*Eva (Johnny)^4 Trawick, Bertha^3 Carter, Ella^2 Hooks, James^1*) was born on 10 March 1948 in Philadelphia, Pennsylvania. She was born on 10 March 1948 in Philadelphia, Pennsylvania. She married **Howard Edward McCall Jr.** on 30 January 1971 in Philadelphia, Pennsylvania.

Children of **Sigrid Ann^5 Thomas** and **Howard Edward McCall Jr.** were as follows:
568.   i. MARK ANTHONY^6 was born on 25 August 1971 in Philadelphia, Pennsylvania.
569.   ii. KEITH HOWARD was born on 15 June 1974 in Philadelphia, Pennsylvania.

356. WANDA EILEEN^5 THOMAS (*Eva (Johnny)^4 Trawick, Bertha^3 Carter, Ella^2 Hooks, James^1*) was born on 12 April 1950 in Philadelphia, Pennsylvania. She married **John 'Donald' Bird** in Philadelphia, Pennsylvania.

Children of **Wanda Eileen^5 Thomas** and **John 'Donald' Bird** were:
570.   i. HEATHER^6 was born on 27 December 1981 in Philadelphia, Pennsylvania.

363. ALTON^5 BUTTS (*Mary Julia^4 Carter, Jeff^3, Ella^2 Hooks, James^1*) was born on 28 October 1934 in Sandersville, Georgia. He married **Marlyn Farley.** He died on 19 May 2003 in Philadelphia, Pennsylvania, at age 68.

Children of **Alton^5 Butts** and **Marlyn Farley** were as follows:
+ 571.   i. VERONA^6, born 3 December 1963 in Philadelphia, Pennsylvania.
+ 572.   ii. MARSHA, born 20 October 1967 in Philadelphia, Pennsylvania.
+ 573.   iii. TERESE, born 10 February 1970 in Philadelphia, Pennsylvania.

365. MIRIAM^5 CHEEVES (*Lillian Arthur^4 Carter, Jeff^3, Ella^2 Hooks, James^1*) was born in Sandersville, Washington County, Georgia.

Children of **Miriam^5 Cheeves** include:
574.   i. CLARA BELLE^6 was born on 2 February 1979 in Tacoma, Washington.

366. GLORIA^5 CHEEVES (*Lillian Arthur^4 Carter, Jeff^3, Ella^2 Hooks, James^1*) was born on 4 July 1941 in Sandersville, Washington County, Georgia. She married **Charles Graham.**

Children of **Gloria^5 Cheeves** and **Charles Graham** were as follows:
+ 575.   i. CHARLES DAVID^6, born 20 May 1969 in Philadelphia, Pennsylvania; married **Lorrie Hatten.**
+ 576.   ii. MELISSA AVA, born 21 April 1970 in Philadelphia, Pennsylvania.
577.   iii. JENNIFER ANNETTE was born on 21 February 1979 in Philadelphia, Pennsylvania.

367. HORACE^5 **CHEEVES** (*Lillian Arthur*^{4}*Carter, Jeff*^{3}, *Ella*^{2}*Hooks, James*^{1}) was born on 4 September 1943 in Sandersville, Washington County, Georgia. He married **Fannie Pearl Williams**, daughter of **Coleman Williams** and **Florence Rogers**, on 6 July 1971 in Philadelphia, Pennsylvania.

Children of **Horace**^{5} **Cheeves** and **Fannie Pearl Williams** were:
578.   i. DENISE NICOLE^6 was born on 20 February 1972 in Philadelphia, Pennsylvania.

368. FOREST^5 **CHEEVES** (*Lillian Arthur*^{4}*Carter, Jeff*^{3}, *Ella*^{2}*Hooks, James*^{1}) was born on 4 September 1943 in Sandersville, Washington County, Georgia. He married **Karen Kennedy** in Philadelphia, Pennsylvania. He died on 27 March 1987 in Detroit, Michigan, at age 43.

Children of **Forest**^{5} **Cheeves** and **Karen Kennedy** were as follows:
+ 579.   i. BARRY STEVEN^6, born 29 June 1960 in Philadelphia, Pennsylvania; married **Andrea Benita 'Nita' Hyden.**
+ 580.   ii. FORREST TROY, born 22 February 1962 in Philadelphia, Pennsylvania.
+ 581.   iii. DARNELL FRANK, born 17 February 1963 in Philadelphia, Pennsylvania; married **Diana 'Ann' Marie Johnson;** married **Pat Young.**
+ 582.   iv. BRUCE KENNETH, born 12 May 1964 in Philadelphia, Pennsylvania; married **Audrey Miree.**

372. MICHELLE^5 **COTTON** (*Ruby Clyde*^{4}*Carter, Jeff*^{3}, *Ella*^{2}*Hooks, James*^{1}) was born on 23 February 1958 in Detroit, Michigan. She died on 16 March 1993 in Philadelphia, Pennsylvania, at age 35.

Children of **Michelle**^{5} **Cotton** and **Stan Johnson** were:
+ 583.   i. VENICE GERVENIA^6, born 23 November 1982 in Philadelphia, Pennsylvania.

373. HERMAN^5 **NELSON** (*Ruby Clyde*^{4}*Carter, Jeff*^{3}, *Ella*^{2}*Hooks, James*^{1}) was born on 4 November 1943 in Philadelphia, Pennsylvania. He married **Dallay Yvonne Graham** on 14 March 1963 in Philadelphia, Pennsylvania.

Children of **Herman**^{5} **Nelson** and **Dallay Yvonne Graham** were as follows:
+ 584.   i. JAMES ANTHONY 'TONY'^{6}, born 1 March 1968 in Burlington County, New Jersey; married **Marsha Phillips.**
585.   ii. HYMAN TERELL 'HYMIE' was born on 27 October 1979 in Philadelphia, Pennsylvania.

Children of **Herman**^{5} **Nelson** and **Dorothy Faraby** were:
586.   i. KENISA^6 was born circa 1973 in Philadelphia, Pennsylvania.

Children of **Herman⁵ Nelson** and **Louise Bouche** were:

587. i. CHRISTOPHER **'CB'⁶** was born on 14 July 1982 in Philadelphia, Pennsylvania.

Children of **Herman⁵ Nelson** and **Joanne Jaworski** were:

588. i. TIFFANY ANNE⁶ was born on 25 February 1989 in Philadelphia, Pennsylvania.

382. SHARON **'SHERRY'⁵** CARTER *(Jeff Raymond⁴, Jeff³, Ella² Hooks, James¹)* was born on 18 April 1949 in Philadelphia, Pennsylvania.

Children of **Sharon 'Sherry'⁵ Carter** and **Arthur Malcolm Wright** were as follows:

+ 589. i. ARTHUR MALCOLM **'SAM'⁶**, born 23 December 1967 in Philadelphia, Pennsylvania; married **Valerie Jean McMahon.**
+ 590. ii. JUAN MALCOLM **'JOHNNY'**, born 12 January 1969 in Philadelphia, Pennsylvania.
+ 591. iii. APRIL DANEEN, born 8 June 1973 in Philadelphia, Pennsylvania; married **Shawn Tyrone Smith.**

Children of **Sharon 'Sherry'⁵ Carter** and **Willie 'Butch' Pannell** were:

592. i. SHARON **'PIGGY'⁶** was born on 13 July 1987 in Philadelphia, Pennsylvania.

383. JEFF RAYMOND **'BROTHER'⁵** CARTER JR. *(Jeff Raymond⁴, Jeff³, Ella² Hooks, James¹)* was born on 1 July 1950 in Philadelphia, Pennsylvania. He married **Sujuan Williams** on 4 May 1968 in Philadelphia, Pennsylvania.

Children of **Jeff Raymond 'Brother'⁵ Carter Jr.** and **Sujuan Williams** were as follows:

+ 593. i. KIM PATRICE⁶, born 26 October 1968 in Philadelphia, Pennsylvania.
+ 594. ii. CRYSTAL LARIN, born 4 July 1974 in Philadelphia, Pennsylvania.

Children of **Jeff Raymond 'Brother'⁵ Carter Jr.** and **Tia Council** were as follows:

+ 595. i. JEFF RAYMOND ISAAC COUNCILL⁶, born 16 September 1975 in Philadelphia, Pennsylvania.
+ 596. ii. NATHANIEL IAN COUNCILL, born 15 March 1977 in Philadelphia, Pennsylvania.
597. iii. JASON ADAM PERSON COUNCILL was born on 6 March 1986 in Philadelphia, Pennsylvania.

385. DENNIS⁵ CARTER *(Jeff Raymond⁴, Jeff³, Ella² Hooks, James¹)* was born on 25 December 1952 in Philadelphia, Pennsylvania. He married **Marcia Earlene Jackson.**

Children of **Dennis⁵ Carter** and **Marcia Earlene Jackson** were as follows:

598. i. ELI⁶ was born on 7 November 1978 in Philadelphia, Pennsylvania.
+ 599. ii. EARL, born 7 November 1978 in Philadelphia, Pennsylvania.

Children of **Dennis^5 Carter** and **Sonya Bernice Thompson** were:

600.   i. DENNIS^6 JR. was born on 27 April 1973 in Philadelphia, Pennsylvania. He died on 12 October 1993 in Philadelphia, Pennsylvania, at age 20.

389. SHIRLEY^5 FISHER (*Elizabeth^{4}Dawson, Lora Ella 'Laura^{3}Carter, Ella^{2}Hooks, James^1*) was born on 29 March. She married **Edward Brent.**

Children of **Shirley^5 Fisher** and **Edward Brent** were:

+ 601.   i. ROBIN^6, born 21 June 1962; married **Joseph Phelps.**

391. BRENDA^5 DAWSON (*Timothy^4, Lora Ella 'Laura^{3}Carter, Ella^{2}Hooks, James^1*) was born on 18 September in Sandersville, Georgia. She married **Mark Scott.**

Children of **Brenda^5 Dawson** and **Mark Scott** were as follows:

602.   i. VALISE^6 was born on 25 July.
603.   ii. VALENE was born on 25 September 1986.

392. BENNIE LAWSON^5 DAWSON (*Timothy^4, Lora Ella 'Laura^{3}Carter, Ella^{2}Hooks, James^1*) was born on 6 July 1947 in Sandersville, Georgia. He married **Barbara Jones.**

Children of **Bennie Lawson^5 Dawson** and **Barbara Jones** were as follows:

604.   i. LIZ^6 was born on 23 June 1970.
605.   ii. PHILIP was born on 4 November 1982.

395. LORETTA^5 DAWSON (*Timothy^4, Lora Ella 'Laura^{3}Carter, Ella^{2}Hooks, James^1*) was born on 30 August 1952 in Sandersville, Georgia. She married **Aubrey Jones.**

Children of **Loretta^5 Dawson** and **Aubrey Jones** were as follows:

606.   i. AUBRINA^6.
607.   ii. GAYLA.
608.   iii. CRISTEN NOEL was born on 15 December 1981.

396. PAULINE^5 DAWSON (*Timothy^4, Lora Ella 'Laura^{3}Carter, Ella^{2}Hooks, James^1*) was born on 12 November 1954 in Sandersville, Georgia. She married **Alfred Ford.**

Children of **Pauline^5 Dawson** and **Alfred Ford** were:

609.   i. TORRANCE^6 was born on 2 November 1982.

399. GRACE HARRIS^5 SPARKS (*Deborah^{4}Dawson, Lora Ella 'Laura^{3}Carter, Ella^{2}Hooks, James^1*) was born on 22 March 1944 in Sandersville, Georgia. She married **Hugh Bryant.**

Children of **Grace Harris**^{5} **Sparks** and **Hugh Bryant** were as follows:
610.   i. HUGH JASON^6 was born on 5 December 1976.
611.   ii. KIRA LAUREN was born on 2 January 1979.

405. GWENDOLYN^5 GORDY (*Eloise 'Honey'^{4}Dawson, Lora Ella 'Laura'^{3}Carter, Ella^{2}Hooks, James^1*) was born on 12 March 1947 in Utica, New York. She married **Julius Murphy.**

Children of **Gwendolyn^5 Gordy** and **Julius Murphy** were as follows:
612.   i. SONIA JOY^6 was born on 13 June 1976 in Albany, Georgia.
613.   ii. ASHLEY was born on 21 December 1984 in Macon, Georgia.

407. DAVID^5 GORDY (*Eloise 'Honey'^{4}Dawson, Lora Ella 'Laura'^{3}Carter, Ella^{2}Hooks, James^1*) was born on 13 April 1952 in Sandersville, Georgia. He married **DeLois Turner.** He married **Darlene Robinson.**

Children of **David^5 Gordy** and **DeLois Turner** were as follows:
614.   i. DEBORAH^6 was born on 14 January 1971 in Augusta, Georgia.
615.   ii. DAVINA was born on 2 June 1972 in Augusta, Georgia.
616.   iii. DENISE was born on 13 June 1975 in Augusta, Georgia.
617.   iv. JOSHUA DAVID was born on 9 February 1987 in Augusta, Georgia.

Children of **David^5 Gordy** and **Darlene Robinson** were:
618.   i. DAYNA LYNN^6 was born on 14 August 1997 in Milledgeville, Georgia.

408. DEBORAH ANNE^5 GORDY (*Eloise 'Honey'^{4}Dawson, Lora Ella 'Laura'^{3}Carter, Ella^{2}Hooks, James^1*) was born on 6 January 1954 in Sandersville, Georgia. She married **Samuel Duggan** on 9 June 1979.

Children of **Deborah Anne^5 Gordy** and **Samuel Duggan** were as follows:
619.   i. LORA ANNE^6 was born on 17 July 1982 in Milledgeville, Georgia.
620.   ii. LORETTA DENISE was born on 12 March 1985 in Milledgeville, Georgia.

409. MARY LUCY^5 GORDY (*Eloise 'Honey'^{4}Dawson, Lora Ella 'Laura'^{3}Carter, Ella^{2}Hooks, James^1*) was born on 17 July 1956 in Sandersville, Georgia. She married **Tony Owen Hurt Sr.** on 7 July 1979.

Children of **Mary Lucy^5 Gordy** and **Tony Owen Hurt Sr.** were as follows:
621.   i. TONY OWEN^6 JR. was born on 19 April 1982 in Milledgeville, Georgia.
622.   ii. KARI LOUCYE was born on 17 February 1985 in Milledgeville, Georgia.
623.   iii. BRAXTON GORDY was born on 7 June 1992 in Macon, Georgia.

411. BERRY RENARD^5 GORDY (*Eloise 'Honey'^{4}Dawson, Lora Ella 'Laura'^{3}Carter, Ella^{2}Hooks, James^1*) was born on 10 September 1958 in Sandersville, Georgia. He married **Brenda Lee Lord Barlow Cardy.**

Children of **Berry Renard^5 Gordy** and **Brenda Lee Lord Barlow Cardy** were:
   624.   i. JALEN BERRY^6 was born on 19 October 1991 in Augusta, Georgia.

412. CATHERINE LORETTA^5 DAWSON (*Homer^4, Lora Ella 'Laura'^{3}Carter, Ella^{2}Hooks, James^1*) was born on 4 February 1951 in West Palm Beach, Florida. She married **Douglas Fulton.**

Children of **Catherine Loretta^5 Dawson** and **Douglas Fulton** were as follows:
   625.   i. LAURIE^6 was born on 14 August 1972.
   626.   ii. ASHLEY was born on 30 September 1980.
   627.   iii. WHITNEY BLAIR was born on 6 September 1987.

413. HOMER 'BILLY'^{5} DAWSON III (*Homer^4, Lora Ella 'Laura'^{3}Carter, Ella^{2}Hooks, James^1*) was born on 9 April 1953 in West Palm Beach, Florida. He married **Brenda McCullom.**

Children of **Homer 'Billy'^{5} Dawson III** and **Brenda McCullom** were as follows:
   628.   i. HOMER^6.
   629.   ii. TANYA was born on 25 June 1973.
   630.   iii. ANTONIO was born on 7 August 1978.
   631.   iv. ALBERT was born on 25 October 1980.

415. WENDELL^5 DAWSON (*Homer^4, Lora Ella 'Laura'^{3}Carter, Ella^{2}Hooks, James^1*) was born on 31 January 1957 in West Palm Beach, Florida. He married **Deborah Davis.**

Children of **Wendell^5 Dawson** and **Deborah Davis** were:
   632.   i. LESLIE CANELIA^6 was born on 24 November 1989 in Nashville, Tennessee.

416. NATALIE JEAN^5 DAWSON (*Homer^4, Lora Ella 'Laura'^{3}Carter, Ella^{2}Hooks, James^1*) was born on 6 April 1958 in West Palm Beach, Florida. She married **Robert Smith.**

Children of **Natalie Jean^5 Dawson** and **Robert Smith** were as follows:
   633.   i. NICOLE^6 was born on 29 September 1979.
   634.   ii. NATALIE RENEE was born on 17 May 1987.
   635.   iii. (FEMALE).

417. BEVERLY^5 DAWSON (*Cornelius^4, Lora Ella 'Laura'^{3}Carter, Ella^{2}Hooks, James^1*) was born on 5 February 1955 in East Palatka, Florida.

Children of **Beverly^5 Dawson** include:
636.   i. HOPE^6 was born on 12 January 1975 in West Palm Beach, Florida.
637.   ii. ANTARIO.

418. WANDA^5 DAWSON (*Cornelius^4, Lora Ella 'Laura^3 Carter, Ella^2 Hooks, James^1*) was born on 1 November 1959 in West Palm Beach, Florida. She married **Tim Hunt.**

Children of **Wanda^5 Dawson** and **Tim Hunt** were as follows:
638.   i. JULIAN^6 was born on 17 August 1995 in Miami, Florida.
639.   ii. JUSTIN was born in February 1997 in Miami, Florida.

421. KAREN ' KAY' ELIZABETH^5 DAVIS ROSS (*Wilhelmina 'Candy^4 Dawson, Lora Ella 'Laura^3 Carter, Ella^2 Hooks, James^1*) was born on 14 May 1956 in West Palm Beach, Florida. She married **Willie Neal.**

Children of **Karen ' Kay' Elizabeth^5 Davis Ross** and **Bernard Jackson** were:
+ 640.   i. KIMBERLY CORNELIA^6, born 19 June 1976 in Florida.

Children of **Karen ' Kay' Elizabeth^5 Davis Ross** and **Willie Neal** were:
641.   i. LINDSEY^6 was born on 1 August 1987 in Florida.

432. AVA DIANE^5 CARTER (*Ruth Mildred^4, Virgil 'Virge^3, Ella^2 Hooks, James^1*) was born on 28 June 1957 in Brooklyn, New York. She married **Ricky Holden.**

Children of **Ava Diane^5 Carter** and **Ricky Holden** were as follows:
642.   i. LESLIE NEVON^6 was born on 8 September 1986 in Colorado.
643.   ii. MALCOLM was born on 4 November 1988 in Colorado.

433. RICHARD CARTER^5 GREEN (*Anne^4 Carter, Virgil 'Virge^3, Ella^2 Hooks, James^1*) was born on 28 October 1947 in Brooklyn, New York. He married **Elaine Parson** on 4 January 1968 in Brooklyn, New York.

Children of **Richard Carter^5 Green** and **Joy Bernard** were:
644.   i. ANTHONY^6 was born on 25 October 1967 in Brooklyn, New York.

Children of **Richard Carter^5 Green** and **Elaine Parson** were as follows:
+ 645.   i. DAMANI SAEED TALE'^{6}, born 18 February 1974 in Dayton, Ohio.
646.   ii. TAIESHA TENE' TALE' was born on 29 July 1976 in Dayton, Ohio.
647.   iii. KHALID ABDULLAH TALE' was born on 3 September 1980 in Dayton, Ohio.

435. BARI LYN^5 SNYDER (*Teresa^4 Carter, Virgil 'Virge^3, Ella^2 Hooks, James^1*) was born on 6 February 1961 in Brooklyn, New York.

Children of **Bari Lyn^5 Snyder** and **Alvin White** were as follows:
648.   i. EVAN BRION^6 was born on 14 August 1993 in Brooklyn, New York.
649.   ii. DARNELL TYREE was born on 30 January 1996 in Brooklyn, New York.

436. DERON KEITH^5 SNYDER (*Teresa^{4}Carter, Virgil 'Virge^3, Ella^{2}Hooks, James^1*) was born on 16 September 1962 in Brooklyn, New York.

Children of **Deron Keith^5 Snyder** and **Vanessa Williams** were:
650.   i. SIERRA NGOZI^6 was born on 9 July 1996 in Washington, D.C.

Generation Six

452. KAREN^6 MOORE (*Joyce^{5}Lawson, Mamie^{4}Gaudy, Mamie^{3}Hooks, Robert^2, James^1*) was born on 11 February 1967.

Children of **Karen^6 Moore** include:
651.   i. ELI^7.
652.   ii. TYLER.

462. EUGENE^6 ANDERSON (IV) (*Florence^{5}Gaudy, John^4, Mamie^{3}Hooks, Robert^2, James^1*) married **Kimberly (———)**.

Children of **Eugene^6 Anderson (IV)** and **Kimberly (———)** were:
653.   i. KAYLA^7.

466. KENDRA^6 MARTIN (*Valerie^{5}Gaudy, John^4, Mamie^{3}Hooks, Robert^2, James^1*).

Children of **Kendra^6 Martin** include:
654.   i. JAMAR^7.

496. LATOYA MERTRICE^6 LEMON (*Howard Lovell^5, Lula Mae^{4}Gaudy, Mamie^{3}Hooks, Robert^2, James^1*) was born on 20 October 1976 in Detroit, Michigan. She married **Henry James** in 1998 in Detroit, Michigan.

Children of **LaToya Mertrice^6 Lemon** and **Henry James** were:
655.   i. CHRISTOPHER^7 was born in April 1998 in Detroit, Michigan.

497. SHEILA RENE^6 GREEN (*Patricia M.^{5}Lemon, Lula Mae^{4}Gaudy, Mamie^{3}Hooks, Robert^2, James^1*).

Children of **Sheila Rene^6 Green** include:
656.   i. ERIC^7.

657. ii. ANTOINE.
658. iii. ZACHERY.
659. iv. MICHAEL.

500. **SONJA DENISE^6 GREEN** (*Patricia M.^{5}Lemon, Lula Mae^{4}Gaudy, Mamie^{3}Hooks, Robert^2, James^1*).

Children of **Sonja Denise^6 Green** include:
660. i. KAYLA^7.
661. ii. KIEARA.
662. iii. CHRISTOPHER.
663. iv. ISAIAH.

567. **KEIA^6 CONNELLY** (*Sandra Carol^{5}Thomas, Eva (Johnny)^{4}Trawick, Bertha^{3}Carter, Ella^{2}Hooks, James^1*) was born on 13 March 1971 in Philadelphia, Pennsylvania.

Children of **Keia^6 Connelly** and **Rob Baker** were:
664. i. HANNAH^7 was born on 5 January 1997 in Philadelphia, Pennsylvania.

571. **VERONA^6 BUTTS** (*Alton^5, Mary Julia^{4}Carter, Jeff^3, Ella^{2}Hooks, James^1*) was born on 3 December 1963 in Philadelphia, Pennsylvania.

Children of **Verona^6 Butts** and **Craig Walker** were:
665. i. TERON BUTTS^7 was born on 21 July 1989 in Philadelphia, Pennsylvania.

572. **MARSHA^6 BUTTS** (*Alton^5, Mary Julia^{4}Carter, Jeff^3, Ella^{2}Hooks, James^1*) was born on 20 October 1967 in Philadelphia, Pennsylvania.

Children of **Marsha^6 Butts** and **Bryan Ford** were:
666. i. NATASHA BUTTS^7 was born on 27 June 1984 in Philadelphia, Pennsylvania.

573. **TERESE^6 BUTTS** (*Alton^5, Mary Julia^{4}Carter, Jeff^3, Ella^{2}Hooks, James^1*) was born on 10 February 1970 in Philadelphia, Pennsylvania.

Children of **Terese^6 Butts** and **Damont Heckstall** were:
667. i. ASHTON BUTTS^7 was born on 3 May 1989 in Ft. Lauderdale, Fla.

575. **CHARLES DAVID^6 GRAHAM** (*Gloria^{5}Cheeves, Lillian Arthur^{4}Carter, Jeff^3, Ella^{2}Hooks, James^1*) was born on 20 May 1969 in Philadelphia, Pennsylvania. He married **Lorrie Hatten** on 5 September 1992 in Philadelphia, Pennsylvania.

Children of **Charles David**[6] **Graham** include:

668.   i. NOLAN LEWIS PAUL[7] was born on 29 May 1984 in Philadelphia, Pennsylvania.

There were no children of **Charles David**[6] **Graham** and **Lorrie Hatten**.

576. **MELISSA AVA**[6] **GRAHAM** (*Gloria*[5]*Cheeves, Lillian Arthur*[4]*Carter, Jeff*[3]*, Ella*[2]*Hooks, James*[1]) was born on 21 April 1970 in Philadelphia, Pennsylvania.

Children of **Melissa Ava**[6] **Graham** and **Carlos Kinslow** were:

669.   i. BRANDON ALEXANDER[7] was born on 28 March 1996 in Philadelphia, Pennsylvania.

579. **BARRY STEVEN**[6] **CHEEVES** (*Forest*[5]*, Lillian Arthur*[4]*Carter, Jeff*[3]*, Ella*[2]*Hooks, James*[1]) was born on 29 June 1960 in Philadelphia, Pennsylvania. He married **Andrea Benita 'Nita' Hyden**, daughter of **Ronald Hyden** and **Judy Ryder**, on 30 April 1988 in Philadelphia, Pennsylvania.

Children of **Barry Steven**[6] **Cheeves** and **Andrea Benita 'Nita' Hyden** were as follows:

+ 670.   i. RASETA NICOLE[7], born 7 May 1982 in Philadelphia, Pennsylvania.

671.   ii. RANIKA MICHELLE was born on 2 February 1990 in Philadelphia, Pennsylvania.

Children of **Barry Steven**[6] **Cheeves** and **Diane Johnson** were:

672.   i. BARRY STEVEN[7] JR. was born on 25 August 1996 in Philadelphia, Pennsylvania.

580. **FORREST TROY**[6] **CHEEVES** (*Forest*[5]*, Lillian Arthur*[4]*Carter, Jeff*[3]*, Ella*[2]*Hooks, James*[1]) was born on 22 February 1962 in Philadelphia, Pennsylvania.

Children of **Forrest Troy**[6] **Cheeves** and **Sue Wilson** were as follows:

673.   i. FORREST TROY[7] JR. was born on 30 March 1988 in Philadelphia, Pennsylvania.

674.   ii. ALEXANDER DOMINIC was born on 19 May 1989 in Philadelphia, Pennsylvania.

581. **DARNELL FRANK**[6] **CHEEVES** (*Forest*[5]*, Lillian Arthur*[4]*Carter, Jeff*[3]*, Ella*[2]*Hooks, James*[1]) was born on 17 February 1963 in Philadelphia, Pennsylvania. He married **Diana 'Ann' Marie Johnson**. He married **Pat Young** on 19 December 1997 in Philadelphia, Pennsylvania.

Children of **Darnell Frank**[6] **Cheeves** and **Diana 'Ann' Marie Johnson** were as follows:

675.   i. SHANAY LANELL[7] was born on 30 October 1985 in Philadelphia, Pennsylvania.

676.   ii. SHEENA MONIQUE was born on 5 November 1989 in Philadelphia, Pennsylvania.

Children of **Darnell Frank**[6] **Cheeves** and **Pat Young** were:

677.   i. DARNELL FRANK[7] JR. was born on 20 March 1993 in Philadelphia, Pennsylvania.

582. BRUCE KENNETH[6] CHEEVES (*Forest[5], Lillian Arthur[4] Carter, Jeff[3], Ella[2] Hooks, James[1]*) was born on 12 May 1964 in Philadelphia, Pennsylvania. He married **Audrey Miree** on 17 July 1998 in Philadelphia, Pennsylvania.

Children of **Bruce Kenneth[6] Cheeves** and **Audrey Miree** were as follows:
678.   i. BRUCE KENNETH[7] JR. was born on 24 October 1989 in Philadelphia, Pennsylvania.
679.   ii. KAREN was born on 13 July 1991 in Philadelphia, Pennsylvania.

583. VENICE GERVENIA[6] COTTON (*Michelle[5], Ruby Clyde[4] Carter, Jeff[3], Ella[2] Hooks, James[1]*) was born on 23 November 1982 in Philadelphia, Pennsylvania.

Children of **Venice Gervenia[6] Cotton** and **Ronald Terrell Mordecai** were:
680.   i. CYIR ISRAEL[7] was born on 28 July 2000 in Philadelphia, Pennsylvania.

584. JAMES ANTHONY 'TONY'[6] NELSON (*Herman[5], Ruby Clyde[4] Carter, Jeff[3], Ella[2] Hooks, James[1]*) was born on 1 March 1968 in Burlington County, New Jersey. He married **Marsha Phillips** on 4 August 1991 in Enid, Oklahoma.

Children of **James Anthony 'Tony'[6] Nelson** and **Marsha Phillips** were:
681.   i. JASHA MIANA[7] was born on 23 May 1995 in Tokyo, Japan.

589. ARTHUR MALCOLM 'SAM'[6] WRIGHT (*Sharon 'Sherry'[5] Carter, Jeff Raymond[4], Jeff[3], Ella[2] Hooks, James[1]*) was born on 23 December 1967 in Philadelphia, Pennsylvania. He married **Valerie Jean McMahon** on 3 November 1986 in Tampa, Florida.

Children of **Arthur Malcolm 'Sam'[6] Wright** and **Valerie Jean McMahon** were as follows:
682.   i. ALEXIS DANEEN[7] was born on 23 March 1991 in Clearwater, Florida.
683.   ii. DANIELLE MARIE was born on 4 July 1992 in Clearwater, Florida.
684.   iii. TIFFANY ELIZABETH was born on 4 April 1994 in Clearwater, Florida.

590. JUAN MALCOLM 'JOHNNY'[6] WRIGHT (*Sharon 'Sherry'[5] Carter, Jeff Raymond[4], Jeff[3], Ella[2] Hooks, James[1]*) was born on 12 January 1969 in Philadelphia, Pennsylvania.

Children of **Juan Malcolm 'Johnny'[6] Wright** include:
685.   i. JUAN VALDEZ[7] was born on 28 July 1987.

591. APRIL DANEEN[6] WRIGHT (*Sharon 'Sherry'[5] Carter, Jeff Raymond[4], Jeff[3], Ella[2] Hooks, James[1]*) was born on 8 June 1973 in Philadelphia, Pennsylvania. She married **Shawn Tyrone Smith** in February 2000 in Philadelphia, Pennsylvania.

242

Children of **April Daneen⁶ Wright** and **Gary McCalla** were:
686. i. LESHAUN DANEEN MCCALLA⁷ was born on 14 September 1989 in Philadelphia, Pennsylvania.

Children of **April Daneen⁶ Wright** and **Darryl Nesmith** were:
687. i. DASHINA⁷ was born on 12 July 1995 in Philadelphia, Pennsylvania.

Children of **April Daneen⁶ Wright** and **Shawn Tyrone Smith** were:
688. i. SHAWN TYRONE⁷ JR. was born on 15 June 1997 in Philadelphia, Pennsylvania.

593. KIM PATRICE⁶ CARTER (*Jeff Raymond 'Brother'⁵, Jeff Raymond⁴, Jeff³, Ella²Hooks, James¹*) was born on 26 October 1968 in Philadelphia, Pennsylvania.

Children of **Kim Patrice⁶ Carter** and **Jujuan Falana** were as follows:
689. i. SYEET⁷ was born on 22 January 1988 in Philadelphia, Pennsylvania.
690. ii. SUPREE was born on 27 April 1989 in Philadelphia, Pennsylvania.

594. CRYSTAL LARIN⁶ CARTER (*Jeff Raymond 'Brother'⁵, Jeff Raymond⁴, Jeff³, Ella²Hooks, James¹*) was born on 4 July 1974 in Philadelphia, Pennsylvania.

Children of **Crystal Larin⁶ Carter** and **Keemen Copeland** were:
691. i. TAHIRAH KADIJAH⁷ was born on 17 December 1996 in Philadelphia, Pennsylvania.

595. JEFF RAYMOND ISAAC COUNCILL⁶ CARTER (*Jeff Raymond 'Brother'⁵, Jeff Raymond⁴, Jeff³, Ella²Hooks, James¹*) was born on 16 September 1975 in Philadelphia, Pennsylvania.

Children of **Jeff Raymond Isaac Councill⁶ Carter** and **Tina Cole** were:
692. i. DIAMOND JANETTE⁷ was born on 12 June 1992 in Philadelphia, Pennsylvania.

Children of **Jeff Raymond Isaac Councill⁶ Carter** and **Sherisa Dennis** were:
693. i. SHIANNA CHARLENE MALIKA⁷ was born on 28 August 1993 in Philadelphia, Pennsylvania.

596. NATHANIEL IAN COUNCILL⁶ CARTER (*Jeff Raymond 'Brother'⁵, Jeff Raymond⁴, Jeff³, Ella²Hooks, James¹*) was born on 15 March 1977 in Philadelphia, Pennsylvania.

Children of **Nathaniel Ian Councill⁶ Carter** and **Dora Street** were:
694. i. KOREY DERELL⁷ was born on 17 May 1996 in Philadelphia, Pennsylvania.

Children of **Nathaniel Ian Councill**^{6} **Carter** and **Nikkia Thompson** were:

695.   i. **NATHANIEL IAN JEFF**^{7} was born on 28 May 2001 in Philadelphia, Pennsylvania.

599. **EARL**^{6} **CARTER** (*Dennis*^{5}, *Jeff Raymond*^{4}, *Jeff*^{3}, *Ella*^{2}*Hooks, James*^{1}) was born on 7 November 1978 in Philadelphia, Pennsylvania.

Children of **Earl**^{6} **Carter** and **Myteesha Elaine Reynolds** were as follows:

696.   i. **EARL**^{7} **JR.** was born on 7 May 2000 in Philadelphia, Pennsylvania.

697.   ii. **ELI** was born on 7 May 2000 in Philadelphia, Pennsylvania.

601. **ROBIN**^{6} **BRENT** (*Shirley*^{5}*Fisher, Elizabeth*^{4}*Dawson, Lora Ella 'Laura*^{3}*Carter, Ella*^{2}*Hooks, James*^{1}) was born on 21 June 1962. She married **Joseph Phelps.**

Children of **Robin**^{6} **Brent** and **Joseph Phelps** were as follows:

698.   i. **JOEY**^{7}.

699.   ii. **ROMAN.**

640. **KIMBERLY CORNELIA**^{6} **JACKSON** (*Karen ' Kay' Elizabeth*^{5}*Davis Ross, Wilhelmina 'Candy*^{4}*Dawson, Lora Ella 'Laura*^{3}*Carter, Ella*^{2}*Hooks, James*^{1}) was born on 19 June 1976 in Florida.

Children of **Kimberly Cornelia**^{6} **Jackson** and **Adrian Davis** were:

700.   i. **ALEXANDRIA MONIQUE**^{7} was born on 14 August 1998 in Fort Lauderdale, Florida.

645. **DAMANI SAEED TALE'**^{6} **GREEN** (*Richard Carter*^{5}, *Anne*^{4}*Carter, Virgil 'Virge*^{3}, *Ella*^{2}*Hooks, James*^{1}) was born on 18 February 1974 in Dayton, Ohio.

Children of **Damani Saeed Tale'**^{6} **Green** and **Katheryn Kirkland** were:

701.   i. **KEVIN MICHAEL**^{7} was born on 2 December 1995 in Dayton, Ohio.

Generation Seven

670. **RASETA NICOLE**^{7} **CHEEVES** (*Barry Steven*^{6}, *Forest*^{5}, *Lillian Arthur*^{4}*Carter, Jeff*^{3}, *Ella*^{2}*Hooks, James*^{1}) was born on 7 May 1982 in Philadelphia, Pennsylvania.

Children of **Raseta Nicole**^{7} **Cheeves** and **James Kennedy** were:

702.   i. **NICHOLAS SEMAJ**^{8} was born on 6 March 2001 in Philadelphia, Pennsylvania.

Descendants of Bybe Butts

Milas Butts, 1920 Census

Descendants of Bybe Butts

Generation One

1. BYBE^1 BUTTS.

Children of **Bybe**^{1} **Butts** and **Catherine** (———) were as follows:
+ 2.   i. FREDDIE^2, married **Carrie** (———).
+ 3.   ii. WILLIAM 'LUMP', married **Jessie Renfrow**.
+ 4.   iii. LULA
+ 5.   iv. EPHRAIM, married **Mamye** (———).
+ 6.   v. THOMAS 'TOMMIE'
  7.   vi. MATTIE.
+ 8.   vii. MILAS (SR.), born 4 July 1883; married **Roeanor Dawson**.
+ 9.   viii. BEVERLY 'LEE'

Generation Two

2. FREDDIE^2 BUTTS (*Bybe^1*) married **Carrie** (———). He died on 30 March 1961.

Children of **Freddie**^{2} **Butts** and **Carrie** (———) were as follows:
+ 10.   i. BEATRICE^3, married **Mr. Lewis**.
  11.   ii. ETHEL LEE died on 12 June 1982 in Detroit, Michigan.
+ 12. iii. IRENE, married (—?—) **Miller**.
+ 13. iv. WILLIAM 'BRO', married **Lucille** (———).
+ 14.   v. TOMMIE SR., born 29 December 1910; married **Pinkey** (———).
+ 15. vi. FREDDIE MAE, born 15 July 1923; married **Abner Miller**; married **Beverly Butts**.

3. WILLIAM 'LUMP'^{2} BUTTS (*Bybe^1*) married **Jessie Renfrow**.

Children of **William 'Lump'**^{2} **Butts** and **Jessie Renfrow** were:
+ 16.   i. WILLIE PEARL^3

4. LULA^2 BUTTS (*Bybe^1*).

Children of **Lula**^{2} **Butts** and **Eddie Smith** were:
+ 17.   i. EULA 'TANG'^{3}, married **Lil Mason**.

Children of **Lula**^{2} **Butts** include:
  18.   i. JOHNNIE^3.
+ 19.   ii. DUKE
  20. iii. KATIE.

5. EPHRAIM^2 BUTTS (*Bybe^1*) married **Mamye** (———).

Children of **Ephraim^2 Butts** and **Mamye** (———) were as follows:
+ 21. i. LULA 'SHIMA'^{3}, married **Fishie Ford.**
+ 22. ii. GEORGE 'HOOT', married **Maude** (—?—).

6. THOMAS 'TOMMIE'^{2} BUTTS (*Bybe^1*).

Children of **Thomas 'Tommie'^{2} Butts** include:
  23. i. LIZZIE^3.
  24. ii. MATTIE MAE.

8. MILAS^2 BUTTS SR. (*Bybe^1*) was born on 4 July 1883. He married **Roeanor Dawson**, daughter of **Issac Dawson** and **Carmela Trawick Butts**, on 3 January 1903. He died on 11 March 1942 at age 58.

Children of **Milas^2 Butts (Sr.)** and **Roeanor Dawson** were as follows:
+ 25. i. KATIE^3, born 26 October 1908; married **Charlie Renfrow.**
+ 26. ii. FREDDIE, born 10 March 1910; married **Eula Mae Smith;** married **Rose Marie Richardson.**
+ 27. iii. MILAS JR., born 6 April 1913 in Sandersville, Washington County, Georgia; married **Mary Julia Carter.**
+ 28. iv. ROSA MAE, born 23 February 1916.
+ 29. v. SIDNEY C., born 6 February 1918; married **Julia Inez Trawick;** married **Ella Fuller.**
+ 30. vi. NATHANIEL 'NATHAN', born 3 February 1920; married **Evelyn** (———).
+ 31. vii. BOB WILLIS, born 11 April 1924; married **Mamye Dorothy 'Mary' Trawick.**
+ 32. viii. DAWSON 'SONNIE' (SR.), born 13 June 1928; married **Butha Larkin.**
  33. ix. HENRETTA.
  34. x. ANNIE MAE.
+ 35. xi. SALLIE LEE, born 31 December 1914; married **James Renfrow.**
+ 36. xii. THELMA, born 25 December 1925; married **George Davis.**

9. BEVERLY 'LEE'^{2} BUTTS (*Bybe^1*) died in 1931 in Akron, Ohio.

Children of **Beverly 'Lee'^{2} Butts** and **Fannie Hooks** were as follows:
+ 37. i. ETHEL JANE^3, born 5 March 1896; married **Charles Johnson.**
  38. ii. DAVID 'DAVE' was born on 1 May 1899. He married **Vertise Massengale.** He died on 2 August 1979 at age 80.
  39. iii. LEON.
  40. iv. SOLOMON was born on 28 April 1901. He died on 20 January 1933 at age 31.
+ 41. v. LEMON SR., born 16 January 1905; married **Emily Kelsey.**

42. vi. CLEMON LEE was born in 1906. He married **Harriet** (—?—). He died on 14 May 1933.
43. vii. FANNY ARRUS was born on 6 July 1912. She married **Christopher Tolbert.** She died on 10 May 1966 at age 53.

Generation Three

10. BEATRICE^3 BUTTS (*Freddie^2, Bybe^1*) married **Mr. Lewis.**

Children of **Beatrice^3 Butts** and **Mr. Lewis** were as follows:
44. i. DOROTHY LEE^4.
45. ii. EMMA JOAN.

12. IRENE^3 BUTTS (*Freddie^2, Bybe^1*) married (—?—) **Miller.** She died on 28 May 1967 in Detroit, Michigan.

Children of **Irene^3 Butts** and (—?—) **Miller** were:
46. i. EMMA JOAN^4.

13. WILLIAM 'BRO'^{3} BUTTS (*Freddie^2, Bybe^1*) married **Lucille** (———).

Children of **William 'Bro'^{3} Butts** and **Lucille** (———) were as follows:
47. i. WILLIAM^4 (JR.).
48. ii. STANLEY K. was born on 23 September 1967.

14. TOMMIE^3 BUTTS SR. (*Freddie^2, Bybe^1*) was born on 29 December 1910. He married **Pinkey** (———).

Children of **Tommie^3 Butts Sr.** and **Pinkey** (———) were as follows:
+ 49. i. TOMMIE^4 JR., born 16 August 1932; married **Marlene** (—?—).
+ 50. ii. EVELYN, born 23 July 1934; married **Mr. Johnson.**

15. FREDDIE MAE^3 BUTTS (*Freddie^2, Bybe^1*) was born on 15 July 1923. She married **Abner Miller.** She married **Beverly Butts,** son of **Lemon Butts Sr.** and **Emily Kelsey.** She died on 12 January 1963 at age 39.

Children of **Freddie Mae^3 Butts** and **Abner Miller** were as follows:
51. i. DAVID^4.
52. ii. KELVIN.
53. iii. DOROTHY.
54. iv. LAURA ANN.

Children of **Freddie Mae**^{3} **Butts** and **Beverly Butts** were as follows:
55.   i. SHERLY^4.
56.   ii. SONDRA.
57.   iii. WONDA.

16. WILLIE PEARL^3 **BUTTS** (*William 'Lump'*^{2}, *Bybe*^{1}).

Children of **Willie Pearl**^{3} **Butts** and **Mr. Butts** were as follows:
58.   i. (———)^4.
59.   ii. DELORES.

17. EULA 'TANG'^{3} **SMITH** (*Lula*^{2}*Butts*, *Bybe*^{1}) married **Lil Mason.**

Children of **Eula 'Tang'**^{3} **Smith** and **Lil Mason** were as follows:
60.   i. BUDDY^4.
61.   ii. LEOLA.

19. DUKE^3 **BUTTS** (*Lula*^{2}, *Bybe*^{1}).

Children of **Duke**^{3} **Butts** include:
62.   i. JOHNNIE^4.
63.   ii. ARTHER.
64.   iii. LEE.
65.   iv. ELIZ.
66.   v. CHARLES.

21. LULA 'SHIMA'^{3} **BUTTS** (*Ephraim*^{2}, *Bybe*^{1}) married **Fishie Ford.**

Children of **Lula 'Shima'**^{3} **Butts** and **Fishie Ford** were:
+ 67.   i. BUDDY^4

22. GEORGE 'HOOT'^{3} **BUTTS** (*Ephraim*^{2}, *Bybe*^{1}) married **Maude (—?—).**

Children of **George 'Hoot'**^{3} **Butts** and **Maude (—?—)** were as follows:
+ 68.   i. ROSAMAE^4
+ 69.   ii. GEORGE BILLY JR., married **Lillian Reeves.**
  70.   iii. EVELYN was born on 4 May 1930. She died on 12 July 1944 at age 14.

25. KATIE^3 **BUTTS** (*Milas*^{2}, *Bybe*^{1}) was born on 26 October 1908. She married **Charlie Renfrow**, son of **Thomas Renfrow** and **Georgianne Davis.** She died on 13 August 1972 at age 63.

Children of **Katie³ Butts** and **Charlie Renfrow** were as follows:
+ 71.   i. YVETTE⁴, married **Wendell Harris.**
  72. ii. LORRAINE.
  73. iii. CHARMAINE.
  74. iv. LAMONT.
+ 75.   v. EDWARD, married **Donna** (——).
+ 76. vi. DELIA, married **James Davis.**
  77. vii. CHARLES.
+ 78. viii. GERALD WAYNE, born 10 October 1945; married **Diane** (——); married **Connie** (——).
+ 79. ix. WILSON, born 10 March 1953.

26. FREDDIE³ BUTTS (*Milas²*, *Bybe¹*) was born on 10 March 1910. He married **Eula Mae Smith.** He married **Rose Marie Richardson.** He died in 1972.

Children of **Freddie³ Butts** and **Eula Mae Smith** were as follows:
  80.   i. VINCENT⁴ was born on 26 July 1937.
  81. ii. RICHARD EDWARD was born on 11 September 1942. He married **Sharon Antonia Scott.**
+ 82. iii. ELSIE MARIE, born 13 February 1944; married **David Leroy Oliver.**

Children of **Freddie³ Butts** and **Rose Marie Richardson** were as follows:
+ 83.   i. FREDDIE⁴ JR., born 11 October 1933; married **Mae Bell** (——).
+ 84. ii. ERNEST LEE 'DUKE', born 24 March 1936; married **Dorothy 'Dot' Johnson.**
  85. iii. DEBBIE was born on 16 May 1953.
  86. iv. ANGIE 'BUDDY' was born on 31 January 1955.

27. MILAS³ BUTTS JR. (*Milas²*, *Bybe¹*) was born on 6 April 1913 in Sandersville, Washington County, Georgia. He married **Mary Julia Carter**, daughter of **Jeff Carter Jr.** and **Gervenia Fisher.** He died on 23 November 1988 at age 75.

Children of **Milas³ Butts Jr.** and **Mary Julia Carter** were as follows:
+ 87.   i. ALTON⁴, born 28 October 1934 in Sandersville, Georgia; married **Marlyn Farley.**
  88. ii. VIVIAN.

28. ROSA MAE³ BUTTS (*Milas²*, *Bybe¹*) was born on 23 February 1916.

Children of **Rosa Mae³ Butts** and **Burley Lord (Sr.)** were as follows:
  89.   i. BERINE⁴.
+ 90. ii. MARY L., born 5 November 1935; married **Ronald Robinson;** married **John Goodson.**

+ 91. iii. BURLEY 'SYTES' (JR.), born 6 July 1938; married **Mary Edith Hall;** married **Gloria 'Glo' Louise Trawick.**
+ 92. iv. JEROME, born 1 April 1940; married **Priscilla Miles;** married **Patricia Pitts.**
+ 93. v. MELVIN, born 1 October 1941; married **Anita 'Cookie' Smith;** married **Conchetta Brewer;** married **Denise Johnson.**
+ 94. vi. RONALD C. (SR.), born 4 February 1944; married **Grace Corn.**
  95. vii. ETHEL JEAN was born on 9 January 1946.
+ 96. viii. JACQUELINE 'JACKI', born 15 May 1948; married **Edward English.**
+ 97. ix. JOAN, born 21 May 1949; married **Charles Moore.**

29. SIDNEY C.^{3} BUTTS (*Milas^2, Bybe^1*) was born on 6 February 1918. He married **Julia Inez Trawick,** daughter of **Dock 'Whale' Trawick** and **Mary 'Ma-Mae' Ollie Cheeves.** He married **Ella Fuller.** He died in 1987.

Children of **Sidney C.^{3} Butts** and **Julia Inez Trawick** were as follows:
+ 98.   i. CHESTER^4, born 13 September 1938; married **Joan Holmes;** married **Anna Gray.**
+ 99.   ii. JANICE, born 18 October 1940; married **William Williams (Sr.);** married **James Rogers;** married **Edward Davis.**
+ 100. iii. ROZEINE, born 5 December 1942; married **Anthony Armstrong;** married **Robert Ruckey;** married **Walter Wyatt.**
+ 101. iv. CURTIS, born 18 December 1943; married **Thelma Lamar.**
  102. v. KENNETH was born on 27 February 1950. He married **Rochelle McLaurin.**
  103. vi. SIDNEY ALLEN was born on 27 February 1955.

Children of **Sidney C.^{3} Butts** and **Ella Fuller** were as follows:
  104.   i. DAISY^4.
  105.   ii. DAVID.
  106.   iii. JOSEPH.
  107.   iv. ALEX.
  108.   v. STANLEY.

30. NATHANIEL 'NATHAN'^{3} BUTTS (*Milas^2, Bybe^1*) was born on 3 February 1920. He married **Evelyn (———).** He died in 1969.

Children of **Nathaniel 'Nathan'^{3} Butts** and **Evelyn (———)** were as follows:
  109.   i. ALLISON^4.
  110.   ii. NATHANIEL (JR.).
  111.   iii. STANLEY 'SIMMONS'.

31. BOB WILLIS^3 BUTTS (*Milas^2, Bybe^1*) was born on 11 April 1924. He married **Mamye Dorothy 'Mary' Trawick,** daughter of **Dock 'Whale' Trawick** and **Mary 'Ma-Mae' Ollie Cheeves.**

Children of **Bob Willis**^{3} **Butts** and **Mamye Dorothy 'Mary' Trawick** were as follows:
+ 112.   i. DELORES^4, born 3 January 1942; married **Edward Smithwick.**
+ 113.   ii. DORIS, born 4 July 1944; married **John Alcorn.**
+ 114.   iii. GWENDOLYN 'GWEN', born 12 August 1945; married **Gene Holliway.**
+ 115.   iv. OLIVIA, born 21 May 1950; married **Bernard Hines.**

32. DAWSON 'SONNIE'^{3} **BUTTS (SR.)** (*Milas*^{2}, *Bybe*^{1}) was born on 13 June 1928. He married **Butha Larkin.**

Children of **Dawson 'Sonnie'**^{3} **Butts (Sr.)** and **Butha Larkin** were as follows:
+ 116.   i. JACQUELINE^4, born 21 August 1951; married **Nathaniel Forney Sr.**
  117.   ii. SHIRLEY was born on 1 November 1952. She married **Mr. Hill.**
+ 118.   iii. GENESE, born 26 October 1959; married **Jimmy Swint.**
  119.   iv. DAWSON (JR.) was born on 8 August 1961. He died on 8 March 1964 at age 2.
+ 120.   v. VIVIAN, born 27 October 1966; married **Alvin Edwards.**
  121.   vi. DAVID was born on 3 November 1967.

35. SALLIE LEE^3 **BUTTS** (*Milas*^{2}, *Bybe*^{1}) was born on 31 December 1914. She married **James Renfrow.**

Children of **Sallie Lee**^{3} **Butts** and **James Renfrow** were as follows:
+ 122.   i. DELORES^4, born 17 June 1943; married **Griffin Washington.**
+ 123.   ii. MARION, born 16 January 1947; married **Billie Medley.**
+ 124.   iii. CURTIS, born 21 October 1950; married **Lisa** (——); married **Beverly Myers.**
+ 125.   iv. ALICE, born 12 June 1954; married **Lee Kinley;** married **Dezi Scruggs.**
+ 126.   v. MICHAEL, born 26 September 1954; married **Tina Harris;** married **Michelle** (-).
  127.   vi. THOMAS BROWN was born on 8 May 1958.
+ 128.   vii. GRACE RANDOLPH, born 28 June 1959; married **David James.**
+ 129.   viii. JOHN RANDOLPH, born 27 September 1960; married **Rosyln Myers;** married **Lisa Hicks.**

36. THELMA^3 **BUTTS** (*Milas*^{2}, *Bybe*^{1}) was born on 25 December 1925. She married **George Davis.**

Children of **Thelma**^{3} **Butts** and **George Davis** were as follows:
  130.   i. LARRY MILAS^4 was born on 18 June 1952. He died on 23 February 1987 at age 34.
+ 131.   ii. GEORGE 'GARY', born 16 October 1953; married **Shery Ann Stewart.**
+ 132.   iii. THERESA ROMONA, born 17 August 1961; married **Dale Thompson.**

37. ETHEL JANE^3 **BUTTS** (*Beverly 'Lee*^{2}, *Bybe*^{1}) was born on 5 March 1896. She married **Charles Johnson.** She died on 31 May 1968 at age 72.

Children of **Ethel Jane³ Butts** and **Charles Johnson** were as follows:
133.   i. MOSLEY⁴.
134.   ii. SILAS.

41. LEMON³ BUTTS SR. (*Beverly 'Lee²*, *Bybe¹*) was born on 16 January 1905. He married **Emily Kelsey**. He died on 13 October 1966 at age 61.

Children of **Lemon³ Butts Sr.** and **Emily Kelsey** were as follows:
+ 135.   i. ROSEANN⁴
+ 136.   ii. EUGENE SR., married **Diane** (———).
+ 137.   iii. BEVERLY, married **Freddie Mae Butts**.
+ 138.   iv. LEMON JR., married **Betty** (———).
+ 139.   v. CORNELIUS, married **Thelma** (———).
+ 140.   vi. DANIEL, born 17 January 1931; married **Virginia** (—?—).
+ 141.   vii. LEON, born 14 February 1933; married **Catherine** (—?—).

Generation Four

49. TOMMIE⁴ BUTTS JR. (*Tommie³*, *Freddie²*, *Bybe¹*) was born on 16 August 1932. He married **Marlene** (—?—). He died on 24 March 1986 at age 53.

Children of **Tommie⁴ Butts Jr.** and **Marlene** (—?—) were as follows:
+ 142.   i. CYNTHIA⁵, born 13 February 1952; married **William Wallace**.
143.   ii. LEVONIA was born on 20 February 1953.
144.   iii. YVONNE was born on 5 August 1955.
+ 145.   iv. MICHELLE, born 5 January 1958.
146.   v. KIMBERLY was born on 22 June 1964.
147.   vi. STEVEN was born on 15 September 1966.
148.   vii. DARREN was born on 2 November 1969.
149.   viii. ERIC was born on 5 June 1973.

50. EVELYN⁴ BUTTS (*Tommie³*, *Freddie²*, *Bybe¹*) was born on 23 July 1934. She married **Mr. Johnson**.

Children of **Evelyn⁴ Butts** and **Mr. Johnson** were:
150.   i. ANTHONY 'TONIE'⁵ was born on 19 August 1954.

67. BUDDY⁴ FORD (*Lula 'Shima³ Butts*, *Ephraim²*, *Bybe¹*).

Children of **Buddy⁴ Ford** include:
151.   i. EVELYN⁵.
152.   ii. (———).

68. ROSAMAE^4 **BUTTS** (*George 'Hoot*^{3}, *Ephraim*^{2}, *Bybe*^{1}).

Children of **Rosamae**^{4} **Butts** include:
153. i. JOSH^5 was born on 6 June 1954.

69. GEORGE BILLY^4 **BUTTS JR.** (*George 'Hoot*^{3}, *Ephraim*^{2}, *Bybe*^{1}) married **Lillian Reeves.**

Children of **George Billy**^{4} **Butts Jr.** and **Lillian Reeves** were as follows:
154. i. EARL^5.
155. ii. BRUCE.
156. iii. MICHELLE.
157. iv. JOHNNIE.
158. v. WAYNE.
159. vi. BARBARA.
160. vii. SPENCER.
161. viii. GARY.
162. ix. GEORGE III.
163. x. WANDA.
+ 164. xi. JOAN 'TOOTIE', born 22 November 1955; married (—?—) **Newkirk.**

71. YVETTE^4 **RENFROW** (*Katie*^{3}*Butts*, *Milas*^{2}, *Bybe*^{1}) married **Wendell Harris.**

Children of **Yvette**^{4} **Renfrow** include:
165. i. KENYATTA^5.

There were no children of **Yvette**^{4} **Renfrow** and **Wendell Harris.**

75. EDWARD^4 **RENFROW** (*Katie*^{3}*Butts*, *Milas*^{2}, *Bybe*^{1}) married **Donna** (———).

Children of **Edward**^{4} **Renfrow** and **Donna** (———) were:
166. i. NICOLE^5.

76. DELIA^4 **RENFROW** (*Katie*^{3}*Butts*, *Milas*^{2}, *Bybe*^{1}) married **James Davis.**

Children of **Delia**^{4} **Renfrow** include:
167. i. QUINZEL^5.

There were no children of **Delia**^{4} **Renfrow** and **James Davis.**

78. GERALD WAYNE^4 **RENFROW** (*Katie*^{3}*Butts*, *Milas*^{2}, *Bybe*^{1}) was born on 10 October 1945. He married **Diane** (———). He married **Connie** (———).

Children of **Gerald Wayne**[4] **Renfrow** and **Diane** (———) were:

168.   i. BOBATAYA[5] was born on 12 August 1969.

Children of **Gerald Wayne**[4] **Renfrow** and **Connie** (———) were as follows:

169.   i. NICOLE[5] was born on 14 February 1970.

170.   ii. AMIR was born on 17 November 1979.

79. WILSON[4] **RENFROW** (*Katie*[3]*Butts, Milas*[2], *Bybe*[1]) was born on 10 March 1953.

Children of **Wilson**[4] **Renfrow** include:

171.   i. SENATE[5].

82. ELSIE MARIE[4] **BUTTS** (*Freddie*[3], *Milas*[2], *Bybe*[1]) was born on 13 February 1944. She married **David Leroy Oliver.**

Children of **Elsie Marie**[4] **Butts** and **David Leroy Oliver** were as follows:

+ 172.   i. DARREN LAMONT[5], born 15 May 1962; married **Barbara Radford.**

173.   ii. DERRICK LEROY was born on 16 April 1963.

+ 174.   iii. DE'ANDRE LEE, born 30 March 1964; married **Rochelle Williams.**

83. FREDDIE[4] **BUTTS JR.** (*Freddie*[3], *Milas*[2], *Bybe*[1]) was born on 11 October 1933. He married **Mae Bell** (———).

Children of **Freddie**[4] **Butts Jr.** and **Mae Bell** (———) were as follows:

175.   i. WONDA[5].

+ 176.   ii. TONI O., married **Sandy** (———).

84. ERNEST LEE 'DUKE'[4] **BUTTS** (*Freddie*[3], *Milas*[2], *Bybe*[1]) was born on 24 March 1936. He married **Dorothy 'Dot' Johnson.**

Children of **Ernest Lee 'Duke'**[4] **Butts** and **Dorothy 'Dot' Johnson** were as follows:

+ 177.   i. ERNEST NATHANIEL 'LITTLE DUKE'[5], born 9 September 1957; married **Florena Williamson.**

+ 178.   ii. ANTHONY 'ANT' LEE, born 6 February 1969; married **Cindy** (———).

87. ALTON[4] **BUTTS** (*Milas*[3], *Milas*[2], *Bybe*[1]) was born on 28 October 1934 in Sandersville, Georgia. He married **Marlyn Farley.** He died on 19 May 2003 in Philadelphia, Pennsylvania, at age 68.

Children of **Alton**[4] **Butts** and **Marlyn Farley** were as follows:

+ 179.   i. VERONA[5], born 3 December 1963 in Philadelphia, Pennsylvania.

+ 180.   ii. MARSHA, born 20 October 1967 in Philadelphia, Pennsylvania.

+ 181.   iii. TERESE, born 10 February 1970 in Philadelphia, Pennsylvania.

90. MARY L.^{4} LORD (*Rosa Mae^{3}Butts, Milas^2, Bybe^1*) was born on 5 November 1935. She married **Ronald Robinson**. She married **John Goodson**.

Children of **Mary L.^{4} Lord** and **Ronald Robinson** were as follows:
+ 182.   i. MICHAEL^5, born 17 February 1953; married **Olivia Poole**.
+ 183.   ii. CAROL LOVE, born 21 June 1954; married **Anthony Hailey**.

Children of **Mary L.^{4} Lord** and **John Goodson** were:
184.   i. TRACEY JAVELLE^5 was born on 23 September 1968.

91. BURLEY 'SYTES'^{4} LORD (JR.) (*Rosa Mae^{3}Butts, Milas^2, Bybe^1*) was born on 6 July 1938. He married **Mary Edith Hall**. He married **Gloria 'Glo' Louise Trawick**, daughter of **Sam Trawick** and **Mary 'Ma-Mae' Ollie Cheeves**. He died on 25 June 1997 in Philadelphia, Pennsylvania, at age 58.

Children of **Burley 'Sytes'^{4} Lord (Jr.)** and **Mary Edith Hall** were:
185.   i. BURLEY STEFAN^5 was born on 6 August 1960.

There were no children of **Burley 'Sytes'^{4} Lord (Jr.)** and **Gloria 'Glo' Louise Trawick**.

92. JEROME^4 LORD (*Rosa Mae^{3}Butts, Milas^2, Bybe^1*) was born on 1 April 1940. He married **Priscilla Miles**. He married **Patricia Pitts**.

Children of **Jerome^4 Lord** and **Priscilla Miles** were as follows:
+ 186.   i. CHERYL ELIZABETH^5, born 13 January 1963; married **William Hacken**; married **Ronald Crosby**.
187.   ii. JEFFREY was born on 18 December 1964.
188.   iii. HOPE was born on 26 October 1965.
189.   iv. LISA was born on 27 October 1967.
190.   v. GERALD FONTAIN was born on 13 September 1969.

Children of **Jerome^4 Lord** and **Patricia Pitts** were:
191.   i. JEROME^5 (JR.) was born on 14 May 1958.

93. MELVIN^4 LORD (*Rosa Mae^{3}Butts, Milas^2, Bybe^1*) was born on 1 October 1941. He married **Anita 'Cookie' Smith**. He married **Conchetta Brewer**. He married **Conchetta Brewer**. He married **Conchetta Brewer**. He married **Denise Johnson**.

Children of **Melvin^4 Lord** and **Anita 'Cookie' Smith** were as follows:
192.   i. ALENCIA SMITH^5 was born on 22 January 1965.

193. ii. ALEX SMITH was born on 3 May 1967.
194. iii. ARLEN SMITH was born on 19 April 1968.
195. iv. ALLISON SMITH was born on 27 April 1969.

Children of **Melvin^4 Lord** and **Conchetta Brewer** were as follows:
+ 196. i. ALONDA^5, born 28 September 1961; married **Martin Harris**.
197. ii. MARQUETT was born on 13 August 1963.
198. iii. TOWANDA.

Children of **Melvin^4 Lord** and **Denise Johnson** were:
199. i. ATRA LORD^5 was born on 6 September 1984.

94. RONALD C.^{4} LORD (SR.) (*Rosa Mae^{3}Butts, Milas^2, Bybe^1*) was born on 4 February 1944. He married **Grace Corn**.

Children of **Ronald C.^{4} Lord (Sr.)** and **Grace Corn** were as follows:
+ 200. i. TINA R.^{5}, born 3 May 1963; married **Emory K. Copeland**.
+ 201. ii. RONALD RODNEY, born 8 August 1965; married **Kisha Mapp**; married **Jucinta Bursch**.
+ 202. iii. RONDA, born 8 August 1965; married **Harold E. Hall**.
+ 203. iv. KAREN A., born 17 October 1967; married **Antoine Johnson**.

96. JACQUELINE 'JACKI'^{4} LORD (*Rosa Mae^{3}Butts, Milas^2, Bybe^1*) was born on 15 May 1948. She married **Edward English**.

Children of **Jacqueline 'Jacki'^{4} Lord** and **Edward English** were:
204. i. LAVADA^5 was born on 12 February 1970.

97. JOAN^4 LORD (*Rosa Mae^{3}Butts, Milas^2, Bybe^1*) was born on 21 May 1949. She married **Charles Moore**.

Children of **Joan^4 Lord** and **Charles Moore** were:
+ 205. i. KELLY S.^{5}, born 30 May 1969; married **Mark Stukes**.

98. CHESTER^4 BUTTS (*Sidney C.^{3}, Milas^2, Bybe^1*) was born on 13 September 1938. He married **Joan Holmes**. He married **Anna Gray**.

Children of **Chester^4 Butts** and **Joan Holmes** were as follows:
+ 206. i. EDDIE HOLMES^5, born 4 October 1954; married **Shirley Holmes**; married **Zina Holmes**.
+ 207. ii. CURTIS, born 27 April 1966; married **Sheila** (———); married **Crystle** (———).
208. iii. KEVIN was born on 4 April 1967.

+ 209.   iv. DARYL, born 19 July 1968; married **Nichelle** (———).
  210.   v. DARNELL was born on 3 March 1970.

Children of **Chester**[4] **Butts** and **Anna Gray** were:
  211.   i. YALONDA[5] was born on 16 April 1970.

99. JANICE[4] **BUTTS** (*Sidney C.*[3], *Milas*[2], *Bybe*[1]) was born on 18 October 1940. She married **Edward Davis**. She married **William Williams (Sr.)**. She married **James Rogers**. She died on 10 September 1989 at age 48.

Children of **Janice**[4] **Butts** and **William Williams (Sr.)** were as follows:
+ 212.   i. WILLIAM[5] (JR.), born 19 January 1958.
+ 213.   ii. KENNETH 'HUCKY', born 13 July 1960; married **Sylvita Barbour;** married **Deborah Lynn** (———).
+ 214.   iii. HERRELL A., born 23 May 1967; married **Stephanie Y Anderson;** married **Nadine Jackson.**
+ 215.   iv. ALONZO LONNIE, born 2 August 1969.
  216.   v. TYNEEK was born on 23 April 1976.

There were no children of **Janice**[4] **Butts** and **James Rogers.**

There were no children of **Janice**[4] **Butts** and **Edward Davis.**

100. ROZEINE[4] **BUTTS** (*Sidney C.*[3], *Milas*[2], *Bybe*[1]) was born on 5 December 1942. She married **Anthony Armstrong**. She married **Robert Ruckey**. She married **Walter Wyatt.**

Children of **Rozeine**[4] **Butts** and **Anthony Armstrong** were:
  217.   i. SEAN[5] was born on 15 November 1967.

Children of **Rozeine**[4] **Butts** and **Robert Ruckey** were:
  218.   i. ROBERT[5] was born on 11 January 1969.

Children of **Rozeine**[4] **Butts** and **Walter Wyatt** were:
  219.   i. JUNITA[5] was born on 7 July 1975.

101. CURTIS[4] **BUTTS** (*Sidney C.*[3], *Milas*[2], *Bybe*[1]) was born on 18 December 1943. He married **Thelma Lamar.**

Children of **Curtis**[4] **Butts** and **Thelma Lamar** were as follows:
  220.   i. DANIELLE MARIE[5] was born on 31 May 1969.
  221.   ii. LAMAR CRAIGE was born on 1 October 1970.

222. iii. LAMONTE DAWSON was born on 2 May 1974.

223. iv. BRANDEN LAVAR was born on 2 July 1978.

112. DELORES^4 BUTTS (*Bob Willis^3, Milas^2, Bybe^1*) was born on 3 January 1942. She married **Edward Smithwick.**

Children of **Delores^4 Butts** and **Edward Smithwick** were as follows:

224. i. DERON^5 was born on 19 July 1965.

225. ii. DEAN was born on 24 January 1968.

226. iii. DENENA was born on 14 September 1970.

113. DORIS^4 BUTTS (*Bob Willis^3, Milas^2, Bybe^1*) was born on 4 July 1944. She married **John Alcorn.**

Children of **Doris^4 Butts** and **John Alcorn** were as follows:

+ 227. i. SABRINA LYNN^5, born 5 February 1967; married **Derrick Girard McCann Sr.**

228. ii. DARLA RAE was born on 13 March 1970.

229. iii. ROOSEVELT.

114. GWENDOLYN 'GWEN'^{4} BUTTS (*Bob Willis^3, Milas^2, Bybe^1*) was born on 12 August 1945. She married **Gene Holliway.**

Children of **Gwendolyn 'Gwen'^{4} Butts** and **Gene Holliway** were as follows:

+ 230. i. TANYA^5, born 9 February 1964; married **Todd Bell.**

231. ii. TERRANCE 'TERRY' was born on 31 July 1968.

115. OLIVIA^4 BUTTS (*Bob Willis^3, Milas^2, Bybe^1*) was born on 21 May 1950. She married **Bernard Hines.**

Children of **Olivia^4 Butts** and **Bernard Hines** were as follows:

232. i. COURTLAND^5 was born on 27 July 1970.

233. ii. ARIC was born on 2 January 1975.

116. JACQUELINE^4 BUTTS (*Dawson 'Sonnie^3, Milas^2, Bybe^1*) was born on 21 August 1951. She married **Nathaniel Forney Sr.**

Children of **Jacqueline^4 Butts** and **Nathaniel Forney Sr.** were as follows:

234. i. MICHELLE^5 was born on 17 August 1972.

235. ii. FELICIA was born on 29 September 1976.

236. iii. NATHANIEL JR. was born on 1 December 1978.

118. GENESE[4] BUTTS (*Dawson 'Sonnie*[3], *Milas*[2], *Bybe*[1]) was born on 26 October 1959. She was born on 26 October 1959. She married **Jimmy Swint.**

Children of **Genese[4] Butts** and **Jimmy Swint** were as follows:
237.   i. SHENEKA[5] was born on 11 September.
238.   ii. JIMMY JEREL was born on 17 August 1978.

120. VIVIAN[4] BUTTS (*Dawson 'Sonnie*[3], *Milas*[2], *Bybe*[1]) was born on 27 October 1966. She married **Alvin Edwards** on 28 July 1990.

Children of **Vivian[4] Butts** include:
239.   i. ALQUETIN[5] was born on 22 March 1988.

There were no children of **Vivian[4] Butts** and **Alvin Edwards.**

122. DELORES[4] RENFROW (*Sallie Lee*[3]*Butts, Milas*[2], *Bybe*[1]) was born on 17 June 1943. She married **Griffin Washington.**

Children of **Delores[4] Renfrow** and **Griffin Washington** were as follows:
240.   i. GRIFFIN[5] (JR.) was born on 5 September 1968.
241.   ii. CORDELL was born on 30 September 1974.
242.   iii. TIANT was born on 10 July 1976.

123. MARION[4] RENFROW (*Sallie Lee*[3]*Butts, Milas*[2], *Bybe*[1]) was born on 16 January 1947. She married **Billie Medley.**

Children of **Marion[4] Renfrow** and **Billie Medley** were as follows:
243.   i. BILLY L.[5] (JR.) was born on 29 August 1964.
244.   ii. SAVOR was born on 26 November 1967. He died in 1992.

124. CURTIS[4] RENFROW (*Sallie Lee*[3]*Butts, Milas*[2], *Bybe*[1]) was born on 21 October 1950. He married **Lisa** (———). He married **Beverly Myers.**

Children of **Curtis[4] Renfrow** and **Lisa** (———) were as follows:
245.   i. PERRIN[5] was born on 15 July 1977.
246.   ii. TERESA MYERS.

There were no children of **Curtis[4] Renfrow** and **Beverly Myers.**

125. ALICE[4] RENFROW (*Sallie Lee*[3]*Butts, Milas*[2], *Bybe*[1]) was born on 12 June 1954. She married **Lee Kinley.** She married **Dezi Scruggs.**

Children of **Alice⁴ Renfrow** include:
247.   i. YAMIKA⁵ was born on 28 May 1971.

Children of **Alice⁴ Renfrow** and **Lee Kinley** were as follows:
248.   i. KYLE⁵ was born on 23 December 1974.
249.   ii. RAVIN was born on 22 November 1976.

Children of **Alice⁴ Renfrow** and **Dezi Scruggs** were as follows:
250.   i. DEZI A.⁵ was born on 18 February 1985.
251.   ii. DESTINCE was born on 18 February 1989.

126. MICHAEL⁴ RENFROW (*Sallie Lee³Butts, Milas², Bybe¹*) was born on 26 September 1954. He married **Tina Harris**. He married **Michelle** (———).

Children of **Michael⁴ Renfrow** and **Tina Harris** were:
252.   i. MICHAEL HARRIS⁵ was born on 17 October 1974.

Children of **Michael⁴ Renfrow** and **Michelle** (———) were:
253.   i. NASTASCIA V.⁵ was born on 4 October 1983.

128. GRACE RANDOLPH⁴ RENFROW (*Sallie Lee³Butts, Milas², Bybe¹*) was born on 28 June 1959. She married **David James**.

Children of **Grace Randolph⁴ Renfrow** and **David James** were:
254.   i. DAVID JAMES⁵ was born on 28 December 1987.

129. JOHN RANDOLPH⁴ RENFROW (*Sallie Lee³Butts, Milas², Bybe¹*) was born on 27 September 1960. He married **Rosyln Myers**. He married **Lisa Hicks**.

Children of **John Randolph⁴ Renfrow** and **Rosyln Myers** were:
255.   i. JEANIN RANDOLPH⁵ was born on 23 January 1982.

Children of **John Randolph⁴ Renfrow** and **Lisa Hicks** were:
256.   i. AMOYA LASHAY RANDOLPH⁵ was born on 11 September 1987.

131. GEORGE 'GARY'⁴ DAVIS (*Thelma³Butts, Milas², Bybe¹*) was born on 16 October 1953. He married **Shery Ann Stewart**.

Children of **George 'Gary'⁴ Davis** and **Shery Ann Stewart** were as follows:
257.   i. ANTOINETTE BERNADETTE ROGERS⁵ was born on 11 June 1970.
258.   ii. KHALID LATEEF STEWART was born on 22 May 1979.
259.   iii. ZAKIA HAZEL JOSIE STEWART was born on 1 April 1981.

260. iv. RAHEEM CHAZZ STEWART was born on 15 November 1982.
261. v. FATIMA NANYAMKA STEWART was born on 7 March 1987.

132. THERESA ROMONA^4 DAVIS (*Thelma^3 Butts, Milas^2, Bybe^1*) was born on 17 August 1961. She married **Dale Thompson.**

Children of **Theresa Romona^4 Davis** and **Dale Thompson** were:
262. i. VENESHIA MONIQUE^5 was born on 2 January 1980.

135. ROSEANN^4 BUTTS (*Lemon^3, Beverly 'Lee^2, Bybe^1*).

Children of **Roseann^4 Butts** and **Alonzo Felton** were as follows:
263. i. RAMONA^5.
264. ii. LARRY.
265. iii. PATTIE married **Alonzo Felton.**
266. iv. RENIECE.

136. EUGENE^4 BUTTS SR. (*Lemon^3, Beverly 'Lee^2, Bybe^1*) married **Diane** (———).

Children of **Eugene^4 Butts Sr.** and **Diane** (———) were as follows:
267. i. EUGENE^5 JR..
268. ii. DALIESSA 'LISA' married **Mr. Bradford.**
269. iii. DALE.

137. BEVERLY^4 BUTTS (*Lemon^3, Beverly 'Lee^2, Bybe^1*) married **Freddie Mae Butts**, daughter of **Freddie Butts** and **Carrie** (———).

Children of **Beverly^4 Butts** and **Freddie Mae Butts** were as follows:
270. i. SHERLY^5.
271. ii. SONDRA.
272. iii. WONDA.

138. LEMON^4 BUTTS JR. (*Lemon^3, Beverly 'Lee^2, Bybe^1*) married **Betty** (———).

Children of **Lemon^4 Butts Jr.** and **Betty** (———) were as follows:
+ 273. i. CURTIS^5, married **Diane** (———).
274. ii. BRENDA.
275. iii. SHIRLY.
+ 276. iv. DENNIS
+ 277. v. OTELIA, married **Joe Simmons III.**
278. vi. AIRON.
279. vii. LORETTA.

139. CORNELIUS^4 BUTTS (*Lemon^3, Beverly 'Lee^2, Bybe^1*) married **Thelma** (———).

Children of **Cornelius^4 Butts** and **Thelma** (———) were:
280.   i. DEBBIE^5.

140. DANIEL^4 BUTTS (*Lemon^3, Beverly 'Lee^2, Bybe^1*) was born on 17 January 1931. He married **Virginia** (—?—).

Children of **Daniel^4 Butts** and **Virginia** (—?—) were as follows:
281.   i. MARK^5.
282.   ii. ROSEANN.
+ 283.   iii. LINDA, married **Leroy Garner.**
284.   iv. KEVIN.
+ 285.   v. BEVERLY, born 23 May 1955; married **Mr. Sipp.**

141. LEON^4 BUTTS (*Lemon^3, Beverly 'Lee^2, Bybe^1*) was born on 14 February 1933. He married **Catherine** (—?—) on 18 August 1962.

Children of **Leon^4 Butts** and **Catherine** (—?—) were as follows:
286.   i. ELLEN KELSEY^5.
+ 287.   ii. REGINALD DALTON

Generation Five

142. CYNTHIA^5 BUTTS (*Tommie^4, Tommie^3, Freddie^2, Bybe^1*) was born on 13 February 1952. She married **William Wallace.**

Children of **Cynthia^5 Butts** and **William Wallace** were as follows:
288.   i. LAINIA MASON^6 was born on 27 October 1970.
289.   ii. WILLIAM (JR.) was born on 8 October 1973.
290.   iii. TAWIA was born on 19 July 1975.

145. MICHELLE^5 BUTTS (*Tommie^4, Tommie^3, Freddie^2, Bybe^1*) was born on 5 January 1958.

Children of **Michelle^5 Butts** include:
291.   i. ANTHONY^6 was born on 4 April 1979.

164. JOAN 'TOOTIE'^{5} BUTTS (*George Billy^4, George 'Hoot^3, Ephraim^2, Bybe^1*) was born on 22 November 1955. She married (—?—) **Newkirk.**

Children of **Joan 'Tootie'^{5} Butts** and (—?—) **Newkirk** were as follows:
292.   i. MARLOW^6 was born on 24 October 1975.
293.   ii. SOJOURNER BAYMON was born on 11 July 1979.

172. **DARREN LAMONT^5 OLIVER** (*Elsie Marie^4 Butts, Freddie^3, Milas^2, Bybe^1*) was born on 15 May 1962. He married **Barbara Radford.**

Children of **Darren Lamont^5 Oliver** and **Barbara Radford** were:
294.   i. SHEILAH LYNN^6 was born on 28 June 1985.

174. **DE'ANDRE LEE^5 OLIVER** (*Elsie Marie^4 Butts, Freddie^3, Milas^2, Bybe^1*) was born on 30 March 1964. He married **Rochelle Williams.**

Children of **De'Andre Lee^5 Oliver** and **Rochelle Williams** were:
295.   i. ANGELA MARCIA^6 was born on 7 April 1983.

176. **TONI O.^{5} BUTTS** (*Freddie^4, Freddie^3, Milas^2, Bybe^1*) married **Sandy** (———).

Children of **Toni O.^{5} Butts** and **Sandy** (———) were as follows:
296.   i. ANTONIA^6 was born on 24 December 1981.
297.   ii. JAMIE was born on 10 October 1984.
298.   iii. STEVE was born on 24 November 1986.

177. **ERNEST NATHANIEL 'LITTLE DUKE'^{5} BUTTS** (*Ernest Lee 'Duke'^{4}, Freddie^3, Milas^2, Bybe^1*) was born on 9 September 1957. He married **Florena Williamson.**

Children of **Ernest Nathaniel 'Little Duke'^{5} Butts** and **Florena Williamson** were as follows:
299.   i. ERICA NICHELL^6 was born on 18 November 1983.
300.   ii. ERNEST III was born on 15 August 1988.

178. **ANTHONY 'ANT' LEE^5 BUTTS** (*Ernest Lee 'Duke'^{4}, Freddie^3, Milas^2, Bybe^1*) was born on 6 February 1969. He married **Cindy** (———).

Children of **Anthony 'Ant' Lee^5 Butts** and **Cindy** (———) were:
301.   i. WAYDIA^6 was born on 2 September 1986.

179. **VERONA^5 BUTTS** (*Alton^4, Milas^3, Milas^2, Bybe^1*) was born on 3 December 1963 in Philadelphia, Pennsylvania.

Children of **Verona^5 Butts** and **Craig Walker** were:
302.   i. TERON BUTTS^6 was born on 21 July 1989 in Philadelphia, Pennsylvania.

180. MARSHA^5 **BUTTS** (*Alton*^{4}, *Milas*^{3}, *Milas*^{2}, *Bybe*^{1}) was born on 20 October 1967 in Philadelphia, Pennsylvania.

Children of **Marsha**^{5} **Butts** and **Bryan Ford** were:
303.   i. NATASHA BUTTS^6 was born on 27 June 1984 in Philadelphia, Pennsylvania.

181. TERESE^5 **BUTTS** (*Alton*^{4}, *Milas*^{3}, *Milas*^{2}, *Bybe*^{1}) was born on 10 February 1970 in Philadelphia, Pennsylvania.

Children of **Terese**^{5} **Butts** and **Damont Heckstall** were:
304.   i. ASHTON BUTTS^6 was born on 3 May 1989 in Fort Lauderdale, Florida.

182. MICHAEL^5 **ROBINSON** (*Mary L.*^{4}*Lord*, *Rosa Mae*^{3}*Butts*, *Milas*^{2}, *Bybe*^{1}) was born on 17 February 1953. He married **Olivia Poole**.

Children of **Michael**^{5} **Robinson** and **Olivia Poole** were:
305.   i. MELISSA^6 was born on 9 April 1976.

183. CAROL LOVE^5 **ROBINSON** (*Mary L.*^{4}*Lord*, *Rosa Mae*^{3}*Butts*, *Milas*^{2}, *Bybe*^{1}) was born on 21 June 1954. She married **Anthony Hailey**.

Children of **Carol Love**^{5} **Robinson** and **Anthony Hailey** were:
306.   i. ANTIRA LOVE ROBINSON^6 was born on 4 February 1987.

186. CHERYL ELIZABETH^5 **LORD** (*Jerome*^{4}, *Rosa Mae*^{3}*Butts*, *Milas*^{2}, *Bybe*^{1}) was born on 13 January 1963. She married **William Hacken**. She married **Ronald Crosby** on 27 May 1989.

Children of **Cheryl Elizabeth**^{5} **Lord** include:
307.   i. BRANDON S.^{6} was born on 3 May 1982.

There were no children of **Cheryl Elizabeth**^{5} **Lord** and **William Hacken**.

There were no children of **Cheryl Elizabeth**^{5} **Lord** and **Ronald Crosby**.

196. ALONDA^5 **LORD** (*Melvin*^{4}, *Rosa Mae*^{3}*Butts*, *Milas*^{2}, *Bybe*^{1}) was born on 28 September 1961. She married **Martin Harris**.

Children of **Alonda**^{5} **Lord** and **Martin Harris** were:
308.   i. MARTIN^6 (JR.) was born on 2 September 1983.

200. TINA R.^{5} **LORD** (*Ronald C.*^{4}*, Rosa Mae*^{3}*Butts, Milas*^{2}*, Bybe*^{1}) was born on 3 May 1963. She married **Emory K. Copeland.**

Children of **Tina R.**^{5} **Lord** and **Emory K. Copeland** were:
309.   i. EMORY T. LORD^6 was born on 17 September 1984.

201. RONALD RODNEY^5 **LORD** (*Ronald C.*^{4}*, Rosa Mae*^{3}*Butts, Milas*^{2}*, Bybe*^{1}) was born on 8 August 1965. He married **Kisha Mapp.** He married **Jucinta Bursch.**

Children of **Ronald Rodney**^{5} **Lord** and **Kisha Mapp** were:
310.   i. HAKIM LAMAR LORD^6 was born on 14 November 1986.

Children of **Ronald Rodney**^{5} **Lord** and **Jucinta Bursch** were:
311.   i. JAHLIL^6 was born on 4 May 1988.

202. RONDA^5 **LORD** (*Ronald C.*^{4}*, Rosa Mae*^{3}*Butts, Milas*^{2}*, Bybe*^{1}) was born on 8 August 1965. She married **Harold E. Hall.**

Children of **Ronda**^{5} **Lord** and **Harold E. Hall** were as follows:
312.   i. HAROLD M. LORD^6 was born on 8 June 1986.
313.   ii. MARQUES LORD was born on 2 October 1988.

203. KAREN A.^{5} **LORD** (*Ronald C.*^{4}*, Rosa Mae*^{3}*Butts, Milas*^{2}*, Bybe*^{1}) was born on 17 October 1967. She married **Antoine Johnson.**

Children of **Karen A.**^{5} **Lord** and **Antoine Johnson** were:
314.   i. SHERRIA A. LORD^6 was born on 4 August 1988.

205. KELLY S.^{5} **MOORE** (*Joan*^{4}*Lord, Rosa Mae*^{3}*Butts, Milas*^{2}*, Bybe*^{1}) was born on 30 May 1969. She married **Mark Stukes.**

Children of **Kelly S.**^{5} **Moore** include:
315.   i. BRYON TRACEY CHARLES^6 was born on 15 January 1986.

There were no children of **Kelly S.**^{5} **Moore** and **Mark Stukes.**

206. EDDIE HOLMES^5 **BUTTS** (*Chester*^{4}*, Sidney C.*^{3}*, Milas*^{2}*, Bybe*^{1}) was born on 4 October 1954. He married **Shirley Holmes.** He married **Zina Holmes.**

Children of **Eddie Holmes**^{5} **Butts** and **Shirley Holmes** were:
316.   i. TAMIKA^6 was born on 3 March 1974.

Children of **Eddie Holmes**[5] **Butts** and **Zina Holmes** were:
317.   i. ASHLEY[6] was born on 13 June 1987.

207. CURTIS[5] **BUTTS** (*Chester*[4], *Sidney C.*[3], *Milas*[2], *Bybe*[1]) was born on 27 April 1966. He married **Sheila** (———). He married **Crystle** (———).

Children of **Curtis**[5] **Butts** and **Sheila** (———) were:
318.   i. BRYON[6] was born on 14 September 1987.

Children of **Curtis**[5] **Butts** and **Crystle** (———) were:
319.   i. CHRISTIA[6] was born on 31 October 1985.

209. DARYL[5] **BUTTS** (*Chester*[4], *Sidney C.*[3], *Milas*[2], *Bybe*[1]) was born on 19 July 1968. He married **Nichelle** (———).

Children of **Daryl**[5] **Butts** and **Nichelle** (———) were:
320.   i. SHAUNICE[6] was born on 24 August 1985.

212. WILLIAM[5] **WILLIAMS (JR.)** (*Janice*[4]*Butts*, *Sidney C.*[3], *Milas*[2], *Bybe*[1]) was born on 19 January 1958.

Children of **William**[5] **Williams (Jr.)** include:
321.   i. LATICHIA[6].

213. KENNETH 'HUCKY'[5] **WILLIAMS** (*Janice*[4]*Butts*, *Sidney C.*[3], *Milas*[2], *Bybe*[1]) was born on 13 July 1960. He married **Sylvita Barbour.** He married **Deborah Lynn** (———).

Children of **Kenneth 'Hucky'**[5] **Williams** and **Sylvita Barbour** were:
322.   i. KINETA[6] was born on 12 February 1977.

Children of **Kenneth 'Hucky'**[5] **Williams** and **Deborah Lynn** (———) were as follows:
323.   i. RAHEEM ANTHONY[6] was born on 13 July 1980.
324.   ii. LATOYA DENISE was born on 6 March 1981.
325.   iii. KENNETH JAMELL was born on 3 March 1982.

214. HERRELL A.[5] **WILLIAMS** (*Janice*[4]*Butts*, *Sidney C.*[3], *Milas*[2], *Bybe*[1]) was born on 23 May 1967. He married **Stephanie Y. Anderson.** He married **Nadine Jackson.**

Children of **Herrell A.**[5] **Williams** and **Stephanie Y. Anderson** were:
326.   i. KIAUNA YVONNE[6] was born on 28 May 1985.

Children of Herrell A.[5] Williams and Nadine Jackson were:
327.   i. SHERRELL VIOLA[6] was born on 4 April 1989.

215. ALONZO LONNIE[5] WILLIAMS (*Janice*[4]*Butts, Sidney C.*[3], *Milas*[2], *Bybe*[1]) was born on 2 August 1969.

Children of Alonzo Lonnie[5] Williams and Trina Straike were:
328.   i. TRANIKA[6] was born on 9 March 1987.

Children of Alonzo Lonnie[5] Williams and Nicole King were:
329.   i. NATASHA[6] was born on 20 November 1987.

Children of Alonzo Lonnie[5] Williams and Barbara M. Rock were:
330.   i. ALONZO ALLEN ROCK[6] was born on 21 April 1989.

227. SABRINA LYNN[5] ALCORN (*Doris*[4]*Butts, Bob Willis*[3], *Milas*[2], *Bybe*[1]) was born on 5 February 1967. She married Derrick Girard McCann (Sr.).

Children of Sabrina Lynn[5] Alcorn and Derrick Girard McCann (Sr.) were:
331.   i. DERRICK GIRARD[6] (JR.) was born on 4 May 1990.

230. TANYA[5] HOLLIWAY (*Gwendolyn 'Gwen'*[4]*Butts, Bob Willis*[3], *Milas*[2], *Bybe*[1]) was born on 9 February 1964. She married Todd Bell.

Children of Tanya[5] Holliway include:
332.   i. T J[6] was born circa 1990.
333.   ii. TIANA was born circa 1990.

Children of Tanya[5] Holliway and Todd Bell were as follows:
334.   i. TIFFANY[6] was born on 31 August 1983.
335.   ii. TODD (JR.) was born on 26 February 1985.

273. CURTIS[5] BUTTS (*Lemon*[4], *Lemon*[3], *Beverly 'Lee'*[2], *Bybe*[1]) married Diane (———).
He died on 13 March 1988.

Children of Curtis[5] Butts and Diane (———) were:
336.   i. KATHEY[6].

276. DENNIS[5] BUTTS (*Lemon*[4], *Lemon*[3], *Beverly 'Lee'*[2], *Bybe*[1]).

Children of Dennis[5] Butts include:
337.   i. J.R.[6].

338.   ii. PAUL.

277. OTELIA^5 BUTTS (*Lemon^4, Lemon^3, Beverly 'Lee^2, Bybe^1*) married **Joe Simmons III.**

Children of **Otelia^5 Butts** and **Joe Simmons III** were as follows:
339.   i. ELAINE^6.
340.   ii. NICKIE.

283. LINDA^5 BUTTS (*Daniel^4, Lemon^3, Beverly 'Lee^2, Bybe^1*) married **Leroy Garner.**

Children of **Linda^5 Butts** and **Leroy Garner** were as follows:
341.   i. DEWANY^6.
+ 342.   ii. ADELE
343.   iii. TORRENCE.
344.   iv. ANTHONY.

285. BEVERLY^5 BUTTS (*Daniel^4, Lemon^3, Beverly 'Lee^2, Bybe^1*) was born on 23 May 1955. She married **Mr. Sipp.**

Children of **Beverly^5 Butts** and **Mr. Sipp** were:
345.   i. DANIEL^6.

287. REGINALD DALTON^5 BUTTS (*Leon^4, Lemon^3, Beverly 'Lee^2, Bybe^1*).

Children of **Reginald Dalton^5 Butts** include:
346.   i. REGINALD DANTE^6.

Generation Six

342. ADELE^6 GARNER (*Linda^5 Butts, Daniel^4, Lemon^3, Beverly 'Lee^2, Bybe^1*).

Children of **Adele^6 Garner** include:
347.   i. JUSTINE^7.

Descendants of Mr. Trawick

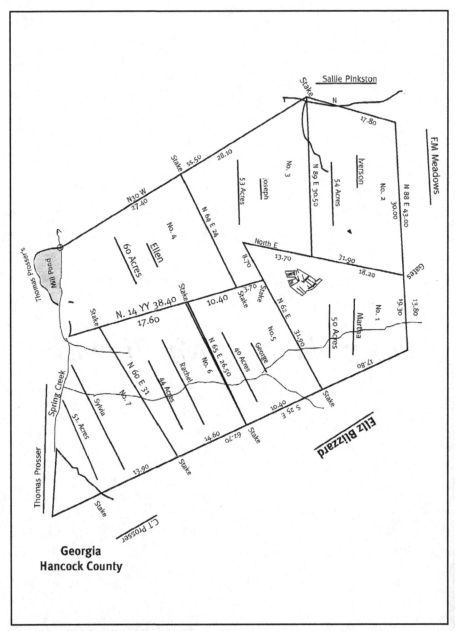

Plat of the Division of Jack Trawick's Property
Hancock County, Georgia, October 1892

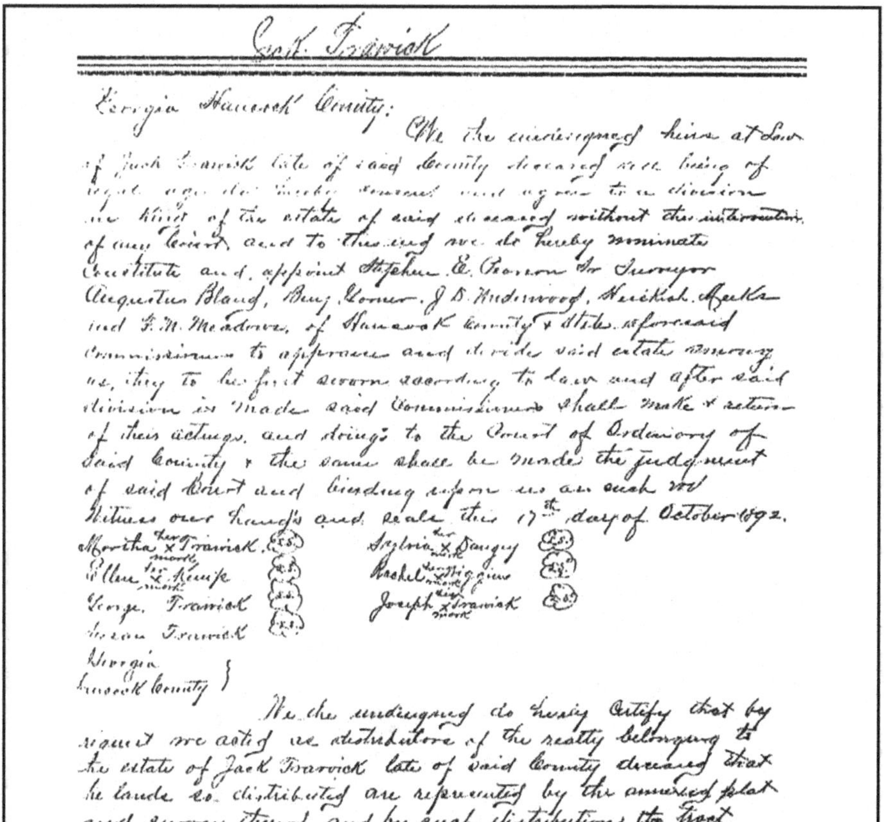

Jack Trawick

Georgia Hancock County:

We the undersigned heirs at Law of Jack Trawick late of said County deceased are being of legal age do hereby consent and agree to a division in kind of the estate of said deceased without the intervention of any Court and to this end we do hereby nominate constitute and appoint Stephen E. Pearson Co Surveyor Augustus Bland, Benj. Gomer, J. D. Underwood, Hezekiah Meeks and F. M. Meadows, of Hancock County & State aforesaid Commissioners to appraise and divide said estate among us, they to be first sworn according to law and after said division is made said Commissioners shall make & return of their actings and doings to the Court of Ordinary of said County & the same shall be made the judgment of said Court and binding upon us as such &c

Witness our hands and seals this 17th day of October 1892.

Martha her x mark Trawick (L.S.) Sylvia her x mark Dangey (L.S.)
Ellen her x mark Kemp (L.S.) Rachel her x mark Wiggins (L.S.)
George Trawick (L.S.) Joseph his x mark Trawick (L.S.)
Susan Trawick (L.S.)

Georgia
Hancock County }

We the undersigned do hereby certify that by request we acted as distributors of the realty belonging to the estate of Jack Trawick late of said County deceased that the lands so distributed are represented by the annexed plat and survey thereof and by such distribution the tract designated in such survey as Lot.

Lot No. 1 was assigned to Martha Trawick
" " 2 " " " Susan Trawick
" " 3 " " " Joseph Trawick
" " 4 " " " Ellen Kemp
" " 5 " " " George Trawick
" " 6 " " " Rachel Wiggins
" " 7 " " " Silvia Dangey

These being the names of the several parties at interest as submitted to us these assignments being made to the several parties by lot & the several tracts being in our judgment of equal value In witness whereof we have hereunto set our hands & seals this " day of 1892.

F. M. Meadows Com.
J. D. Underwood Com
Benjamin Gomer Com
A. C. Bland Com.

The Heirs of Jack Trawick

1870 Census Wash Co Ga   Bartes Dist #98   p/7

133-133

Traywick, Samuel 30 M B   farm lab   Ga   16, 17, 19

    Fannie   31   KH   16, 17

    Morgan   16   "   "   16, 17

    Dock   14   "   "   16, 17

    Rolla   15   17

    Mark   10   17

    Ga   10 F   17

    Laura   9

1870 Census Wash Co Ga   Bartes Dist #98   P 16/17

132-132

    Trawick, John   48 M B   farm lab   Ga   16, 17, 19

       Martha   28   KH   16, 17

       George   19   farm worker   16, 17

       Joseph   16   "   "   16, 17

       Dilora   12 FB   "   "   16, 17

       Rachel   10

       Iverson   7 M B

Samuel and John Trawick, 1870 Census

1880 CENSUS p 421   Dist 95   2802

Trawick, Ben   B   m   45
    Julia   38
    Sam   15
    Lucy   14
    James   12
    Mattie   10
    John   8
    Corrie   6
    Crawford   4
    Kissie   2   F

1880 CENSUS p 421   Dist 98   2803

Trawick, Sam   B   m   43
    Fannie   42
    Dock   m   22
    Rella   n   21
    Mark   19
    Virgen   m   23
    Ga   7   20
    Laura   17
    Dick   26
    Sam Jr   3

Ben and Sam Trawick, 1880 Census

MICROFILM ROLL NUMBER T623, Roll 207

1900 CENSUS – UNITED STATES

STATE Georgia **TOWN/TOWNSHIP** 117 Dist. G.M. **SUPV. DIST. NO.** 10 **SHEET NUMBER** 8

COUNTY Hancock **CALL NUMBER** **DATE** 15 June 1990 **ENUM. DIST. NO.** 19 **PAGE NUMBER**

Street	House Number	Dwelling Number	Family Number	NAME of each person whose place of abode on June 1, 1900, was in this family	Relation to Head of family	Color	Sex	Month of birth	Year of birth	Age	Single, married, widowed, divorced	Number of years married	Mother of how many children	Number of these children living	Place of birth	Place of birth of father	Place of birth of mother	Year of immigration to United States	No. of years in U.S.	Naturalization	OCCUPATION Type	Number of months not employed	Attended school (months)	Can read	Can write	Can speak English	Home owned or rented	Home owned free or mortgaged	Farm or house
	141	141	Trawick, Joe		H	B	M	May 1850	50	M	25				Ga	Ga	Ga				Farmer	0		No	No	Yes			F
			— Nattie		W	B	F	Apr 1855	45	M	25	11	1		Ga	Ga	Ga							No	No	Yes			
			— Mary E.		D	B	F	June 1880	19	S					Ga	Ga	Ga				Farming	0		Y	Y	Y			
			— Lucy		D	B	F	Jan 1882	18	S					Ga	Ga	Ga				Farming	0		Y	Y	Y			
			— Luas		D	B	F	Apr 1883	17	S					Ga	Ga	Ga				Farming	0		Y	Y	Y			
			— Clara B		D	B	F	Nov 1884	13	S					Ga	Ga	Ga				at school	5		Y	Y	Y			
			— Jennie A		S	B	M	Sep 1888	11	S					Ga	Ga	Ga				at school	5		Y	Y	Y			
			— George W.		S	B	M	Mar 1892	7	S					Ga	Ga	Ga												
			— ? izzie		d	B	F	Dec 1894	5	S					Ga	Ga	Ga												
			Ella		N	B	F	Apr 1896	4	S					Ga	Ga	Ga												

NATIONAL ARCHIVES AND RECORDS ADMINISTRATION NA 14087 (10-86)

Joe Trawick, 1900 Census

```
TRAWICK   DOCK
Mayo Funeral Home Book 6  # 190
Died 1/27/1928 at home  Buried Jordan Grave Yard  Age 25  Married
Father Dock Trawick Wash Co
Mother Violet Young   "    "
Charge to Home Union Work society & wife May Ollie
```

```
TRAWICK, VIOLET
Mayo Funeral Home Book 9  # 525
Born Wash Co ?  died 12/23/1930 at home, buried at home, age 80
Father Ned James  Ga
Charge to Home Union Workers Society      Informant Tom Trawick
                                                          Deepstep
```

Dock Trawick, 1920 Census

Descendants of Mr. Trawick

Generation One

1. MR.*¹* TRAWICK.

Children of **Mr.*¹* Trawick** include:
+ 2. i. JACK 'JOHN'*²*, born circa 1822 in Washington County, Georgia.
+ 3. ii. BENJAMIN, born circa 1835 in Washington County, Georgia; married **Julia** (————).
+ 4. iii. SAMUEL, born 1840 in Washington County, Georgia; married **Fannie** (————).

Generation Two

2. JACK 'JOHN'*²* TRAWICK (*Mr.¹*) was born circa 1822 in Washington County, Georgia. He died before October 1892 in Hancock County, Georgia.

Children of **Jack 'John'*²* Trawick** include:
5. i. ELLEN*³* was born in Washington County, Georgia. She married **Mr. Kemp** in Washington County, Georgia.
6. ii. MARTHA was born circa 1842 in Washington County, Georgia.
7. iii. GEORGE was born circa 1851 in Washington County, Georgia.
+ 8. iv. JOSEPH 'JOE', born May 1854 in Washington County, Georgia; married **Mattie Young.**
9. v. SILVIA was born circa 1858 in Washington County, Georgia. She married **Elijah Dangey** in Washington County, Georgia.
10. vi. RACHEL was born in 1860 in Washington County, Georgia. She married **Walter Wiggins** in Washington County, Georgia.
11. vii. IVERSON was born in 1863 in Washington County, Georgia.

3. BENJAMIN*²* TRAWICK (*Mr.¹*) was born circa 1835 in Washington County, Georgia. He married **Julia** (————) in Washington County, Georgia.

Children of **Benjamin*²* Trawick** and **Julia** (————) were as follows:
12. i. SAMUEL*³* was born in 1862 in Washington County, Georgia.
13. ii. JANE was born circa 1865 in Washington County, Georgia.
14. iii. LUCY was born in 1866 in Washington County, Georgia.
15. iv. JAMES was born in 1868 in Washington County, Georgia.
16. v. MATTIE was born in 1870 in Washington County, Georgia.
17. vi. JOHN was born in 1872 in Washington County, Georgia.
18. vii. CARRIE was born in 1874 in Washington County, Georgia.
19. viii. CRAWFORD was born in 1876 in Washington County, Georgia.
20. ix. KISSIE was born in 1878 in Washington County, Georgia.

4. SAMUEL² TRAWICK (*Mr.¹*) was born in 1840 in Washington County, Georgia. He married **Fannie** (———) in Washington County, Georgia.

Children of **Samuel² Trawick** and **Fannie** (———) were as follows:
21.   i. MORGAN³ was born circa 1854 in Washington County, Georgia.
22.   ii. DICK was born in 1854 in Washington County, Georgia.
23.   iii. VIRGE was born in 1857 in Washington County, Georgia.
+ 24.   iv. DOCK, born March 1859 in Washington County, Georgia; married **Violet Young.**
25.   v. MARK was born circa 1860 in Washington County, Georgia.
26.   vi. ROLLA was born circa 1860 in Washington County, Georgia.
27.   vii. GEORGIA ANN was born in 1860 in Washington County, Georgia.
28.   viii. LAURA was born in 1863 in Washington County, Georgia.
29.   ix. SAMUEL 'SAM' JR. was born in 1877 in Washington County, Georgia.

Generation Three

8. JOSEPH 'JOE'³ TRAWICK (*Jack John²*, *Mr.¹*) was born in May 1854 in Washington County, Georgia. He married **Mattie Young** in Georgia. He died in 1919 in Hancock County, Georgia.

Children of **Joseph 'Joe'³ Trawick** and **Mattie Young** were as follows:
+ 30.   i. TOMMY⁴
31.   ii. SISSIE was born in Georgia.
32.   iii. LUCY was born in January 1882 in Georgia.
+ 33.   iv. VIRGINIA 'GINNY', married **Mr. Adams.**
+ 34.   v. MARY ELLA, born June 1880 in Hancock County, Georgia.
+ 35.   vi. LEANNE 'LOU', born April 1883 in Hancock County, Georgia.
+ 36.   vii. CLARA BELL, born 12 December 1886 in Hancock County, Georgia; married **Henry Cheeves Jr.**
+ 37.   viii. LOBELA
+ 38.   ix. JIMMIE A., born September 1888 in Hancock County, Georgia.
39.   x. GEORGE W. was born in January 1893 in Georgia.
+ 40.   xi. ELIZABETH 'KIZZIE', born August 1894 in Hancock County, Georgia; married **Mr. Hall.**

24. DOCK³ TRAWICK (*Samuel²*, *Mr.¹*) was born in March 1859 in Washington County, Georgia. He married **Violet Young** in Georgia. He died on 16 March 1928 in Washington County, Georgia

Children of **Dock³ Trawick** and **Violet Young** were as follows:
+ 41.   i. KIZZIE⁴, born September 1880 in Washington County, Georgia; married **Adam 'Add' Hooks.**

+ 42. ii. TEXANN, born July 1882 in Georgia; married **Joseph 'Joe' Smith Sr.**
+ 43. iii. MARY, born July 1884 in Washington County, Georgia.
+ 44. iv. JOHNNIE, born October 1886 in Washington County, Georgia; married **Bertha Carter.**
  45. v. ELIZABETH was born in May 1888 in Georgia.
+ 46. vi. ELISHA, born September 1890 in Georgia; married **Mary Lucy Ann Barlow;** married **Mattie Adolphus.**
+ 47. vii. TOM, born October 1892 in Georgia; married **Melissa Williams;** married **Irene Rushin.**
+ 48. viii. LAURA, born October 1894 in Washington County, Georgia; married **Oscar Renfroe.**
+ 49. ix. SAM, born December 1896 in Washington County, Georgia; married **Mary 'Ma-Mae' Ollie Cheeves.**
+ 50. x. DOCK 'WHALE', born January 1899 in Georgia; married **Mary 'Ma-Mae' Ollie Cheeves.**
  51. xi. IRENE was born circa 1902 in Washington County, Georgia. She married **Morris Grady** in Washington County, Georgia.

Generation Four

30. TOMMY^4 TRAWICK (*Joseph 'Joe'^{3}, Jack 'John'^{2}, Mr.^{1}*) died in September 1961.

Children of **Tommy^4 Trawick** include:
  52. i. DAISY^5.
  53. ii. MARIE.
  54. iii. ROBERT.
  55. iv. HOLMES.

33. VIRGINIA 'GINNY'^{4} TRAWICK (*Joseph 'Joe'^{3}, Jack 'John'^{2}, Mr.^{1}*) married **Mr. Adams.**

Children of **Virginia 'Ginny'^{4} Trawick** and **Mr. Adams** were as follows:
  56. i. MATTIE^5.
  57. ii. ANNIE CLYDE.

34. MARY ELLA^4 TRAWICK (*Joseph 'Joe'^{3}, Jack 'John'^{2}, Mr.^{1}*) was born in June 1880 in Hancock County, Georgia.

Children of **Mary Ella^4 Trawick** include:
  58. i. ANNIE BELLE^5.

35. LEANNE 'LOU'^{4} TRAWICK (*Joseph 'Joe'^{3}, Jack 'John'^{2}, Mr.^{1}*) was born in April 1883 in Hancock County, Georgia. She died in 1962.

Children of **Leanne 'Lou'**[4] **Trawick** include:
59.   i. TILDA MAE[5].
60.   ii. ESSIE BELLE.
61.   iii. LOU ETHER.
62.   iv. PROFESSOR WOMBLE.

36. **CLARA BELL**[4] **TRAWICK** (*Joseph 'Joe'*[3], *Jack 'John'*[2], *Mr.*[1]) was born on 12 December 1886 in Hancock County, Georgia. She married **Henry Cheeves Jr.**, son of **Henry Cheeves Sr.** and **Mary Ann Wise**, in Washington County, Georgia. She died on 20 July 1969 in Philadelphia, Pennsylvania, at age 82.

Children of **Clara Bell**[4] **Trawick** and **Henry Cheeves Jr.** were as follows:
63.   i. JOSEPH 'JOE'[5] was born on 8 July 1905 in Sandersville, Georgia. He married **Beatrice Veal.** He married **Eva Mae Jordan.** He died in 1990 in Georgia.
+ 64.   ii. HENRIETTA, born 30 May 1907 in Sandersville, Georgia; married **Willie Smith;** married **Willie W. Hooks.**
+ 65.   iii. MATTIE LOU, born 24 June 1909 in Sandersville, Georgia; married **Bobby Lee Shenoster;** married **Oreain Johnson.**
+ 66.   iv. HENRY HOLMES, born 18 February 1918 in Sandersville, Washington County, Georgia; married **Lillian Arthur Carter.**
67.   v. CARRIE ANN was born on 6 November 1920 in Sandersville, Georgia. She died on 26 April 1921 in Sandersville, Washington County, Georgia.

37. **LOBELA**[4] **TRAWICK** (*Joseph 'Joe'*[3], *Jack 'John'*[2], *Mr.*[1]).

Children of **Lobela**[4] **Trawick** include:
68.   i. BEULAH[5].

38. **JIMMIE A.**[4] **TRAWICK** (*Joseph 'Joe'*[3], *Jack 'John'*[2], *Mr.*[1]) was born in September 1888 in Hancock County, Georgia.

Children of **Jimmie A.**[4] **Trawick** include:
69.   i. VIOLA[5].
70.   ii. GLADYS married **Mr. Spikes.**
71.   iii. SAM 'SAMMY'.
72.   iv. LAURA DEE married **Mr. Desseau.**

40. **ELIZABETH 'KIZZIE'**[4] **TRAWICK** (*Joseph 'Joe'*[3], *Jack 'John'*[2], *Mr.*[1]) was born in August 1894 in Hancock County, Georgia. She was born in August 1894 in Hancock, Georgia. She was born in August 1894 in Hancock, Georgia. She married **Mr. Hall.**

Children of **Elizabeth 'Kizzie'^{4} Trawick** and **Mr. Hall** were as follows:

   73.   i. MARY^5.

   74.   ii. ANNA MELISSA.

41. **KIZZIE^4 TRAWICK** (*Dock^3, Samuel^2, Mr.^{1}*) was born in September 1880 in Washington County, Georgia. She married **Adam 'Add' Hooks**, son of **James Hooks** and **Ella Kelsey**, on 26 December 1894 in Washington County, Georgia.

Children of **Kizzie^4 Trawick** and **Adam 'Add' Hooks** were as follows:

   75.   i. LEE^5 was born in September 1895 in Georgia. He married **Eunice O'Neal**.

   76.   ii. SYLVESTER was born on 2 September 1899 in Georgia. He married **Lucille Smith**.

+ 77.   iii. JOE, married **Fannie Smith**.

   78.   iv. INEZ married **Mr. Garcia**.

42. **TEXANN^4 TRAWICK** (*Dock^3, Samuel^2, Mr.^{1}*) was born in July 1882 in Georgia. She married **Joseph 'Joe' Smith Sr.**, son of **James Smith Sr.** and **Milly Carter**.

Children of **Texann^4 Trawick** and **Joseph 'Joe' Smith Sr.** were as follows:

+ 79.   i. JAMES BERYL 'BUDDY'^{5}, born 9 February 1909 in Sandersville, Washington County, Georgia; married **Mildred West**; married **Mary Scott**.

   80.   ii. JOSEPH D. 'JOE' (JR.) was born circa 1912 in Washington County, Georgia. He died in 1990.

   81.   iii. VIRGIL was born in 1914 in Washington County, Georgia. He died in 1953.

   82.   iv. MILLICENSE 'MYLIE' was born circa 1915 in Washington County, Georgia. She married **Mr. Howard**. She died in 1996.

   83.   v. MARY ANN was born on 11 September 1916 in Washington County, Georgia. She married **Mr. Rayford**.

   84.   vi. JULIA was born in 1920 in Washington County, Georgia. She married **Mr. Fussel**. She died in 1985.

+ 85.   vii. KENNETH PAUL, born 16 August 1922 in Washington County, Georgia; married **Evelyn** (———).

43. **MARY^4 TRAWICK** (*Dock^3, Samuel^2, Mr.^{1}*) was born in July 1884 in Washington County, Georgia.

Children of **Mary^4 Trawick** include:

   86.   i. ED^5 was born circa 1910.

   87.   ii. JACK was born circa 1910.

44. **JOHNNIE^4 TRAWICK** (*Dock^3, Samuel^2, Mr.^{1}*) was born in October 1886 in Washington County, Georgia. He married **Bertha Carter**, daughter of **Jeff Carter Sr.** and **Ella Hooks**.

Children of **Johnnie**[4] **Trawick** and **Bertha Carter** were:
+ 88.   i. **EVA (JOHNNY)**[5], born 31 January 1920 in Sandersville, Washington County, Georgia; married **Matthew Thomas.**

46. **ELISHA**[4] **TRAWICK** (*Dock*[3], *Samuel*[2], *Mr.*[1]) was born in September 1890 in Georgia. He married **Mary Lucy Ann Barlow**, daughter of **Eldridge Barlow** and **Elsie Canty.** He married **Mary Lucy Ann Barlow**, daughter of **Eldridge Barlow** and **Elsie Canty.** He married **Mattie Adolphus.**

Children of **Elisha**[4] **Trawick** and **Mary Lucy Ann Barlow** were as follows:
+ 89.   i. **JOHN**[5], born 9 June 1917 in Sandersville, Georgia; married **Vera Peeler.**
   90.   ii. **JOSEPH** married **Josephine** (—?—).
   91.   iii. **ELIZABETH** married **Mr. Mathis.**

Children of **Elisha**[4] **Trawick** and **Mattie Adolphus** were as follows:
   92.   i. **HARVEY**[5].
   93.   ii. **BURLEY.**
   94.   iii. **WILLIE.**
   95.   iv. **LEE DOCK.**
   96.   v. **TEXANN** married **Mr. Ingram.**
   97.   vi. **GEORGIA ANNE** married **Mr. Sanford.**

47. **TOM**[4] **TRAWICK** (*Dock*[3], *Samuel*[2], *Mr.*[1]) was born in October 1892 in Georgia. He married **Melissa Williams**, daughter of **Ed Williams** and **Nancy Boyer,** in Georgia. He married **Irene Rushin.** He died on 5 December 1980 at age 88.

Children of **Tom**[4] **Trawick** and **Melissa Williams** were as follows:
+ 98.   i. **VERNON 'BUD'**[5], born 29 September 1926 in Philadelphia, Pennsylvania; married **Mary Pearl 'Town' Gordy Cheeves.**
   99.   ii. **ORIAN.**
+ 100.   iii. **NANCY**
+ 101.   iv. **VIVIAN 'TUET'**, born 29 September 1926 in Philadelphia, Pennsylvania.
   102.   v. **LENWOOD.**
+ 103.   vi. **THOMAS**
   104.   vii. **SAMUEL.**
   105.   viii. **DOCK.**

There were no children of **Tom**[4] **Trawick** and **Irene Rushin.**

48. **LAURA**[4] **TRAWICK** (*Dock*[3], *Samuel*[2], *Mr.*[1]) was born in October 1894 in Washington County, Georgia. She married **Oscar Renfroe.** She died in October 1969.

Children of **Laura**^{4} **Trawick** and **Oscar Renfroe** were as follows:

+ 106.   i. **ADAM**^{5}, born 27 January 1916 in Sandersville, Washington County, Georgia; married **Athele 'Jacy' Maxwell.**

107.   ii. **NATHANIEL** was born circa 1918 in Washington County, Georgia.

+ 108.   iii. **EVALENE**, married **W. Louis Hodges.**

+ 109.   iv. **JOHNNIE DARK,** born 1 April 1922 in Sandersville, Georgia; married **Mae Will Williams.**

110.   v. **ANNIE JULIA** married **Mr. Kendricks.**

111.   vi. **ORETHA.**

112.   vii. **SALLIE** married **Mr. Daniels.**

113.   viii. **RUTH** married **Mr. Stevens.**

114.   ix. **HATTIE** married **Mr. Cooper.**

49. SAM^4 **TRAWICK** (*Dock*^{3}, *Samuel*^{2}, *Mr.*^{1}) was born in December 1896 in Washington County, Georgia. He married **Mary 'Ma-Mae' Ollie Cheeves**, daughter of **David 'Coot' Cheeves** and **Hattie Johnson.** He died in October 1927 at age 30.

Children of **Sam**^{4} **Trawick** and **Mary 'Ma-Mae' Ollie Cheeves** were as follows:

115.   i. **MYRIAN**^{5} married **Mr. Hall.**

116.   ii. **LAURTY.**

117.   iii. **GLORIA 'GLO' LOUISE** married **Burley 'Sytes' Lord** (Jr.), son of **Burley Lord** (Sr.) and **Rosa Mae Butts.**

50. DOCK 'WHALE'^{4} **TRAWICK** (*Dock*^{3}, *Samuel*^{2}, *Mr.*^{1}) was born in January 1899 in Georgia. He married **Mary 'Ma-Mae' Ollie Cheeves**, daughter of **David 'Coot' Cheeves** and **Hattie Johnson.** He died in January 1928.

Children of **Dock 'Whale'**^{4} **Trawick** and **Mary 'Ma-Mae' Ollie Cheeves** were as follows:

+ 118.   i. **JULIA INEZ**^{5}, born 24 January 1920; married **Sidney C. Butts.**

119.   ii. **CLYDE 'BUDDY'.**

+ 120.   iii. **MAMYE DOROTHY 'MARY'**, born 16 January 1925; married **Bob Willis Butts.**

+ 121.   iv. **JUANITA EASTER MAE**, married **Cleophus Crumbly;** married **Mr. Elliott.**

122.   v. **JULIA** married **Mr. Elliott.**

Generation Five

64. HENRIETTA^5 **CHEEVES** (*Clara Bell*^{4} *Trawick, Joseph 'Joe'*^{3}, *Jack 'John'*^{2}, *Mr.*^{1}) was born on 30 May 1907 in Sandersville, Georgia. She married **Willie Smith.** She married **Willie W. Hooks**, son of **Mitchell Hooks** and **Love Andrews.** She died on 12 May 1969 in Augusta, Georgia, at age 61.

Children of **Henrietta**^{5} **Cheeves** and **Willie Smith** were:

123.   i. **WILLIE C.**^{6} was born in Sandersville, Georgia. He married **Inez** (———).

Children of **Henrietta**^{5} **Cheeves** and **Willie W. Hooks** were as follows:

+ 124.   i. **MITCHELL**^{6}, born 7 March 1933 in Sandersville, Georgia; married **Delores Hooks.**

+ 125.   ii. **CHEEVES,** born 4 April 1935 in Washington County, Georgia; married **Myrtistine Cullens.**

126.   iii. **WILLIE WALTER (JR.)** was born on 30 June 1937 in Washington County, Georgia. He married **Annie** (———). He married **Gussie** (———).

+ 127.   iv. **MARION,** born 1 July 1940 in Sandersville, Georgia; married **Annie** (———); married **Christine** (—?—).

+ 128.   v. **ORALENE,** born 4 April 1943 in Sandersville, Georgia; married **Frank Pierce.**

65. MATTIE LOU^5 **CHEEVES** (*Clara Bell*^{4} *Trawick, Joseph 'Joe'*^{3}*, Jack 'John'*^{2}*, Mr.*^{1}) was born on 24 June 1909 in Sandersville, Georgia. She married **Bobby Lee Shenoster.** She married **Oreain Johnson.** She died on 5 March 1995 in Philadelphia, Pennsylvania, at age 85.

Children of **Mattie Lou**^{5} **Cheeves** and **Bobby Lee Shenoster** were as follows:

+ 129.   i. **ZELMA**^{6}, born 10 January 1932 in Sandersville, Georgia.

+ 130.   ii. **KATHERINE,** born 19 April 1934 in Milledgeville, Georgia; married **John Benjamin Douglass (Sr.).**

There were no children of **Mattie Lou**^{5} **Cheeves** and **Oreain Johnson.**

66. HENRY HOLMES^5 **CHEEVES** (*Clara Bell*^{4} *Trawick, Joseph 'Joe'*^{3}*, Jack 'John'*^{2}*, Mr.*^{1}) was born on 18 February 1918 in Sandersville, Washington County, Georgia. He married **Lillian Arthur Carter,** daughter of **Jeff Carter Jr.** and **Gervenia Fisher.** He died on 15 September 2001 in Philadelphia, Pennsylvania, at age 83.

Children of **Henry Holmes**^{5} **Cheeves** and **Lillian Arthur Carter** were as follows:

+ 131.   i. **MIRIAM**^{6}, born in Sandersville, Washington County, Georgia

+ 132.   ii. **GLORIA,** born 4 July 1941 in Sandersville, Washington County, Georgia; married **Charles Graham.**

+ 133.   iii. **HORACE,** born 4 September 1943 in Sandersville, Washington County, Georgia; married **Fannie Pearl Williams.**

+ 134.   iv. **FOREST,** born 4 September 1943 in Sandersville, Washington County, Georgia; married **Karen Kennedy.**

135.   v. **HENRY** was born on 8 September 1948 in Sandersville, Washington County, Georgia

136.   vi. **DAVID** was born on 10 November 1954 in Philadelphia, Pennsylvania. He died on 17 August 1995 in Detroit, Michigan, at age 40.

137.   vii. **ANNETTE GAIL** was born on 7 August 1958 in Philadelphia, Pennsylvania.

77. JOE⁵ HOOKS (*Kizzie⁴ Trawick, Dock³, Samuel², Mr.¹*) married **Fannie Smith.**

Children of **Joe⁵ Hooks** and **Fannie Smith** were as follows:
+ 138. i. FRANK⁶, married **Bertha** (——).
   139. ii. HAROLD.

79. JAMES BERYL 'BUDDY'⁵ SMITH (*Texann⁴ Trawick, Dock³, Samuel², Mr.¹*) was born on 9 February 1909 in Sandersville, Washington County, Georgia. He married **Mildred West.** He married **Mary Scott.** He died on 17 October 1981 in Camden, New Jersey, at age 72.

Children of **James Beryl 'Buddy'⁵ Smith** and **Mildred West** were:
+ 140. i. JEAN⁶, born 7 August 1934 in Philadelphia, Pennsylvania; married **Arnold Dixon Jackson Sr.**

Children of **James Beryl 'Buddy'⁵ Smith** and **Mary Scott** were:
   141. i. DRESSLER⁶ was born on 14 September 1958 in Philadelphia, Pennsylvania. She married **Crandall Richard.**

85. KENNETH PAUL⁵ SMITH (*Texann⁴ Trawick, Dock³, Samuel², Mr.¹*) was born on 16 August 1922 in Washington County, Georgia. He married **Evelyn** (——). He died on 22 October 1996 at age 74.

Children of **Kenneth Paul⁵ Smith** and **Evelyn** (——) were:
+ 142. i. EVETTE⁶

88. EVA (JOHNNY)⁵ TRAWICK (*Johnnie⁴, Dock³, Samuel², Mr.¹*) was born on 31 January 1920 in Sandersville, Washington County, Georgia. She married **Matthew Thomas.**

Children of **Eva (Johnny)⁵ Trawick** and **Matthew Thomas** were as follows:
+ 143. i. SANDRA CAROL⁶, born 31 May 1946 in Philadelphia, Pennsylvania; married **Herb Connelly.**
+ 144. ii. SIGRID ANN, born 10 March 1948 in Philadelphia, Pennsylvania; married **Howard Edward McCall Jr.**
+ 145. iii. WANDA EILEEN, born 12 April 1950 in Philadelphia, Pennsylvania; married **John 'Donald' Bird.**

89. JOHN⁵ TRAWICK (*Elisha⁴, Dock³, Samuel², Mr.¹*) was born on 9 June 1917 in Sandersville, Georgia. He married **Vera Peeler,** daughter of **Cleveland Peeler** and **Leola Rogers,** on 22 June 1947 in Sandersville, Georgia. He died on 6 July 1991 in Sandersville, Georgia, at age 74.

Children of **John**^{5} **Trawick** and **Vera Peeler** were as follows:

146. i. MALVIN^6 was born on 22 October 1947 in Sandersville, Georgia. He married **Jacqueline Parklin.**

+ 147. ii. ALTON, born 18 January 1949 in Sandersville, Georgia; married **Joanne Washington.**

148. iii. LINDA JOYCE was born on 15 May 1950 in Sandersville, Georgia. She married **Samual Chandle.**

149. iv. BEVERLY LAVERNE was born on 1 July 1953 in Sandersville, Georgia.

+ 150. v. CATHY ANN, born 3 January 1955 in Sandersville, Georgia; married **Leo Suggs.**

151. vi. JOHN RICKY was born on 19 September 1959 in Sandersville, Georgia. He died in December 1995 in St. Paul, Minnesota, at age 36.

+ 152. vii. LYDIA JEAN, born 3 February 1961 in Sandersville, Georgia; married **Willie James Woodard.**

98. VERNON 'BUD'^{5} **TRAWICK** (*Tom*^{4}, *Dock*^{3}, *Samuel*^{2}, *Mr.*^{1}) was born on 29 September 1926 in Philadelphia, Pennsylvania. He married **Mary Pearl 'Town' Gordy Cheeves,** daughter of **Samuel 'Sam' Gordy Jr.** and **Sarah Ella 'SC' Hopkins,** on 19 November 1948 in Sandersville, Georgia. He died on 26 March 2001 in Philadelphia, Pennsylvania, at age 74.

Children of **Vernon 'Bud'**^{5} **Trawick** and **Mary Pearl 'Town' Gordy Cheeves** were as follows:

153. i. VERNON^6 JR. was born on 10 April 1950 in Sandersville, Washington County, Georgia

+ 154. ii. BERNARD, born 14 December 1951 in Philadelphia, Pennsylvania; married **Kenya Wilson.**

155. iii. MARVIN was born on 6 November 1954 in Philadelphia, Pennsylvania.

156. iv. VERONICA was born on 17 February 1957 in Philadelphia, Pennsylvania.

+ 157. v. CYNTHIA, born 12 November 1958 in Philadelphia, Pennsylvania; married **William Boyer.**

100. NANCY^5 **TRAWICK** (*Tom*^{4}, *Dock*^{3}, *Samuel*^{2}, *Mr.*^{1}).

Children of **Nancy**^{5} **Trawick** include:

+ 158. i. RHONDA^6

101. VIVIAN 'TUET'^{5} **TRAWICK** (*Tom*^{4}, *Dock*^{3}, *Samuel*^{2}, *Mr.*^{1}) was born on 29 September 1926 in Philadelphia, Pennsylvania.

Children of **Vivian 'Tuet'**^{5} **Trawick** include:

159. i. VIVIAN^6.

160. ii. GREGORY.

161. iii. ANTHONY.

162. iv. GAIL.
163. v. GERALDINE.
164. vi. NANCY.

103. THOMAS^5 TRAWICK (*Tom^4, Dock^3, Samuel^2, Mr.^{1}*).

Children of Thomas^5 Trawick include:
165. i. RALPH^6.

106. ADAM^5 RENFROE (*Laura^4 Trawick, Dock^3, Samuel^2, Mr.^{1}*) was born on 27 January 1916 in Sandersville, Washington County, Georgia. He married Athele 'Jacy' Maxwell. He died on 5 September 1996 in Philadelphia, Pennsylvania, at age 80.

Children of Adam^5 Renfroe and Athele 'Jacy' Maxwell were as follows:
166. i. ADAM 'RENNY'^{6} JR..
167. ii. KEITH.
+ 168. iii. PATRICIA 'PATTY', married Chaka Fattah.

108. EVALENE^5 RENFROE (*Laura^4 Trawick, Dock^3, Samuel^2, Mr.^{1}*) married W. Louis Hodges.

Children of Evalene^5 Renfroe and W. Louis Hodges were as follows:
169. i. GENE^6 married Janice (—?—).
170. ii. EDITH.
171. iii. WILLIE.
172. iv. W. LOUIS (II).
173. v. KENYA.

109. JOHNNIE DARK^5 RENFROE (*Laura^4 Trawick, Dock^3, Samuel^2, Mr.^{1}*) was born on 1 April 1922 in Sandersville, Georgia. He married Mae Will Williams, daughter of Lee Williams and Mae Will Rogers, on 31 December 1943 in Philadelphia, Pennsylvania.

Children of Johnnie Dark^5 Renfroe and Mae Will Williams were as follows:
+ 174. i. CAROLINE^6, born 7 July 1943 in Detroit, Michigan; married William Johnson.
175. ii. JOHNNIE DARK JR. was born on 31 January 1945 in Detroit, Michigan.
+ 176. iii. PEGGY, born 4 November 1946 in Detroit, Michigan; married Bobby Walton.
+ 177. iv. HAROLD, born 28 August 1947 in Detroit, Michigan; married Catherine Lynch.
178. v. OSCAR LEE was born on 11 September 1966 in Detroit, Michigan.

118. JULIA INEZ^5 TRAWICK (*Dock 'Whale*^{4}, *Dock*^{3}, *Samuel*^{2}, *Mr.*^{1}) was born on 24 January 1920. She married **Sidney C. Butts**, son of **Milas Butts (Sr.)** and **Roeanor Dawson**.

Children of **Julia Inez**^{5} **Trawick** and **Sidney C. Butts** were as follows:
+ 179. i. CHESTER^6, born 13 September 1938; married **Joan Holmes**; married **Anna Gray**.
+ 180. ii. JANICE, born 18 October 1940; married **William Williams (Sr.)**; married **James Rogers**; married **Edward Davis**.
+ 181. iii. ROZEINE, born 5 December 1942; married **Anthony Armstrong**; married **Robert Ruckey**; married **Walter Wyatt**.
+ 182. iv. CURTIS, born 18 December 1943; married **Thelma Lamar**.
183. v. KENNETH was born on 27 February 1950. He married **Rochelle McLaurin**.
184. vi. SIDNEY ALLEN was born on 27 February 1955.

120. MAMYE DOROTHY 'MARY'^{5} TRAWICK (*Dock 'Whale*^{4}, *Dock*^{3}, *Samuel*^{2}, *Mr.*^{1}) was born on 16 January 1925. She married **Bob Willis Butts**, son of **Milas Butts (Sr.)** and **Roeanor Dawson**.

Children of **Mamye Dorothy 'Mary'**^{5} **Trawick** and **Bob Willis Butts** were as follows:
+ 185. i. DELORES^6, born 3 January 1942; married **Edward Smithwick**.
+ 186. ii. DORIS, born 4 July 1944; married **John Alcorn**.
+ 187. iii. GWENDOLYN 'GWEN', born 12 August 1945; married **Gene Holliway**.
+ 188. iv. OLIVIA, born 21 May 1950; married **Bernard Hines**.

121. JUANITA EASTER MAE^5 TRAWICK (*Dock 'Whale*^{4}, *Dock*^{3}, *Samuel*^{2}, *Mr.*^{1}) married **Cleophus Crumbly**. She married **Mr. Elliott**.

Children of **Juanita Easter Mae**^{5} **Trawick** and **Cleophus Crumbly** were:
189. i. EDGAR^6.

There were no children of **Juanita Easter Mae**^{5} **Trawick** and **Mr. Elliott**.

Generation Six

124. MITCHELL^6 HOOKS (*Henrietta*^{5}*Cheeves*, *Clara Bell*^{4}*Trawick*, *Joseph 'Joe*^{3}, *Jack 'John*^{2}, *Mr.*^{1}) was born on 7 March 1933 in Sandersville, Georgia. He married **Delores Hooks**, daughter of **Robert J. Hooks Jr.** and **Carrie B. Lawson**.

Children of **Mitchell**^{6} **Hooks** include:
190. i. SARAH D.^{7}.

Children of **Mitchell⁶ Hooks** and **Delores Hooks** were as follows:
+ 191.   i. MICHAEL D.⁷, born 25 December 1956; married **Carol Anderson.**
  192. ii. RHONDA was born on 17 January 1958. She married **George Ashison.**
  193. iii. MONICA was born on 26 August 1970.

125. CHEEVES⁶ HOOKS (*Henrietta⁵ Cheeves, Clara Bell⁴ Trawick, Joseph 'Joe³, Jack 'John²,*
  Mr.¹) was born on 4 April 1935 in Washington County, Georgia. He married
  Myrtistine Cullens on 11 May 1958 in Washington County, Georgia. He died
  on 17 February 1997 in Milledgeville, Baldwin County, Georgia, at age 61.

Children of **Cheeves⁶ Hooks** and **Myrtistine Cullens** were as follows:
+ 194.   i. ROSALIND LINETTE⁷, born 4 January 1959; married **Thomas Victor Brown.**
  195. ii. CHARLES ANDRIE was born on 16 November 1961.
  196. iii. TRACY CHEEVES was born on 14 November 1964.

127. MARION⁶ HOOKS (*Henrietta⁵ Cheeves, Clara Bell⁴ Trawick, Joseph 'Joe³, Jack 'John²,*
  Mr.¹) was born on 1 July 1940 in Sandersville, Georgia. He married **Annie** (———).
  He married **Christine** (—?—).

Children of **Marion⁶ Hooks** and **Annie** (———) were as follows:
  197.   i. MAXINE⁷.
  198. ii. MARVIN S..
  199. iii. QUILLIAN E..
  200. iv. CHARLES T..

There were no children of **Marion⁶ Hooks** and **Christine** (—?—).

128. ORALENE⁶ HOOKS (*Henrietta⁵ Cheeves, Clara Bell⁴ Trawick, Joseph 'Joe³, Jack*
  'John², Mr.¹) was born on 4 April 1943 in Sandersville, Georgia. She married
  Frank Pierce on 25 December 1962 in Sandersville, Georgia.

Children of **Oralene⁶ Hooks** and **Frank Pierce** were as follows:
  201.   i. RAYNELL TYSON⁷ was born on 10 March 1963 in Sandersville, Georgia.
+ 202. ii. PATRICE ISLENE, born 25 January 1966 in New Haven, Connecticut; married
  Nathaniel Balkcom III.
  203. iii. FRANK MYRON was born on 1 October 1973 in New Haven, Connecticut.

129. ZELMA⁶ SHENOSTER (*Mattie Lou⁵ Cheeves, Clara Bell⁴ Trawick, Joseph 'Joe³, Jack*
  'John², Mr.¹) was born on 10 January 1932 in Sandersville, Georgia.

Children of **Zelma**^{6} **Shenoster** and **Ennis Carter** were:
204.   i. DONALD 'DUCK'^{7} was born on 29 September 1948 in Philadelphia, Pennsylvania. He died on 29 June 2001 in Philadelphia, Pennsylvania, at age 52.

Children of **Zelma**^{6} **Shenoster** and **Rufus Hall** were:
+ 205.   i. SAUNDRA ERICKA^7, born 30 June 1950 in Philadelphia, Pennsylvania.

Children of **Zelma**^{6} **Shenoster** and **Jesse James McLean** were as follows:
+ 206.   i. ANTHONY^7, born 27 November 1958 in Philadelphia, Pennsylvania; married **Linda Star Woodson.**
+ 207.   ii. JESSE JAMES (JR.), born 5 October 1960 in Philadelphia, Pennsylvania; married **Antoinette Coto.**

130. **KATHERINE**^{6} **SHENOSTER** (*Mattie Lou*^{5}*Cheeves, Clara Bell*^{4}*Trawick, Joseph 'Joe*^{3}, *Jack 'John*^{2}, *Mr.*^{1}) was born on 19 April 1934 in Milledgeville, Georgia. She married **John Benjamin Douglass (Sr.)** on 7 February 1959 in Maryland.

Children of **Katherine**^{6} **Shenoster** and **John Benjamin Douglass (Sr.)** were as follows:
208.   i. CAROL LYNNE^7 was born on 1 May 1962 in Philadelphia, Pennsylvania.
+ 209.   ii. JOHN BENJAMIN (JR.), born 4 April 1965 in Philadelphia, Pennsylvania; married **Tykeia Giles.**

131. **MIRIAM**^{6} **CHEEVES** (*Henry Holmes*^{5}, *Clara Bell*^{4}*Trawick, Joseph 'Joe*^{3}, *Jack 'John*^{2}, *Mr.*^{1}) was born in Sandersville, Washington County, Georgia

Children of **Miriam**^{6} **Cheeves** include:
210.   i. CLARA BELLE^7 was born on 2 February 1979 in Tacoma, Washington.

132. **GLORIA**^{6} **CHEEVES** (*Henry Holmes*^{5}, *Clara Bell*^{4}*Trawick, Joseph 'Joe*^{3}, *Jack 'John*^{2}, *Mr.*^{1}) was born on 4 July 1941 in Sandersville, Washington County, Georgia. She married **Charles Graham.**

Children of **Gloria**^{6} **Cheeves** and **Charles Graham** were as follows:
+ 211.   i. CHARLES DAVID^7, born 20 May 1969 in Philadelphia, Pennsylvania; married **Lorrie Hatten.**
+ 212.   ii. MELISSA AVA, born 21 April 1970 in Philadelphia, Pennsylvania.
213.   iii. JENNIFER ANNETTE was born on 21 February 1979 in Philadelphia, Pennsylvania.

133. **HORACE**^{6} **CHEEVES** (*Henry Holmes*^{5}, *Clara Bell*^{4}*Trawick, Joseph 'Joe*^{3}, *Jack 'John*^{2}, *Mr.*^{1}) was born on 4 September 1943 in Sandersville, Washington County, Georgia. He married **Fannie Pearl Williams**, daughter of **Coleman Williams** and **Florence Rogers**, on 6 July 1971 in Philadelphia, Pennsylvania.

Children of **Horace**[6] **Cheeves** and **Fannie Pearl Williams** were:

214. i. **DENISE NICOLE**[7] was born on 20 February 1972 in Philadelphia, Pennsylvania.

134. FOREST[6] **CHEEVES** (*Henry Holmes*[5], *Clara Bell*[4] *Trawick, Joseph 'Joe*[3], *Jack 'John*[2], *Mr.*[1]) was born on 4 September 1943 in Sandersville, Washington County, Georgia. He married **Karen Kennedy** in Philadelphia, Pennsylvania. He died on 27 March 1987 in Detroit, Michigan, at age 43.

Children of **Forest**[6] **Cheeves** and **Karen Kennedy** were as follows:

+ 215. i. **BARRY STEVEN**[7], born 29 June 1960 in Philadelphia, Pennsylvania; married **Andrea Benita 'Nita' Hyden.**

+ 216. ii. **FORREST TROY**, born 22 February 1962 in Philadelphia, Pennsylvania.

+ 217. iii. **DARNELL FRANK**, born 17 February 1963 in Philadelphia, Pennsylvania; married **Diana 'Ann' Marie Johnson;** married **Pat Young.**

+ 218. iv. **BRUCE KENNETH**, born 12 May 1964 in Philadelphia, Pennsylvania; married **Audrey Miree.**

138. FRANK[6] **HOOKS** (*Joe*[5], *Kizzie*[4] *Trawick, Dock*[3], *Samuel*[2], *Mr.*[1]) married **Bertha** (———).

Children of **Frank**[6] **Hooks** and **Bertha** (———) were as follows:

219. i. **GERALD**[7].

220. ii. **JOSEPH.**

221. iii. **CHARLIE.**

140. JEAN[6] **SMITH** (*James Beryl 'Buddy*[5], *Texann*[4] *Trawick, Dock*[3], *Samuel*[2], *Mr.*[1]) was born on 7 August 1934 in Philadelphia, Pennsylvania. She married **Arnold Dixon Jackson Sr.** on 23 September 1961 in Philadelphia, Pennsylvania.

Children of **Jean**[6] **Smith** and **Arnold Dixon Jackson Sr.** were as follows:

222. i. **LISA**[7] was born on 24 April 1962 in Philadelphia, Pennsylvania.

223. ii. **ARNOLD JR.** was born on 4 December 1963 in Philadelphia, Pennsylvania.

+ 224. iii. **LAURIE**, born 20 March 1965 in Philadelphia, Pennsylvania; married **Mark Darby.**

225. iv. **LYNETTE** was born on 21 November 1969 in Philadelphia, Pennsylvania.

226. v. **LESLIE** was born on 31 December 1970 in Philadelphia, Pennsylvania.

142. EVETTE[6] **SMITH** (*Kenneth Paul*[5], *Texann*[4] *Trawick, Dock*[3], *Samuel*[2], *Mr.*[1]).

Children of **Evette**[6] **Smith** include:

227. i. **FALLON**[7].

228. ii. **PATRELL.**

143. SANDRA CAROL^6 THOMAS (*Eva (Johnny)^5 Trawick, Johnnie^4, Dock^3, Samuel^2, Mr.^{1}*) was born on 31 May 1946 in Philadelphia, Pennsylvania. She married **Herb Connelly** circa 1970 in Philadelphia, Pennsylvania.

Children of **Sandra Carol^6 Thomas** and **Herb Connelly** were as follows:
229.   i. KEISHA^7 was born on 13 March 1971 in Philadelphia, Pennsylvania.
+ 230.   ii. KEIA, born 13 March 1971 in Philadelphia, Pennsylvania.

144. SIGRID ANN^6 THOMAS (*Eva (Johnny)^5 Trawick, Johnnie^4, Dock^3, Samuel^2, Mr.^{1}*) was born on 10 March 1948 in Philadelphia, Pennsylvania. She was born on 10 March 1948 in Philadelphia, Pennsylvania. She married **Howard Edward McCall Jr.** on 30 January 1971 in Philadelphia, Pennsylvania.

Children of **Sigrid Ann^6 Thomas** and **Howard Edward McCall Jr.** were as follows:
231.   i. MARK ANTHONY^7 was born on 25 August 1971 in Philadelphia, Pennsylvania.
232.   ii. KEITH HOWARD was born on 15 June 1974 in Philadelphia, Pennsylvania.

145. WANDA EILEEN^6 THOMAS (*Eva (Johnny)^5 Trawick, Johnnie^4, Dock^3, Samuel^2, Mr.^{1}*) was born on 12 April 1950 in Philadelphia, Pennsylvania. She married **John 'Donald' Bird** in Philadelphia, Pennsylvania.

Children of **Wanda Eileen^6 Thomas** and **John 'Donald' Bird** were:
233.   i. HEATHER^7 was born on 27 December 1981 in Philadelphia, Pennsylvania.

147. ALTON^6 TRAWICK (*John^5, Elisha^4, Dock^3, Samuel^2, Mr.^{1}*) was born on 18 January 1949 in Sandersville, Georgia. He married **Joanne Washington** on 21 September 1974 in Atlanta, Georgia.

Children of **Alton^6 Trawick** and **Joanne Washington** were:
234.   i. BRANDON ALTUS^7 was born on 8 January 1978 in Rochester, New York.

150. CATHY ANN^6 TRAWICK (*John^5, Elisha^4, Dock^3, Samuel^2, Mr.^{1}*) was born on 3 January 1955 in Sandersville, Georgia. She married **Leo Suggs** on 29 June 1984 in Elkhart, Indiana.

Children of **Cathy Ann^6 Trawick** and **Leo Suggs** were as follows:
235.   i. LEO DEON^7 was born on 16 October 1986 in Atlanta, Georgia.
236.   ii. INDIA SHARNAE was born on 9 June 1990 in South Bend, Indiana.

152. LYDIA JEAN^6 TRAWICK (*John^5, Elisha^4, Dock^3, Samuel^2, Mr.^{1}*) was born on 3 February 1961 in Sandersville, Georgia. She married **Willie James Woodard**.

Children of **Lydia Jean**[6] **Trawick** and **Willie James Woodard** were as follows:

237.   i. VICTORIA DANIELLE[7] was born on 25 March 1984 in Atlanta, Georgia.
238.   ii. ASHLEY NICOLE was born on 1 November 1987 in Atlanta, Georgia.
239.   iii. WILLIE JAMES JR. was born on 5 August 1991 in Atlanta, Georgia.

154. **BERNARD**[6] **TRAWICK** (*Vernon 'Bud'*[5], *Tom*[4], *Dock*[3], *Samuel*[2], *Mr.*[1]) was born on
     14 December 1951 in Philadelphia, Pennsylvania. He married **Kenya Wilson.**

Children of **Bernard**[6] **Trawick** and **Kenya Wilson** were as follows:
240.   i. TAFT[7] was born on 25 April 1986 in Winston-Salem, North Carolina.
241.   ii. JASON was born on 14 December 1987 in Philadelphia, Pennsylvania.

157. **CYNTHIA**[6] **TRAWICK** (*Vernon 'Bud'*[5], *Tom*[4], *Dock*[3], *Samuel*[2], *Mr.*[1]) was born on
     12 November 1958 in Philadelphia, Pennsylvania. She married **William Boyer.**

Children of **Cynthia**[6] **Trawick** and **William Boyer** were as follows:
242.   i. AJA MARIE[7] was born on 9 June 1982 in Philadelphia, Pennsylvania.
243.   ii. TODD was born on 20 January 1984 in Philadelphia, Pennsylvania.
244.   iii. JENNA DANIELLE was born on 14 August 1989 in Philadelphia, Pennsylvania.
245.   iv. WILLIAM 'BJ' JR. was born on 16 December 1997 in Philadelphia, Pennsylvania.

158. **RHONDA**[6] **TRAWICK** (*Nancy*[5], *Tom*[4], *Dock*[3], *Samuel*[2], *Mr.*[1]).

Children of **Rhonda**[6] **Trawick** include:
246.   i. ROBBIE[7] was born circa 1965.

168. **PATRICIA 'PATTY'**[6] **RENFROE** (*Adam*[5], *Laura*[4] *Trawick*, *Dock*[3], *Samuel*[2], *Mr.*[1])
     married **Chaka Fattah.**

Children of **Patricia 'Patty'**[6] **Renfroe** and **Chaka Fattah** were:
247.   i. CHRISTIAN[7].

174. **CAROLINE**[6] **RENFROE** (*Johnnie Dark*[5], *Laura*[4] *Trawick*, *Dock*[3], *Samuel*[2], *Mr.*[1])
     was born on 7 July 1943 in Detroit, Michigan. She married **William Johnson.**

Children of **Caroline**[6] **Renfroe** and **William Johnson** were as follows:
248.   i. RENITA[7] was born on 18 July 1962 in Detroit, Michigan.
249.   ii. WILLIAM JR. was born on 4 August 1964 in Detroit, Michigan.

176. **PEGGY**[6] **RENFROE** (*Johnnie Dark*[5], *Laura*[4] *Trawick*, *Dock*[3], *Samuel*[2], *Mr.*[1]) was
     born on 4 November 1946 in Detroit, Michigan. She married **Bobby Walton.**

Children of **Peggy⁶ Renfroe** and **Bobby Walton** were as follows:
+ 250.   i. LASHAY⁷, born 30 April 1967 in Detroit, Michigan.
  251.   ii. MARY LATRICE was born on 27 July 1972 in Detroit, Michigan.

177. HAROLD⁶ RENFROE (*Johnnie Dark⁵, Laura⁴ Trawick, Dock³, Samuel², Mr.¹*) was born on 28 August 1947 in Detroit, Michigan. He married **Catherine Lynch** on 11 March in Detroit, Michigan.

Children of **Harold⁶ Renfroe** and **Catherine Lynch** were as follows:
  252.   i. HAROLD⁷ JR. was born on 7 July 1968 in Detroit, Michigan.
  253.   ii. DION was born in 1981 in Detroit, Michigan.
  254.   iii. NATHAN was born in December 1982 in Detroit, Michigan.

179. CHESTER⁶ BUTTS (*Julia Inez⁵ Trawick, Dock 'Whale⁴, Dock³, Samuel², Mr.¹*) was born on 13 September 1938. He married **Joan Holmes**. He married **Anna Gray.**

Children of **Chester⁶ Butts** and **Joan Holmes** were as follows:
+ 255.   i. EDDIE HOLMES⁷, born 4 October 1954; married **Shirley Holmes**; married **Zina Holmes.**
+ 256.   ii. CURTIS, born 27 April 1966; married **Sheila** (———); married **Crystle** (———).
  257.   iii. KEVIN was born on 4 April 1967.
+ 258.   iv. DARYL, born 19 July 1968; married **Nichelle** (———).
  259.   v. DARNELL was born on 3 March 1970.

Children of **Chester⁶ Butts** and **Anna Gray** were:
  260.   i. YALONDA⁷ was born on 16 April 1970.

180. JANICE⁶ BUTTS (*Julia Inez⁵ Trawick, Dock 'Whale⁴, Dock³, Samuel², Mr.¹*) was born on 18 October 1940. She married **Edward Davis**. She married **William Williams (Sr.)**. She married **James Rogers**. She died on 10 September 1989 at age 48.

Children of **Janice⁶ Butts** and **William Williams (Sr.)** were as follows:
+ 261.   i. WILLIAM⁷ (JR.), born 19 January 1958.
+ 262.   ii. KENNETH 'HUCKY', born 13 July 1960; married **Sylvita Barbour**; married **Deborah Lynn** (———).
+ 263.   iii. HERRELL A., born 23 May 1967; married **Stephanie Y Anderson**; married **Nadine Jackson.**
+ 264.   iv. ALONZO LONNIE, born 2 August 1969.
  265.   v. TYNEEK was born on 23 April 1976.

There were no children of **Janice⁶ Butts** and **James Rogers**.

There were no children of **Janice**[6] **Butts** and **Edward Davis**.

181. ROZEINE[6] **BUTTS** (*Julia Inez*[5] *Trawick, Dock 'Whale*[4], *Dock*[3], *Samuel*[2], *Mr.*[1]) was born on 5 December 1942. She married **Anthony Armstrong**. She married **Robert Ruckey**. She married **Walter Wyatt**.

Children of **Rozeine**[6] **Butts** and **Anthony Armstrong** were:
266.   i. SEAN[7] was born on 15 November 1967.

Children of **Rozeine**[6] **Butts** and **Robert Ruckey** were:
267.   i. ROBERT[7] was born on 11 January 1969.

Children of **Rozeine**[6] **Butts** and **Walter Wyatt** were:
268.   i. JUNITA[7] was born on 7 July 1975.

182. CURTIS[6] **BUTTS** (*Julia Inez*[5] *Trawick, Dock 'Whale*[4], *Dock*[3], *Samuel*[2], *Mr.*[1]) was born on 18 December 1943. He married **Thelma Lamar**.

Children of **Curtis**[6] **Butts** and **Thelma Lamar** were as follows:
269.   i. DANIELLE MARIE[7] was born on 31 May 1969.
270.   ii. LAMAR CRAIGE was born on 1 October 1970.
271.   iii. LAMONTE DAWSON was born on 2 May 1974.
272.   iv. BRANDEN LAVAR was born on 2 July 1978.

185. DELORES[6] **BUTTS** (*Mamye Dorothy 'Mary*[5] *Trawick, Dock 'Whale*[4], *Dock*[3], *Samuel*[2], *Mr.*[1]) was born on 3 January 1942. She married **Edward Smithwick**.

Children of **Delores**[6] **Butts** and **Edward Smithwick** were as follows:
273.   i. DERON[7] was born on 19 July 1965.
274.   ii. DEAN was born on 24 January 1968.
275.   iii. DENENA was born on 14 September 1970.

186. DORIS[6] **BUTTS** (*Mamye Dorothy 'Mary*[5] *Trawick, Dock 'Whale*[4], *Dock*[3], *Samuel*[2], *Mr.*[1]) was born on 4 July 1944. She married **John Alcorn**.

Children of **Doris**[6] **Butts** and **John Alcorn** were as follows:
+ 276.   i. SABRINA LYNN[7], born 5 February 1967; married **Derrick Girard McCann (Sr.)**.
277.   ii. DARLA RAE was born on 13 March 1970.
278.   iii. ROOSEVELT.

187. GWENDOLYN 'GWEN'[6] **BUTTS** (*Mamye Dorothy 'Mary*[5] *Trawick, Dock 'Whale*[4], *Dock*[3], *Samuel*[2], *Mr.*[1]) was born on 12 August 1945. She married **Gene Holliway**.

Children of **Gwendolyn 'Gwen'**^{6} **Butts** and **Gene Holliway** were as follows:
+ 279.   i. TANYA^7, born 9 February 1964; married **Todd Bell**.
  280.   ii. TERRANCE 'TERRY' was born on 31 July 1968.

188. OLIVIA^6 BUTTS (*Mamye Dorothy 'Mary'^{5} Trawick, Dock 'Whale'^{4}, Dock^3, Samuel^2, Mr.^{1}*) was born on 21 May 1950. She married **Bernard Hines**.

Children of **Olivia^6 Butts** and **Bernard Hines** were as follows:
  281.   i. COURTLAND^7 was born on 27 July 1970.
  282.   ii. ARIC was born on 2 January 1975.

Generation Seven

191. MICHAEL D.^{7} HOOKS (*Mitchell^6, Henrietta^5 Cheeves, Clara Bell^4 Trawick, Joseph 'Joe'^{3}, Jack 'John'^{2}, Mr.^{1}*) was born on 25 December 1956. He married **Carol Anderson**.

Children of **Michael D.^{7} Hooks** and **Carol Anderson** were:
  283.   i. KIRA LYNN^8.

194. ROSALIND LINETTE^7 HOOKS (*Cheeves^6, Henrietta^5 Cheeves, Clara Bell^4 Trawick, Joseph 'Joe'^{3}, Jack 'John'^{2}, Mr.^{1}*) was born on 4 January 1959. She married **Thomas Victor Brown**.

Children of **Rosalind Linette^7 Hooks** and **Thomas Victor Brown** were:
  284.   i. CAMILLE VICTORIA^8.

202. PATRICE ISLENE^7 PIERCE (*Oralene^6 Hooks, Henrietta^5 Cheeves, Clara Bell^4 Trawick, Joseph 'Joe'^{3}, Jack 'John'^{2}, Mr.^{1}*) was born on 25 January 1966 in New Haven, Connecticut. She married **Nathaniel Balkcom III** on 11 March 1988 in Sandersville, Georgia.

Children of **Patrice Islene^7 Pierce** and **Teddy Butler** were:
  285.   i. KRISTEN JANA'^{8} was born on 22 September 1986 in Augusta, Georgia.

Children of **Patrice Islene^7 Pierce** and **Nathaniel Balkcom III** were:
  286.   i. NICHOLAS NATHANIEL^8 was born on 13 March 1998 in Georgia.

205. SAUNDRA ERICKA^7 SHENOSTER (*Zelma^6, Mattie Lou^5 Cheeves, Clara Bell^4 Trawick, Joseph 'Joe'^{3}, Jack 'John'^{2}, Mr.^{1}*) was born on 30 June 1950 in Philadelphia, Pennsylvania. She died in December 1985 in Philadelphia, Pennsylvania, at age 35.

Children of **Saundra Ericka^7 Shenoster** include:

287.   i. DONALD DANTE'^{8} was born on 26 November 1967 in Philadelphia, Pennsylvania.

288.   ii. MICHAEL LAMONT was born on 9 July 1974 in Philadelphia, Pennsylvania.

Children of **Saundra Ericka^7 Shenoster** and **Barry Hilton** were:

289.   i. BARRY ANTHONY^8 was born on 17 July 1969 in Philadelphia, Pennsylvania.

206. ANTHONY^7 MCLEAN (*Zelma^{6}Shenoster, Mattie Lou^{5}Cheeves, Clara Bell^{4}Trawick, Joseph 'Joe^3, Jack 'John^2, Mr.^{1}*) was born on 27 November 1958 in Philadelphia, Pennsylvania. He married **Linda Star Woodson** on 18 June 1994 in Philadelphia, Pennsylvania.

Children of **Anthony^7 McLean** and **Gwendolyn Carmella Bond** were:

290.   i. NACHE' ANTOINETTE^8 was born on 12 June 1988 in Philadelphia, Pennsylvania.

There were no children of **Anthony^7 McLean** and **Linda Star Woodson**.

207. JESSE JAMES^7 MCLEAN (JR.) (*Zelma^{6}Shenoster, Mattie Lou^{5}Cheeves, Clara Bell^{4}Trawick, Joseph 'Joe^3, Jack 'John^2, Mr.^{1}*) was born on 5 October 1960 in Philadelphia, Pennsylvania. He married **Antoinette Coto** on 9 July 1988 in Philadelphia, Pennsylvania.

Children of **Jesse James^7 McLean (Jr.)** and **Antoinette Coto** were:

291.   i. JESSE JAMES^8 (III) was born on 30 March 1986 in Philadelphia, Pennsylvania.

209. JOHN BENJAMIN^7 DOUGLASS (JR.) (*Katherine^{6}Shenoster, Mattie Lou^{5}Cheeves, Clara Bell^{4}Trawick, Joseph 'Joe^3, Jack 'John^2, Mr.^{1}*) was born on 4 April 1965 in Philadelphia, Pennsylvania. He married **Tykeia Giles** in Philadelphia, Pennsylvania.

Children of **John Benjamin^7 Douglass (Jr.)** and **Tykeia Giles** were:

292.   i. SHAUN SHAQUOI^8 was born on 2 October 1992 in Philadelphia, Pennsylvania.

211. CHARLES DAVID^7 GRAHAM (*Gloria^{6}Cheeves, Henry Holmes^5, Clara Bell^{4}Trawick, Joseph 'Joe^3, Jack 'John^2, Mr.^{1}*) was born on 20 May 1969 in Philadelphia, Pennsylvania. He married **Lorrie Hatten** on 5 September 1992 in Philadelphia, Pennsylvania.

Children of **Charles David^7 Graham** include:

293.   i. NOLAN LEWIS PAUL^8 was born on 29 May 1984 in Philadelphia, Pennsylvania.

There were no children of **Charles David^7 Graham** and **Lorrie Hatten**.

212. MELISSA AVA[7] GRAHAM (*Gloria[6]Cheeves, Henry Holmes[5], Clara Bell[4]Trawick, Joseph 'Joe'[3], Jack 'John'[2], Mr.[1]*) was born on 21 April 1970 in Philadelphia, Pennsylvania.

Children of Melissa Ava[7] Graham and Carlos Kinslow were:
294.   i. BRANDON ALEXANDER[8] was born on 28 March 1996 in Philadelphia, Pennsylvania.

215. BARRY STEVEN[7] CHEEVES (*Forest[6], Henry Holmes[5], Clara Bell[4]Trawick, Joseph 'Joe'[3], Jack 'John'[2], Mr.[1]*) was born on 29 June 1960 in Philadelphia, Pennsylvania. He married Andrea Benita 'Nita' Hyden, daughter of Ronald Hyden and Judy Ryder, on 30 April 1988 in Philadelphia, Pennsylvania.

Children of Barry Steven[7] Cheeves and Andrea Benita 'Nita' Hyden were as follows:
+ 295.   i. RASETA NICOLE[8], born 7 May 1982 in Philadelphia, Pennsylvania.
296.   ii. RANIKA MICHELLE was born on 2 February 1990 in Philadelphia, Pennsylvania.

Children of Barry Steven[7] Cheeves and Diane Johnson were:
297.   i. BARRY STEVEN[8] JR. was born on 25 August 1996 in Philadelphia, Pennsylvania.

216. FORREST TROY[7] CHEEVES (*Forest[6], Henry Holmes[5], Clara Bell[4]Trawick, Joseph 'Joe'[3], Jack 'John'[2], Mr.[1]*) was born on 22 February 1962 in Philadelphia, Pennsylvania.

Children of Forrest Troy[7] Cheeves and Sue Wilson were as follows:
298.   i. FORREST TROY[8] JR. was born on 30 March 1988 in Philadelphia, Pennsylvania.
299.   ii. ALEXANDER DOMINIC was born on 19 May 1989 in Philadelphia, Pennsylvania.

217. DARNELL FRANK[7] CHEEVES (*Forest[6], Henry Holmes[5], Clara Bell[4]Trawick, Joseph 'Joe'[3], Jack 'John'[2], Mr.[1]*) was born on 17 February 1963 in Philadelphia, Pennsylvania. He married Diana 'Ann' Marie Johnson. He married Pat Young on 19 December 1997 in Philadelphia, Pennsylvania.

Children of Darnell Frank[7] Cheeves and Diana 'Ann' Marie Johnson were as follows:
300.   i. SHANAY LANELL[8] was born on 30 October 1985 in Philadelphia, Pennsylvania.
301.   ii. SHEENA MONIQUE was born on 5 November 1989 in Philadelphia, Pennsylvania.

Children of Darnell Frank[7] Cheeves and Pat Young were:
302.   i. DARNELL FRANK[8] (JR.) was born on 20 March 1993 in Philadelphia, Pennsylvania.

218. BRUCE KENNETH[7] **CHEEVES** (*Forest*[6], *Henry Holmes*[5], *Clara Bell*[4]*Trawick, Joseph 'Joe'*[3], *Jack 'John'*[2], *Mr.*[1]) was born on 12 May 1964 in Philadelphia, Pennsylvania. He married **Audrey Miree** on 17 July 1998 in Philadelphia, Pennsylvania.

Children of **Bruce Kenneth**[7] **Cheeves** and **Audrey Miree** were as follows:

303.   i. BRUCE KENNETH[8] (JR.) was born on 24 October 1989 in Philadelphia, Pennsylvania.

304.   ii. KAREN was born on 13 July 1991 in Philadelphia, Pennsylvania.

224. LAURIE[7] **JACKSON** (*Jean*[6]*Smith, James Beryl 'Buddy'*[5], *Texann*[4]*Trawick, Dock*[3], *Samuel*[2], *Mr.*[1]) was born on 20 March 1965 in Philadelphia, Pennsylvania. She married **Mark Darby**.

Children of **Laurie**[7] **Jackson** and **Mark Darby** were as follows:

305.   i. MYAH[8].

306.   ii. DEENA.

230. KEIA[7] **CONNELLY** (*Sandra Carol*[6]*Thomas, Eva (Johnny)*[5]*Trawick, Johnnie*[4], *Dock*[3], *Samuel*[2], *Mr.*[1]) was born on 13 March 1971 in Philadelphia, Pennsylvania.

Children of **Keia**[7] **Connelly** and **Rob Baker** were:

307.   i. HANNAH[8] was born on 5 January 1997 in Philadelphia, Pennsylvania.

250. LASHAY[7] **WALTON** (*Peggy*[6]*Renfroe, Johnnie Dark*[5], *Laura*[4]*Trawick, Dock*[3], *Samuel*[2], *Mr.*[1]) was born on 30 April 1967 in Detroit, Michigan.

Children of **Lashay**[7] **Walton** and **Byron** (—?—) were:

308.   i. BYRON[8] was born on 17 July 1985 in Detroit, Michigan.

255. EDDIE HOLMES[7] **BUTTS** (*Chester*[6], *Julia Inez*[5]*Trawick, Dock 'Whale'*[4], *Dock*[3], *Samuel*[2], *Mr.*[1]) was born on 4 October 1954. He married **Shirley Holmes**. He married **Zina Holmes**.

Children of **Eddie Holmes**[7] **Butts** and **Shirley Holmes** were:

309.   i. TAMIKA[8] was born on 3 March 1974.

Children of **Eddie Holmes**[7] **Butts** and **Zina Holmes** were:

310.   i. ASHLEY[8] was born on 13 June 1987.

256. CURTIS[7] **BUTTS** (*Chester*[6], *Julia Inez*[5]*Trawick, Dock 'Whale'*[4], *Dock*[3], *Samuel*[2], *Mr.*[1]) was born on 27 April 1966. He married **Sheila** (———). He married **Crystle** (———).

Children of **Curtis**[7] **Butts** and **Sheila** (———) were:
311.   i. BRYON[8] was born on 14 September 1987.

Children of **Curtis**[7] **Butts** and **Crystle** (———) were:
312.   i. CHRISTIA[8] was born on 31 October 1985.

258. **DARYL**[7] **BUTTS** (*Chester*[6], *Julia Inez*[5] *Trawick, Dock 'Whale*[4], *Dock*[3], *Samuel*[2], *Mr.*[1]) was born on 19 July 1968. He married **Nichelle** (———).

Children of **Daryl**[7] **Butts** and **Nichelle** (———) were:
313.   i. SHAUNICE[8] was born on 24 August 1985.

261. **WILLIAM**[7] **WILLIAMS (JR.)** (*Janice*[6] *Butts, Julia Inez*[5] *Trawick, Dock 'Whale*[4], *Dock*[3], *Samuel*[2], *Mr.*[1]) was born on 19 January 1958.

Children of **William**[7] **Williams (Jr.)** include:
314.   i. LATICHIA[8].

262. **KENNETH 'HUCKY'**[7] **WILLIAMS** (*Janice*[6] *Butts, Julia Inez*[5] *Trawick, Dock 'Whale*[4], *Dock*[3], *Samuel*[2], *Mr.*[1]) was born on 13 July 1960. He married **Sylvita Barbour**. He married **Deborah Lynn** (———).

Children of **Kenneth 'Hucky'**[7] **Williams** and **Sylvita Barbour** were:
315.   i. KINETA[8] was born on 12 February 1977.

Children of **Kenneth 'Hucky'**[7] **Williams** and **Deborah Lynn** (———) were as follows:
316.   i. RAHEEM ANTHONY[8] was born on 13 July 1980.
317.   ii. LATOYA DENISE was born on 6 March 1981.
318.   iii. KENNETH JAMELL was born on 3 March 1982.

263. **HERRELL A.**[7] **WILLIAMS** (*Janice*[6] *Butts, Julia Inez*[5] *Trawick, Dock 'Whale*[4], *Dock*[3], *Samuel*[2], *Mr.*[1]) was born on 23 May 1967. He married **Stephanie Y. Anderson**. He married **Nadine Jackson**.

Children of **Herrell A.**[7] **Williams** and **Stephanie Y. Anderson** were:
319.   i. KIAUNA YVONNE[8] was born on 28 May 1985.

Children of **Herrell A.**[7] **Williams** and **Nadine Jackson** were:
320.   i. SHERRELL VIOLA[8] was born on 4 April 1989.

264. **ALONZO LONNIE**[7] **WILLIAMS** (*Janice*[6] *Butts, Julia Inez*[5] *Trawick, Dock 'Whale*[4], *Dock*[3], *Samuel*[2], *Mr.*[1]) was born on 2 August 1969.

Children of **Alonzo Lonnie**^{7} **Williams** and **Trina Straike** were:
321.   i. TRANIKA^8 was born on 9 March 1987.

Children of **Alonzo Lonnie**^{7} **Williams** and **Nicole King** were:
322.   i. NATASHA^8 was born on 20 November 1987.

Children of **Alonzo Lonnie**^{7} **Williams** and **Barbara M. Rock** were:
323.   i. ALONZO ALLEN ROCK^8 was born on 21 April 1989.

276. **SABRINA LYNN**^{7} **ALCORN** (*Doris*^{6}*Butts, Mamye Dorothy 'Mary*^{5} *Trawick, Dock 'Whale*^{4}*, Dock*^{3}*, Samuel*^{2}*, Mr.*^{1}) was born on 5 February 1967. She married **Derrick Girard McCann (Sr.)**.

Children of **Sabrina Lynn**^{7} **Alcorn** and **Derrick Girard McCann (Sr.)** were:
324.   i. DERRICK GIRARD^8 (JR.) was born on 4 May 1990.

279. **TANYA**^{7} **HOLLIWAY** (*Gwendolyn 'Gwen*^{6}*Butts, Mamye Dorothy 'Mary*^{5} *Trawick, Dock 'Whale*^{4}*, Dock*^{3}*, Samuel*^{2}*, Mr.*^{1}) was born on 9 February 1964. She married **Todd Bell**.

Children of **Tanya**^{7} **Holliway** include:
325.   i. T J^8 was born circa 1990.
326.   ii. TIANA was born circa 1990.

Children of **Tanya**^{7} **Holliway** and **Todd Bell** were as follows:
327.   i. TIFFANY^8 was born on 31 August 1983.
328.   ii. TODD (JR.) was born on 26 February 1985.

Generation Eight

295. **RASETA NICOLE**^{8} **CHEEVES** (*Barry Steven*^{7}*, Forest*^{6}*, Henry Holmes*^{5}*, Clara Bell*^{4}*Trawick, Joseph 'Joe*^{3}*, Jack 'John*^{2}*, Mr.*^{1}) was born on 7 May 1982 in Philadelphia, Pennsylvania.

Children of **Raseta Nicole**^{8} **Cheeves** and **James Kennedy** were:
329.   i. NICHOLAS SEMAJ^9 was born on 6 March 2001 in Philadelphia, Pennsylvania.

Descendants of Jim Gordy

304

Berry Gordy, 1920 Census

Georgia
Washington County
In the Ordinary of said County.
The petition of Berry Gordy, shows that he
is a citizen of said County and the head of
a family consisting of his wife Lucy Gordy
36 years old, and six minor children to wit
Lula Gordy 14 years old, Esther Gordy 12 ye
old, Mamie Gordy 6 years old, Berry Gordy
5 years old, Lucy Gordy 4 years old, and bo
aged 18 months, and that he desires a Homeste
and exemption of personalty in his property se
apart for his minor children under Section 2
of the Code.
And your petitioner further shows that Sched
a. hereto attached and made part of this
application embraces the property he desires so
set apart.

his
Berry + Gordy
mark

Attest. W. F. Robson

Schedule "a,
One single horse wagon   valued $30.00

Petition of Berry Gordy

Descendants of Jim Gordy

Generation One

1. **JIM** *1* **GORDY**; Jim Gordy was a white plantation owner. Esther Johnson was an enslaved Black woman on the plantation.

Children of **Jim** *1* **Gordy** and **Esther Johnson** were:
+   2.   i. BERRY *2* SR., married **Lucy Hellum**.

Generation Two

2. **BERRY** *2* **GORDY SR.** (*Jim* *1*); Freed from slavery when he was a child. He was raised on a farm outside Oconee now known as Gordy Church area. He married **Lucy Hellum** in Washington County, Georgia. They had twenty-three children; all but nine died before adulthood.

Children of **Berry** *2* **Gordy Sr.** and **Lucy Hellum** were as follows:
     3.   i. MAMIE *3* was born in Sandersville, Washington County, Georgia.
+   4.   ii. JOHN, born in Sandersville, Georgia; married **Mamie Hooks**.
     5.   iii. LULA was born in Sandersville, Washington County, Georgia. She married **Morgan Butts** in Sandersville, Georgia.
+   6.   iv. CHARLIE, born in Washington County, Georgia; married **Pearl Bouyer**.
+   7.   v. BERRY 'POP' JR., married **Bertha Fuller**.
+   8.   vi. JOSEPH 'JOE', married **Lee Alice Reese**.
+   9.   vii. SAMUEL 'SAM', born 1878 in Washington County, Georgia; married **Carrie Cheeves**.
+   10.   viii. EASTER, born circa 1883 in Georgia; married **Jeff Carter Sr.**
+   11.   ix. LUCY 'NIG', born 10 April 1896 in Sandersville, Washington County, Georgia; married **Albert Butts**; married **Mark Lane Wood**.

Generation Three

4. **JOHN** *3* **GAUDY** (*Berry* *2* *Gordy, Jim* *1*) was born in Sandersville, Georgia. He married **Mamie Hooks**, daughter of **Robert Hooks Sr.** and **Clara Lane**.

Children of **John** *3* **Gaudy** and **Mamie Hooks** were as follows:
    12.   i. BENJAMIN *4* was born in Sandersville, Georgia. He married **Barbara** (—?—).
+   13.   ii. CLARA, born in Sandersville, Georgia.
+   14.   iii. MAMIE, born in Sandersville, Georgia; married **Alfred Lawson**.
+   15.   iv. JOHN JR., born in Sandersville, Georgia; married **Florine** (———).
+   16.   v. NAOMIE, born in Sandersville, Georgia; married **Joe Johnson**.

+ 17. vi. BRENDA, born in Sandersville, Georgia; married **Hezekiah McDonald.**
+ 18. vii. THELMA, born in Sandersville, Georgia.
+ 19. viii. RAYMOND, born in Sandersville, Georgia; married **Florence** (———).
  20. ix. ROBERT was born in Sandersville, Washington County, Georgia.
+ 21. x. JOHNNIE LOU, born circa 1918 in Washington County, Georgia; married **William Carithers.**
+ 22. xi. LULA MAE, born 22 November 1919 in Washington County, Georgia; married **William Johnson;** married **David James Lemon Sr.**
+ 23. xii. PORTER, born 2 February 1929 in Sandersville, Washington County, Georgia; married **Frances** (———).

6. CHARLIE³ GORDY (GAUDY) (*Berry²Gordy, Jim¹*); On birth certificate surname appears as Gaudy; was born in Washington County, Georgia. He married **Pearl Bouyer.**

Children of **Charlie³ Gordy (Gaudy)** and **Pearl Bouyer** were as follows:
  24. i. RUTH⁴ married **Mr. Lowery.**
  25. ii. ROOSEVELT.
  26. iii. TIMOTHY.

Children of **Charlie³ Gordy (Gaudy)** include:
  27. i. IDA L.⁴ was born in Michigan.

7. BERRY 'POP'³ GORDY JR. (*Berry², Jim¹*) was born in 1888 in Sandersville, Washington County, Georgia. He married **Bertha Fuller.** He died in 1978.

Children of **Berry 'Pop'³ Gordy Jr.** and **Bertha Fuller** were as follows:
  28. i. BERRY⁴ III was born in Sandersville, Georgia.
  29. ii. ESTHER was born in Sandersville, Washington County, Georgia. She married **Mr. Edwards.**
  30. iii. ANNA was born in Sandersville, Georgia. She married **Marvin Gaye** in Detroit, Michigan.
  31. iv. LUCY was born in Sandersville, Georgia.
  32. v. GEORGE was born in Sandersville, Georgia.
  33. vi. ROBERT was born in Sandersville, Georgia.
  34. vii. GWENDOLYN was born in Sandersville, Georgia. She married **Mr. Fuqua.**
+ 35. viii. FULLER BERRY, born 9 September 1918 in Sandersville, Oconee, Georgia; married **Mildred Hart.**

8. JOSEPH 'JOE'³ GORDY (*Berry², Jim¹*) was born on 7 February 1885 in Sandersville, Georgia. He married **Lee Alice Reese.** He died in 1983 in Detroit, Michigan.

Children of **Joseph 'Joe'**^{3} **Gordy** and **Lee Alice Reese** were as follows:
36.   i. FLETCHER^4 was born in Sandersville, Georgia.
+ 37.   ii. HARVEY, born in Sandersville, Georgia; married **Myrtle Upshaw.**
+ 38.   iii. EARL, born in Sandersville, Georgia.
+ 39.   iv. JOSEPH JR., born in Sandersville, Georgia; married **Berniece** (—?—).
+ 40.   v. GLENNIS, born in Sandersville, Georgia; married **Renardo Harris.**
+ 41.   vi. ISAAC, born in Sandersville, Georgia; married **Janette** (—?—).
+ 42.   vii. MARY FRANCIS, born 18 May 1918 in Sandersville, Georgia; married **Raymond L. Washington.**
+ 43.   viii. MAMIE, born 1920 in Sandersville, Georgia; married **Homer Upshaw.**

9. SAMUEL 'SAM'^{3} **GORDY** (*Berry*^{2}, *Jim*^{1}) was born in 1878 in Washington County, Georgia. He married **Carrie Cheeves**, daughter of **Henry Cheeves Sr.** and **Mary Ann Wise.** He died in June 1947 in Washington County, Georgia.

Children of **Samuel 'Sam'**^{3} **Gordy** and **Carrie Cheeves** were as follows:
+ 44.   i. HENRY BERRY^4, born 3 May 1905 in Sandersville, Georgia; married **Hattie Mae Hooks.**
+ 45.   ii. MARY LUCY, born 10 November 1906 in Sandersville, Georgia; married **Robert Cawthon.**
+ 46.   iii. JOHN, born 3 December 1908 in Sandersville, Georgia; married **Georgia Belle Hodges.**
+ 47.   iv. SAMUEL 'SAM' JR., born 28 October 1910 in Sandersville, Georgia; married **Margaret Sheppard.**
48.   v. LENNIE RUTH was born on 28 June 1914 in Washington County, Georgia. She married **Robert J. Hooks Jr.**, son of **Robert Hooks Sr.** and **Clara Lane.**
49.   vi. DAVID was born on 24 April 1919 in Sandersville, Georgia. He died in September 1950 at age 31.
+ 50.   vii. ANN 'ANNIE' OWEN, born 30 December 1925 in Sandersville, Washington County, Georgia; married **Herman Smith**; married **Maxel Hardy.**
+ 51.   viii. ROBERT DANIEL, born 21 June 1926 in Sandersville, Georgia; married **Eloise 'Honey' Dawson.**

10. EASTER^3 **GORDY** (*Berry*^{2}, *Jim*^{1}) was born circa 1883 in Georgia. She married **Jeff Carter Sr.**, son of **Burrell Carter** and **Mary Ann Lane,** in February 1908 in Washington County, Georgia She died before 1920.

Children of **Easter**^{3} **Gordy** include:
+ 52.   i. WILLIAM ROY^4, born 2 August 1900 in Sandersville, Georgia; married **Clara Walker.**

Children of **Easter^3 Gordy** and **Jeff Carter Sr.** were as follows:
+ 53.   i. RODELL^4, born circa 1911 in Georgia; married **Lillian Lucille 'Seal' Cheeves.**
  54.   ii. ESTHER was born on 7 May 1914 in Sandersville, Washington County, Georgia. She married **Mr. Hinton** in California. She married **I.V. Scott** in 1932 in Detroit, Michigan. She died on 19 October 1985 in Los Angeles, California, at age 71.

11. LUCY 'NIG'^{3} GORDY (*Berry^2, Jim^1*) was born on 10 April 1896 in Sandersville, Washington County, Georgia. She married **Albert Butts.** She married **Mark Lane Wood.**

Children of **Lucy 'Nig'^{3} Gordy** and **Albert Butts** were:
+ 55.   i. JOHN 'JOHNNIE' REASE^4, born 18 August 1915 in Sandersville, Georgia; married **Verneda Lewis.**

Children of **Lucy 'Nig'^{3} Gordy** and **Mark Lane Wood** were:
+ 56.   i. THOMAS 'T.J' JEFFERSON^4, born 26 May 1922 in Sandersville, Georgia; married **Anna Goins;** married **Thomasine Harris.**

Generation Four

13. CLARA^4 GAUDY (*John^3, Berry^2 Gordy, Jim^1*) was born in Sandersville, Georgia.

Children of **Clara^4 Gaudy** and **Leonard Eston** were as follows:
+ 57.   i. LEONARD^5 JR.
+ 58.   ii. DIANE, married **Lamar Riddle.**
  59.   iii. ARMON.

14. MAMIE^4 GAUDY (*John^3, Berry^2 Gordy, Jim^1*) was born in Sandersville, Georgia. She married **Alfred Lawson.**

Children of **Mamie^4 Gaudy** and **Alfred Lawson** were as follows:
+ 60.   i. JOYCE^5, married **Joseph Moore.**
+ 61.   ii. SHARON, married **James E. Garrett.**

15. JOHN^4 GAUDY JR. (*John^3, Berry^2 Gordy, Jim^1*) was born in Sandersville, Georgia. He married **Florine (———).**

Children of **John^4 Gaudy Jr.** and **Florine (———)** were as follows:
+ 62.   i. BERNADETTE^5, married **David Anderson.**
+ 63.   ii. FLORENCE, married **Eugene Anderson.**
  64.   iii. JOHN III.
+ 65.   iv. JANICE, married **Dwight McCarter.**

+ 66.   v. VALERIE, married **Keith Martin**; married **Columbus Sykes.**
+ 67.   vi. JOCELYN, married **Jerry Flowers.**
  68.   vii. ROBERT.

16. NAOMIE[4] GORDY (*John[3]Gaudy, Berry[2]Gordy, Jim[1]*) was born in Sandersville, Georgia. She married **Joe Johnson.**

Children of **Naomie[4] Gordy** and **Joe Johnson** were as follows:
  69.   i. DENISE[5].
+ 70.   ii. CYNTHIA
+ 71.   iii. CHERYL, married **Robert Marshall.**

17. BRENDA[4] GORDY (*John[3]Gaudy, Berry[2]Gordy, Jim[1]*) was born in Sandersville, Georgia. She married **Hezekiah McDonald.**

Children of **Brenda[4] Gordy** and **Hezekiah McDonald** were as follows:
  72.   i. MICHELLE[5].
  73.   ii. HEZEKIAH TROY.

18. THELMA[4] GORDY (*John[3]Gaudy, Berry[2]Gordy, Jim[1]*) was born in Sandersville, Georgia.

Children of **Thelma[4] Gordy** and **James Brooks** were as follows:
+ 74.   i. JAMES[5] (JR.)
+ 75.   ii. KARLA
+ 76.   iii. SEDARA, married **Darryl Stroud.**
+ 77.   iv. SHARRENA, married **Frank Johnson.**
+ 78.   v. LINDA, married **Ken Wells.**

19. RAYMOND[4] GORDY (*John[3]Gaudy, Berry[2]Gordy, Jim[1]*) was born in Sandersville, Georgia. He married **Florence** (———).

Children of **Raymond[4] Gordy** and **Florence** (———) were as follows:
+ 79.   i. BARBARA[5]
  80.   ii. RAYMOND (JR.).
  81.   iii. TRACY.
+ 82.   iv. NICOLE

21. JOHNNIE LOU[4] GORDY (*John[3]Gaudy, Berry[2]Gordy, Jim[1]*) was born circa 1918 in Washington County, Georgia. She married **William Carithers.**

Children of **Johnnie Lou**[4] **Gordy** and **William Carithers** were:

+ 83.   i. GARY[5]

22. LULA MAE[4] **GAUDY** (*John*[3], *Berry*[2]*Gordy*, *Jim*[1]) was born on 22 November 1919 in Washington County, Georgia. She married **William Johnson.** She married **David James Lemon Sr.** in January 1940 in Detroit, Michigan.

There were no children of **Lula Mae**[4] **Gaudy** and **William Johnson.**

Children of **Lula Mae**[4] **Gaudy** and **David James Lemon Sr.** were as follows:

+ 84.   i. HOWARD LOVELL[5], born 26 October 1940 in Detroit, Michigan; married **Sandra Lynn Powell.**
+ 85.   ii. PATRICIA M., born 2 April 1942 in Detroit, Michigan; married **Phil Green.**
+ 86.   iii. DAVID JAMES JR., born 21 November 1944 in Detroit, Michigan; married **Merilyn Ann Bradley.**
+ 87.   iv. RICHARD, born 26 December 1947 in Detroit, Michigan; married **Lorraine** (————); married **Shirley Boyd.**
+ 88.   v. DEBRA, born 6 March 1954 in Detroit, Michigan; married **Jimmy Forrest;** married **Felton Wright.**
+ 89.   vi. SONIA DARLENE, born 22 July 1958 in Detroit, Michigan; married **Cassell Mathews.**

23. PORTER[4] **GORDY** (*John*[3]*Gaudy*, *Berry*[2]*Gordy*, *Jim*[1]) was born on 2 February 1929 in Sandersville, Washington County, Georgia. He married **Frances** (————).

Children of **Porter**[4] **Gordy** and **Frances** (————) were as follows:

90.   i. ABBIE GAIL[5].
+ 91.   ii. CLARENCE
+ 92.   iii. PORTIA
+ 93.   iv. CAROL

35. FULLER BERRY[4] **GORDY** (*Berry 'Pop*[3], *Berry*[2], *Jim*[1]) was born on 9 September 1918 in Sandersville, Oconee, Georgia. He married **Mildred Hart** on 31 January 1942 in Detroit, Michigan. He died on 9 November 1991 in Los Angeles, California, at age 73.

Children of **Fuller Berry**[4] **Gordy** and **Mildred Hart** were:

+ 94.   i. IRIS BERTHA[5], born in Detroit, Michigan; married **Johnny William Bristol.**

37. HARVEY[4] **GORDY** (*Joseph 'Joe*[3], *Berry*[2], *Jim*[1]) was born in Sandersville, Georgia. He married **Myrtle Upshaw.**

Children of **Harvey**^{4} **Gordy** and **Myrtle Upshaw** were:
95.   i. DELORES 'DEE DEE'^{5}.

38. EARL^4 **GORDY** (*Joseph 'Joe*^{3}, *Berry*^{2}, *Jim*^{1}) was born in Sandersville, Georgia.

Children of **Earl**^{4} **Gordy** and **Lenore** (—?—) were:
96.   i. EARL^5 JR..

Children of **Earl**^{4} **Gordy** and **Erma Graham** were:
97.   i. GREGORY^5.

39. JOSEPH^4 **GORDY JR.** (*Joseph 'Joe*^{3}, *Berry*^{2}, *Jim*^{1}) was born in Sandersville, Georgia. He married **Berniece** (—?—).

Children of **Joseph**^{4} **Gordy Jr.** and **Berniece** (—?—) were:
98.   i. ARLETTE^5.

40. GLENNIS^4 **GORDY** (*Joseph 'Joe*^{3}, *Berry*^{2}, *Jim*^{1}) was born in Sandersville, Georgia. She married **Renardo Harris.**

Children of **Glennis**^{4} **Gordy** and **Renardo Harris** were as follows:
99.   i. ROSLYN^5.
100.   ii. RENAY.
101.   iii. RENARDO JR..
102.   iv. STEPHANIE.

41. ISAAC^4 **GORDY** (*Joseph 'Joe*^{3}, *Berry*^{2}, *Jim*^{1}) was born in Sandersville, Georgia. He married **Janette** (—?—).

Children of **Isaac**^{4} **Gordy** and **Janette** (—?—) were:
103.   i. TONY^5.

42. MARY FRANCIS^4 **GORDY** (*Joseph 'Joe*^{3}, *Berry*^{2}, *Jim*^{1}) was born on 18 May 1918 in Sandersville, Georgia. She married **Raymond L. Washington.**

Children of **Mary Francis**^{4} **Gordy** and **Raymond L. Washington** were as follows:
+ 104. i. ALICE RAMONA 'PEACHES'^{5}, born 10 August 1944 in Detroit, Michigan; married **Ralph Jones.**
105.   ii. PHYLLIS 'PEANUT' ELAINE was born on 29 August 1946 in Detroit, Michigan. She married **Antonio David.** She died in 1998 in Detroit, Michigan.

43. MAMIE⁴ GORDY (*Joseph 'Joe'³, Berry², Jim¹*) was born in 1920 in Sandersville, Georgia. She married **Homer Upshaw.**

Children of **Mamie⁴ Gordy** and **Homer Upshaw** were:
106.   i. JACKIE⁵.

44. HENRY BERRY⁴ GORDY (*Samuel 'Sam'³, Berry², Jim¹*) was born on 3 May 1905 in Sandersville, Georgia. He married **Hattie Mae Hooks,** daughter of **Mack Hooks** and **Judy Mason,** on 29 April 1928.

Children of **Henry Berry⁴ Gordy** and **Hattie Mae Hooks** were as follows:
+ 107.   i. HENRY EDWARD⁵, born 2 March 1929 in Sandersville, Georgia; married Jeanetta (—?—).
108.   ii. SAM married **Mary Moses.**
+ 109.   iii. MARGARET JEWEL, married **Isaac King.**
+ 110.   iv. CLAUDETTE, born 9 February 1937; married **Alfred C. Johnson.**
+ 111.   v. CAROLYN, married **Leonard Kennedy.**
+ 112.   vi. LAWRENCE, married **Shirley Palmer.**
113.   vii. GARY.
+ 114.   viii. JOYCE, born 1938 in Sandersville, Georgia; married **Welton Lawrence.**
+ 115.   ix. JAMES HAROLD, born 16 March 1942; married **Donna** (———).

45. MARY LUCY⁴ GORDY (*Samuel 'Sam'³, Berry², Jim¹*) was born on 10 November 1906 in Sandersville, Georgia. She married **Robert Cawthon.** She died in October 1940 at age 33.

Children of **Mary Lucy⁴ Gordy** and **Robert Cawthon** were as follows:
+ 116.   i. EVELYN BERNICE⁵, born circa 1925 in Milledgeville, Georgia; married **William Turner.**
+ 117.   ii. MARY LOUVENIA 'BENIA', born 17 August 1928 in Milledgeville, Georgia; married **Ernest Butts.**
+ 118.   iii. ROBERT 'BOB' JR., born circa 1930 in Milledgeville, Georgia; married **Arlene** (—?—).
119.   iv. BARNEY was born circa 1935 in Milledgeville, Georgia. He died circa 1951.
+ 120.   v. BETTY JEAN, born circa 1940 in Milledgeville, Georgia; married **James Nelson.**

46. JOHN⁴ GORDY (*Samuel 'Sam'³, Berry², Jim¹*) was born on 3 December 1908 in Sandersville, Georgia. He married **Georgia Belle Hodges,** daughter of **Mitchell Hodges.** He died on 28 May 1969 at age 60.

Children of **John**[4] **Gordy** and **Georgia Belle Hodges** were as follows:

121.   i. LAVORA[5] was born in February 1932. He died in January 1995 at age 62.
122.   ii. HODGES BAY was born on 9 January 1935 in Sandersville, Georgia. He died in June 1996 at age 61.
123.   iii. JOHN 'JACK' JR. was born on 15 June 1937 in Sandersville, Georgia.
+ 124.   iv. EVELYN 'SIS', born 4 January 1939 in Sandersville, Georgia.

47. SAMUEL 'SAM'[4] **GORDY JR.** (*Samuel 'Sam'*[3], *Berry*[2], *Jim*[1]) was born on 28 October 1910 in Sandersville, Georgia. He married **Margaret Sheppard.** He died on 31 August 1985 in Sandersville, Georgia, at age 74.

Children of **Samuel 'Sam'**[4] **Gordy Jr.** and **Margaret Sheppard** were as follows:

125.   i. BEVERLY[5] was born in Washington County, Georgia.
126.   ii. CLEAVIE was born in Washington County, Georgia.
127.   iii. SHEILA was born in Washington County, Georgia.
128.   iv. ROY SAMUEL was born circa 1935 in Washington County, Georgia.

Children of **Samuel 'Sam'**[4] **Gordy Jr.** and **Sarah Ella 'SC' Hopkins** were:

+ 129.   i. MARY PEARL 'TOWN'[5] CHEEVES, born 21 January 1930 in Sandersville, Georgia; married **Vernon 'Bud' Trawick.**

50. ANN 'ANNIE' OWEN[4] **GORDY** (*Samuel 'Sam'*[3], *Berry*[2], *Jim*[1]) was born on 30 December 1925 in Sandersville, Washington County, Georgia. She married **Herman Smith.** She married **Maxel Hardy** on 11 August 1951 in Detroit, Michigan. She died on 12 July 1992 in Detroit, Michigan, at age 66.

There were no children of **Ann 'Annie' Owen**[4] **Gordy** and **Herman Smith**.

Children of **Ann 'Annie' Owen**[4] **Gordy** and **Maxel Hardy** were as follows:

+ 130.   i. MAXEL[5] JR., born 10 October 1952 in Detroit, Michigan.
131.   ii. LYNETTE was born on 5 May 1955 in Detroit, Michigan.
+ 132.   iii. CHERYL DENISE, born 20 September 1958 in Detroit, Michigan.

51. ROBERT DANIEL[4] **GORDY** (*Samuel 'Sam'*[3], *Berry*[2], *Jim*[1]) was born on 21 June 1926 in Sandersville, Georgia. He married **Eloise 'Honey' Dawson,** daughter of **Homer Dawson** and **Lora Ella 'Laura' Carter,** on 6 March 1950 in Sandersville, Washington County, Georgia.

Children of **Robert Daniel**[4] **Gordy** and **Eloise 'Honey' Dawson** were as follows:

+ 133.   i. GWENDOLYN[5], born 12 March 1947 in Utica, New York; married **Julius Murphy.**
134.   ii. ROBERT DANIEL JR. was born on 27 July 1950 in Sandersville, Georgia.

+ 135.   iii. DAVID, born 13 April 1952 in Sandersville, Georgia; married DeLois Turner; married Darlene Robinson.
+ 136.   iv. DEBORAH ANNE, born 6 January 1954 in Sandersville, Georgia; married Samuel Duggan.
+ 137.   v. MARY LUCY, born 17 July 1956 in Sandersville, Georgia; married Tony Owen Hurt Sr.
  138.   vi. REGINALD CORNELIUS was born on 5 September 1957 in Sandersville, Georgia. He married Yvette (—?—).
+ 139.   vii. BERRY RENARD, born 10 September 1958 in Sandersville, Georgia; married Brenda Lee Lord Barlow Cardy.

52. WILLIAM ROY^4 GORDY (*Easter^3, Berry^2, Jim^1*) was born on 2 August 1900 in Sandersville, Georgia. He married Clara Walker. He died on 25 March 1985 in Detroit, Michigan, at age 84.

Children of William Roy^4 Gordy and Clara Walker were as follows:
  140.   i. WILLIAM^5 was born in Detroit, Michigan.
+ 141.   ii. MAUDE, born in Detroit, Michigan; married James Casey.
  142.   iii. FRED was born in Detroit, Michigan.
+ 143.   iv. DOROTHY, born 18 October 1926 in Sandersville, Georgia; married George Lowe.

53. RODELL^4 CARTER (*Easter^{3}Gordy, Berry^2, Jim^1*) was born circa 1911 in Georgia. He married Lillian Lucille 'Seal' Cheeves, daughter of David 'Coot' Cheeves and Hattie Johnson.

Children of Rodell^4 Carter and Nora Davis were:
  144.   i. BARBARA 'BOBBY'^{5}.

There were no children of Rodell^4 Carter and Lillian Lucille 'Seal' Cheeves.

55. JOHN 'JOHNNIE' REASE^4 BUTTS (*Lucy 'Nig^{3}Gordy, Berry^2, Jim^1*) was born on 18 August 1915 in Sandersville, Georgia. He married Verneda Lewis on 23 June 1945 in Detroit, Michigan. He died on 14 February 2004 in Detroit, Michigan, at age 88.

Children of John 'Johnnie' Rease^4 Butts and Verneda Lewis were as follows:
+ 145.   i. JOHN REASE^5 JR., born 7 March 1946 in Detroit, Michigan; married Gwendolyn Gambrell.
+ 146.   ii. VERNEDA ELAINE, born 1 May 1947 in Detroit, Michigan; married L.V. Allen.
+ 147.   iii. VINCENT DEROY, born 3 March 1953 in Detroit, Michigan.
  148.   iv. MARK was born on 12 August 1960 in Detroit, Michigan.

56. THOMAS 'T.J' JEFFERSON^4 **WOOD** (*Lucy 'Nig*^{3}*Gordy, Berry*^{2}*, Jim*^{1}) was born on 26 May 1922 in Sandersville, Georgia. He married **Anna Goins** in 1940 in Detroit, Michigan. He married **Thomasine Harris** in 1955 in Detroit, Michigan. He died in January 1992 in Detroit, Michigan, at age 69.

Children of **Thomas 'T.J' Jefferson**^{4} **Wood** and **Anna Goins** were as follows:
+ 149.   i. JEFFREY BERNARD^5, born 15 January 1941 in Detroit, Michigan.
+ 150.   ii. NICKOLE T., born 19 September 1943 in Detroit, Michigan; married **John Pierpont Massey III.**

Children of **Thomas 'T.J' Jefferson**^{4} **Wood** and **Thomasine Harris** were as follows:
151.   i. THOMAS JEFFERSON^5 JR. was born in Detroit, Michigan.
+ 152.   ii. DARRYL PATRICK, born in Detroit, Michigan; married **Erma** (—?—).
+ 153.   iii. WANDA, born in Detroit, Michigan; married **John Donald.**

Generation Five

57. LEONARD^5 **ESTON JR.** (*Clara*^{4}*Gaudy, John*^{3}*, Berry*^{2}*Gordy, Jim*^{1}).

Children of **Leonard**^{5} **Eston Jr.** include:
154.   i. OSCAR^6.

58. DIANE^5 **ESTON** (*Clara*^{4}*Gaudy, John*^{3}*, Berry*^{2}*Gordy, Jim*^{1}) married **Lamar Riddle.**

Children of **Diane**^{5} **Eston** and **Lamar Riddle** were as follows:
155.   i. LATONYA^6.
156.   ii. LAVELLE.

60. JOYCE^5 **LAWSON** (*Mamie*^{4}*Gaudy, John*^{3}*, Berry*^{2}*Gordy, Jim*^{1}) married **Joseph Moore.**

Children of **Joyce**^{5} **Lawson** and **Joseph Moore** were:
+ 157.   i. KAREN^6, born 11 February 1967.

61. SHARON^5 **LAWSON** (*Mamie*^{4}*Gaudy, John*^{3}*, Berry*^{2}*Gordy, Jim*^{1}) married **James E. Garrett.**

Children of **Sharon**^{5} **Lawson** and **James E. Garrett** were as follows:
158.   i. JAMES E.^{6} JR..
159.   ii. JOI.

62. BERNADETTE^5 **GAUDY** (*John*^{4}*, John*^{3}*, Berry*^{2}*Gordy, Jim*^{1}) married **David Anderson.**

Children of **Bernadette**[5] **Gaudy** and **David Anderson** were as follows:
160. i. DAVID[6] (JR.).
161. ii. EUGENE.
162. iii. CAMILE.
163. iv. SIMEON.
164. v. LATRISHA.
165. vi. CINDY.

63. FLORENCE[5] **GAUDY** (*John*[4], *John*[3], *Berry*[2]*Gordy*, *Jim*[1]) married **Eugene Anderson.**

Children of **Florence**[5] **Gaudy** and **Eugene Anderson** were as follows:
166. i. YOLANDA[6].
+ 167. ii. EUGENE (**IV**), married **Kimberly** (———).

65. JANICE[5] **GAUDY** (*John*[4], *John*[3], *Berry*[2]*Gordy*, *Jim*[1]) married **Dwight McCarter.**

Children of **Janice**[5] **Gaudy** and **Dwight McCarter** were as follows:
168. i. JENNIFER[6].
169. ii. JANELLE.
170. iii. DWIGHT (JR.).

66. VALERIE[5] **GAUDY** (*John*[4], *John*[3], *Berry*[2]*Gordy*, *Jim*[1]) married **Keith Martin.** She married **Columbus Sykes.**

Children of **Valerie**[5] **Gaudy** and **Keith Martin** were as follows:
+ 171. i. KENDRA[6]
172. ii. KEITH.
173. iii. VALENTE.
174. iv. ANTWON.
175. v. VINCENT.

There were no children of **Valerie**[5] **Gaudy** and **Columbus Sykes.**

67. JOCELYN[5] **GAUDY** (*John*[4], *John*[3], *Berry*[2]*Gordy*, *Jim*[1]) married **Jerry Flowers.**

Children of **Jocelyn**[5] **Gaudy** and **Jerry Flowers** were as follows:
176. i. CRYSTAL[6].
177. ii. NATHANIEL JEROME.
178. iii. JACQUELINE.
179. iv. ROBERT.

70. CYNTHIA[5] **JOHNSON** (*Naomie*[4]*Gordy*, *John*[3]*Gaudy*, *Berry*[2]*Gordy*, *Jim*[1]).

Children of **Cynthia**[5] **Johnson** include:
180. i. JESSICA[6].

71. **CHERYL**[5] **JOHNSON** (*Naomie*[4]*Gordy, John*[3]*Gaudy, Berry*[2]*Gordy, Jim*[1]) married **Robert Marshall.**

Children of **Cheryl**[5] **Johnson** and **Robert Marshall** were as follows:
181. i. TABITHA[6].
182. ii. ANTHONY.
183. iii. ROBERT.
184. iv. JOE.

74. **JAMES**[5] **BROOKS (JR.)** (*Thelma*[4]*Gordy, John*[3]*Gaudy, Berry*[2]*Gordy, Jim*[1]).

Children of **James**[5] **Brooks (Jr.)** include:
185. i. CHRISTINA[6].
186. ii. KAI.

75. **KARLA**[5] **BROOKS** (*Thelma*[4]*Gordy, John*[3]*Gaudy, Berry*[2]*Gordy, Jim*[1]).

Children of **Karla**[5] **Brooks** include:
187. i. KYLE[6].

76. **SEDARA**[5] **BROOKS** (*Thelma*[4]*Gordy, John*[3]*Gaudy, Berry*[2]*Gordy, Jim*[1]) married **Darryl Stroud.**

Children of **Sedara**[5] **Brooks** and **Darryl Stroud** were as follows:
188. i. MELANIE[6].
189. ii. MELISSA.

77. **SHARRENA**[5] **BROOKS** (*Thelma*[4]*Gordy, John*[3]*Gaudy, Berry*[2]*Gordy, Jim*[1]) married **Frank Johnson.**

Children of **Sharrena**[5] **Brooks** and **Frank Johnson** were as follows:
190. i. BENJAMIN[6].
191. ii. SONYA.
192. iii. KALEB.

78. **LINDA**[5] **BROOKS** (*Thelma*[4]*Gordy, John*[3]*Gaudy, Berry*[2]*Gordy, Jim*[1]) married **Ken Wells.**

Children of **Linda**[5] **Brooks** and **Ken Wells** were as follows:
193. i. MONICA[6].

194. ii. JAMES.

79. BARBARA⁵ GORDY (*Raymond⁴, John³ Gaudy, Berry² Gordy, Jim¹*).

Children of **Barbara⁵** Gordy include:
195. i. DIONNE⁶.

82. NICOLE⁵ GORDY (*Raymond⁴, John³ Gaudy, Berry² Gordy, Jim¹*).

Children of **Nicole⁵** Gordy include:
196. i. JASON⁶.

83. GARY⁵ CARITHERS (*Johnnie Lou⁴ Gordy, John³ Gaudy, Berry² Gordy, Jim¹*).

Children of **Gary⁵ Carithers** include:
197. i. CLAUDETTE⁶.
198. ii. AMANI.

84. HOWARD LOVELL⁵ LEMON (*Lula Mae⁴ Gaudy, John³, Berry² Gordy, Jim¹*) was born on 26 October 1940 in Detroit, Michigan. He married **Sandra Lynn Powell** on 16 May 1970 in Detroit, Michigan.

Children of **Howard Lovell⁵ Lemon** and **Sandra Lynn Powell** were as follows:
199. i. MYRON LOVELL⁶ was born on 3 October 1971 in Detroit, Michigan. He married **Yolanda** (—?—) in Detroit, Michigan.
200. ii. ERICA LYNN was born on 24 August 1974 in Detroit, Michigan. She married **Stacy Gordon** in September 1997 in Detroit, Michigan.
+ 201. iii. LATOYA MERTRICE, born 20 October 1976 in Detroit, Michigan; married **Henry James.**

85. PATRICIA M.⁵ LEMON (*Lula Mae⁴ Gaudy, John³, Berry² Gordy, Jim¹*) was born on 2 April 1942 in Detroit, Michigan. She married **Phil Green.**

Children of **Patricia M.⁵ Lemon** and **Phil Green** were as follows:
+ 202. i. SHEILA RENE⁶
203. ii. CARL ANTHONY.
204. iii. KEVIN LOUIS.
+ 205. iv. SONJA DENISE
206. v. CHRISTOPHER C..

86. DAVID JAMES⁵ LEMON JR. (*Lula Mae⁴ Gaudy, John³, Berry² Gordy, Jim¹*) was born on 21 November 1944 in Detroit, Michigan. He married **Merilyn Ann Bradley.**

Children of **David James**^{5} **Lemon Jr.** and **Merilyn Ann Bradley** were as follows:
207.   i. DEMARCO^6.
208.   ii. KAMRON.
209.   iii. TUAN.

87. **RICHARD**^{5} **LEMON** (*Lula Mae*^{4}*Gaudy, John*^{3}*, Berry*^{2}*Gordy, Jim*^{1}) was born on 26 December 1947 in Detroit, Michigan. He married **Lorraine** (———). He married **Shirley Boyd** in 1970 in Detroit, Michigan.

There were no children of **Richard**^{5} **Lemon** and **Lorraine** (———).

Children of **Richard**^{5} **Lemon** and **Shirley Boyd** were as follows:
210.   i. NAKEMA^6.
211.   ii. LAQUAN.

88. **DEBRA**^{5} **LEMON** (*Lula Mae*^{4}*Gaudy, John*^{3}*, Berry*^{2}*Gordy, Jim*^{1}) was born on 6 March 1954 in Detroit, Michigan. She married **Jimmy Forrest** in Detroit, Michigan. She married **Felton Wright** on 14 February 1998 in Detroit, Michigan.

Children of **Debra**^{5} **Lemon** and **Jimmy Forrest** were as follows:
212.   i. JIMMY QUATRELL^6 was born in September 1977 in Detroit, Michigan.
213.   ii. LOUIS was born in October 1978 in Detroit, Michigan.

There were no children of **Debra**^{5} **Lemon** and **Felton Wright**.

89. **SONIA DARLENE**^{5} **LEMON** (*Lula Mae*^{4}*Gaudy, John*^{3}*, Berry*^{2}*Gordy, Jim*^{1}) was born on 22 July 1958 in Detroit, Michigan. She married **Cassell Mathews** on 3 August 2002 in Detroit, Michigan.

Children of **Sonia Darlene**^{5} **Lemon** and **Dennis Hall** were:
214.   i. LAMAR^6 was born on 19 October 1976 in Detroit, Michigan.

Children of **Sonia Darlene**^{5} **Lemon** and **Kevin Stevenson** were:
215.   i. SONIA^6 was born on 3 October 1990 in Detroit, Michigan.

Children of **Sonia Darlene**^{5} **Lemon** and **Cassell Mathews** were:
216.   i. SHARROD^6 was born on 11 December 1986 in Detroit, Michigan.

91. **CLARENCE**^{5} **GAUDY** (*Porter*^{4}*Gordy, John*^{3}*Gaudy, Berry*^{2}*Gordy, Jim*^{1}).

Children of **Clarence**^{5} **Gaudy** include:
217.   i. FELICIA FRANCIS^6.

218.	ii. JENNIFER LEE.
219.	iii. JASON.
220.	iv. JAMAR.

92. **PORTIA**^{5} **GAUDY** (*Porter*^{4}*Gordy, John*^{3}*Gaudy, Berry*^{2}*Gordy, Jim*^{1}).

Children of **Portia**^{5} **Gaudy** include:
221.	i. STACY^6.

93. **CAROL**^{5} **GAUDY** (*Porter*^{4}*Gordy, John*^{3}*Gaudy, Berry*^{2}*Gordy, Jim*^{1}).

Children of **Carol**^{5} **Gaudy** include:
222.	i. ASHLEY^6.

94. **IRIS BERTHA**^{5} **GORDY** (*Fuller Berry*^{4}*, Berry 'Pop*^{3}*, Berry*^{2}*, Jim*^{1}) was born in Detroit, Michigan. She married **Johnny William Bristol** on 17 April 1964 in Detroit, Michigan.

Children of **Iris Bertha**^{5} **Gordy** and **Johnny William Bristol** were:
+ 223.	i. KARLA DAWN^6, born circa 22 December 1970 in Detroit, Michigan; married **Tyrone Brown**.

104. **ALICE RAMONA 'PEACHES'**^{5} **WASHINGTON** (*Mary Francis*^{4}*Gordy, Joseph 'Joe'*^{3}*, Berry*^{2}*, Jim*^{1}) was born on 10 August 1944 in Detroit, Michigan. She married **Ralph Jones** on 26 September 1966 in Detroit, Michigan.

Children of **Alice Ramona 'Peaches'**^{5} **Washington** and **Ralph Jones** were as follows:
+ 224.	i. SCHAMEL LA NEACE^6, born 4 October 1966 in Detroit, Michigan.
+ 225.	ii. CONSTANCE MONIQUE, born 29 August 1969 in Detroit, Michigan; married **Aphrodion Hamilton**.
+ 226.	iii. MASHANNA IKEYLA, born 24 January 1972 in Detroit, Michigan; married **James Hall**.
227.	iv. BERRY IBN LEROY was born on 17 July 1979 in Detroit, Michigan.

107. **HENRY EDWARD**^{5} **GORDY** (*Henry Berry*^{4}*, Samuel 'Sam'*^{3}*, Berry*^{2}*, Jim*^{1}) was born on 2 March 1929 in Sandersville, Georgia. He married **Jeanetta** (—?—). He died in 1985.

Children of **Henry Edward**^{5} **Gordy** and **Jeanetta** (—?—) were as follows:
+ 228.	i. BRIAN^6, married **Yvonne** (———).
+ 229.	ii. BYRON, married **Willette** (———).
+ 230.	iii. BRUCE, married **Deborah** (———).

+ 231. iv. BRENT, married **Effie** (———).
+ 232. v. BRIDGETTE, married **Bernell Seal.**
  233. vi. BRENDA married **Anthony Berry.**

109. MARGARET JEWEL^5 GORDY (*Henry Berry^4, Samuel 'Sam^3, Berry^2, Jim^1*) married **Isaac King.**

Children of **Margaret Jewel^5 Gordy** and **Isaac King** were as follows:
+ 234. i. KAREN^6, married **Elvin Brooks.**
+ 235. ii. KYRA, married **James Ridgell.**
  236. iii. KEVIN married **Lillie** (—?—).

110. CLAUDETTE^5 GORDY (*Henry Berry^4, Samuel 'Sam^3, Berry^2, Jim^1*) was born on 9 February 1937. She married **Alfred C. Johnson.**

Children of **Claudette^5 Gordy** and **Alfred C. Johnson** were:
  237. i. MARCUS LAVON^6.

111. CAROLYN^5 GORDY (*Henry Berry^4, Samuel 'Sam^3, Berry^2, Jim^1*) married **Leonard Kennedy.**

Children of **Carolyn^5 Gordy** and **Leonard Kennedy** were as follows:
  238. i. STEPHANIE^6 married **James C. Gardner.**
  239. ii. SEAN.
  240. iii. STEVEN.
  241. iv. SHANNON.

112. LAWRENCE^5 GORDY (*Henry Berry^4, Samuel 'Sam^3, Berry^2, Jim^1*) married **Shirley Palmer.**

Children of **Lawrence^5 Gordy** and **Shirley Palmer** were:
  242. i. DWAYNE^6.

114. JOYCE^5 GORDY (*Henry Berry^4, Samuel 'Sam^3, Berry^2, Jim^1*) was born in 1938 in Sandersville, Georgia. She married **Welton Lawrence.**

Children of **Joyce^5 Gordy** and **Welton Lawrence** were as follows:
+ 243. i. DEBORAH^6, married **Lamont McClain.**
+ 244. ii. DOREEN, married **Sam Hughes.**
  245. iii. DAVID.
+ 246. iv. DARIN, married **Shirley** (———).

115. JAMES HAROLD^5 GORDY (*Henry Berry^4, Samuel 'Sam^3, Berry^2, Jim^1*) was born on 16 March 1942. He married **Donna** (———).

Children of **James Harold^5 Gordy** and **Donna** (———) were as follows:
247.   i. SHAWN^6 was born circa 1965.
248.   ii. JA VON was born circa 1965.
249.   iii. NICOLE.
250.   iv. ROBIN married **Timothy Banks.**
251.   v. MARISA.

116. EVELYN BERNICE^5 CAWTHON (*Mary Lucy^4 Gordy, Samuel 'Sam^3, Berry^2, Jim^1*) was born circa 1925 in Milledgeville, Georgia. She married **William Turner.**

Children of **Evelyn Bernice^5 Cawthon** and **William Turner** were:
252.   i. HEATH^6.

117. MARY LOUVENIA 'BENIA'^{5} CAWTHON (*Mary Lucy^4 Gordy, Samuel 'Sam^3, Berry^2, Jim^1*) was born on 17 August 1928 in Milledgeville, Georgia. She married **Ernest Butts.** She died in December 1956 in Hartford, Connecticut, at age 28.

Children of **Mary Louvenia 'Benia'^{5} Cawthon** and **Ernest Butts** were as follows:
+ 253.   i. LINDA^6, born 27 February 1951 in Milledgeville, Georgia; married **Donald Edwin Brooks.**
254.   ii. BRENDA was born on 27 February 1951 in Milledgeville, Georgia.
+ 255.   iii. EVELYN BERNICE 'EBBIE', born 12 April 1954 in Hartford, Connecticut.
+ 256.   iv. CHRISTIE TURNER, born 18 December 1956 in Hartford, Connecticut; married **Joseph Hicks Sr.**

118. ROBERT 'BOB'^{5} CAWTHON JR. (*Mary Lucy^4 Gordy, Samuel 'Sam^3, Berry^2, Jim^1*) was born circa 1930 in Milledgeville, Georgia. He married **Arlene** (—?—).

Children of **Robert 'Bob'^{5} Cawthon Jr.** and **Arlene** (—?—) were as follows:
257.   i. ROBERT^6 III.
258.   ii. JULIE.
259.   iii. LINDA.
260.   iv. DAVID.
261.   v. MICHAEL.

120. BETTY JEAN^5 CAWTHON (*Mary Lucy^4 Gordy, Samuel 'Sam^3, Berry^2, Jim^1*) was born circa 1940 in Milledgeville, Georgia. She married **James Nelson.**

Children of **Betty Jean**^{5} **Cawthon** and **James Nelson** were as follows:
262.   i. MARY DENISE 'NIECY'^{6} was born in Georgia.
263.   ii. JAMES 'JIMMY' JR. was born in July 1958 in Georgia.

124. EVELYN 'SIS'^{5} GORDY (*John*^{4}, *Samuel 'Sam'*^{3}, *Berry*^{2}, *Jim*^{1}) was born on 4 January 1939 in Sandersville, Georgia.

Children of **Evelyn 'Sis'**^{5} **Gordy** include:
264.   i. JOHN C.^{6}.
265.   ii. LINDA was born on 30 May 1955.

129. MARY PEARL 'TOWN'^{5} GORDY CHEEVES (*Samuel 'Sam'*^{4}, *Samuel 'Sam'*^{3}, *Berry*^{2}, *Jim*^{1}) was born on 21 January 1930 in Sandersville, Georgia. She married **Vernon 'Bud' Trawick**, son of **Tom Trawick** and **Melissa Williams**, on 19 November 1948 in Sandersville, Georgia.

Children of **Mary Pearl 'Town'**^{5} **Gordy Cheeves** and **Vernon 'Bud' Trawick** were as follows:
266.   i. VERNON^6 JR. was born on 10 April 1950 in Sandersville, Washington County, Georgia.
+ 267.   ii. BERNARD, born 14 December 1951 in Philadelphia, Pennsylvania; married **Kenya Wilson.**
268.   iii. MARVIN was born on 6 November 1954 in Philadelphia, Pennsylvania.
269.   iv. VERONICA was born on 17 February 1957 in Philadelphia, Pennsylvania.
+ 270.   v. CYNTHIA, born 12 November 1958 in Philadelphia, Pennsylvania; married **William Boyer.**

130. MAXEL^5 HARDY JR. (*Ann 'Annie' Owen*^{4} *Gordy, Samuel 'Sam'*^{3}, *Berry*^{2}, *Jim*^{1}) was born on 10 October 1952 in Detroit, Michigan.

Children of **Maxel**^{5} **Hardy Jr.** and **Laverne Arnette** were:
271.   i. MAXEL^6 III was born on 5 December 1983 in Detroit, Michigan.

132. CHERYL DENISE^5 HARDY (*Ann 'Annie' Owen*^{4} *Gordy, Samuel 'Sam'*^{3}, *Berry*^{2}, *Jim*^{1}) was born on 20 September 1958 in Detroit, Michigan.

Children of **Cheryl Denise**^{5} **Hardy** and **William Desi Richardson** were as follows:
272.   i. WILLIAM ARNAZ^6 was born on 30 November 1988 in Detroit, Michigan.
273.   ii. MALCOLM JAWAN was born on 29 April 1992 in Detroit, Michigan.

133. GWENDOLYN^5 GORDY (*Robert Daniel*^{4}, *Samuel 'Sam'*^{3}, *Berry*^{2}, *Jim*^{1}) was born on 12 March 1947 in Utica, New York. She married **Julius Murphy.**

Children of **Gwendolyn**^{5} **Gordy** and **Julius Murphy** were as follows:
274. i. SONIA JOY^6 was born on 13 June 1976 in Albany, Georgia.
275. ii. ASHLEY was born on 21 December 1984 in Macon, Georgia.

135. DAVID^5 **GORDY** (*Robert Daniel*^{4}, *Samuel 'Sam*^{3}, *Berry*^{2}, *Jim*^{1}) was born on 13 April 1952 in Sandersville, Georgia. He married **DeLois Turner**. He married **Darlene Robinson.**

Children of **David**^{5} **Gordy** and **DeLois Turner** were as follows:
276. i. DEBORAH^6 was born on 14 January 1971 in Augusta, Georgia.
277. ii. DAVINA was born on 2 June 1972 in Augusta, Georgia.
278. iii. DENISE was born on 13 June 1975 in Augusta, Georgia.
279. iv. JOSHUA DAVID was born on 9 February 1987 in Augusta, Georgia.

Children of **David**^{5} **Gordy** and **Darlene Robinson** were:
280. i. DAYNA LYNN^6 was born on 14 August 1997 in Milledgeville, Georgia.

136. DEBORAH ANNE^5 **GORDY** (*Robert Daniel*^{4}, *Samuel 'Sam*^{3}, *Berry*^{2}, *Jim*^{1}) was born on 6 January 1954 in Sandersville, Georgia. She married **Samuel Duggan** on 9 June 1979.

Children of **Deborah Anne**^{5} **Gordy** and **Samuel Duggan** were as follows:
281. i. LORA ANNE^6 was born on 17 July 1982 in Milledgeville, Georgia.
282. ii. LORETTA DENISE was born on 12 March 1985 in Milledgeville, Georgia.

137. MARY LUCY^5 **GORDY** (*Robert Daniel*^{4}, *Samuel 'Sam*^{3}, *Berry*^{2}, *Jim*^{1}) was born on 17 July 1956 in Sandersville, Georgia. She married **Tony Owen Hurt Sr.** on 7 July 1979.

Children of **Mary Lucy**^{5} **Gordy** and **Tony Owen Hurt Sr.** were as follows:
283. i. TONY OWEN^6 JR. was born on 19 April 1982 in Milledgeville, Georgia.
284. ii. KARI LOUCYE was born on 17 February 1985 in Milledgeville, Georgia.
285. iii. BRAXTON GORDY was born on 7 June 1992 in Macon, Georgia.

139. BERRY RENARD^5 **GORDY** (*Robert Daniel*^{4}, *Samuel 'Sam*^{3}, *Berry*^{2}, *Jim*^{1}) was born on 10 September 1958 in Sandersville, Georgia. He married **Brenda Lee Lord Barlow Cardy.**

Children of **Berry Renard**^{5} **Gordy** and **Brenda Lee Lord Barlow Cardy** were:
286. i. JALEN BERRY^6 was born on 19 October 1991 in Augusta, Georgia.

141. MAUDE^5 GORDY (*William Roy^4, Easter^3, Berry^2, Jim^1*) was born in Detroit, Michigan. She married **James Casey.**

Children of **Maude^5 Gordy** and **James Casey** were as follows:
287. i. MELVIN^6 was born in Detroit, Michigan.
288. ii. DENNIS 'PISTOL' was born in Detroit, Michigan.

143. DOROTHY^5 GORDY (*William Roy^4, Easter^3, Berry^2, Jim^1*) was born on 18 October 1926 in Sandersville, Georgia. She married **George Lowe** in July 1945 in Detroit, Michigan. She died on 3 May 1998 in Detroit, Michigan, at age 71.

Children of **Dorothy^5 Gordy** include:
+ 289. i. MARGARET 'COOKIE'^{6}, born 1944; married **Kenneth Whitlock.**
+ 290. ii. RICHARD LEE, born 24 April 1945; married **Katherine 'Kathy'** (—?—).

Children of **Dorothy^5 Gordy** and **George Lowe** were as follows:
+ 291. i. GEORGE RALPH^6, born 27 December 1946 in Detroit, Michigan; married **Lorraine Williams.**
+ 292. ii. SANDRA JEAN, born 7 December 1947 in Detroit, Michigan; married **Charles Owen.**
+ 293. iii. VICKIE, born 3 July 1950 in Detroit, Michigan; married **Albert Lee Shackelford.**
+ 294. iv. JANICE, born 9 September 1951 in Detroit, Michigan; married **Jeffrey Jackson.**
+ 295. v. DARRELL LAWRENCE, born 24 August 1953 in Detroit, Michigan.
+ 296. vi. PHILLIP WARREN, born 6 October 1954 in Detroit, Michigan; married **Jessie** (—?—).
+ 297. vii. KATHERINE ANN, born 24 November 1955 in Detroit, Michigan; married **Dwight Hosey.**

145. JOHN REASE^5 BUTTS JR. (*John 'Johnnie' Rease^4, Lucy 'Nig'^{3}Gordy, Berry^2, Jim^1*) was born on 7 March 1946 in Detroit, Michigan. He married **Gwendolyn Gambrell** in 1977 in Toledo, Ohio.

Children of **John Rease^5 Butts Jr.** and **Jacqueline Carter** were as follows:
298. i. EARLANDO^6 was born on 1 September 1966 in Detroit, Michigan.
+ 299. ii. ALMA JEAN, born 2 September 1967 in Detroit, Michigan; married **James Arthur Price.**

Children of **John Rease^5 Butts Jr.** and **Gwendolyn Gambrell** were as follows:
+ 300. i. SHONA MONIQUE^6, born 15 December 1968 in Detroit, Michigan.
+ 301. ii. JOHN REASE III, born 26 April 1970 in Detroit, Michigan.
302. iii. ANTHONY was born on 16 July 1971 in Detroit, Michigan.

146. VERNEDA ELAINE[5] BUTTS (*John 'Johnnie' Rease[4], Lucy 'Nig[3]Gordy, Berry[2], Jim[1]*) was born on 1 May 1947 in Detroit, Michigan. She married **L.V. Allen** on 16 December 1967 in Detroit, Michigan.

Children of **Verneda Elaine[5] Butts** and **L.V. Allen** were as follows:
+ 303.   i. BRIAN LAMAR[6], born 17 October 1970 in Ann Arbor, Michigan; married **Stephlanie Dobbins.**
+ 304.   ii. TAMARA NIKKOL, born 25 September 1974 in Ann Arbor, Michigan.
+ 305.   iii. TIFFANY RENEE, born 1 January 1979 in Ann Arbor, Michigan.

147. VINCENT DEROY[5] BUTTS (*John 'Johnnie' Rease[4], Lucy 'Nig[3]Gordy, Berry[2], Jim[1]*) was born on 3 March 1953 in Detroit, Michigan. He died on 21 June 1986 in Detroit, Michigan, at age 33.

Children of **Vincent DeRoy[5] Butts** and **Karen Stanford** were:
+ 306.   i. SUSAN LINNETTE[6], born 22 February 1971 in Ypsilanti, Michigan.

Children of **Vincent DeRoy[5] Butts** and **Robin Dalian** were:
+ 307.   i. STACHA[6], born 25 February 1978 in Ann Arbor, Michigan.

149. JEFFREY BERNARD[5] WOOD (*Thomas 'T.J' Jefferson[4], Lucy 'Nig[3]Gordy, Berry[2], Jim[1]*) was born on 15 January 1941 in Detroit, Michigan.

Children of **Jeffrey Bernard[5] Wood** include:
308.   i. DERRICK SCOTT[6] was born in 1941 in Detroit, Michigan.
309.   ii. JEFFREY was born in 1943 in Detroit, Michigan.

150. NICKOLE T.[5] WOOD (*Thomas 'T.J' Jefferson[4], Lucy 'Nig[3]Gordy, Berry[2], Jim[1]*) was born on 19 September 1943 in Detroit, Michigan. She married **John Pierpont Massey III** on 26 May 1961 in Detroit, Michigan.

Children of **Nickole T.[5] Wood** and **John Pierpont Massey III** were as follows:
+ 310.   i. JOHN PIERPONT[6] IV, born 13 September 1962 in Detroit, Michigan; married **Kimberly Colden.**
+ 311.   ii. ANTOINETTE NICKOLE, born 12 August 1963 in Detroit, Michigan.

152. DARRYL PATRICK[5] WOOD (*Thomas 'T.J' Jefferson[4], Lucy 'Nig[3]Gordy, Berry[2], Jim[1]*) was born in Detroit, Michigan. He married **Erma** (—?—) in Detroit, Michigan.

Children of **Darryl Patrick[5] Wood** and **Erma** (—?—) were as follows:
312.   i. BROOKE[6] was born in Detroit, Michigan.
313.   ii. BRITTANY was born in Detroit, Michigan.

314.   iii. BRIDGETT was born in Detroit, Michigan.

153. **WANDA**^{5} **WOOD** (*Thomas 'T.J' Jefferson*^{4}, *Lucy 'Nig*^{3}*Gordy, Berry*^{2}, *Jim*^{1}) was born in Detroit, Michigan. She married **John Donald** in Detroit, Michigan.

Children of **Wanda**^{5} **Wood** and **John Donald** were as follows:
315.   i. ERICA^6 was born in December 1989 in Detroit, Michigan.
316.   ii. BRANDON was born in December 1989 in Detroit, Michigan.

Generation Six

157. **KAREN**^{6} **MOORE** (*Joyce*^{5}*Lawson, Mamie*^{4}*Gaudy, John*^{3}, *Berry*^{2}*Gordy, Jim*^{1}) was born on 11 February 1967.

Children of **Karen**^{6} **Moore** include:
317.   i. ELI^7.
318.   ii. TYLER.

167. **EUGENE**^{6} **ANDERSON (IV)** (*Florence*^{5}*Gaudy, John*^{4}, *John*^{3}, *Berry*^{2}*Gordy, Jim*^{1}) married **Kimberly** (———).

Children of **Eugene**^{6} **Anderson (IV)** and **Kimberly** (———) were:
319.   i. KAYLA^7.

171. **KENDRA**^{6} **MARTIN** (*Valerie*^{5}*Gaudy, John*^{4}, *John*^{3}, *Berry*^{2}*Gordy, Jim*^{1}).

Children of **Kendra**^{6} **Martin** include:
320.   i. JAMAR^7.

201. **LATOYA MERTRICE**^{6} **LEMON** (*Howard Lovell*^{5}, *Lula Mae*^{4}*Gaudy, John*^{3}, *Berry*^{2}*Gordy, Jim*^{1}) was born on 20 October 1976 in Detroit, Michigan. She married **Henry James** in 1998 in Detroit, Michigan.

Children of **LaToya Mertrice**^{6} **Lemon** and **Henry James** were:
321.   i. CHRISTOPHER^7 was born in April 1998 in Detroit, Michigan.

202. **SHEILA RENE**^{6} **GREEN** (*Patricia M.*^{5}*Lemon, Lula Mae*^{4}*Gaudy, John*^{3}, *Berry*^{2}*Gordy, Jim*^{1}).

Children of **Sheila Rene**^{6} **Green** include:
322.   i. ERIC^7.
323.   ii. ANTOINE.

324.   iii. ZACHERY.
325.   iv. MICHAEL.

205. SONJA DENISE^6 GREEN (*Patricia M.^{5}Lemon, Lula Mae^{4}Gaudy, John^3, Berry^{2}Gordy, Jim^1*).

Children of **Sonja Denise^6 Green** include:
326.   i. KAYLA^7.
327.   ii. KIEARA.
328.   iii. CHRISTOPHER.
329.   iv. ISAIAH.

223. KARLA DAWN^6 BRISTOL (*Iris Bertha^{5}Gordy, Fuller Berry^4, Berry 'Pop'^{3}, Berry^2, Jim^1*) was born circa 22 December 1970 in Detroit, Michigan. She married **Tyrone Brown** on 8 July 1990 in Los Angeles, California.

Children of **Karla Dawn^6 Bristol** and **Tyrone Brown** were as follows:
330.   i. KIARRA MICHAUX^7 was born on 13 May 1992 in Los Angeles, California.
331.   ii. MORGAN ASHLEY was born on 5 September 1995 in Atlanta, Georgia.

224. SCHAMEL LA NEACE^6 JONES (*Alice Ramona 'Peaches'^{5}Washington, Mary Francis^{4}Gordy, Joseph 'Joe'^{3}, Berry^2, Jim^1*) was born on 4 October 1966 in Detroit, Michigan.

Children of **Schamel La Neace^6 Jones** and **Maurice Stewart** were:
332.   i. SCHAURICE IMAN^7 was born on 14 March 1987 in Detroit, Michigan.

225. CONSTANCE MONIQUE^6 JONES (*Alice Ramona 'Peaches'^{5}Washington, Mary Francis^{4}Gordy, Joseph 'Joe'^{3}, Berry^2, Jim^1*) was born on 29 August 1969 in Detroit, Michigan. She married **Aphrodion Hamilton**.

Children of **Constance Monique^6 Jones** and **Aphrodion Hamilton** were as follows:
333.   i. LEON CORTEZ^7 was born on 22 September 1989 in Detroit, Michigan.
334.   ii. MICHAEL was born on 5 September 1994 in Detroit, Michigan.
335.   iii. EVAN was born on 30 December 1997 in Detroit, Michigan.
336.   iv. DESTINY was born on 12 June 2000 in Detroit, Michigan.

226. MASHANNA IKEYLA^6 JONES (*Alice Ramona 'Peaches'^{5}Washington, Mary Francis^{4}Gordy, Joseph 'Joe'^{3}, Berry^2, Jim^1*) was born on 24 January 1972 in Detroit, Michigan. She married **James Hall** in Detroit, Michigan.

Children of **Mashanna Ikeyla**^{6} **Jones** and **James Hall** were as follows:

337.   i. JAMES^7 JR. was born on 19 December 1989 in Detroit, Michigan.
338.   ii. JOSHUA was born on 17 December 1990 in Detroit, Michigan.
339.   iii. JEREMIAH was born on 21 November 1992 in Detroit, Michigan.
340.   iv. JAWAN was born on 6 July 1994 in Detroit, Michigan.
341.   v. JAKEYLA was born on 6 November 1997 in Las Vegas, Nevada.
342.   vi. JAQUAZE was born on 23 October 1998 in Las Vegas, Nevada.
343.   vii. JOSAIA was born on 10 May 2000 in Las Vegas, Nevada.
344.   viii. JAZMYNE was born on 20 May 2001 in Las Vegas, Nevada.
345.   ix. JAZELL was born on 23 May 2002 in Las Vegas, Nevada.
346.   x. JANAY was born in July 2003 in Las Vegas, Nevada.

228. BRIAN^6 GORDY (*Henry Edward^5, Henry Berry^4, Samuel 'Sam^3, Berry^2, Jim^1*) married **Yvonne** (———).

Children of **Brian^6 Gordy** and **Yvonne** (———) were as follows:
347.   i. LANITA^7.
348.   ii. BRIANA.

229. BYRON^6 GORDY (*Henry Edward^5, Henry Berry^4, Samuel 'Sam^3, Berry^2, Jim^1*) married **Willette** (———).

Children of **Byron^6 Gordy** and **Willette** (———) were:
349.   i. CHRISTINE^7.

230. BRUCE^6 GORDY (*Henry Edward^5, Henry Berry^4, Samuel 'Sam^3, Berry^2, Jim^1*) married **Deborah** (———).

Children of **Bruce^6 Gordy** and **Deborah** (———) were as follows:
350.   i. MARQITA^7.
351.   ii. APRIL.

231. BRENT^6 GORDY (*Henry Edward^5, Henry Berry^4, Samuel 'Sam^3, Berry^2, Jim^1*) married **Effie** (———).

Children of **Brent^6 Gordy** and **Effie** (———) were:
352.   i. JASMINE^7.

232. BRIDGETTE^6 GORDY (*Henry Edward^5, Henry Berry^4, Samuel 'Sam^3, Berry^2, Jim^1*) married **Bernell Seal**.

Children of **Bridgette**^{6} **Gordy** and **Bernell Seal** were as follows:
- 353.   i. ROBERT^7.
- 354.   ii. RAYNELL.
- 355.   iii. RAYNARD.

234. KAREN^6 KING (*Margaret Jewel^{5}Gordy, Henry Berry^4, Samuel 'Sam^3, Berry^2, Jim^1*) married **Elvin Brooks.**

Children of **Karen**^{6} **King** and **Elvin Brooks** were as follows:
- 356.   i. KYLE^7.
- 357.   ii. KARLIS.
- 358.   iii. KELLUM.
- 359.   iv. KRISTOPHER.
- 360.   v. KENNETH.
- 361.   vi. KARY.
- 362.   vii. KARIS.

235. KYRA^6 KING (*Margaret Jewel^{5}Gordy, Henry Berry^4, Samuel 'Sam^3, Berry^2, Jim^1*) married **James Ridgell.**

Children of **Kyra**^{6} **King** and **James Ridgell** were as follows:
- 363.   i. IAN^7.
- 364.   ii. ETHAN.
- 365.   iii. JULIAN.

243. DEBORAH^6 LAWRENCE (*Joyce^{5}Gordy, Henry Berry^4, Samuel 'Sam^3, Berry^2, Jim^1*) married **Lamont McClain.**

Children of **Deborah**^{6} **Lawrence** and **Lamont McClain** were as follows:
- 366.   i. VANESSA^7.
- 367.   ii. KRISTIN.
- 368.   iii. TASHA.

244. DOREEN^6 LAWRENCE (*Joyce^{5}Gordy, Henry Berry^4, Samuel 'Sam^3, Berry^2, Jim^1*) married **Sam Hughes.**

Children of **Doreen**^{6} **Lawrence** and **Sam Hughes** were:
- 369.   i. DAVID^7.

246. DARIN^6 LAWRENCE (*Joyce^{5}Gordy, Henry Berry^4, Samuel 'Sam^3, Berry^2, Jim^1*) married **Shirley (———).**

Children of **Darin[6] Lawrence** and **Shirley** (———) were as follows:
370. i. BRANDON[7].
371. ii. KEITH.

253. LINDA[6] BUTTS (*Mary Louvenia 'Benia[5] Cawthon, Mary Lucy[4] Gordy, Samuel 'Sam[3], Berry[2], Jim[1]*) was born on 27 February 1951 in Milledgeville, Georgia. She married **Donald Edwin Brooks**, son of **Donald Brooks** and **Ermine Steadman-Johnson**.

Children of **Linda[6] Butts** and **Donald Edwin Brooks** were as follows:
372. i. DAWN ERMINE[7] was born on 11 November 1972 in Meriden, Connecticut.
373. ii. ANITRA LOUVINE was born on 20 July 1975 in Meriden, Connecticut.
374. iii. KAHLIL was born on 28 March 1977 in Meriden, Connecticut.

255. EVELYN BERNICE 'EBBIE'[6] BUTTS (*Mary Louvenia 'Benia[5] Cawthon, Mary Lucy[4] Gordy, Samuel 'Sam[3], Berry[2], Jim[1]*) was born in Hartford, Connecticut. She was born on 12 April 1954 in Hartford, Connecticut.

Children of **Evelyn Bernice 'Ebbie'[6] Butts** include:
+ 375. i. BRITTANY EUGENIA[7], born 5 March 1976 in Middletown, Connecticut; married **Edward Ray Jordan**.
376. ii. ENID JO MCKENZIE was born on 16 December 1984 in Hartford, Connecticut.

256. CHRISTIE[6] BUTTS TURNER (*Mary Louvenia 'Benia[5] Cawthon, Mary Lucy[4] Gordy, Samuel 'Sam[3], Berry[2], Jim[1]*) was born on 18 December 1956 in Hartford, Connecticut. She married **Joseph Hicks Sr.** in Atlanta, Georgia.

Children of **Christie[6] Butts Turner** and **Joseph Hicks Sr.** were:
+ 377. i. JOSEPH 'JOE'[7] JR., born in Atlanta, Georgia.

267. BERNARD[6] TRAWICK (*Mary Pearl 'Town[5] Gordy, Samuel 'Sam[4], Samuel 'Sam[3], Berry[2], Jim[1]*) was born on 14 December 1951 in Philadelphia, Pennsylvania. He married **Kenya Wilson**.

Children of **Bernard[6] Trawick** and **Kenya Wilson** were as follows:
378. i. TAFT[7] was born on 25 April 1986 in Winston-Salem, North Carolina.
379. ii. JASON was born on 14 December 1987 in Philadelphia, Pennsylvania.

270. CYNTHIA[6] TRAWICK (*Mary Pearl 'Town[5] Gordy, Samuel 'Sam[4], Samuel 'Sam[3], Berry[2], Jim[1]*) was born on 12 November 1958 in Philadelphia, Pennsylvania. She married **William Boyer**.

Children of **Cynthia**^{6} **Trawick** and **William Boyer** were as follows:
380.   i. AJA MARIE^7 was born on 9 June 1982 in Philadelphia, Pennsylvania.
381.   ii. TODD was born on 20 January 1984 in Philadelphia, Pennsylvania.
382.   iii. JENNA DANIELLE was born on 14 August 1989 in Philadelphia, Pennsylvania.
383.   iv. WILLIAM 'BJ' JR. was born on 16 December 1997 in Philadelphia, Pennsylvania.

289. MARGARET 'COOKIE'^{6} **GORDY** (*Dorothy*^{5}, *William Roy*^{4}, *Easter*^{3}, *Berry*^{2}, *Jim*^{1}) was born in 1944. She married **Kenneth Whitlock.**

Children of **Margaret 'Cookie'**^{6} **Gordy** and **Kenneth Whitlock** were as follows:
384.   i. ANTHONY^7.
385.   ii. DERRICK.

290. RICHARD LEE^6 **GORDY** (*Dorothy*^{5}, *William Roy*^{4}, *Easter*^{3}, *Berry*^{2}, *Jim*^{1}) was born on 24 April 1945. He married **Katherine 'Kathy'** (—?—). He died on 12 March 1979 in Detroit, Michigan, at age 33.

Children of **Richard Lee**^{6} **Gordy** and **Katherine 'Kathy'** (—?—) were as follows:
386.   i. ROCHELLE^7.
387.   ii. RICHARD LEE JR. was born on 10 April 1971 in Detroit, Michigan.
388.   iii. RICARDO was born on 24 March 1993 in Detroit, Michigan.

291. GEORGE RALPH^6 **LOWE** (*Dorothy*^{5} *Gordy*, *William Roy*^{4}, *Easter*^{3}, *Berry*^{2}, *Jim*^{1}) was born on 27 December 1946 in Detroit, Michigan. He married **Lorraine Williams** in 1955 in Detroit, Michigan.

Children of **George Ralph**^{6} **Lowe** and **Lorraine Williams** were as follows:
+ 389.   i. JOHN^7, born 3 July 1965 in Detroit, Michigan.
390.   ii. BRIAN KEITH was born on 13 September 1966 in Detroit, Michigan.
391.   iii. GEORGE JR. was born on 12 June 1971 in Detroit, Michigan.

292. SANDRA JEAN^6 **LOWE** (*Dorothy*^{5} *Gordy*, *William Roy*^{4}, *Easter*^{3}, *Berry*^{2}, *Jim*^{1}) was born on 7 December 1947 in Detroit, Michigan. She married **Charles Owen** on 28 May 1966 in Detroit, Michigan.

Children of **Sandra Jean**^{6} **Lowe** and **Charles Owen** were as follows:
+ 392.   i. CHARLES^7 JR., born 15 February 1967 in Detroit, Michigan; married **Sharon Roberts.**
+ 393.   ii. DARRELL, born 12 April 1968 in Detroit, Michigan.

293. VICKIE^6 LOWE (*Dorothy^{5}Gordy, William Roy^4, Easter^3, Berry^2, Jim^1*) was born on 3 July 1950 in Detroit, Michigan. She married **Albert Lee Shackelford** on 31 July 1975 in Detroit, Michigan.

Children of **Vickie^6 Lowe** and **Albert Lee Shackelford** were:
394.   i. AISHA PLESHETTE^7 was born on 23 August 1977 in Detroit, Michigan.

294. JANICE^6 LOWE (*Dorothy^{5}Gordy, William Roy^4, Easter^3, Berry^2, Jim^1*) was born on 9 September 1951 in Detroit, Michigan. She married **Jeffrey Jackson** on 18 October 1977.

Children of **Janice^6 Lowe** and **Jeffrey Jackson** were:
+ 395.   i. BRIDGETTE JEAN^7, born 9 December 1974.

295. DARRELL LAWRENCE^6 LOWE (*Dorothy^{5}Gordy, William Roy^4, Easter^3, Berry^2, Jim^1*) was born on 24 August 1953 in Detroit, Michigan.

Children of **Darrell Lawrence^6 Lowe** and **Cynthia** (—?—) were:
396.   i. DARRELL LAWRENCE^7 JR. was born on 18 October 1990 in Cleveland, Ohio.

296. PHILLIP WARREN^6 LOWE (*Dorothy^{5}Gordy, William Roy^4, Easter^3, Berry^2, Jim^1*) was born on 6 October 1954 in Detroit, Michigan. He married **Jessie** (—?—).

Children of **Phillip Warren^6 Lowe** and **Jessie** (—?—) were:
397.   i. PHELAN^7.

297. KATHERINE ANN^6 LOWE (*Dorothy^{5}Gordy, William Roy^4, Easter^3, Berry^2, Jim^1*) was born on 24 November 1955 in Detroit, Michigan. She married **Dwight Hosey** on 1 September 1978 in Detroit, Michigan.

Children of **Katherine Ann^6 Lowe** and **Dwight Hosey** were as follows:
398.   i. MIGNON^7 was born on 24 October 1982 in Detroit, Michigan.
399.   ii. ARIAL was born on 13 June 1984 in Detroit, Michigan.

299. ALMA JEAN^6 CARTER (*John Rease^{5}Butts, John 'Johnnie' Rease^4, Lucy 'Nig'^{3}Gordy, Berry^2, Jim^1*) was born on 2 September 1967 in Detroit, Michigan. She married **James Arthur Price** in June 2003 in Detroit, Michigan.

Children of **Alma Jean^6 Carter** and **James Arthur Price** were as follows:
400.   i. BRIAN KEITH^7 was born on 15 May 1988 in Detroit, Michigan.
401.   ii. JAYLEN LAMAR was born on 2 March 1998 in Detroit, Michigan.

300. SHONA MONIQUE^6 **BUTTS** (*John Rease*^{5}, *John 'Johnnie' Rease*^{4}, *Lucy 'Nig*^{3}*Gordy, Berry*^{2}, *Jim*^{1}) was born on 15 December 1968 in Detroit, Michigan.

Children of **Shona Monique**^{6} **Butts** and **Kareem** (—?—) were as follows:
402.   i. TAVAREZ^7 was born on 8 November 1988 in Detroit, Michigan.
403.   ii. VICTORIA was born on 11 August 1990 in Detroit, Michigan.

301. JOHN REASE^6 **BUTTS III** (*John Rease*^{5}, *John 'Johnnie' Rease*^{4}, *Lucy 'Nig*^{3}*Gordy, Berry*^{2}, *Jim*^{1}) was born on 26 April 1970 in Detroit, Michigan.

Children of **John Rease**^{6} **Butts III** and **Evelyn** (—?—) were as follows:
404.   i. JAMEER^7 was born on 28 August 1998 in Detroit, Michigan.
405.   ii. JARRID was born on 2 April 2000 in Detroit, Michigan.

303. BRIAN LAMAR^6 **ALLEN** (*Verneda Elaine*^{5}*Butts, John 'Johnnie' Rease*^{4}, *Lucy 'Nig*^{3}*Gordy, Berry*^{2}, *Jim*^{1}) was born on 17 October 1970 in Ann Arbor, Michigan. He married **Stephlanie Dobbins** in Ann Arbor, Michigan.

Children of **Brian Lamar**^{6} **Allen** and **Stephlanie Dobbins** were as follows:
406.   i. BRAXTON LAMAR^7 was born on 24 July 1997 in Ann Arbor, Michigan.
407.   ii. BREYDEN was born on 28 March 2002 in Ann Arbor, Michigan.

Children of **Brian Lamar**^{6} **Allen** and **Latrena Wall** were:
408.   i. BRIAN LAMAR^7 JR. was born on 3 May 1990 in Detroit, Michigan.

304. TAMARA NIKKOL^6 **ALLEN** (*Verneda Elaine*^{5}*Butts, John 'Johnnie' Rease*^{4}, *Lucy 'Nig*^{3}*Gordy, Berry*^{2}, *Jim*^{1}) was born on 25 September 1974 in Ann Arbor, Michigan.

Children of **Tamara Nikkol**^{6} **Allen** and **Darren Wheeler** were:
409.   i. BREANNA SIMONE^7 was born on 8 December 1995 in Ann Arbor, Michigan.

305. TIFFANY RENEE^6 **ALLEN** (*Verneda Elaine*^{5}*Butts, John 'Johnnie' Rease*^{4}, *Lucy 'Nig*^{3}*Gordy, Berry*^{2}, *Jim*^{1}) was born on 1 January 1979 in Ann Arbor, Michigan.

Children of **Tiffany Renee**^{6} **Allen** and **Xango Uche Moreland** were:
410.   i. ANAYA SIMONE^7 was born on 15 July 2000 in Baltimore, Maryland.

306. SUSAN LINNETTE^6 **STANFORD** (*Vincent DeRoy*^{5}*Butts, John 'Johnnie' Rease*^{4}, *Lucy 'Nig*^{3}*Gordy, Berry*^{2}, *Jim*^{1}) was born on 22 February 1971 in Ypsilanti, Michigan.

Children of **Susan Linnette**^{6} **Stanford** and **Craig Walter Doyle** were:
411.   i. CRAIGE MICHAEL^7 was born on 5 December 1986 in Lansing, Michigan.

336

Children of **Susan Linnette**[6] **Stanford** and **Lamont Brian Eaton** were as follows:
412.   i. BRYANT CHRISTOPHER[7] was born on 1 April 1989 in Lansing, Michigan.
413.   ii. JAMES AVERY was born on 25 April 1991 in Lansing, Michigan.

Children of **Susan Linnette**[6] **Stanford** and **Nolan Smith** were:
414.   i. JASMINE AMARI[7] was born on 5 March 1996 in Michigan.

307. STACHA[6] **DALIAN** (*Vincent DeRoy*[5]*Butts, John 'Johnnie' Rease*[4], *Lucy 'Nig*[3]*Gordy, Berry*[2], *Jim*[1]) was born on 25 February 1978 in Ann Arbor, Michigan.

Children of **Stacha**[6] **Dalian** and **Eric** (—?—) were:
415.   i. ERICA[7] was born in 1995.

310. JOHN PIERPONT[6] **MASSEY IV** (*Nickole T.*[5]*Wood, Thomas 'T.J' Jefferson*[4], *Lucy 'Nig*[3]*Gordy, Berry*[2], *Jim*[1]) was born on 13 September 1962 in Detroit, Michigan. He married **Kimberly Colden** on 14 October 1994 in Detroit, Michigan.

Children of **John Pierpont**[6] **Massey IV** and **Kimberly Colden** were as follows:
416.   i. LAUREN COLDEN[7] was born on 4 February 1997 in Detroit, Michigan.
417.   ii. JOHN PIERPONT V was born on 6 March 2004 in Detroit, Michigan.

311. ANTOINETTE NICKOLE[6] **MASSEY** (*Nickole T.*[5]*Wood, Thomas 'T.J' Jefferson*[4], *Lucy 'Nig*[3]*Gordy, Berry*[2], *Jim*[1]) was born on 12 August 1963 in Detroit, Michigan.

Children of **Antoinette Nickole**[6] **Massey** and **Jason Justice** were:
418.   i. KENNEDY NICKOLE[7] was born on 12 October 2003 in Detroit, Michigan.

Generation Seven

375. BRITTANY EUGENIA[7] **BUTTS** (*Evelyn Bernice 'Ebbie*[6], *Mary Louvenia 'Benia*[5]*Cawthon, Mary Lucy*[4]*Gordy, Samuel 'Sam*[3], *Berry*[2], *Jim*[1]) was born on 5 March 1976 in Middletown, Connecticut. She married **Edward Ray Jordan** in September 1994 in Middletown, Connecticut.

Children of **Brittany Eugenia**[7] **Butts** and **Edward Ray Jordan** were:
419.   i. NATHANIAL RAY[8] was born on 13 August 1995.

377. JOSEPH 'JOE'[7] **HICKS JR.** (*Christie*[6]*Butts, Mary Louvenia 'Benia*[5]*Cawthon, Mary Lucy*[4]*Gordy, Samuel 'Sam*[3], *Berry*[2], *Jim*[1]) was born in Atlanta, Georgia.

Children of **Joseph 'Joe'**[7] **Hicks Jr.** include:
420.   i. SYDNEY[8] was born in Atlanta, Georgia.

421.   ii. TAJI was born in Atlanta, Georgia.

389. JOHN^7 LOWE (*George Ralph^6, Dorothy^5 Gordy, William Roy^4, Easter^3, Berry^2, Jim^1*) was born on 3 July 1965 in Detroit, Michigan.

Children of **John^7 Lowe** and **Melissa Mercedes** were:
422.   i. MORGAN^8 was born in July 1991 in Minnesota.

392. CHARLES^7 OWEN JR. (*Sandra Jean^6 Lowe, Dorothy^5 Gordy, William Roy^4, Easter^3, Berry^2, Jim^1*) was born on 15 February 1967 in Detroit, Michigan. He married **Sharon Roberts.**

Children of **Charles^7 Owen Jr.** and **Sharon Roberts** were as follows:
423.   i. DANIQUA^8 was born on 26 July 1986 in Los Angeles, California.
424.   ii. DANISHA was born on 27 September 1988 in Los Angeles, California.

393. DARRELL^7 OWEN (*Sandra Jean^6 Lowe, Dorothy^5 Gordy, William Roy^4, Easter^3, Berry^2, Jim^1*) was born on 12 April 1968 in Detroit, Michigan.

Children of **Darrell^7 Owen** and **Beth** (—?—) were:
425.   i. BRIANNA^8 was born on 26 February 1998 in Minnesota.

395. BRIDGETTE JEAN^7 JACKSON (*Janice^6 Lowe, Dorothy^5 Gordy, William Roy^4, Easter^3, Berry^2, Jim^1*) was born on 9 December 1974.

Children of **Bridgette Jean^7 Jackson** and **Terry Thomas** were as follows:
426.   i. CHANEL^8 was born on 11 August 1995 in Minnesota.
427.   ii. JALEN EDWARD was born on 26 February 2001 in Minnesota.

Descendants of Sampson Dawson

340

1910 CENSUS — UNITED STATES

STATE: Georgia
COUNTY: Washington
EXTRACT: Nonie C. Veal
DATE: 1910

Location	Name	Relation	Sex	Color	Age					Place of birth	Place of birth of father	Place of birth of mother				Occupation							
163 103	Dawson Sampson	Head	M	B	52	m	26			GA													
	Mary	wife	F	B	45	m	26	10	7	GA													
	? E. Herman	son	M	B	21	S				GA													
	Homer	son	M	B	18	S				GA													
	? Alpheous	son	M	B	17	S				GA													
	Cireus	son	M	B	14	S				GA													
	Bessie	dau	F	B	12	S				GA													
	Willie Lewis	son	M	B	10	S				GA													
3 3	Trawick Marl?	Head	M	B	67					GA													
	Rachel	wife	F	B	68					GA													
	Ivey	grandson	M	B	16					GA													
	? Della	neice	F	B	18					GA													

Sampson Dawson, 1910 Census

Descendants of Sampson Dawson

Generation One

1. SAMPSON[1] DAWSON married **Mamie Robinson.**

Children of **Sampson[1] Dawson** and **Mamie Robinson** were as follows:
+ 2.   i. HOMER[2], born in Sandersville, Washington County, Georgia; married **Lora Ella 'Laura' Carter.**
+ 3.   ii. HERMAN, born in Sandersville, Washington County, Georgia; married **Effie Walker.**
4.   iii. LILLIAN was born in Sandersville, Washington County, Georgia.
5.   iv. CASSIUS was born in Sandersville, Washington County, Georgia.
6.   v. WILLIE LOUIS was born in Sandersville, Washington County, Georgia.
7.   vi. BESSIE was born in Sandersville, Washington County, Georgia.
8.   vii. ALPHEUS was born in Sandersville, Washington County, Georgia.

Generation Two

2. HOMER[2] DAWSON (*Sampson[1]*) was born in Sandersville, Washington County, Georgia. He married **Lora Ella 'Laura' Carter**, daughter of **Jeff Carter Sr.** and **Ella Hooks.** He died in September 1964 in Philadelphia, Pennsylvania.

Children of **Homer[2] Dawson** and **Lora Ella 'Laura' Carter** were as follows:
9.   i. SAM[3] was born in Sandersville, Washington County, Georgia.
+ 10.   ii. ROBERTA, born circa 5 November 1916 in Sandersville, Washington County, Georgia; married **Wesley Pettis.**
+ 11.   iii. ELIZABETH, born 20 August 1921 in Sandersville, Washington County, Georgia; married **Lucious 'Lewis' Fisher;** married **Booker T. Whitehead.**
+ 12.   iv. TIMOTHY, born 31 August 1924 in Sandersville, Washington County, Georgia; married **Lillie Ruth Wiley.**
+ 13.   v. DEBORAH, born 29 June 1927 in Sandersville, Washington County, Georgia; married **Edward Sparks.**
+ 14.   vi. ELOISE 'HONEY', born 27 September 1929 in Sandersville, Washington County, Georgia; married **Robert Daniel Gordy.**
+ 15.   vii. HOMER (JR.), born 4 January 1932 in Sandersville, Washington County, Georgia; married **Bettye Tanner.**
+ 16.   viii. CORNELIUS, born 5 November 1933 in Sandersville, Washington County, Georgia; married **Delores Pinkston.**
+ 17.   ix. WILHELMINA 'CANDY', born 29 September 1936 in Sandersville, Washington County, Georgia; married **Amos Ross;** married **Frank Davis.**

3. HERMAN^2 DAWSON (*Sampson^1*) was born in Sandersville, Washington County, Georgia. He married **Effie Walker.**

Children of **Herman^2 Dawson** and **Effie Walker** were as follows:
  18. i. EMORY^3 was born on 20 February 1924. He married **Mary Lou** (—?—).
  19. ii. MATTHEW was born on 25 June 1928. He married **Estella** (—?—).
  20. iii. EUGENE was born on 1 January 1930. He married **Berniece** (—?—).

Generation Three

10. ROBERTA^3 DAWSON (*Homer^2, Sampson^1*) was born circa 5 November 1916 in Sandersville, Washington County, Georgia. She married **Wesley Pettis.** She died in December 1954 in West Palm Beach, Florida.

Children of **Roberta^3 Dawson** and **Wesley Pettis** were as follows:
  21. i. CALVIN^4.
  22. ii. JOYCE.

11. ELIZABETH^3 DAWSON (*Homer^2, Sampson^1*) was born on 20 August 1921 in Sandersville, Washington County, Georgia. She married **Lucious 'Lewis' Fisher.** She married **Booker T. Whitehead.**

Children of **Elizabeth^3 Dawson** include:
+ 23. i. SHIRLEY^4, born 29 March; married **Edward Brent.**

There were no children of **Elizabeth^3 Dawson** and **Lucious 'Lewis' Fisher.**

There were no children of **Elizabeth^3 Dawson** and **Booker T. Whitehead.**

12. TIMOTHY^3 DAWSON (*Homer^2, Sampson^1*) was born on 31 August 1924 in Sandersville, Washington County, Georgia. He married **Lillie Ruth Wiley** in 1949. He died on 26 April 1995 in Philadelphia, Pennsylvania, at age 70.

Children of **Timothy^3 Dawson** and **Lillie Ruth Wiley** were as follows:
  24. i. JEFFREY^4 was born on 6 August in Sandersville, Georgia.
+ 25. ii. BRENDA, born 18 September in Sandersville, Georgia; married **Mark Scott.**
+ 26. iii. BENNIE LAWSON, born 6 July 1947 in Sandersville, Georgia; married **Barbara Jones.**
  27. iv. TIMOTHY (JR.) was born on 11 November 1950 in Sandersville, Georgia. He married **Volanda** (—?—).
  28. v. EMORY was born on 21 June 1951 in Sandersville, Georgia. He married **Patricia Pates.**

+ 29. vi. LORETTA, born 30 August 1952 in Sandersville, Georgia; married **Aubrey Jones.**
+ 30. vii. PAULINE, born 12 November 1954 in Sandersville, Georgia; married **Alfred Ford.**
  31. viii. ROBERTA was born on 19 April 1956 in Sandersville, Georgia.
  32. ix. LILLIAN was born on 6 August 1957 in Sandersville, Georgia. She married **Eddie Pulliam.**

13. DEBORAH^3 DAWSON (*Homer^2, Sampson^1*) was born on 29 June 1927 in Sandersville, Washington County, Georgia. She married **Edward Sparks.**

Children of **Deborah^3 Dawson** and **Edward Sparks** were as follows:
+ 33. i. GRACE HARRIS^4, born 22 March 1944 in Sandersville, Georgia; married **Hugh Bryant.**
  34. ii. EDWARD TRACY was born on 28 September 1958 in Syracuse, New York.
  35. iii. MICHAEL was born on 31 October 1959 in Syracuse, New York.
  36. iv. GARY was born on 13 October 1960 in Syracuse, New York.
  37. v. WILLIAM 'BILLY' KENNETH was born on 29 January 1962 in Syracuse, New York.
  38. vi. RICHARD was born on 17 July 1965 in Syracuse, New York.

14. ELOISE 'HONEY'^{3} DAWSON (*Homer^2, Sampson^1*) was born on 27 September 1929 in Sandersville, Washington County, Georgia. She married **Robert Daniel Gordy**, son of **Samuel 'Sam' Gordy** and **Carrie Cheeves**, on 6 March 1950 in Sandersville, Washington County, Georgia.

Children of **Eloise 'Honey'^{3} Dawson** and **Robert Daniel Gordy** were as follows:
+ 39. i. GWENDOLYN^4, born 12 March 1947 in Utica, New York; married **Julius Murphy.**
  40. ii. ROBERT DANIEL JR. was born on 27 July 1950 in Sandersville, Georgia.
+ 41. iii. DAVID, born 13 April 1952 in Sandersville, Georgia; married **DeLois Turner;** married **Darlene Robinson.**
+ 42. iv. DEBORAH ANNE, born 6 January 1954 in Sandersville, Georgia; married **Samuel Duggan.**
+ 43. v. MARY LUCY, born 17 July 1956 in Sandersville, Georgia; married **Tony Owen Hurt Sr.**
  44. vi. REGINALD CORNELIUS was born on 5 September 1957 in Sandersville, Georgia. He married **Yvette (—?—).**
+ 45. vii. BERRY RENARD, born 10 September 1958 in Sandersville, Georgia; married **Brenda Lee Lord Barlow Cardy.**

15. HOMER^3 DAWSON (JR.) (*Homer^2, Sampson^1*) was born on 4 January 1932 in Sandersville, Washington County, Georgia. He married **Bettye Tanner.**

Children of **Homer³ Dawson** (Jr.) and **Bettye Tanner** were as follows:

+ 46.   i. CATHERINE LORETTA⁴, born 4 February 1951 in West Palm Beach, Florida; married **Douglas Fulton.**

+ 47.   ii. HOMER 'BILLY' III, born 9 April 1953 in West Palm Beach, Florida; married **Brenda McCullom.**

   48.   iii. JEFFREY was born on 4 June 1954 in West Palm Beach, Florida. He married Bernice (—?—).

+ 49.   iv. WENDELL, born 31 January 1957 in West Palm Beach, Florida; married **Deborah Davis.**

+ 50.   v. NATALIE JEAN, born 6 April 1958 in West Palm Beach, Florida; married **Robert Smith.**

16. CORNELIUS³ DAWSON (*Homer²*, *Sampson¹*) was born on 5 November 1933 in Sandersville, Washington County, Georgia. He married **Delores Pinkston.**

Children of **Cornelius³ Dawson** and **Delores Pinkston** were as follows:

+ 51.   i. BEVERLY⁴, born 5 February 1955 in East Palatka, Florida.

+ 52.   ii. WANDA, born 1 November 1959 in West Palm Beach, Florida; married **Tim Hunt.**

   53.   iii. ROBBYN was born on 2 November 1961 in West Palm Beach, Florida.

   54.   iv. ERIC was born on 25 November 1967 in West Palm Beach, Florida.

17. WILHELMINA 'CANDY'³ DAWSON (*Homer²*, *Sampson¹*) was born on 29 September 1936 in Sandersville, Washington County, Georgia. She married **Amos Ross.** She married **Frank Davis.**

There were no children of **Wilhelmina 'Candy'³ Dawson** and **Amos Ross.**

Children of **Wilhelmina 'Candy'³ Dawson** and **Frank Davis** were as follows:

+ 55.   i. KAREN ' KAY' ELIZABETH⁴, born 14 May 1956 in West Palm Beach, Florida; married **Willie Neal.**

   56.   ii. GWENETH 'RUTHIE' was born on 29 September 1957.

Generation Four

23. SHIRLEY⁴ FISHER (*Elizabeth³Dawson, Homer², Sampson¹*) was born on 29 March. She married **Edward Brent.**

Children of **Shirley⁴ Fisher** and **Edward Brent** were:

+ 57.   i. ROBIN⁵, born 21 June 1962; married **Joseph Phelps.**

25. BRENDA⁴ DAWSON (*Timothy³, Homer², Sampson¹*) was born on 18 September in Sandersville, Georgia. She married **Mark Scott.**

Children of **Brenda**^{4} **Dawson** and **Mark Scott** were as follows:
58. i. VALISE^5 was born on 25 July.
59. ii. VALENE was born on 25 September 1986.

26. **BENNIE LAWSON**^{4} **DAWSON** (*Timothy*^{3}, *Homer*^{2}, *Sampson*^{1}) was born on 6 July 1947 in Sandersville, Georgia. He married **Barbara Jones.**

Children of **Bennie Lawson**^{4} **Dawson** and **Barbara Jones** were as follows:
60. i. LIZ^5 was born on 23 June 1970.
61. ii. PHILIP was born on 4 November 1982.

29. **LORETTA**^{4} **DAWSON** (*Timothy*^{3}, *Homer*^{2}, *Sampson*^{1}) was born on 30 August 1952 in Sandersville, Georgia. She married **Aubrey Jones.**

Children of **Loretta**^{4} **Dawson** and **Aubrey Jones** were as follows:
62. i. AUBRINA^5.
63. ii. GAYLA.
64. iii. CRISTEN NOEL was born on 15 December 1981.

30. **PAULINE**^{4} **DAWSON** (*Timothy*^{3}, *Homer*^{2}, *Sampson*^{1}) was born on 12 November 1954 in Sandersville, Georgia. She married **Alfred Ford.**

Children of **Pauline**^{4} **Dawson** and **Alfred Ford** were:
65. i. TORRANCE^5 was born on 2 November 1982.

33. **GRACE HARRIS**^{4} **SPARKS** (*Deborah*^{3}*Dawson*, *Homer*^{2}, *Sampson*^{1}) was born on 22 March 1944 in Sandersville, Georgia. She married **Hugh Bryant.**

Children of **Grace Harris**^{4} **Sparks** and **Hugh Bryant** were as follows:
66. i. HUGH JASON^5 was born on 5 December 1976.
67. ii. KIRA LAUREN was born on 2 January 1979.

39. **GWENDOLYN**^{4} **GORDY** (*Eloise 'Honey*^{3}*Dawson*, *Homer*^{2}, *Sampson*^{1}) was born on 12 March 1947 in Utica, New York. She married **Julius Murphy.**

Children of **Gwendolyn**^{4} **Gordy** and **Julius Murphy** were as follows:
68. i. SONIA JOY^5 was born on 13 June 1976 in Albany, Georgia.
69. ii. ASHLEY was born on 21 December 1984 in Macon, Georgia.

41. **DAVID**^{4} **GORDY** (*Eloise 'Honey*^{3}*Dawson*, *Homer*^{2}, *Sampson*^{1}) was born on 13 April 1952 in Sandersville, Georgia. He married **DeLois Turner.** He married **Darlene Robinson.**

Children of **David**[4] **Gordy** and **DeLois Turner** were as follows:

70.   i. DEBORAH[5] was born on 14 January 1971 in Augusta, Georgia.

71.   ii. DAVINA was born on 2 June 1972 in Augusta, Georgia.

72.   iii. DENISE was born on 13 June 1975 in Augusta, Georgia.

73.   iv. JOSHUA DAVID was born on 9 February 1987 in Augusta, Georgia.

Children of **David**[4] **Gordy** and **Darlene Robinson** were:

74.   i. DAYNA LYNN[5] was born on 14 August 1997 in Milledgeville, Georgia.

42. DEBORAH ANNE[4] **GORDY** (*Eloise 'Honey'*[3]*Dawson, Homer*[2], *Sampson*[1]) was born on 6 January 1954 in Sandersville, Georgia. She married **Samuel Duggan** on 9 June 1979.

Children of **Deborah Anne**[4] **Gordy** and **Samuel Duggan** were as follows:

75.   i. LORA ANNE[5] was born on 17 July 1982 in Milledgeville, Georgia.

76.   ii. LORETTA DENISE was born on 12 March 1985 in Milledgeville, Georgia.

43. MARY LUCY[4] **GORDY** (*Eloise 'Honey'*[3]*Dawson, Homer*[2], *Sampson*[1]) was born on 17 July 1956 in Sandersville, Georgia. She married **Tony Owen Hurt Sr.** on 7 July 1979.

Children of **Mary Lucy**[4] **Gordy** and **Tony Owen Hurt Sr.** were as follows:

77.   i. TONY OWEN[5] JR. was born on 19 April 1982 in Milledgeville, Georgia.

78.   ii. KARI LOUCYE was born on 17 February 1985 in Milledgeville, Georgia.

79.   iii. BRAXTON GORDY was born on 7 June 1992 in Macon, Georgia.

45. BERRY RENARD[4] **GORDY** (*Eloise 'Honey'*[3]*Dawson, Homer*[2], *Sampson*[1]) was born on 10 September 1958 in Sandersville, Georgia. He married **Brenda Lee Lord Barlow Cardy.**

Children of **Berry Renard**[4] **Gordy** and **Brenda Lee Lord Barlow Cardy** were:

80.   i. JALEN BERRY[5] was born on 19 October 1991 in Augusta, Georgia.

46. CATHERINE LORETTA[4] **DAWSON** (*Homer*[3], *Homer*[2], *Sampson*[1]) was born on 4 February 1951 in West Palm Beach, Florida. She married **Douglas Fulton.**

Children of **Catherine Loretta**[4] **Dawson** and **Douglas Fulton** were as follows:

81.   i. LAURIE[5] was born on 14 August 1972.

82.   ii. ASHLEY was born on 30 September 1980.

83.   iii. WHITNEY BLAIR was born on 6 September 1987.

47. HOMER 'BILLY'[4] **DAWSON III** (*Homer*[3], *Homer*[2], *Sampson*[1]) was born on 9 April 1953 in West Palm Beach, Florida. He married **Brenda McCullom.**

Children of **Homer 'Billy'^{4} Dawson III** and **Brenda McCullom** were as follows:
84.   i. HOMER^5.
85.   ii. TANYA was born on 25 June 1973.
86.   iii. ANTONIO was born on 7 August 1978.
87.   iv. ALBERT was born on 25 October 1980.

49. **WENDELL^4 DAWSON** (*Homer^3, Homer^2, Sampson^1*) was born on 31 January 1957 in West Palm Beach, Florida. He married **Deborah Davis.**

Children of **Wendell^4 Dawson** and **Deborah Davis** were:
88.   i. LESLIE CANELIA^5 was born on 24 November 1989 in Nashville, Tennessee.

50. **NATALIE JEAN^4 DAWSON** (*Homer^3, Homer^2, Sampson^1*) was born on 6 April 1958 in West Palm Beach, Florida. She married **Robert Smith.**

Children of **Natalie Jean^4 Dawson** and **Robert Smith** were as follows:
89.   i. NICOLE^5 was born on 29 September 1979.
90.   ii. NATALIE RENEE was born on 17 May 1987.
91.   iii. (FEMALE).

51. **BEVERLY^4 DAWSON** (*Cornelius^3, Homer^2, Sampson^1*) was born on 5 February 1955 in East Palatka, Florida.

Children of **Beverly^4 Dawson** include:
92.   i. HOPE^5 was born on 12 January 1975 in West Palm Beach, Florida.
93.   ii. ANTARIO.

52. **WANDA^4 DAWSON** (*Cornelius^3, Homer^2, Sampson^1*) was born on 1 November 1959 in West Palm Beach, Florida. She married **Tim Hunt.**

Children of **Wanda^4 Dawson** and **Tim Hunt** were as follows:
94.   i. JULIAN^5 was born on 17 August 1995 in Miami, Florida.
95.   ii. JUSTIN was born in February 1997 in Miami, Florida.

55. **KAREN ' KAY' ELIZABETH^4 DAVIS ROSS** (*Wilhelmina 'Candy'^{3} Dawson, Homer^2, Sampson^1*) was born on 14 May 1956 in West Palm Beach, Florida. She married **Willie Neal.**

Children of **Karen ' Kay' Elizabeth^4 Davis Ross** and **Bernard Jackson** were:
+ 96.   i. KIMBERLY CORNELIA^5, born 19 June 1976 in Florida.

348

Children of **Karen ' Kay' Elizabeth**[4] **Davis Ross** and **Willie Neal** were:
97.   i. LINDSEY[5] was born on 1 August 1987 in Florida.

Generation Five

57. **ROBIN**[5] **BRENT** (*Shirley*[4]*Fisher, Elizabeth*[3]*Dawson, Homer*[2], *Sampson*[1]) was born on 21 June 1962. She married **Joseph Phelps.**

Children of **Robin**[5] **Brent** and **Joseph Phelps** were as follows:
98.   i. JOEY[6].
99.   ii. ROMAN.

96. **KIMBERLY CORNELIA**[5] **JACKSON** (*Karen ' Kay' Elizabeth*[4]*Davis Ross, Wilhelmina 'Candy*[3]*Dawson, Homer*[2], *Sampson*[1]) was born on 19 June 1976 in Florida.

Children of **Kimberly Cornelia**[5] **Jackson** and **Adrian Davis** were:
100.   i. ALEXANDRIA MONIQUE[6] was born on 14 August 1998 in Fort Lauderdale, Florida.

Descendants of William 'Tump' Peeler

Descendants of William 'Tump' Peeler

Generation One

1. WILLIAM 'TUMP'*1* PEELER was born in North Carolina. He married Susie Temple. He died in 1912 in Washington County, Georgia.

Children of William 'Tump'*1* Peeler and Susie Temple were as follows:
+   2.   i. MAUDE*2*, born in Washington County, Georgia.
+   3.   ii. BERNIECE, born in Washington County, Georgia.
+   4.   iii. CLAUDIA, born in Washington County, Georgia; married Walter Wiggins.
    5.   iv. BOOKER was born in Washington County, Georgia.
+   6.   v. DONNIE, born in Washington County, Georgia.
    7.   vi. JOHN was born in Washington County, Georgia.
    8.   vii. FREDDIE was born in Washington County, Georgia.
+   9.   viii. CLEVELAND, born 25 December 1889 in Sandersville, Washington County, Georgia; married Leola Rogers.

Generation Two

2. MAUDE*2* PEELER (*William 'Tump'1*) was born in Washington County, Georgia.

Children of Maude*2* Peeler include:
+   10.   i. RUBY*3*

3. BERNIECE*2* PEELER (*William 'Tump'1*) was born in Washington County, Georgia.

Children of Berniece*2* Peeler include:
    11.   i. LILA*3*.
    12.   ii. BERNIECE (JR.).
    13.   iii. CARRIE.

4. CLAUDIA*2* PEELER (*William 'Tump'1*) was born in Washington County, Georgia. She married Walter Wiggins.

Children of Claudia*2* Peeler and Mr. Williams were as follows:
    14.   i. NUMANZELLE*3*.
+   15.   ii. CHARLES
+   16.   iii. HERMAN

Children of **Claudia**^{2} **Peeler** and **Walter Wiggins** were as follows:

17.   i. ARMY G.^{3}.
+ 18.   ii. IVORY
  19.   iii. THEODIS.
  20.   iv. CLAUDIA.
  21.   v. WALTER JR..

6. DONNIE^2 **PEELER** (*William 'Tump'*^{1}) was born in Washington County, Georgia.

Children of **Donnie**^{2} **Peeler** include:

22.   i. DEEMERY^3.

9. CLEVELAND^2 **PEELER** (*William 'Tump'*^{1}) was born on 25 December 1889 in Sandersville, Washington County, Georgia. He married **Leola Rogers**, daughter of **Randall Rogers** and **Dovie Cheeves**. He died on 9 June 1963 in Dublin, Georgia, at age 73.

Children of **Cleveland**^{2} **Peeler** and **Leola Rogers** were as follows:

+ 23.   i. RUBY^3, born 28 December 1918 in Milledgeville, Georgia; married **William Jamison**.
+ 24.   ii. ROGERS, born 4 September 1920 in Milledgeville, Georgia; married **Mary Helen McBride**.
  25.   iii. CLEVELAND JR. was born on 1 June 1922 in Milledgeville, Georgia. He died in December 1941 in Great Lake, Illinois, at age 19.
+ 26.   iv. SUSIE, born 7 April 1924 in Milledgeville, Georgia; married **Grady Jones**.
+ 27.   v. VERA, born 10 May 1926 in Milledgeville, Georgia; married **John Trawick**.
  28.   vi. LEOLA was born on 24 May 1928 in Milledgeville, Georgia. She married **Mr. Banks**. She died in October 1986 in Detroit, Michigan, at age 58.
+ 29.   vii. DOVIE ONEAIN, born 19 April 1930 in Sandersville, Georgia; married **Frank Williams**.
+ 30.   viii. THOMAS JAMES 'TJ', born 22 May 1933 in Sandersville, Georgia.

Generation Three

10. RUBY^3 **ROBINSON** (*Maude*^{2}*Peeler, William 'Tump'*^{1}).

Children of **Ruby**^{3} **Robinson** include:

31.   i. AUSTIN W.^{4}.
32.   ii. DELORES.

15. CHARLES^3 **WILLIAMS** (*Claudia*^{2}*Peeler, William 'Tump'*^{1}).

Children of **Charles**^{3} **Williams** include:
 33. i. BETTY^4.

16. HERMAN^3 **WILLIAMS** (*Claudia*^{2}*Peeler, William 'Tump'*^{1}).

Children of **Herman**^{3} **Williams** include:
 34. i. VIVIAN^4.

18. IVORY^3 **WIGGINS** (*Claudia*^{2}*Peeler, William 'Tump'*^{1}).

Children of **Ivory**^{3} **Wiggins** include:
 35. i. KENNETH^4.
 36. ii. RANDY.
 37. iii. IVORY (JR.).

23. RUBY^3 **PEELER** (*Cleveland*^{2}, *William 'Tump'*^{1}) was born on 28 December 1918 in Milledgeville, Georgia. She married **William Jamison**. She died on 29 June 1963 in Detroit, Michigan, at age 44.

Children of **Ruby**^{3} **Peeler** include:
+ 38. i. CYNTHIA^4, born 2 December 1951 in Detroit, Michigan.

There were no children of **Ruby**^{3} **Peeler** and **William Jamison**.

24. ROGERS^3 **PEELER** (*Cleveland*^{2}, *William 'Tump'*^{1}) was born on 4 September 1920 in Milledgeville, Georgia. He married **Mary Helen McBride**. He died on 6 August 1991 in Macon, Georgia, at age 70.

Children of **Rogers**^{3} **Peeler** and **Mary Helen McBride** were as follows:
 39. i. GARY^4 was born on 30 December 1959 in Sandersville, Georgia.
 40. ii. TANGA ANN was born on 26 June 1963 in Sandersville, Georgia.

Children of **Rogers**^{3} **Peeler** and **Laura Jean Hopkins** were:
+ 41. i. WANDA JEAN^4, born 11 October 1957 in Washington, DC.

26. SUSIE^3 **PEELER** (*Cleveland*^{2}, *William 'Tump'*^{1}) was born on 7 April 1924 in Milledgeville, Georgia. She married **Grady Jones**.

Children of Susie^3 Peeler and Grady Jones were as follows:

+ 42.   i. GRADY^4 JR., born 9 December 1953 in Detroit, Michigan; married Jacqueline Denise Major.
+ 43.   ii. MICHAEL, born 26 September 1955 in Detroit, Michigan; married Gertrude Hawthorn.
+ 44.   iii. SHIRLEY JEAN, born 5 April 1957 in Detroit, Michigan; married Alvin Brezzell.
+ 45.   iv. PAULA, born 27 July 1963 in Detroit, Michigan; married Marco Henry.

27. VERA^3 PEELER (*Cleveland^2, William 'Tump'^{1}*) was born on 10 May 1926 in Milledgeville, Georgia. She married John Trawick, son of Elisha Trawick and Mary Lucy Ann Barlow, on 22 June 1947 in Sandersville, Georgia.

Children of Vera^3 Peeler and John Trawick were as follows:

46.   i. MALVIN^4 was born on 22 October 1947 in Sandersville, Georgia. He married Jacqueline Parklin.
+ 47.   ii. ALTON, born 18 January 1949 in Sandersville, Georgia; married Joanne Washington.
48.   iii. LINDA JOYCE was born on 15 May 1950 in Sandersville, Georgia. She married Samual Chandle.
49.   iv. BEVERLY LAVERNE was born on 1 July 1953 in Sandersville, Georgia.
+ 50.   v. CATHY ANN, born 3 January 1955 in Sandersville, Georgia; married Leo Suggs.
51.   vi. JOHN RICKY was born on 19 September 1959 in Sandersville, Georgia. He died in December 1995 in St. Paul, Minnesota, at age 36.
+ 52.   vii. LYDIA JEAN, born 3 February 1961 in Sandersville, Georgia; married Willie James Woodard.

29. DOVIE ONEAIN^3 PEELER (*Cleveland^2, William 'Tump'^{1}*) was born on 19 April 1930 in Sandersville, Georgia. She married Frank Williams on 14 May 1950 in Detroit, Michigan.

Children of Dovie Oneain^3 Peeler and Frank Williams were as follows:

+ 53.   i. BELINDA^4, born 23 April 1949 in Detroit, Michigan.
+ 54.   ii. ROCHELLE, born 13 December 1951 in Detroit, Michigan.
+ 55.   iii. FRAUN, born 3 December 1954 in Detroit, Michigan; married Bernard Delmas Foster Sr.
+ 56.   iv. VIVIAN, born 26 October 1957 in Detroit, Michigan; married Wendel Burch.
+ 57.   v. WENDY, born 26 October 1959 in Detroit, Michigan; married Scott Rose.
+ 58.   vi. FRANK JR., born 28 December 1964 in St. Paul, Minnesota; married Titka (—?—).
59.   vii. RODNEY BOONE was born on 27 March 1967 in St. Paul, Minnesota.

30. THOMAS JAMES 'TJ'^{3} PEELER (*Cleveland*^{2}, *William 'Tump'*^{1}) was born on 22 May 1933 in Sandersville, Georgia. He died on 16 July 2001 in Milledgeville, Georgia, at age 68.

Children of **Thomas James 'TJ'**^{3} **Peeler** include:

60.   i. CHRISTOPHER^4 was born in Milledgeville, Georgia.
61.   ii. JON was born in Milledgeville, Georgia.
62.   iii. CORNELIUS was born in Milledgeville, Georgia.
63.   iv. NEIL was born in Milledgeville, Georgia.

Generation Four

38. CYNTHIA^4 PEELER (*Ruby*^{3}, *Cleveland*^{2}, *William 'Tump'*^{1}) was born on 2 December 1951 in Detroit, Michigan.

Children of **Cynthia**^{4} **Peeler** include:

64.   i. PAUL MICHAEL^5 was born on 29 September 1986.

41. WANDA JEAN^4 THOMAS (*Rogers*^{3}*Peeler, Cleveland*^{2}, *William 'Tump'*^{1}) was born on 11 October 1957 in Washington, DC.

Children of **Wanda Jean**^{4} **Thomas** include:

65.   i. ZACHARY ROGERS^5 was born on 31 October 1991.

42. GRADY^4 JONES JR. (*Susie*^{3}*Peeler, Cleveland*^{2}, *William 'Tump'*^{1}) was born on 9 December 1953 in Detroit, Michigan. He married **Jacqueline Denise Major**.

Children of **Grady**^{4} **Jones Jr.** and **Jacqueline Denise Major** were:

66.   i. EMERY EDMOND^5 was born on 15 April 1987.

43. MICHAEL^4 JONES (*Susie*^{3}*Peeler, Cleveland*^{2}, *William 'Tump'*^{1}) was born on 26 September 1955 in Detroit, Michigan. He married **Gertrude Hawthorn**.

Children of **Michael**^{4} **Jones** and **Gertrude Hawthorn** were:

67.   i. LEBREE SINCLAIR^5 was born on 7 January 1987.

44. SHIRLEY JEAN^4 JONES (*Susie*^{3}*Peeler, Cleveland*^{2}, *William 'Tump'*^{1}) was born on 5 April 1957 in Detroit, Michigan. She married **Alvin Brezzell**.

Children of **Shirley Jean**[4] **Jones** and **Alvin Brezzell** were as follows:

68.   i. CLARISSA[5].

69.   ii. NICHOLS GRADY was born on 10 December 1980.

45. PAULA[4] JONES (*Susie*[3]*Peeler, Cleveland*[2], *William 'Tump'*[1]) was born on 27 July 1963 in Detroit, Michigan. She married **Marco Henry**.

Children of **Paula**[4] **Jones** and **Marco Henry** were as follows:

70.   i. SYDNEY[5].

71.   ii. PAIGE.

47. ALTON[4] TRAWICK (*Vera*[3]*Peeler, Cleveland*[2], *William 'Tump'*[1]) was born on 18 January 1949 in Sandersville, Georgia. He married **Joanne Washington** on 21 September 1974 in Atlanta, Georgia.

Children of **Alton**[4] **Trawick** and **Joanne Washington** were:

72.   i. BRANDON ALTUS[5] was born on 8 January 1978 in Rochester, New York.

50. CATHY ANN[4] TRAWICK (*Vera*[3]*Peeler, Cleveland*[2], *William 'Tump'*[1]) was born on 3 January 1955 in Sandersville, Georgia. She married **Leo Suggs** on 29 June 1984 in Elkhart, Indiana.

Children of **Cathy Ann**[4] **Trawick** and **Leo Suggs** were as follows:

73.   i. LEO DEON[5] was born on 16 October 1986 in Atlanta, Georgia.

74.   ii. INDIA SHARNAE was born on 9 June 1990 in South Bend, Indiana.

52. LYDIA JEAN[4] TRAWICK (*Vera*[3]*Peeler, Cleveland*[2], *William 'Tump'*[1]) was born on 3 February 1961 in Sandersville, Georgia. She married **Willie James Woodard**.

Children of **Lydia Jean**[4] **Trawick** and **Willie James Woodard** were as follows:

75.   i. VICTORIA DANIELLE[5] was born on 25 March 1984 in Atlanta, Georgia.

76.   ii. ASHLEY NICOLE was born on 1 November 1987 in Atlanta, Georgia.

77.   iii. WILLIE JAMES JR. was born on 5 August 1991 in Atlanta, Georgia.

53. BELINDA[4] WILLIAMS (*Dovie Oneain*[3]*Peeler, Cleveland*[2], *William 'Tump'*[1]) was born on 23 April 1949 in Detroit, Michigan.

Children of **Belinda**[4] **Williams** and **Larry Brown** were:

78.   i. BRETT[5] was born on 3 November 1979 in St. Paul, Minnesota.

54. ROCHELLE^4 **WILLIAMS** (*Dovie Oneain*^{3}*Peeler, Cleveland*^{2}, *William 'Tump'*^{1}) was born on 13 December 1951 in Detroit, Michigan.

Children of **Rochelle**^{4} **Williams** and **Mitchell Adams** were:

79. i. ELLIETTE O'NEIL^5 was born on 20 February 1991 in St. Paul, Minnesota.

55. FRAUN^4 **WILLIAMS** (*Dovie Oneain*^{3}*Peeler, Cleveland*^{2}, *William 'Tump'*^{1}) was born on 3 December 1954 in Detroit, Michigan. She married **Bernard Delmas Foster Sr.** on 15 October 1972.

Children of **Fraun**^{4} **Williams** and **Bernard Delmas Foster Sr.** were as follows:

80. i. BERNARD DELMAS^5 JR. was born on 25 November 1973 in St. Paul, Minnesota.
81. ii. BRANDON DAMONE was born on 15 November 1978 in St. Paul, Minnesota.
82. iii. BRENT DEMITRI was born on 22 July 1981 in St. Paul, Minnesota.

56. VIVIAN^4 **WILLIAMS** (*Dovie Oneain*^{3}*Peeler, Cleveland*^{2}, *William 'Tump'*^{1}) was born on 26 October 1957 in Detroit, Michigan. She married **Wendel Burch** on 9 March 1975 in St. Paul, Minnesota.

Children of **Vivian**^{4} **Williams** and **Wendel Burch** were as follows:

83. i. TYLER ONEAIN^5 was born on 26 October 1977 in St. Paul, Minnesota.
84. ii. KELLEN RYAN was born on 22 September 1981 in St. Paul, Minnesota.
85. iii. KIRSTEN NICOLE was born on 22 December 1985 in St. Paul, Minnesota.

57. WENDY^4 **WILLIAMS** (*Dovie Oneain*^{3}*Peeler, Cleveland*^{2}, *William 'Tump'*^{1}) was born on 26 October 1959 in Detroit, Michigan. She married **Scott Rose.**

Children of **Wendy**^{4} **Williams** include:

86. i. KYLE^5 was born on 31 May 1988 in St. Paul, Minnesota.
87. ii. DANNY was born on 18 April 1995 in St. Paul, Minnesota.

There were no children of **Wendy**^{4} **Williams** and **Scott Rose.**

58. FRANK^4 **WILLIAMS JR.** (*Dovie Oneain*^{3}*Peeler, Cleveland*^{2}, *William 'Tump'*^{1}) was born on 28 December 1964 in St. Paul, Minnesota. He married **Titka** (—?—).

Children of **Frank**^{4} **Williams Jr.** and **Titka** (—?—) were as follows:

88. i. EMANUEL FRANTE^5 was born on 8 September 1992 in St. Paul, Minnesota.
89. ii. PAYTON was born in October 1996 in St. Paul, Minnesota.

Printed in the United States
by Baker & Taylor Publisher Services